THE JACOBITE PEERAGE

THE
JACOBITE PEERAGE
BARONETAGE, KNIGHTAGE AND GRANTS OF HONOUR

EXTRACTED, BY PERMISSION, FROM THE STUART PAPERS
NOW IN POSSESSION OF HIS MAJESTY THE KING AT
WINDSOR CASTLE, AND SUPPLEMENTED BY BIOGRAPHICAL
AND GENEALOGICAL NOTES, BY THE

MARQUIS OF RUVIGNY AND RAINEVAL

AUTHOR OF 'THE BLOOD ROYAL OF BRITAIN,' ETC.

DEI GRATIA SED NON VOLUNTATE HOMINUM

CLEARFIELD

Originally published:
Edinburgh, Scotland, 1904
Reprinted: Genealogical Publishing Co., Inc.
Baltimore, Maryland, 2003

Library of Congress Catalog Card Number 2002114475

Reprinted for Clearfield Company by
Genealogical Publishing Company
Baltimore, Maryland, 2013

ISBN 978-0-8063-1716-8

Made in the United States of America

CONTENTS

	PAGE
PREFACE.	vii
ENGLISH TITLES .	xv
SCOTTISH TITLES	xvi
IRISH TITLES	xvii

PART I

PEERAGE AND BARONETAGE	1

PART II

KNIGHTS.	191
KNIGHTS OF THE GARTER .	193
KNIGHTS OF THE THISTLE	194
DECLARATIONS OF NOBLESSE, Etc.	195
SECRETARIES OF STATE	214
HOUSEHOLD APPOINTMENTS	216
ECCLESIASTICAL NOMINATIONS .	226
DIPLOMATIC APPOINTMENTS	232
CONSULAR APPOINTMENTS, Etc. .	235
PARDONS, Etc. .	237
MILITARY AND NAVAL COMMISSIONS .	238
VARIOUS APPOINTMENTS .	246
ALPHABETICAL LIST OF SURNAMES OF PEERS AND BARONETS .	251
INDEX TO PART II .	257

PREFACE

'One of the publications recommended by the Royal Commission
'appointed for the examination of the *Stuart Papers* in its second
'report in the year 1827 was a work which should contain,
'*inter alia*, a full account of the Grants of Honour, Peerages,
'Baronetcies, and Knighthoods bestowed upon the adherents of
'the Stuarts by James II after his abdication, and by his son
'and grandson. Some progress was made by the Commission
'towards the carrying out of this recommendation; but the dis-
'solution of the Commission in 1829, and the death of the King
'the following year, seems to have brought it to an abrupt close.
'A few additions to the collections of Mr. Pulman made by
'Mr. Glover, lately librarian to the Queen at Windsor, are all
'the indications which remain to show that the project did not die
'with the Commission. The interest awakened by the publica-
'tion in the *Times* of 28th December 1864 of some passages from
'the *Stuart Papers* relating to Prince Charles Edward shows,
'however, that there are many persons and families for whom
'this proposed publication would have more than an antiquarian
'value; whilst it needs must possess a peculiar value for heralds
'and genealogists.

'The Commissioners add, after speaking of the valuable
'genealogical material to be found in the warrants for the house-
'hold, other civil appointments, the naval and military commis-
'sions, and the appointments and instructions of the agents at
'foreign courts, the following :—

'" The Certificates of Gentility are very numerous, and appear
'" to have been issued in reward for services and with a view
'" to secure to the individuals, who are the objects of them,
'" certain privileges, which in France and Italy were limited to
'" persons who were of the class of noblesse : many of these

PREFACE

'"documents contain considerable genealogical details, which are curious, if not important, as matters of family interest."'
—Extract from a letter of B. B. Woodward, the Queen's librarian at Windsor Castle, in *Notes and Queries* for 27th January 1866.

Appended to the same letter was the list drawn up by the Royal Commissioners of those persons who were known to have received titles from the Stuarts, and Mr. Woodward invited information to enable him to prepare a Jacobite Peerage.

He does not, however, appear to have proceeded with the matter, and nothing more was done until 1897, when in the course of his address to the Scottish History Society at Edinburgh on the 23rd November Lord Rosebery said :—

'Before the history of the Stuarts can be written there is a
' book which must be compiled, and which will not easily be
' compiled. I suppose you all know the book called Haydn's
' *Book of Dignities*, which has been continued in a later edition
' by Mr. Ockerly, and published by Messrs. Allen and Sons. It
' contains all the prominent honours and dignities and ministries
' which have been conferred by the monarchy during the whole
' period of our history; but what is wanted is a book of those
' dignities that were conferred by the Stuarts after their de-
' parture from England in 1689. During almost all that time
' they had their Secretaries of State, their peerages, their knight-
' hoods, and dignities, and a list of that kind would be of the
' most invaluable assistance to any historian of the Stuarts. I
' quite admit that the first edition might not be a very complete
' book, because I can see there would be some difficulty in the
' compilation; but the first edition would bring out so many sug-
' gestions, and put their editor on the track of so many papers,
' that the second, third, and fourth editions would be works of
' incalculable value to historians. I dare say you may say, What
' is the use of such a book when the dignities died with the
' people, and when they were not of much interest while they
' existed? But that is not the fact. Historians, with all respect
' be it said to them, are not sufficiently careful in matters of
' detail. They do not give us the actual date of resignations of
' power and accessions to power, and in the majority of histories,

PREFACE

'if anybody wishes to read them accurately, they have to read
'them with some sort of calendar of dignities with exact dates
'by their side. And I think with such a book as I suggest
'there is also this to be said, that whereas dignities and minis-
'tries are perhaps of an ephemeral interest when conferred by
'dynasties that are actually existing, there is an element of
'sympathetic pathos about them when they represent nothing
'but a faded, abdicated, and banished past. I am not sure that
'the whole calendar of the melancholy Court of the Stuarts,
'their shadowy Secretaries of State, and their purely nominal
'dignities, would not be of greater interest both for the historian
'and the student of human nature than that book of Haydn's
'to which I have referred, which tells you of those who enjoyed
'power and substantial reign.'

In the present work an attempt has been made to carry out the suggestions of the Royal Commission and Lord Rosebery, and though the Editor is fully aware that there are many who are much better qualified to deal with the subject than he is, still he ventures to hope that the present work may be found of some assistance to historians of the Stuart period, and to a certain extent supply the want long felt, as is shown by the numerous letters and inquiries in the various genealogical and antiquarian publications for some work of the kind.

The titles treated of are those which were conferred by James II and VII and his son and grandson after the Revolution of 1688, and in the majority of cases the particulars, which are now for the first time published, are taken direct from the Warrant Books (five in number) among the *Stuart Papers* at Windsor Castle. These Warrant Books, however, are unfortunately not complete, and do not contain the patents of some well-known titles. Particulars concerning these are taken from the correspondence or from the authorities quoted. In a few other cases it is difficult to determine the remainder owing to the warrant not being entered in full.

The first part contains an alphabetical list of all titles known to have been conferred between the 11th December 1688, the date on which James II and VII was (by the English Convention)

PREFACE

declared to have abdicated the throne, and the 4th November 1784, the date of the last title conferred by Charles III (Prince Charles Edward). The Editor has ventured to follow very closely the plan adopted by G. E. C. in *The Complete Peerage*.

A biographical and genealogical account, as far as obtainable, is given of each peer and baronet, together with the names of their children, except in the cases of those peers who appear under some other title in the current peerages. In these cases it has been thought unnecessary to set out their descendants further than was necessary to show the descent of the title.

The names of all the titles held by each peer are given, together with the date of the creation, and the letters E, S, I, G B, and U K are added to show whether the Peerages are English, Scottish, or Irish, or those of Great Britain or the United Kingdom.

The Jacobite titles are printed throughout in italics.

It is possible that further researches may bring to light some more creations, but as far as the Editor has been able to ascertain, the total number of persons who received hereditary titles from the Stuarts during these ninety-six years was one hundred and twelve,[1] and the total number of titles conferred some two hundred and fourteen. Of these, however, ninety-one were merely minor titles (*i.e.* a Barony conferred with a Viscounty, or a Barony and Viscounty conferred with an Earldom, etc.), so that the actual number of distinct titles granted was only one hundred and twenty-three,[2] and as four of these, viz. the Earldoms of Bath [E] and Inverness [S], and the Baronies of Castle

---

[1] The difference between the number of persons (one hundred and twelve) who received titles and the number of distinct titles (one hundred and twenty-three) conferred is made up as follows: the Earl of Melfort received two, a Scottish Dukedom and an English Barony; the Earl of Mar received three, a Scottish Dukedom, an Irish Dukedom, and an English Earldom; John Græme received two, a Scottish Baronetcy, and afterwards an Earldom; Lord Lansdown two, an English Earldom, and afterwards a Dukedom; the Hon. John Hay three, a Scottish Earldom, and afterwards a Dukedom and an English Barony; Colonel Daniel O'Brien two, an Irish Barony, and afterwards an Earldom; Owen O'Rourke two, an Irish Barony, and afterwards a Viscounty; Peter Redmond two, an English Baronetcy and an Irish Barony; and the Hon. A. Dillon two, a Scottish Earldom and an Irish Viscounty.

[2] During the same period two hundred and ninety-two Peerages or steps in the peerage were conferred by the reigning sovereigns.

PREFACE

Lyons and O'Rourke [I], were subsequently merged in the Dukedoms of Albemarle [E] and Inverness [S], and the Earldom of Lismore and Viscounty of Breffney [I] respectively, the total number is reduced to one hundred and nineteen,[1] viz. eighty-five[2] Peerages and thirty-four Baronetcies,[3] of which twenty-six (twenty-five Peerages and one Baronetcy) were conferred by James II and VII, ninety (fifty-nine Peerages and thirty-one Baronetcies) by James III and VIII, and three (one Peerage and two Baronetcies) by Charles III.[4]

Of these one hundred and nineteen titles, thirty-seven were English, forty-one Scottish, and forty-one Irish.

Dealing with the English titles first, it is not known whether representatives still exist of the seven Baronetcies and of the thirty Peerages, of which five were conferred on pre-Revolution peers, four on post-Revolution peers, five on Scottish peers, and one on a post-Revolution Irish peer: twenty-five are extinct, of one (Baron Kilpee) nothing is known, and of the remaining four, one (Earl of Jersey) is merged in the post-Revolution Earldom of the same name, and two others (Earldoms of Falkland and Westminster) are held by the Scottish Lords Falkland and Elibank, so that the only actual addition is the **Viscounty of Goring**. See Table I, p. xv.

In Scotland the declaration declaring James to have abdicated the throne was not made until the 4th April 1689, and the first title conferred by him after that date was the Dukedom of Melfort, created 17th April 1694. He had in the interval, however, between the 11th December 1688 and 4th April 1689, conferred one title, that of Countess of Almond, on 3rd January 1689. Of the twenty-nine Scottish Peerages, of which six were

---

[1] The evidence for the creation of five of these, however, viz. Marquis of Trelessick [E], Earl of O'Callaghan [I], Baron Loughmore [I], Baron Kilpee [E], and Robertson of Struan, Baronet [S], is extremely slender.
[2] Of these eighty-five, nineteen were conferred on holders of pre-Revolution and five on holders of post-Revolution Peerages (see Tables I, II, III), and one on the heir-apparent of the (pre-Revolution) Earl and (post-Revolution) Duke of Atholl.
[3] Two of these, Græme [S] and Redmond [E], were afterwards created peers.
[4] His brother and heir, Henry IX (the Cardinal Duke of York), is not known to have conferred any titles.

PREFACE

conferred on pre-Revolution peers, nine are extinct, of four it is not known whether heirs exist or not, and of the sixteen existing, five are held by actual Scottish peers, two (Earl of Dillon and Baron Sleat) by Irish Peers (Viscount Dillon and Lord Macdonald), and one (Earl of Dunbar) by the Earl of Mansfield [G B].

The net addition to the peerage would therefore be but seven. See Table II, p. xvi.

In Ireland, James remained *de facto* as well as *de jure* King until the battle of the Boyne, 12th July 1690, and between 11th December 1688 and this date he created seven Irish peers,[1] concerning whom G. E. C. says in *The Complete Peerage*, vol. i. p. 60:
'Such Irish Peerages, however, as were created by James II in
'1689—at a time when he was in full possession of all his Regal
'Rights as King of Ireland, *all* of which creations, moreover,
'were *duly enrolled* on the *Patent Rolls* of that Kingdom, from
'which they have *never* been *erased*—stand in a very different
'category from other Peerages created by that King since his
'(so called) "abdication" of the throne of England on 11th
'December 1688.' These creations were, however, not recognised by William of Orange or by his successors.[2] The first creation by James after the battle of the Boyne would seem to have been the Viscounty of Cahiravahilla. Taking the twenty-six Irish Peerages, it will be seen that fourteen are extinct, of the heirs of eight nothing is known, and the remaining four are all vested in actual Irish peers. See Table III, p. xvii.

The total number of Jacobite Peerages of which representatives are known to exist is therefore twenty-three, and as the

---

[1] Viz. one Duke (Tyrconnell), three Viscounts (Kenmare, Mountcashell, and Mount Leinster), and three Barons (Fitton of Gosworth, Bourke of Bophin, and Nugent of Riverston). Of these, Tyrconnell, Mountcashell, Mount Leinster, and Fitton of Gosworth became extinct on the death of the grantees, Bourke of Bophin and Nugent of Riverston merged in the Earldoms of Clanricarde and Westmeath in 1705 and 1871 respectively, and the fifth (Jacobite) Viscount Kenmare, was in 1798 created a peer by George III, by the same titles which had been conferred on his ancestor by James II and VII one hundred and nine years before.

[2] See p. 132, note 3.

PREFACE

representatives of fourteen of these are actual peers, the net addition to the peerage would be but nine.

The second part contains lists of the Knights created by the Stuarts, of persons to whom certificates of noblesse were granted, of the Household, Diplomatic, and Consular appointments, of the Catholic Archbishops, Bishops, and Vicars-Apostolic nominated by James II and VII and James III and VIII, and of those who received Naval and Military Commissions, etc. etc. It will be observed that the list of Irish Bishops considerably supplements that given in Gam's *Series Episcoporum Ecclesiæ Catholicæ*, and makes it clear that the Stuarts maintained and exercised their right of nomination to the Irish churches and to the English and Scottish vicariates for over three-quarters of a century after the Revolution, James III and VIII nominating Philip MacDavett as Bishop of Derry on 21st December 1765, only ten days before his own death.

The lists of the Household, Diplomatic, and Consular appointments, and of those who received Naval and Military Commissions, only contain the particulars found among the *Stuart Papers*, and could doubtless be considerably supplemented from other sources.

It may appear to many that some apology is needed for this work, treating as it does of titles which are neither claimed nor used,[1] which died with the dynasty by whom they were conferred, and which are now at most merely of historical interest. Still, though this be the case, the representatives of the families here treated of, no matter to which side their sympathies may incline, are surely justly entitled to be proud of the titles that were won by their ancestors for loyalty to the Princes whom they regarded as their rightful sovereigns.

In dealing with these titles the Editor has endeavoured to avoid any expression of opinion, confining himself merely to chronicling facts. It is true he has accorded their kingly styles to the son and grandsons of James II and VII, but in a work of

---

[1] The last Jacobite title known to have been used was that of Earl Walsh, which became extinct 23rd January 1881.

PREFACE

this nature a different course could hardly have been pursued, and he would point out that a similar course is followed as regards James III and VIII in the *Calendar of Stuart Papers* issued by the Historical Manuscripts Commission; indeed, it is difficult to see on what grounds it can be refused him, when it is remembered that he was recognised as a sovereign by the Continental powers, and that his ambassadors were received and the titles he conferred recognised by them.

In conclusion, the Editor desires to thank all those who have so kindly assisted him while preparing this work. His thanks are particularly due to Mr. F. H. Blackburne Daniell, the editor of the *Stuart Papers*, both for his assistance in obtaining permission to inspect the papers and for his uniform kindness and courtesy to him when making extracts; to the French Minister of War and to M. Lequeux, Consul-General of France in London, for furnishing him with statements of the services of the Jacobite officers in the French army; and to Mr. W. B. Blaikie, author of *The Itinerary of Prince Charles Edward*, for much assistance concerning the Highland chiefs of the '45 period. He is also indebted for many valuable notes to G. E. Cokayne, Clarenceux King-of-Arms; Sir James Balfour Paul, Lyon King-of-Arms; and Sir Arthur Vicars, K.C.V.O., Ulster King-of-Arms; and he has to thank Mr. Keith Murray for a note of the minor titles conferred with the Dukedom of Rannoch.

THE STUART SUCCESSION AFTER 1688

The following dates may be found useful when consulting this work:—

JAMES II and VII died at St. Germains, 16th September 1701, and was succeeded by his son,

JAMES III and VIII, (Chevalier de St. George), who died at Rome, 1st January 1766, and was succeeded by his son,

CHARLES III, (Prince Charles Edward), who died at Rome, *s.p.l.*, 31st January 1788, and was succeeded by his brother,

HENRY IX and I. (Cardinal Duke of York), who died at Rome, *s.p.*, 13th July 1807.

PREFACE

TABLE I
ENGLISH TITLES

Date.	Name of Title.	If conferred on a Peer.	If existing or extinct.
	Dukes.		
1689	Powis, . . .	Marquis of Powis [E], .	extinct 1748.
1696	Albemarle, . .	... ...	,, 1702.
1716	Northumberland, .	Marquis (1715) and Baron (1544) Wharton [E].	,, 1731.
1721	Albemarle, .	Lord Lansdown (1712) [GB],	,, 1776.
1722	Arran, . . .	Earl of Arran (1693) [I],	,, 1758.
1722	Strafford, . .	Earl of Strafford (1711) [GB], Baron Raby (1640) [E].	,, 1691.
1733	York, . . .	... ...	,, 1807.
	Marquis.		
1715	Trelessick, . .	... ...	,, on death of grantee.
	Earls.		
1689	Dover, . . .	Lord Dover (1685) [E], .	,, 1708.
1689	Portland, . .	... ...	,, 1698.
1692	Tenterden, . .	... ...	,, 1829.
1701	Monmouth . .	Earl of Middleton (1660) [S],	,, 1747.
1715	Bolingbroke, . .	Viscount Bolingbroke (1712) [GB].	,, 1751.
1716	Jersey (Countess) .	Dowager-Countess of Jersey (1697) [E].	,, 1735.
1716	Jersey, . . .	Earl of Jersey (1697) [E], .	present Earl of Jersey [E].
1717	Mar (Duke [S and I])	Earl of Mar (1115) [S], .	extinct 1766.
1720	Chester, . . .	... ...	,, 1784.
1722	North, . . .	Lord North (1554) and Grey (1673) [E].	,, 1734.
1722	Falkland, . .	Viscount Falkland (1620) [S].	present Viscount Falkland [S].
17 ?	Macclesfield, . .	... ...	apparently extinct 1841.
1759	Westminster, . .	... ...	present Lord Elibank [S].
	Viscount.		
1722	Goring, . . .	... ...	present Sir Henry Goring, Baronet [E].
	Barons.		
1689	Cleworth (Duke of Melfort [S]).	Earl of Melfort (1686) [S],	extinct 1902.
1689	Esk, . . .	Viscount Preston (1681) [S],	,, 1739.
1690	Kilpee, . . .	... ...	?
16 ?	Borlase of Mitchell,	... ...	,, 1709.
1699	Caryll of Durford, .	... ...	apparently extinct 1788.
1716	Cottington, . .	... ...	,, 1758.
1717	Oglethorpe, . .	... ...	extinct 1785.
1727	Hay (Duke of Inverness [S]).	... ...	,, 1740.
	Baronets.		
1692	Ashton, . . .	... ...	?
1715	Ronchi, . . .	... ...	?
1717	Redmond (Baron Redmond [I]).	... ...	?
1722	Ronchi, . . .	... ...	?
1732	Connock, . .	... ...	?
1743	Butler, . . .	... ...	?
1753	Constable, . .	... ...	?

PREFACE

TABLE II

SCOTTISH TITLES

Date.	Name of Title.	If conferred on a Peer.	If existing or extinct.
	Dukes.		
1694	Melfort (Baron Cleworth [E]).	Earl of Melfort (1686) [S],	extinct 1902.
1701	Perth, . . .	Earl of Perth (1605) [S], .	present Viscount Strathallan [S].
1715	Mar (Earl [E] and Duke [I]).	Earl of Mar (1115) [S], .	present Earl of Mar [S].
1717	Castleblanco and St. Andrews.	... ...	present heir in Spain.
1717	Rannoch, . .	Marquis of Tullybardine, son and heir of Duke (1703) and Marquis (1676) of Atholl [S].	present Duke of Atholl [S].
1727	Inverness (Baron Hay [E]).	... ...	extinct 1740.
1740	Fraser, . . .	Lord Lovat (1464) [S], .	„ 1815.
1783	Albany, . . .	... ...	„ 1789.
	Marquis.		
1690	Seaforth, . .	Earl of Seaforth (1623) [S],	„ 1815.
	Earls.		
1689	Almond (Countess),	... ...	„ on death of grantee.
1698	Almond, . . .	... ...	?
1705	Dundee, . . .	... ...	?
1721	Dunbar, . . .	... ...	present Earl of Mansfield [G B].
1721	Nairne, . . .	Lord Nairne (1681) [S], .	present Earl of Dunmore [S].
1721	Dillon (Viscount Dillon [I]).	... ...	present Viscount Dillon [I].
1760	Alford, . . .	... ...	extinct 1773.
	Barons.		
1716	Clanranald (Bss.), .	... ...	„ 1743.
1716	Clanranald, . .	... ...	A. D. Macdonald of Clanranald.
1716	MacLeod, . .	... ...	Capt. Norman MacLeod of that ilk.
1716	Macdonell, . .	... ...	E. R. Macdonell of Glengarry.
1716	Maclean, . .	... ...	Sir Fitzroy D. Maclean, Baronet [S].
1716	Sleat, . . .	... ...	Lord MacDonald [I].
1717	Mackintosh, . .	... ...	Col. A. D. Mackintosh.
1717	Lochiel, . . .	... ...	Donald Cameron of Lochiel.
1721	Grant, . . .	... ...	present Earl of Seafield [S].
1723	Fraser of Muchalls,	... ...	present Lord Lovat [S].
1725	Sempill, . . .	... ...	?
1743	Appin, . . .	... ...	R. B. Stewart of Appin.
1760	Oliphant, . .	... ...	extinct 1847.

PREFACE

TABLE II—*continued*
SCOTTISH TITLES

Date.	Name of Title.	If conferred on a Peer.	If existing or extinct.
	Baronets.		
1723	MacLeod, . .	... ...	Bannatyne MacLeod, I.C.S.
1725	Robertson of Fascally.	... ...	?
1725	Robertson of Struan,	... ...	A. S. Robertson of Struan.
1726	Græme (Earl of Alford [S], 1760).	... ...	extinct 1773.
1729	Forester, . . .	... ...	?
1735	Ramsay, . . .	... ...	?
1740	Lumisden, . .	... ...	extinct 1751.
1740	MacGregor, . .	... ...	?
1743	Macdonell of Keppoch.	... ...	?
1747	Hay, . . .	... ...	?
1766	Hay, . . .	... ...	Sir Hector Hay, Baronet [S].
1784	Stuart, . . .	... ...	?

TABLE III
IRISH TITLES

Date.	Name of Title.	If conferred on a Peer.	If existing or extinct.
	Dukes.		
1689	Tyrconnell, . .	Earl of Tyrconnell (1685) [I],	extinct 1691.
1722	Mar (Duke [S] and Earl [I]).	Earl of Mar (1115) [S], .	,, 1766.
	Earls.		
1691	Lucan, . . .	... ...	,, 1719.
1692	Newcastle, . .	Viscount Galmoye (1646) [I],	,, 1740.
1722	Oglethorpe (Ctss.), .	... ...	,, 1776.
1726	Browne, . . .	... ...	heir probably in Russia or Austria.
17 ?	O'Callaghan, . .	... ...	?
1745	Walsh, . . .	... ...	extinct 1884.
1746	Moenmoyne, . .	... ...	,, 1830.
1746	Lismore, . . .	... ...	apparently extinct 1789.
	Viscounts.		
1689	Kenmare, . .	... ...	present Earl of Kenmare [I].
1689	Mountcashell, .	... ...	extinct 1694.
1689	Mount Leinster, .	... ...	,, 1709.
1690	Cahiravahilla, .	... ...	?

PREFACE

TABLE III—continued
IRISH TITLES

Date.	Name of Title.	If conferred on a Peer.	If existing or extinct.
	Viscounts—contd.		
1717	Dillon,	... ...	present Viscount Dillon [I].
1721	Redmond,	... ...	apparently extinct before 1732.
1723	Everard,	... ...	extinct 1740.
1731	Breffney,	... ...	heir probably in Austria.
	Barons.		
1689	Fitton of Gosforth,	... ...	extinct 1698.
1689	Bourke of Dophin,	... ...	present Marquis of Clanricarde [I].
1689	Nugent of Riverston,	... ...	present Earl of Westmeath [I].
1690	Loughmore,	... ...	?
1708	Hooke,	... ...	extinct 1744.
1727	Butler,	... ...	?
1727	Bourke,	... ...	?
1728	Crone,	... ...	?
	Baronets.		
1707	Lally (Earl of Moenmoyne [I]).	... ...	extinct 1830.
1716	Sherlock,	... ...	?
1719	Wogan,	... ...	Baron Tannequy de Wogan.
1723	O'Brien,	... ...	?
1724	Higgins,	... ...	?
1726	Sheridan,	... ...	extinct 1746.
1727	O'Gara,	... ...	?
1728	Hely,	... ...	?
1733	Worth,	... ...	?
1734	Forstal,	... ...	?
1743	Gaydon,	... ...	?
1745	Macdonald,	... ...	?
1746	Warren,	... ...	extinct 1775.
1748	Rutledge,	... ...	?
1753	O'Sullivan,	... ...	extinct 1895.

PART I

PEERAGE AND BARONETAGE

THE JACOBITE PEERAGE

AIRD, Viscount of the [S].

i.e. '*AIRD,*' VISCOUNTY OF THE (Fraser), created 14th March 1740, with '*FRASER,*' DUKEDOM OF, which see; extinct 8th December 1815.

ALBANY, Duchess of [S].

I. CHARLOTTE STUART, illegitimate daughter of King Charles III, by Clementina, COUNTESS OF ALBERSTROF [H.R.H.], youngest of the ten daughters of John Walkinshaw of Camlachie and Barrowfield, co. Lanark, by his third wife, Katharine, daughter of Sir Hugh Paterson of Bannockburn, Baronet [S], was born and baptized at Liége, in the parish church of 'la Bienheureuse Vierge 'Marie des Fonts,' 29th October 1753,[1] educated at the Abbey of Notre Dame de Meaux in Brie, was on or before 23/24 March 1783 created DUCHESS OF ALBANY [S] by her father, being so styled in his will of that date, and was *legitimated*, 30th March following, by a deed recorded in the Parliament of Paris, 6th September 1787. She joined her father at Florence, October 1784, and on St. Andrew's Day was invested with the green ribbon as a *K.T.* She died unmarried at Bologna, from the effects of a fall from her horse, 14th November 1789.

1783
—
1789

ALBEMARLE, Duke of [E].

I. HENRY FITZJAMES, second son and youngest of the five illegitimate children of James II and VII, by Arabella Churchill, spinster, sister to John (Churchill), Duke of Marlborough [E],

1696
—
1702

---

[1] The entry of her baptism is as follows:—'L'an du Seigneur, 1753, a été baptisée 'dans notre église paroissiale de la Bienheureuse Vierge Marie des Fonts de la ville 'de Liége, Charlotte, fille de Noble Seigneur Guillaume Johnson et de Noble Dame 'Charlotte Pit. Le parrain a été Noble Seigneur Georges Frementen, au nom de 'Noble Seigneur André Giffard' (see *Miscellany of the Scottish History Society*, 1904, ii. p. 437, where her will is printed in full).

I

ALBEMARLE

and only daughter of Sir Winston Churchill, was born August 1673. At the age of sixteen he was made Colonel of a regiment of infantry, which he headed at the battle of the Boyne. In 1695 he, who was generally known as 'the Grand Prior,' and his gallant brother, the Duke of Berwick, were *outlawed* by the government of William III. On 13th January 1696 he was created by (his father) James II and VII (when in exile) BARON OF ROMNEY, EARL OF ROCHFORD, and DUKE OF ALBEMARLE [E],[1] with remainder to the heirs-male of his body, and he was shortly afterwards placed in command of the Toulon fleet designed to invade England. He was in 1702 made a Lieutenant-General and Admiral in France. He died 17/27 December 1702, at Bagnolles in Languedoc, when all his honours became *extinct*. He married, 20th July 1700, Marie Gabrielle, only daughter and heiress of John (d'Audibert), second Count of Lussan [F], Knight of the St. Esprit, by his wife, Marie Frances, daughter of Henry (Raymond), Seigneur de Brignon, Senilloc and Rosières. She, who was born about 1675, married secondly[2] [Colonel Mahony, and thirdly], 12th March 1707, John (Drummond), second DUKE OF PERTH [S], who died 1754. She died at the Chateau of St. Germains-en-Laye, 15th May 1741, aged about sixty-six. He had issue an only daughter:—

1. LADY [   ] FitzJames, a nun, died young.

1721 — 1735

II. GEORGE GRANVILLE, second (but in 1706 first surviving) son of Bernard Granville, Groom of the Bedchamber, by Anne, daughter of and heiress of Cuthbert Morley of Hornby, co. York, which Bernard was younger brother to John (Granville), Earl of Bath, Viscount Granville of Lansdown, etc. [E]. He was born 1667; educated in France and at Trinity College, Cambridge; M.A., 1679; M.P. for Fawey 1702, and for Cornwall 1710; Secretary of War to Anne, September 1710, and was by her, 1st January 1711/2, created BARON LANSDOWN OF BIDEFORD, co. DEVON [G B], being one of the twelve peers created in five

---

[1] He had had a grant from his father (when in exile), 22nd July 1701, of the lands at Old and New Deal, Kent, formerly recovered from the sea, and now or late in the occupation of Henry Sidney or his under-tenants, in tail male, with remainder to James, Duke of Berwick, in tail male, at the yearly rent of 40s. a year, reserving power to charge the premises with £9000 sterling for the portion of Ignatia FitzJames, the King's natural daughter (*Calendar of Stuart Papers*, i. p. 160).

[2] 'Le mariage fut tenu caché, afin qu'elle pût conserver le titre de Duchesse d'Albemarle' (*Dict. de la Noblesse par La Chenaye des Bois*).

ALBEMARLE

days to secure a majority in the House of Lords,[1] P.C., and Comptroller of the Household, 1712; Treasurer of the Household, 1713 to 11th October 1714, when he was removed therefrom and imprisoned as a suspected person in the Tower of London, 26th September 1715 to 8th February 1717. He was restored to his seat in Parliament, but soon afterwards went abroad. On 6th October 1721 he was as 'George Granville, Esq.,' created by James III and VIII LORD OF LANSDOWN, co. Devon, VISCOUNT OF [   ], co. [   ], and EARL OF BATH, co. Somerset [E], with remainder to his heirs-male, and shortly afterwards, 3rd November following, as 'George Granville commonly called ' Lord Lansdown, Earl of Corbeil and Lord of Thorigny and ' Granville,' he was further created[2] BARON LANSDOWN OF BIDEFORD, co. Devon, VISCOUNT BEVEL, EARL OF BATH, MARQUIS MONK AND FITZHEMON, and DUKE OF ALBEMARLE [E], with

---

[1] See *The Complete Peerage* under Lansdown of Bideford, from which the particulars as to the first Duke, other than his Jacobite titles, are taken.

[2] The preamble sets forth: 'Whereas in consideration of the joint merit of the late ' General Monck, afterwards Duke of Albemarle, and of Sir John Granville, late Earl ' of Bathe, and of Bernard Granville, brother of the said Earl, in negociating and ' effecting the restoration of the Royal Family, It appears to us to have been the ' Gracious intention of our Royal Uncle, King Charles II, at the request of the said ' Duke of Albemarle, that in case of failure of issue male, from the body of the said ' Duke, or of his son Christopher, Lord Torrington, then living, that the said Dukedom, ' together with the title of Lord Monk, should descend to the said Earl of Bath, and ' be continued in the male line of the Granvilles, and whereas our said Royal Uncle ' did not only by warrant under his sign manual, bearing date 13th June 1667, promise ' to perform the same himself in case the same should so happen during his Reign, ' but otherwise strictly and expressly enjoin to his heirs and successors, and whereas ' George Granville, commonly called Lord Lansdowne, Earl of Corbeil, Thorigni, and ' Granville, in France and Normandy, son of the said Bernard, who was the person ' charged with the invitation to our Royal Uncle, to return to his Dominions, without ' any condition imposed upon him, is now become the chief heir-male surviving of the ' said ancient and loyal family of the Granvilles. In conformity therefore to the gracious ' intentions and injunctions of our Royal Uncle, and as a farther encouragement to ' Virtue and loyalty, and to perpetuate as far as in us lyes, the memory of persons so ' principally concerned in that happy and Glorious work of the Restoration, and likewise ' in consideration of the steady adherence and faithful services of the said George ' Granville to us and our Royall Father of blessed memory in our greatest distress— ' Know ye.' In *The Complete Peerage*, i. p. 59, is the following note: 'So popular was ' this title of ALBEMARLE, that, in 1661 (only a year after it had been conferred on ' George Monck), on the petition of John (GRANVILLE), EARL OF BATH (so created ' 20th April 1661), "the King passed a warrant, under the privy seal, whereby he obliged ' " himself and recommended it to his successors, that, in case of failure of male issue to ' " General Monck, the title of DUKE OF ALBEMARLE should descend to the said EARL ' " OF BATH, and be continued in his family" (*see* Heylin's *Help to English History*, ' edition 1783, p. 163). In 1688 this event happened; but no further steps appear to ' have been taken by the family of GRANVILLE in the matter. The validity of the ' King's warrant had expired with his Majesty in 1685, so that a royal recommendation ' to his successor was all that remained.'

3

ALBEMARLE

remainder to the heirs-male of his body, whom failing to his brother Bernard Granville, and the heirs-male of his body. Nominated by James, one of the nine LORDS REGENT [E] to manage affairs until his arrival, 26th May 1722.[1] He died *s.p.m.* 30th January 1734/5, in Hanover Square, and was buried at St. Clement Danes, when the Barony of Lansdown conferred on him by Anne became extinct. Admon., 6th May 1737, is full of genealogical details. He married, 1711, Lady Mary, widow of Thomas Thynne, daughter of Edward (Villiers), first Earl of Jersey [E], by Barbara, daughter of William Chiffinch. She died (two weeks before her husband), 17th January 1734/5, and was buried in St. Clement Danes. He had issue :—

1. LADY Anne Granville, Bedchamber-woman to the Duchess of Cumberland, 1745, died unmarried 18th October 1767.
2. LADY Mary Granville, married 1730 William Graham of Platten, near Drogheda, and died November 1735.
3. LADY Grace Granville, married 28th March 1740 Thomas Foley of Stoke, co. Hereford, afterwards (1776) created (by George III) Baron Foley of Kidderminster [G B]. She died 1st November 1769, leaving issue.
4. LADY Elizabeth Granville, Maid of Honour 1742-1756, and afterwards Bedchamber-woman to the Princess of Wales, died unmarried 1790.

1735
—
1776

III. BERNARD (GRANVILLE), second *DUKE OF ALBEMARLE*, etc., nephew and heir-male, being elder son of Bernard Granville of Buckland, co. Gloucester, M.P., by Mary, daughter of Sir Martin Westcombe, Knight Baronet [E]; which Bernard was younger brother to the first *DUKE*. He was born

---

[1] They were :—
  James (Butler), second Duke of Ormonde [E and I], etc.
  Charles (Butler), first *Duke of Arran* [I].
  Thomas (Wentworth), first *Duke of Strafford* [E].
  Robert (Harley), first Earl of Oxford and Mortimer [E].
  Charles (Boyle), fourth Earl of Orrery [I], etc.
  Francis (Atterbury), Bishop of Rochester [E].
  ? Lord Gore [? John (Leveson-Gower), second Baron [E] and afterwards first Earl [G B] Gower].
  William (North), sixth Lord North and second Lord Grey [E].
  George (Granville), first Lord Lansdown, *Duke of Albemarle* [E].
They had power (five making a quorum) to add four to their number. The entry is endorsed, '26 Aug. 1722'; this commission was returned, and is destroyed.

ALBERSTROF

1700, served for some time in the army; succeeded his father 8th December 1723, and his uncle 30th January 1734/5, when he retired from the army and established himself in Hollis Street. The same year he succeeded to a portion of the Duchess of Albemarle's estate, and in 1738 purchased from the Fleetwoods the estate of Calwich Abbey, co. Stafford. On 6th December 1752 he further acquired the Westcombe property by the death *s.p.* of his uncle, Sir Anthony Westcombe. He died unmarried at Calwich, 2nd July 1776, and was buried in Ellaston Church, when the DUKEDOM OF ALBEMARLE, MARQUISATES OF MONK AND FITZHEMON, EARLDOM OF BATH (of the 3rd November), VISCOUNTY OF BEVEL, and BARONY OF LANSDOWN became extinct, while the EARLDOM OF BATH (6th October), the VISCOUNTY OF [   ], and LORDSHIP OF LANSDOWN devolved on his heir-male.[1]

ALBERSTROF, Countess of.

i.e. title sometimes, but erroneously, included among Jacobite creations, having been an Imperial title[2] conferred by the Emperor Francis I on Clementina Walkinshaw, mistress of Charles III (see ALBANY, Duchess of), and used by her from the time she left him, 22nd July 1760, to her death unmarried at Fribourg in Switzerland, November 1805.

---

[1] His only brother, the Rev. Bevel Granville, born 1707; educated at Westminster School; married, 24th July 1722, in the Fleet Prison, Mary Ann Rose of Weedon; took Holy Orders and emigrated to Carolina, 1731, where he died *s.p.* 1736. She died at Weedon, 8th September 1776, aged seventy-six, and was buried in Wingrave Parish Church, Bucks, M.I. In the autobiography of Augustus Bozzi (in 1806) Granville, M.D., F.R.S., he describes his parentage thus:—'My mother, Maria Antoinetta, was 'one of the four daughters of the Chevalier Rapazinni, who filled an important post under 'Government in the Secretary of State department (in Milan). Rapazinni, in 1761, took 'for a second wife a very young English lady, born in Italy, whither her father, Bevil 'Granville, a Cornish gentleman, implicated in some political troubles, had withdrawn, 'and where his wife, Rosa Granville, had presented him with a daughter. This daughter, 'also named Rosa, grew up and was educated in a convent, which she left at the age of 'fifteen to become the wife of Rapazinni and the mother of his daughter, Maria 'Antoinetta, who in due time married Carlo Bozzi and was my mother.' See *A History of the Granville Family*, by Richard Granville, p. 439, where, however, the writer points out that Rosa Granville was not born till 1746, while Bevel Granville died in 1736. Of his sisters, the elder, Mary, so well known for her literary acquirements, was born at Coulston, Wilts, 14th May 1700; married first, 1717, Alexander Pendarves of Roscrow, co. Cornwall, and secondly the Very Rev. Patrick Delany, D.D., Dean of Down, and died *s.p.* 15th April 1788; and the younger, Anne, born 1707, married August 1740 John D'Ewes of Wellesbourne (who died 30th August 1780, aged eighty-six), and died at Bristol 16th July 1761, leaving, with other issue, a third son, the Rev. John D'Ewes, who succeeded his uncle and thereupon assumed the names and arms of Granville.

[2] *See* p. 190, note 2.

ALBEVILLE

ALBEVILLE, Marquis of.

i.e. title sometimes, but erroneously, included among Jacobite creations, being a Marquisate of the Holy Roman Empire, possessed by Sir Ignatius White, Baronet [E], sometime Envoy Extraordinary from James II and VII to the States of Holland, and afterwards his Secretary of State [I].

ALFORD, Earl of [S].

1760 — 1773

I. JOHN GRÆME,[1] eldest son and heir[2] of James Græme of Newton, Solicitor-General for Scotland 1688, by Elizabeth, daughter of Robert Moray of Abercairney, and grandson of Colonel Patrick Graham of Inchbrakie, the celebrated Royalist, was, 6th September 1726, created a *KNIGHT* and *BARONET* [S] by James III and VIII in reward for his services at the Court of Vienna, and the same day was appointed Minister at that Court. In April 1727, on the resignation of *LORD INVERNESS*, he was appointed *CHIEF SECRETARY OF STATE*. On 20th January 1734 he had a grant of a coat of augmentation, viz., the royal arms of Scotland on the field and cross of St. Andrew, counterchanged, and of supporters, viz., two horses bridled. He had a disposition of Newton from his father 1737, and took sasine 1740, the latter being then dead. He sold the estate to Moray of Abercairney 27th January [N S] 1744.[3] In 1745-1747 he was in attendance on the Duke of York in Paris, and on the Duke's flight he was taken into the household of the Prince of Wales, and fell into disgrace with the King, who held him responsible for the disorderly household of Prince Charles and for his mischief-making between the two princes. He afterwards repented, left the Prince, and was pardoned by James. He was received into the Catholic Church at Dijon 1751; succeeded *LORD LISMORE*, who died October 1759, as *SECRETARY OF STATE*, and was, 20th January 1760, created a Lord and Peer of Parliament as *LORD*

---

[1] He may have been the Brigadier Græme who had a commission as Major-General, 31st January 1722.

[2] For assistance in ascertaining the parentage of this John Græme, the writer has to thank Sir James Balfour Paul, Lyon King, and Mr. J. Maitland Thomson.

[3] The disposition was signed at Avignon, the witnesses being Alexander Falconer, Esq., Master of Haulkertouns, Edward Lisle of Moyles Court, in the county of Gloucester, Esq., and a servant. The seller signs 'Jo Græme.' Information kindly supplied by Miss L. Græme, who has compiled a history of the Inchbrakie family.

ALMOND

Newton, Viscount of Falkirk and *Earl of Alford* [S],[1] with remainder to the heirs-male of his body. He resigned the Secretaryship in 1763 on account of his age and infirmity, and retired to Paris. He died in the Scots College there, 3rd January 1773, apparently *s.p.*[2]

ALLOA, Baron [S].

i.e. '*Alloa,*' *Barony of* (Erskine), created 22nd October 1715, with '*Mar*,' *Dukedom of*, which see.

ALLOWAY, Earl of [S].

i.e. '*Alloway,*' *Earldom of*, title said, but erroneously, to have been conferred, 22nd October 1715, on John (Erskine), twenty-seventh Earl of Mar, with the *Dukedom of Mar*.

ALMOND, Countess of [S].

I. DONNA ANNA VICTORIA DAVIA-MONTECUCULI, probably daughter or sister of [ ] Marquis of Montecuculi[3] [Modena], who accompanied the Queen on her escape from Whitehall, 9th December 1688. She, who was 'the companion of the childhood and the friend of the 'maturer years' of Mary Beatrice of Modena, Queen Consort of James II and VII, accompanied the Queen on her escape to France, with her infant son, from Whitehall, soon after midnight, Sunday, 9th December 1688, and was by James II and VII (when in exile at St. Germains), 3/13 January 1689, created *Countess of Almond* [S] for life. On 30th October 1701 she was appointed, with the Duchess of Perth, Lady of the Bedchamber in Ordinary

1689
–
1703

---

[1] The preamble speaks of his family having been out with Montrose, and as having greatly contributed to the victory of Alford.

[2] His brother, David Græme, in Scotland was his heir, and inherited his money, about eighteen hundred francs, and furniture. Lumisden, writing to Dr. J. Murray at Rome, December 1770, says: 'The assistance that friendship and regard are capable of is, at 'a certain age, the greatest of comforts. Sensible of it, Lord Alford proposes to leave 'his elegant house and garden and to spend the few years he may have to live at the 'Scots College' (*see* Dennistoun's *Memoir of Sir Robert Strang*, ii. p. 149).

[3] An old Modenese family. A Marchioness of Montecuculi was a correspondent of Mary of Modena. In December 1696 the Queen writes to her, condoling with her on the loss of her son, 'of whom she has been deprived in the flower of his age.'

7

APPIN

to the Queen, with whom she remained 'till (to the great grief of 'her Royal Mistress)'[1] she died at St. Germains, April 1703.

1698 — 17

II. SIGNOR VIRGILIO DAVIA,[2] Senator of Bologna, husband of the preceding, was by James II and VII (when in exile at St. Germains), 9th and 12th April 1698, created BARON DAVIA, VISCOUNT OF MONEYDIE, and EARL OF ALMOND [S], with remainder to the heirs-male of his body. The preamble states that the honour was conferred on account of his own services to the Queen, but chiefly on account of the 'extraordinary merits' of his wife, DONNA VICTORIA DAVIA-MONTECUCULI, and her having 'attended on the person of our said dearest Consort even from 'her infancy with great zeal and fidelity, and particularly her 'having waited on our dearest Consort in her hazardous passage 'out of England into France at the beginning of the late Revolu-'tion, and shared in all the many and great dangers and diffi-'culties of her evasion, and that, as the misfortunes of our Royal 'Family increased, she has redoubled her endeavours to be still 'more and more useful in performing all the duties of a faithful 'servant passionately concerned in whatsoever regarded the 'Queen's service and person.'

APPIN, Baron [S].

1743 — 1769

I. DUGALD STEWART, ninth CHIEF OF APPIN,[3] second but only surviving son and heir of Robert Stewart, eighth

---

[1] *The Complete Peerage*, i. p. 74.

[2] Members of this family are frequently mentioned in the *Stuart Papers*. On 10th April 1695 the young Marquis D'Avia is referred to as being a prisoner at Constantinople, to the great affliction of his poor mother. Count Antonio Davia was appointed Groom of the Bedchamber to the King, 6th February 1702; John Anthony Davia, born at Bologna 12th October 1660, was created a Cardinal 18th March 1712, nominated Protector of England by King James 1727, and died at Rome 10th June 1740.

[3] The Stewarts of Appin, who were among the most loyal of the clans, are descended from Sir James Stewart of Pierston, fourth son of Sir John Stewart of Bonkyl, second son of Alexander, fourth High Steward of Scotland, whose eldest son James was ancestor of the royal family of Scotland. Duncan Stewart, eighth of Appin, served at the head of his clan under Montrose at Inverlochy. His estates were confiscated by Cromwell, but were restored at the Restoration. Robert Stewart, ninth of Appin, was at Killiecrankie, and was 'forfaulted' 16th July 1690. He was at the raising of the Standard at Braemar in 1715, and led his clan at Sheriffmuir. Duncan Stewart, second of Ardsheal, was an officer in the Appin regiment under Montrose. John Stewart, third of Ardsheal, as Tutor of Appin, held Castle Stalcaire for King James until October 1690. John Stewart, fourth of Ardsheal, was at Sheriffmuir and was attainted 1716, but obtained the restoration of his estates in 1717. His son Charles Stewart, fifth of Ard-

APPIN

Chief of Appin, by his second wife Anne, daughter of Sir Duncan Campbell of Lochnell, succeeded his father in the Chiefship, and was by James III and VIII, 6th June 1743, created a Lord and Peer of Parliament as BARON APPIN [S], with remainder to his heirs-male. When the Prince landed in 1745, he did not join him, but the clan was led by his cousin, Charles Stewart, fifth of Ardsheal, and he consequently escaped attainder. He sold Appin in 1765, and died *s.p.m.* 1769, being the last Chief of the direct male line. He married Mary, daughter of [LORD Alexander] Mackenzie, and had issue an only daughter :—

1. HON. Anne Stewart, married David Loch of Over Carnbee, Fifeshire.

II. ALEXANDER (STEWART), second BARON APPIN, eleventh of Appin, sixth of Ardsheal, cousin and heir-male, being second but eldest surviving son and heir of Charles, fifth of Ardsheal, by Isabel, daughter of John Haldane of Lanrick, which Charles Stewart was son and heir of John Stewart of the same, son and heir of another John Stewart of the same, son and heir of Duncan Stewart of the same, son and heir of John Stewart, first of Ardsheal, younger son of John Stewart, fifth of Appin, which last John Stewart was great-great-great-grandfather of the first LORD APPIN. He was in the service of the H.E.I.C.; succeeded his father 15th March 1757, and his cousin, the first LORD APPIN, in the PEERAGE and Chiefship of the clan in 1769. He died *s.p.* the same year. 1769

III. DUNCAN (STEWART), third BARON APPIN, twelfth of Appin and seventh of Ardsheal, next brother and heir of the preceding. The family estates having been forfeited on account of his father's share in the '45, he emigrated to America and settled in Connecticut, where he was appointed Collector of Customs. He served as a loyalist during the American Civil War, and after the peace retired to Bermuda, where for two years he was Collector of Customs. He had succeeded his elder brother in the PEERAGE and Chiefship, 1769, and in 1782 1769 - 1793

---

sheal, was an enthusiastic Jacobite, and took a leading part in the correspondence with Prince Charles as to his chances of success in Scotland. He was at Prestonpans, Falkirk, and Culloden, was attainted 1746, and his estates again confiscated. The Appin Stewarts are said to have been very nearly included with their neighbours of Glencoe in the massacre. As to this see a most interesting article, entitled 'The Clans of Culloden,' by Henry Jenner, F.S.A., in *The Royalist*, iii. p. 140.

APPIN

obtained the restoration of Ardsheal, when he returned to Scotland. He died at Ardsheal in 1793. He married, 1767, Anne, daughter of the Hon. John Erving, one of the Council for Connecticut (before 1776), and had issue :—
  1. Charles, MASTER OF APPIN, his heir.
  2. HON. John Stewart, Collector of Customs and President of the Council of Bermuda, born 3rd February 1769; died 3rd February 1832; married, 2nd April 1789, Sarah, daughter of Hon. Daniel Leonard, Chief-Justice of Bermuda, and had issue :—
     (1) Duncan Stewart, Attorney-General for Bermuda, born 3rd September 1795; died 9th February 1861; married Sarah Amelia, daughter of Richard Darrell of Montpelier, Bermuda, and had issue :—
        (1) John Stewart, who succeeded as sixth LORD APPIN.
        (2) Duncan Stewart, Barrister-at-Law, of Lincoln's Inn, Master of the Court of Bankruptcy in London, born 29th January 1825; died 12th September 1887; married, 21st February 1863, Florence Emma, daughter of the Rev. Charles Mackenzie of Torridon, Ross-shire, a Prebendary of St. Paul's, London, and had issue.
        (3) Leonard Stewart, Barrister-at-Law, born 7th December 1826, died unmarried 19th January 1894.
        (4) James Stewart, born 24th December 1828; died 16th March 1879; married first, Julia Bransom, daughter of Edward Pringle; secondly, Jane, daughter of I. Bell, by whom he had issue.
        (5) Richard Darrell Stewart, born 25th September 1830, died unmarried 19th September 1865.
        (6) Harvey Darrell Stewart, Barrister-at-Law of the Inner Temple, born 5th August 1823.
        (7) Rev. Charles Edward Stewart, M.A.

APPIN

Magd. Hall, Oxford, Rector of St. James's, Manchester, born 23rd October 1839; married, 2nd August 1881, Margaret Katherine, daughter of Andrew Davies Bird, and has issue.
 (8) Sarah Darrell Stewart, died 11th November 1896; married, 7th September 1841, Major A. F. W. Papillon, R.A., and had issue.
 (9) Emily Clementina Stewart, died unmarried December 1902.
 (10) Mary Catherine Darrell Stewart.
 (11) Anne Margaret Stewart, died unmarried.
 (12) Esther Mary Darrell Stewart.
 (13) Frederica Harriet Papillon Leonard Stewart.
(2) Leonard Stewart, M.D., died unmarried.
(3) James Stewart, Barrister-at-Law, M.P. for Honiton 1837-1841, born 17th August 1805; died 26th September 1860; married, 12th August 1834, his cousin, Margaret Emily, third daughter of Duncan Stewart of Glenbuckie, Perthshire, and had issue :—
 (1) James Stewart, born 19th August 1837.
 (2) Duncan John Stewart, Major Indian army, born 1st November 1840.
 (3) Mary Stewart, died unmarried.
 (4) Margaret Stewart, died 30th August 1844.
 (5) Alice Charlotte Stewart.
(4) Emily Clementina Stewart, married, 10th March 1818, Edward Witherington, and had issue.
(5) Anne Stewart, married, 12th October 1819, William S. Cumming, and had issue.
(6) Sarah Joanna Stewart, married, 10th April 1827, Edward Winslow of Lincoln's Inn, Barrister-at-Law, and had issue.

3. *Hon.* George Stewart, died an infant.
4. Rev. THE *Hon.* James Haldane Stewart, M.A., Rector of Limpsfield, Surrey, born 1778; died 22nd October

APPIN

1854; married Mary, daughter of David Dale, and had issue :—
  (1) William Cadogan Stewart, died unmarried.
  (2) Rev. David Dale Stewart, M.A., Canon of Rochester, for long Rector of Maidstone, Kent, afterwards Rector of Coulsdon, Surrey, born 1819; died *s.p.*; married, 8th August 1854, Cecilia, daughter of the Rev. Henry Raikes, Chancellor of Chester.
  (3) Rev. James Haldane Stewart, M.A., Rector of Brightwell, Berks, born 1821; died 24th February 1879; married, 22nd May 1866, Emily, eldest daughter of William Leveson-Gower of Titsey Place, and had issue.
  (4) Anne Erving Stewart, died unmarried.
  (5) Mary Dale Stewart, died unmarried.
5. *Hon.* William George Erving Stewart, settled in Lima, and left issue.
6. *Hon.* Anne Stewart, married John M'Nab of Balquidder, and had issue.
7. *Hon.* Margaret Stewart, married Captain Duncan Stewart of Glenbuckie, and had issue.
8. *Hon.* Charlotte Stewart, married Colonel Charles Alexander Stewart.
9. *Hon.* Sophia Stewart, married John Campbell, and had issue.
10. *Hon.* Isabella Stewart, died unmarried.

1793 – 1844
IV. CHARLES (STEWART), fourth *Baron Appin*, twelfth of Appin and eighth of Ardsheal, son and heir of the preceding; died 1844; married Rebecca, daughter of William Sinclair of Deer Park, Armagh and Strabane, Tyrone, and by her had issue :—
  1. Charles, *Master of Appin*, his heir.
  2. *Hon.* Annette Stewart, married Major Robert Stewart, 94th regiment, and had issue.

1844 – 1882
V. CHARLES (STEWART), fifth *Baron Appin*, thirteenth of Appin and ninth of Ardsheal, only son and heir of the preceding, born 1805; sold the estates, and died unmarried 23rd January 1882.

ARRAN

VI. JOHN (STEWART), sixth *Baron Appin*, etc., next heir-male of the preceding, being son and heir of Duncan Stewart, Attorney-General of Bermuda, and grandson of the *Hon.* John Stewart, next younger brother to the fourth *Lord*; born 11th January 1822, Barrister-at-Law of Lincoln's Inn; died 16th November 1890; buried at Hanworth, Middlesex. He married, 4th January 1859, Anne, fourth daughter of Thomas Forbes Winslow, and had issue:— 1882 - 1890

1. Donald Charles, *Master of Appin*, born 12th December 1859, died unmarried *v.p.* 13th September 1885.
2. Robert Bruce, *Master of Appin*, his heir.
3. *Hon.* Alan Winslow Stewart, born 19th April 1865.
4. *Hon.* Haldane Campbell Stewart, B.A. Magd. Coll., Oxon., born 28th February 1868.

VII. ROBERT BRUCE (STEWART), seventh *Baron Appin*, representative of the Stewarts of Lorn, Appin, and Ardsheal, B.A. Magd. Coll., Oxon., second but elder surviving son and heir of the preceding, born 23rd April 1863, succeeded his father 16th November 1890. 1890

ARRAN, Duke of [E].

I. CHARLES BUTLER, second and youngest surviving son of Thomas Butler, Earl of Ossory (son and heir-apparent of James (Butler), first Duke of Ormonde [I]), by Amelia, eldest daughter of Henry (de Nassau), Lord of Auverquerque [Holland], was born 4th September 1671, and like his brother, the Duke of Ormonde, accepted the Revolution settlement, and was made Lord of the Bedchamber to William of Orange, and Colonel of a regiment of horse. On 8th March 1693 he was created (by William) Baron of Cloughgrenan, Viscount of Tullogh, and Earl of Arran [I],[1] and the following year, 23rd January, Baron Butler of Weston, co. Huntingdon [E]. He was Governor of Dover Castle; Master of the Ordnance, 1712-1714; Chancellor of the University of Oxford, 10th September 1715; and High Steward of Westminster, 28th February 1715/6. By Act of Parliament [E], 21st June 1721, he was enabled to purchase his 1722 - 1758

---

[1] These same titles had been conferred by Charles II, 13th May 1662, on his uncle, Lord Richard Butler, and had become extinct on the latter's death *s.p.m.s.* 25th January 1685/6.

ASHTON

brother's estates, which he had forfeited for his share in the '15. On the 2nd January 1722 he was, as 'Charles Butler,' created by James III and VIII DUKE OF [? ARRAN] [E], with remainder to the heirs-male of his body, and on the 26th May following he was one of the nine noblemen appointed by James to be LORDS REGENT [E] during his absence.[1] On 16th November 1745 he succeeded his elder brother as third DUKE (1661) and MARQUIS (1642) and fourteenth EARL (1328) OF ORMONDE [I], third DUKE OF ORMONDE (1682), EARL OF BRECKNOCK (1660), and BARON BUTLER OF LLANTHONY (1660) [E], and seventh EARL OF OSSORY (1527) and sixth VISCOUNT THURLES (1535) [I], and third BARON BUTLER OF MOORE PARK (1666) [E], and, on 20th April 1750, his niece as fourth BARON DINGWALL (1609) [S]; but notwithstanding ' he appears never to have styled himself otherwise than as Earl ' of Arran [I], the popular idea at that time being that the *Irish* ' [and *Scottish*] titles (as well as the English) of his said brother ' had been forfeited by the Act of Attainder of the *English* ' Parliament.'[2] He married, 18th September 1721, the Hon. Elizabeth, daughter and co-heir of Thomas (Crewe), second Lord Crewe of Steane [E], by his second wife, Anne, daughter and co-heir of Sir William Airmine, Baronet [E]. She died, 21st May 1756, aged seventy-seven, and was buried at Steane, co. Northampton. He died *s.p.*, 17th December 1758, at his lodgings next the Tilt Yard, Whitehall, aged eighty-eight, and was buried on the 23rd at St. Margaret's, Westminster, when the DUKEDOM OF ARRAN, as well as all his other honours, except the Earldoms of Ormonde and Ossory, the Viscounty of Thurles [I], the Barony of Dingwall [S], and the Barony of Butler of Moore Park [E], became extinct.

ASHTON.

1692 —
I. [   ] ASHTON, son and heir of John Ashton,[3] sometime Clerk of the Closet to Mary of Modena, who was executed

---

[1] See p. 4, note 1.
[2] See *The Complete Peerage*, i. p. 135.
[3] He is described in the indictment as 'late of the parish of St. Paul's, Covent ' Garden.' On the scaffold he handed the sheriff a paper declaring himself a Protestant, and happy in losing his life in James's service, 'from whom he had received ' favours for 16 years past.' This document, which well exemplified the depth of the sincerity of James's supporters in England, was published in England, France, and Holland, and greatly alarmed the authorities.

BATH

at Tyburn 28th January 1690/1 for his loyalty to James II and VII, by his wife [   ],[1] daughter of [   ] Rigby, retired to France after his father's death, and was created a *BARONET* [E][2] by King James.

BALLYHIGUE, Baron.

i.e. title sometimes, but erroneously, included among Jacobite creations, but which was in reality a French Barony conferred by Louis Philip, by letters patent dated 18th November 1839, on Anthony Sylvain de Cantillon, Knight of St. Louis and of the second class of St. Ferdinand of Spain, Colonel of Hussars, a great-grandson of James Cantillon of Ballyhigue and Belview, co. Kerry, born 1650; a Captain in the army of James II and VII, whom he followed to France after the Revolution.[3]

BALLYMOLE, Viscount of [I].

i.e. '*BALLYMOLE,*' *VISCOUNTY OF* (Lally), created 1746, with '*MOENMOYNE,*' *EARLDOM OF*, which see.

BANNO, Baron [I].

i.e. '*BANNO,*' co. Wexford, *BARONY OF* (Cheevers), created 23rd August 1689, with '*MOUNT LEINSTER,*' *VISCOUNTY OF*, which see.

BASS, Viscount of [S].

i.e. '*BASS,*' *VISCOUNTY OF* (de Bozas), created 4th February 1717, with '*ST. ANDREWS,*' *DUKEDOM OF*, which see.

BATH, Earl of [E].

I. GEORGE GRANVILLE, first surviving son of Bernard Granville, and nephew of John (Granville), first Earl of Bath [E],   1721 - 1735

---

[1] She died at St. Germains 1694, her body being sent to England for burial (*Dictionary of National Biography*).

[2] 8th November 1692. 'Mrs. Ashton, wife to him lately executed, with her son went to France, and at her arrival at Paris King James made him a baronet.'—*Luttrell's Diary*, for calling his attention to which the Editor has to thank G. E. Cokayne, Clarenceux King of Arms.

[3] See a pedigree of the family in Burke's *Heraldic Illustrations*, p. 51.

BEAUFORT

was on 1st January 1711/2 created by Anne BARON LANSDOWN OF BIDEFORD, co. Devon [E], and by James III and VIII, 6th October 1721, LORD OF LANSDOWN, VISCOUNT [   ], and EARL OF BATH [E], with remainder to his heirs-male, and, 3rd November following, BARON LANSDOWN OF BIDEFORD, co. Devon, VISCOUNT BEVEL, EARL OF BATH, MARQUIS MONK AND FITZHEMON, and DUKE OF ALBEMARLE [E], with remainder to the heirs-male of his body, whom failing to his brother, Bernard Granville, and the heirs-male of his body. He died *s.p.m.* 30th January 1734/5.

1735 – 1776

II. BERNARD GRANVILLE, second DUKE OF ALBEMARLE, EARL OF BATH, etc., nephew and heir-male, being son and heir of Bernard Granville above named, younger brother of the first Peer. He died unmarried 1776, when the DUKEDOM OF ALBEMARLE, MARQUISATES OF MONK AND FITZHEMON, EARLDOM OF BATH (of the 3rd November), VISCOUNTY OF BEVEL, and BARONY OF LANSDOWN (of the 3rd November) became extinct; while the EARLDOM OF BATH (of the 6th October), VISCOUNTY OF [   ], and LORDSHIP OF LANSDOWN (of the 6th October) passed to his next heir-male.

See fuller particulars under '*ALBEMARLE*,' DUKEDOM OF.

BEAUFORT, Marquis of [S].

i.e. '*BEAUFORT*,' MARQUISATE OF (Fraser), created 14th March 1740, with '*FRASER*,' DUKEDOM OF, which see.

BEAULY, Baron [S].

i.e. '*BEAULY*,' BARONY OF (Fraser), created 14th March 1740, with '*FRASER*,' DUKEDOM OF, which see.

BEVEL, Viscount [E].

i.e. '*BEVEL*,' VISCOUNTY OF (Granville), created 3rd November 1721, with '*ALBEMARLE*,' DUKEDOM OF, which see.

BLAIR, Marquis of [S].

i.e. '*BLAIR*,' co. Perth, MARQUISATE OF (Murray), created 1st February 1717, with '*RANNOCH*,' DUKEDOM OF, which see.

BOLINGBROKE

BOLINGBROKE, Earl of [E].

I. HENRY ST. JOHN, son and heir of Sir Henry St. John, fourth Baronet [E] (afterwards created by George I, 2nd July 1716, Viscount St. John [E], with remainder to his second son), by Lady Mary, second daughter and co-heir of Robert (Rich), second Earl of Warwick [E]; the celebrated statesman and writer; baptized, 10th October 1678, at Battersea, Surrey; M.P. for Wootton Bassett, 1701-1705; for Berks, 1710-1712; Secretary of War, 1704-1708; P.C., 1710; Secretary of State, 1710-1714; was, 7th July 1712, created by Anne BARON ST. JOHN of LYDIARD TREGOZE, Wilts, and VISCOUNT BOLINGBROKE, co. Lincoln [G B], with special remainder, failing his issue-male, to his father and the heirs-male of his body. On 27th July 1714 (by the removal of the Earl of Oxford) he became virtually Prime Minister, but the appointment of the Duke of Shrewsbury as Treasurer, followed by the death of Anne, 1st August, upset the plans he is supposed to have formed for the restoration of King James. On the accession of King George I he was dismissed, and being defeated in the House of Commons, 22nd March, on a motion in answer to the King's speech, by sixty-six votes to thirty-three, he retired to France, 27th March. He was impeached 10th June, and attainted 18th August following. On or shortly before the 26th July 1715[1] he was created, by King James III and VIII, *EARL OF BOLINGBROKE* [E], having a few days before been appointed *SECRETARY OF STATE*. He was dismissed, however, the following March, being accused, though unjustly, of having betrayed his party to the Hanoverian Government. By an Act of the English Parliament he was restored (though in blood only), 31st May 1725, and returning to England, died there, *s.p.s.* 12th, and was buried 15th December 1751, at Battersea. Will dated 22nd November 1751, proved 5th March 1752. He had succeeded his father, April 1742, as fifth Baronet [E], but in consequence of his attainder was not recog-

1715
–
1751

---

[1] James writes to him from Bar that day as follows: 'I find too much solid reason and sincere zeal in yours of the 23rd that I cannot but dayly more and more applaude myself for the choice I have mad of you; I cannot, you know, as yett give you very essentiall proofs of my kindness, but the least I cann do for so good and faithfull a servant, is at least in sending you the inclosed warrant, which raises you a degree higher than my sister had done before, and which will fix your rank with me beyond dispute; I hope you will take this mark of my favour as kindly as I meane it.'

BORLASE

nised as such by the *de facto* government. He married first, in 1700, Frances, first daughter and co-heir of Sir Henry Winchcombe, Baronet [E], by his wife, [   ], daughter of [   ] Rolls. She died November 1718. He married, secondly, at Aix-la-Chapelle, May 1720,[1] Marie Claire, Dowager-Marchioness of Villette [F], daughter and co-heir of Armand (des Champs), Seigneur of Marcilly [F], by his wife, Elizabeth Indrot. She was born 9th September 1675, was received into St. Cyr, after having proved the nobility of her family since Erard des Champs, her ancestor in the sixth degree,[2] and died 18th March 1750, aged seventy-four, and was buried at Battersea. On his death the EARLDOM OF BOLINGBROKE presumably became extinct; the BARONY OF ST. JOHN of Lydiard Tregoze (1712) and the VISCOUNTY OF BOLINGBROKE (1712) under the special remainder devolved on his nephew, while the BARONETCY (1611), being considered under attainder, remained dormant.

BORLASE OF BORLASE, Baron [E].

See MITCHELL, BARON [E].

BOURKE OF BOPHIN [I], Baron.

1689
–
1722

I. HON. JOHN BOURKE, second son of William (Bourke), seventh Earl of Clanricarde [I], by Lettice, daughter of Sir Henry Shirley, second Baronet [E], born 1642; was Colonel of a regiment of infantry in the service of James II and VII, and was created by that King, 2nd April 1689[3] (some four months after the revolution in England, but while still *de facto*, as well as *de jure*, King of Ireland), BARON BOURKE OF BOPHIN, co. Galway [I], with remainder to the heirs-male of his body. He was taken prisoner at the battle of Aughrim, 12th July 1691, and was attainted. A bill for his restoration in 1698 was

---

[1] *The Complete Peerage* gives the date as 1718, and Dean Swift, in a letter dated 11th December 1718, mentions a rumour of his having married the Marchioness of Villette (see, however, the *Dictionary of National Biography*). She or her first husband was a relation of Madame de Maintenon.

[2] *Dict. de la Noblesse*, by La Chenaye des Bois.

[3] This was one of the seven Irish peerages created by James II and VII after the Revolution in England, but while he was still *de facto* as well as *de jure* King of Ireland, all of which creations were duly enrolled on the Patent Rolls of that kingdom, from which they have never been erased (see Preface, p. xii.).

BOURKE

rejected, but by an Act, 1 Anne (1702), the attainder was reversed. He succeeded his elder brother as ninth Earl of Clanricarde and Baron of Dunkellin [I], and sixth Viscount Bourke of Clanmories [I] after November 1702, and died 17th October 1722.

II. MICHAEL (BOURKE), tenth EARL OF CLANRICARDE, second *BARON BOURKE OF BOPHIN*, etc., son and heir of the preceding, born about 1786, and died 28th November 1736.[1]

1722 – 1736

III. JOHN SMYTH (BOURKE, afterwards (13th May 1752) DE BURGH), eleventh EARL OF CLANRICARDE, third *BARON BOURKE OF BOPHIN*, etc., second but first surviving son and heir of the preceding, born 11th November 1720, died 21st April 1782.

1736 – 1782

IV. HENRY (DE BURGH), twelfth EARL OF CLANRICARDE, fourth *BARON BOURKE OF BOPHIN*, etc., son and heir of the preceding, born 9th January, and baptized 9th February 1742/3; K.P., 5th February 1783, being one of the fifteen original knights of that order. On 17th August 1789 he was by George III created MARQUIS OF CLANRICARDE [I]. He died *s.p.* 8th December 1797.

1782 – 1797

V. JOHN THOMAS (DE BURGH), thirteenth EARL OF CLANRICARDE, fifth *BARON BOURKE OF BOPHIN*, etc., only brother and heir of the preceding, born 22nd September 1744. On 29th December 1800 he was by George III created EARL OF CLANRICARDE [I], with remainder, failing his issue-male, to his daughters and their issue-male. He died 27th July 1808.

1797 – 1808

VI. ULICK JOHN (DE BURGH), fourteenth EARL OF CLANRICARDE, sixth *BARON BOURKE OF BOPHIN*, etc., only son and heir of the preceding, born 20th December 1802; K.P., October 1831. On 26th November 1825 he was created by George IV MARQUIS OF CLANRICARDE [I], and on 13th December 1826 (by the same King) BARON SOMERHILL of Somerhill, co. Kent [U K]. He died 10th April 1874.

1808 – 1874

---

[1] For a fuller account of this peer and of his successors, see the extant peerages under Clanricarde.

BOURKE

1874   VII. HUBERT GEORGE (DE BURGH, afterwards (9th July 1862) DE BURGH-CANNING), fifteenth EARL (1543) and second MARQUIS (1825) OF CLANRICARDE [I], third EARL OF CLANRICARDE (1800) [I], twelfth VISCOUNT BOURKE OF CLANMORIES (1629) [I], fifteenth BARON DUNKELLIN (1543) [I], and seventh *BARON BOURKE OF BOPHIN* (1689) [I], second BARON SOMERHILL [U K], second but only surviving son and heir, born 30th November 1832. He is unmarried, and failing any issue-male of his body, the Barony of Bourke of Bophin will become extinct on his death.

BOURKE, Baron [I].

1727 – 17   I. TOBY [THEOBALD] BOURKE, descended from the Bourkes of Clanricarde, was, 5th September 1697, recommended to the protection of the Princess of Carignano, by Queen Mary, as 'a young Irish gentleman of merit and good family.' He entered the Spanish army, and, being then in Spain, had a certificate from King James, dated August 1702, that he was descended from the old and noble family of Bourke of Clanricarde. He may have been the Theobald Bourke, Knight of the Spanish Order of St. James, who was sworn a Gentleman of the Privy Chamber, 7th January 1704; and he was knighted before 16th April 1705, when he was sent by King James as his Minister to the Court of Madrid, which post he still held 12th June 1712. On 3rd February 1727 he was created by James III and VIII *BARON BOURKE* [I], with remainder to the heirs-male of his body.

BREFFNEY, Viscount of [I].

1731 – 17   I. OWEN (otherwise AUDEONUS or EUGENIUS) O'ROURKE,[1] of Carha, co. Leitrim, served King James II and VII faithfully in his Irish wars, and afterwards followed him to France. On the Peace of Ryswick, 10th September 1697, the regiment in which he served having been disbanded, he entered the Duke of Lorraine's service, and after having served that Prince as Major of his Body Guards and as a Gentleman of his Bedchamber,

---

[1] He was probably the 'Mr. O'Roerk' who had a declaration of his noblesse from James III and VIII, January 1709.

BREFFNEY

he was made a P.C. by him. On 18th April 1727 he was (as Audeonus O'Rourke) appointed Ambassador from King James III and VIII to the Court of Vienna,[1] and on the 24th May following was created (by that King) BARON O'ROURKE, of Carha, co. Leitrim [I], with remainder to the heirs-male of his body. On the 31st July 1731 he had a fresh patent of the same date, but with a new preamble,[2] and on the same day (31st July 1731) was further created VISCOUNT OF BREFFNEY, in Connaught [I], with the same remainder. His appointment at the Court of Vienna was renewed 'at his desire of the same date, but with 'the change of the name Audeonus to Eugenius,' 18th August 1731, and in July 1742 he had, 'as a special mark of the Royal 'favour, he having no children, and his lady being past the age 'of having any,' a new patent,[3] but with precedency of the former, as BARON OF CARHA and VISCOUNT OF BREFFNEY [I], with remainder, failing heirs-male of his body, to his cousin-german, Constantine O'Rourke, of Carha, Esquire, and the heirs-male of his body.

---

[1] He had possibly been on a mission to the Emperor in 1715, for on the 1st March 1715 the Duke of Berwick writes to King James : 'We are assured M. 11, 13, 55, 11, 29 ' (Ruerk) is a man of sense, and would be a fitter person to employ near M. Erington (the ' Emperor)'; and again, 10th March : 'I am glad your Majesty is resolved sending ' O'R[uer]k to M. Alain (Germany), but I humbly conceive his business will not only be to ' treat about 25, 11, 46, 28, 87, 55, 87, 96, 11, 21, 55, 69, 12, 96, 13, 20, 37, 55, 11 (Prince Carles' ' daug[h]ter), but also about M. Erington's (the Emperor's) 69, 46, 69, 37, 55, 11 (sister), ' and for to watch an occasion to make a friendshipp betwixt M. Robinson (James) and ' M. Erington. These points are certainly very essential.' On the 15th March, however, he writes : 'I cannot think M. O'R[uer]k's journey to Mr. Erington (the Emperor) ' useless, for all people at Alencon (England) and at M. Fredeling's (France) write ' continually of the great advantages could be had by a friendship or alliance with Mr. ' Erington. 'Tis worth while at least to try'—as if the King had changed his mind (*Calendar of Stuart Papers*, i. p. 351 *et seq.*).

[2] This sets forth his services as above, and is endorsed : '*N.B.*—The two above ' warrants were both signed by the King the 13 July 1731, and the Preambles are in ' Mr. O'Rouerke's own words contained in a letter he writ Lord Dunbar,' and in another handwriting : 'This warrant was renewed again with alterations, *vide* t other Book of ' Entries.'

[3] This is endorsed : 'The Preamble of this warrant is drawn exactly from that of a ' former one of the same date entered in the other Book of Entry's, and from a letter ' Mr. O'Rouerke now writes to Lord Dunbar. The present warrant was signed by the ' King in July 1742, but of the same date as the former one above mentioned, viz. ' 13 July 1731, which former one was returned by Mr. O'Rouerke to the King and · destroyed by H.M.'

This Owen O'Rourke was a well-known general in the armies of Maria Theresa, as were also others of his name. Count John O'Rourke was a distinguished officer in the armies of Russia, Poland, and France between 1760 and 1780, and another Count Owen O'Rourke married a niece of General de Lacy (see Walker's *Hibernian Magazine*, 1782, p. 144).

BROWNE

BROWNE, Earl of [I].

1726 — 17

I. GEORGE BROWNE or BROWN, COUNT OF THE HOLY ROMAN EMPIRE, Lieutenant-General of the armies of His Imperial and Catholic Majesty, Counsellor of War, and Colonel of a regiment of infantry in his said Majesty's service, a Jacobite exile descended from the family of Browne of Camus,[1] co. Limerick, was on the 12th April 1726 created by King James III and VIII *BARON OF* [   ], *VISCOUNT OF* [   ], and *EARL OF* [*BROWNE*] [I], with remainder, failing heirs-male of his body, to his brother, Ulysses Browne,[2] and the heirs-

---

[1] See Ferrar's *History of Limerick*, p. 348, where there is a somewhat confused account of this family.

[2] This ULYSSES BROWNE, an Irish Jacobite exile, was a colonel of cavalry in the Austrian army, and was made a Baron of the Empire by the Emperor Charles VI (not Charles V, as in the *Dictionary of National Biography*) for his military services. He was father of

ULYSSES MAXIMILIAN BROWNE or BROWN, *Count of the Holy Roman Empire, Baron of Camus and Mountany*, and Field-Marshal in the Imperial service, who was born at Basle (*Dictionary of National Biography*) or at Limerick (Dalton, p. 322), 23rd October 1705, was probably educated at Limerick Diocesan School, and in 1715 was invited to Hungary by his uncle, the *Earl of Browne*, who was in command of an infantry regiment there. He was present at the siege of Belgrade, and was a Colonel at twenty in 1725. He accompanied his uncle in the expedition to Corsica in 1730, and at twenty-nine in 1734 was in command of an infantry regiment in Italy, being the same year appointed by the Emperor Charles VI a member of the Aulic Council of War. On the accession of the Empress Queen Maria Theresa he was made Field-Marshal Lieutenant, and given command of the army in Silesia; P.C. 1743. In the campaign in Italy, 1743-1748, he greatly distinguished himself at the battle of Piacenza, 15th June 1745, and was in command of the Imperial troops who crossed the Var and entered France, afterwards conducting a masterly retreat. On the Convention of Nizza, 1749, he returned to Vienna, and was in command in Transylvania and afterwards in Bohemia; Knight of the Polish Order of the White Eagle, 1752; Field-Marshal, 1753. He was struck by a cannon-ball while heading a bayonet charge of grenadiers on the Prussian lines before the walls of Prague, 6th May 1757, which shattered one of his legs. He was carried from the field, and died of his wounds at Prague 26th June following (a few minutes after hearing of the victory of Kollin, won on the 18th by his cousin *Earl Browne*), leaving behind him 'the reputation of a consummate general and an able and successful ' negociator.' His life was published in French and German, 1757. He married, when twenty-one, in 1726, the Countess Maria Philipine von Martinez, daughter of George Adam, Count of Martinez, sometime Viceroy of Naples, by whom, who was granted a pension by the Empress, he had two sons (see *Dictionary of National Biography* and D'Alton's *King James' Irish Army List*, 1689). See also Ferrar's *History of Limerick*, p. 348, where mention is made of George, Baron Brown, Governor of Deva in Transylvania, who married the Countess of Rohdt, niece of the Prince of Constance; of a Colonel George Brown, killed at the battle of Guastalla in Italy; and of a Colonel Brown who served with the French at Savannah in America and was killed there, and whose uncle, Marshal Brown, died at Vienna 1784. Concerning the above-named Colonel Brown, the French military records show that Thomas Browne, born 18th October 1732 at Castelloffre (*sic*), Ireland, entered the Dillon regiment as a cadet 1st June 1747, and was dangerously wounded at the battle of Laufeld 2nd July that year; became

BROWNE

male of his body. In 1715 he was Colonel of an infantry regiment in Hungary, and in 1730 was in command of the Imperial forces that invested Corsica. He was apparently the father of

II. GEORGE (BROWNE), second EARL OF [BROWNE], etc. [I], and COUNT OF THE HOLY ROMAN EMPIRE, son and heir of the preceding, born at Limerick, 15th June 1698, educated at Limerick Diocesan School. In his twenty-seventh year he entered the service of the Elector Palatine, from which he passed in 1730 to that of Russia. He distinguished himself in the Polish, French, and Turkish wars, and had risen to the rank of General, with command of 30,000 men, when he was taken prisoner by the Turks at Krolke in 1738. After being three times sold as a slave he obtained his freedom through the intercession of the French Ambassador, Villeneuve; and remaining some time in Constantinople in his slave's costume, succeeded in discovering some important state secrets, which he carried to St. Petersburg. In recognition of this special service he was raised by the Empress Anna to the rank of Major-General, and in this capacity accompanied General Lacy on his first expedition to Finland. On the outbreak of the Swedish war his tactical skill was displayed to great advantage, and in the seven years' war he rendered important assistance as Lieutenant-General under his cousin, Field-Marshal Browne. His fortunate diversion of the enemy's attack at Kollin, 18th June 1757, and again at Zorndorf, 25th August 1758, chiefly contributed to those victories. By Peter III he was made a Field-Marshal, and given chief command in the Danish War. Governor of Livonia, 1762 to (his death[1] in) 1792, where he administered affairs 'with ' remarkable practical sagacity and with great advantage, both ' to the supreme Government and to the varied interests of ' the inhabitants.' He died 18th February 1792.[2] He married

17 - 1792

Lieutenant *réformé* 12th November following; Foot Lieutenant 1st August 1756; 2nd Captain 1st June 1757; Knight of St. Louis 18th February 1763; Captain *réformé* 23rd March 1763; Aide-Major 1st January 1766; given a company 31st December 1766; Colonel in the army 23rd January 1771; Captain-commandant of a company of chasseurs 5th June 1776; Major ditto 30th January 1778, and was killed at siege of Savannah 9th October 1779.

[1] Some time before his death he handed his resignation to the Empress Catherine, 'Monsieur le Comte, répondit-elle, rien ne doit nous séparer que la mort.'

[2] *Dictionary of National Biography.* Other accounts give the date of his death as 18th September.

BURNTISLAND

[   ], fourth daughter of Peter, Count Lacy, Field-Marshal in the Russian service (born 1698, died 1751), by the Countess Martha Feuchen de Loeser. He had issue, two sons.[1]

1792 — III. [   ] (BROWNE), third *EARL OF BROWNE*, etc. [I], and COUNT OF THE HOLY ROMAN EMPIRE, elder son and heir.

BURNTISLAND, Earl of [S].

i.e. '*BURNTISLAND*,' *EARLDOM OF* (Drummond), created 17th April 1692, with '*MELFORT*,' *DUKEDOM OF*, which see.

BUTLER, Baron [I].

1727 — 17   I. RICHARD BUTLER was on the 1st April 1727 created by King James III and VIII *BARON BUTLER* [I], with remainder to the heirs-male of his body.[2]

BUTLER, Baronet [E].

1743 — 1   I. JAMES BUTLER was on the 23rd December 1743 created by King James III and VIII a *KNIGHT* and *BARONET* [E], for special service in that country.

BULLINGHEL, Baron [E].

i.e. '*BULLINGHEL*,' *BARONY OF* (Goring), created 2nd January 1722, with '*GORING*,' *VISCOUNTY OF*, which see.

CARHA, Baron of [I].

i.e. '*CARHA*,' co. Leitrim, *BARONY OF* (O'Rourke), created July 1742, with '*BREFFNEY*,' *VISCOUNTY OF*, which see.

---

[1] Farrer says (p. 349) General and Colonel Brown, now (1787) in the Emperor's service.

[2] He was probably either the Richard Butler, 'the son of gentle parents of co. 'Kilkenny,' who had a declaration of his noblesse from James III and VIII, 23rd March 1703, or the one 'residing at St. Malo, and descended from the old and gentle 'house of Paulstown, co. Kilkenny,' who had a similar declaration, 18th July 1712. In the St. Germains Registers, 26th October 1692, is a note of the baptism of James Francis Richard, son of Captain Richard Butler, the Prince of Wales being sponsor.

CARYLL

CAHIRAVAHILLA, Viscount of [I].

I. DOMINICK ROCHE, Alderman of Limerick, son of Jordan Oge Roche, Mayor of Limerick (in 1639), by his wife Marne O'Brien, widow of a Butler surnamed Moura Trowla,[1] presented a petition on the Restoration to the Court of Claims, praying that the estates of Newcastle, Mungrel, and Cahiravahilla, all within the liberties of Limerick, and which had been confiscated under Cromwell, might be restored to him. He is said to have been created by King James II and VII, when in Ireland in 1689 or 1690, BARON TARBERT and VISCOUNT OF CAHIRAVAHILLA [I]. He married Agnes Burke of Cahirmakel,[1] and had issue.[2]

1689/90
—
1

CARGILL, Viscount [S].

i.e. 'CARGILL,' VISCOUNTY OF (Drummond), created 1701, with 'PERTH,' DUKEDOM OF, which see.

CARYLL OF DURFORD, Baron [E].

I. JOHN CARYLL of Goodward, and Lady Holt in Harting, Sussex,[3] eldest son and heir of John Caryll of Lady Holt and West Grinstead, by the Hon. Catherine, fourth and youngest daughter of William (Petre), second Baron Petre [E], was baptized at Harting, 2nd November 1626, educated at St. Omer, and succeeded his father 15th August 1681. As a Roman Catholic

1698/9
—
1711

---

[1] *Aylward*, 397, Ulster Office.

[2] See Farrer's *History of Limerick*, 1787, p. 352, where his grandsons are stated to have been Thomas Roche of Dublin, Esq., and Sir Boyle Roche, first Baronet [I]. This latter, according to the *Dictionary of National Biography* (which is, however, silent as to his parentage), was born 1743, entered the army, and distinguished himself in the American War; was M.P. for Tralee 1776-1777, for Gowran 1777-1783, for Portarlington 1783-1790, for Tralee again 1790-1797, and for Old Leighton 1798-1801; was created a Baronet [I], 30th November 1782; and died *s.p.* at Eccle Street, Dublin, 5th June 1807, having married Mary, eldest daughter of Admiral Sir Thomas Frankland of Great Thirkleby Hall, Yorks.... In a MS. pedigree of the family (*Aylward*, 397) in the Ulster Office, for sending him a copy of which the Editor has to thank Sir Arthur Vicars, Dominick Roche, *Lord Cahiravahilla*, is said to have had a son, Jordan Roche, who, by his wife Eleanor, daughter of Colonel John White of Rahagogan, co. Limerick, was father of Sir Boyle Roche, Baronet.

[3] The Carylls had been seated at Harting since the end of the sixteenth century. *Lord Caryll's* father was a noted Royalist and suffered heavily during the Commonwealth. He compounded for his estates by payment of £3020, the largest amount paid by any Sussex gentleman.

CARYLL

he fell under suspicion in the panic at the time of the alleged Popish Plot of 1679, and was committed to the Tower, but was shortly released on bail. On the accession of King James II and VII he was selected as the English agent at the Court of Rome, where, says Macaulay, he 'acquitted himself of his ' delicate errand with good sense and good feeling. The business ' confided in him was well done; but he assumed no public ' character, and carefully avoided all display.' His mission, therefore, put the government to scarcely any charge and excited scarcely any murmurs. Being recalled in 1686, he was appointed Secretary to the Queen Consort, Mary of Modena, and early the following year was with other Roman Catholics put into the commission of the peace. On the Revolution he followed the Royal Family into exile, being much esteemed by both the King and Queen. At James's special request his estates were exempted by William of Orange from confiscation; but in 1696, on the discovery of the so-called Assassination Plot, it being found that he had supplied Sir George Barclay with a sum of money to purchase horses and arms, he was attainted and his property seized by the Crown. It was afterwards redeemed by his nephew, on payment of £6000. He was joint SECRETARY OF STATE with the Earl of Middleton [S], 1694-1696, and before the 29th January 1698/9[1] was created BARON CARYLL OF DUNFORD [*i.e.* Durford], in Harting, Sussex [E], with apparently special remainder to the issue-male of his brothers. After the death of King James II and VII he appears again as Secretary to the Queen Regent, Mary of Modena, which post he continued to hold until his death *s.p.* at St. Germains-en-Laye, 4th September 1711, aged eighty-six. He was buried, near King James, in the church of the English Dominicans at Paris. A tablet was erected to his memory in the Scots College.[2] Will, dated 9th November 1707, with codicils of the 16th December 1707, 2nd September 1708, 9th October 1708, 4th April 1711, and 9th July 1711. He married

---

[1] When he signs a warrant 'Dunford.'
[2] The inscription is printed in full in the *Coll. Top. et Gen.*, vii. p. 42. Pope wrote an epitaph on him, and sent it to his nephew, which began—

> 'A manly form; a bold, yet modest mind;
> Sincere, though prudent; constant, yet resigned;
> Honour unchanged, a principle professed
> Fixed to one side, but moderate to the rest:
> An honest courtier, and a patriot too;
> Just to his prince, and to his country true.'

CARYLL

early in life Margaret, daughter and co-heir of Sir Maurice Drummond, who died in 1656. LORD CARYLL figures among the minor poets of Charles II's time. Macaulay says that he was 'known to his contemporaries as a man of fortune and fashion, 'and the author of two successful plays.' In 1700 he published anonymously an English version of the Psalms, probably designed more particularly for the use of the Royal Household.

II. JOHN (CARYLL), second BARON CARYLL OF DURFORD, nephew and heir-male of the preceding, being eldest son and heir of Richard Caryll of West Grinstead Place, Sussex, by Johanna, second daughter of Sir Henry Bedingfeld, first Baronet [E], by Margaret, daughter and heiress of Edward Paston of Appleton, Norfolk; which Richard was fifth, but next brother, who had issue, of the first LORD CARYLL. He was born at West Grinstead 9th, and baptized 12th, December 1667; succeeded his father at West Grinstead 1st May 1701, and his uncle at Lady Holt in Harting 4th September 1711. He lived quietly on his estate, and is chiefly distinguished as the friend of Pope. He died April 1736, being buried at Harting the 17th of that month. He married, 2nd January 1686, Elizabeth, daughter of John Harrington of Orle Place, Sussex, and by her, who died and was buried at Harting 25th October 1723, he had issue:—

1711 – 1736

1. HON. John Caryll, baptized at West Grinstead 28th December 1687, died *v.p.* 6th, and was buried at Harting 8th, April 1718. He married (marriage-settlement dated 12th July), 1712, Lady Mary, only daughter of Kenneth (Mackenzie), fourth Earl and first MARQUIS of Seaforth [S], K.T., by Lady Frances, second daughter of William (Herbert), first DUKE OF POWIS [E], and by her, who remarried Francis (Sempill), second LORD SEMPILL [S], and died in London 14th April, and was buried at Harting in the Caryll Chapel 16th April 1740,[1] he had issue:—
    (1) John Baptist Caryll, third BARON CARYLL.
    (2) A child died at birth.

---

[1] The following curious document is preserved among the Caryll Correspondence (Add. MSS. 28, 230, p. 34): 'Vous estes priez d'assister au Service pour le repos de 'l'Ame de Haute et Puissante Dame, Madame Marie Mackenzie, Veuve de My Lord 'Caryll, Baron de Dunford, Seignur de Lady Holt et autres Lieux, Pair d'Angleterre, décédée a Londres le 14º du present mois; qui se sera Mardy 26 Avril 1740, a neuf

CARYLL

 (3) Elizabeth Caryll, born 1713; died unmarried 1767.
 (4) Agnes Caryll, born 21st January 1718; died unmarried 1728.
 (5) Catherine Caryll (twin with her sister), born 21st January 1718; died 1747, about three months after her marriage with the Hon. J. F. Gage, commonly called Count Gage.

2. *Hon.* Richard Caryll, S. J., born 1692; entered the Society of Jesus, 7th September 1711; Priest at Lady's Holt, 1718, known as Paul Kelly; died at Stapehill, 18th February 1750, buried at Hampreston, *s.p.*

3. *Hon.* Edward Caryll, born 1695, buried at Harting, 2nd June 1766; married, first, before 1743, Catherine, daughter of Nathaniel Pigott of Whitton, co. Surrey, and by her, who died 1747, and was buried at Harting, he had a daughter.

 (1) Elizabeth Caryll, buried at Harting, 13th April 1743.

He married, secondly, Anne, daughter of Richard Harcourt, by the Hon. Henrietta, daughter of Henry (Browne), fifth Viscount Montagu [E], but appears to have had no further issue.

4. *Hon.* Henry Caryll, Page to the King of Poland, the father of Mary Leczinska, Queen Consort of Louis xv., born 1702; died 1726.

5. *Hon.* Elizabeth Caryll, born 1686/7; professed, 1708; nun of the Holy Sepulchre at Liége, 1713; died 1758.

6. *Hon.* Catherine Caryll, baptized 13th October 1686; died unmarried 26th May 1759.

7. *Hon.* Mary Caryll, a nun (Dame Romana), O.S.B. at Dunkirk; died 18th July 1758.

' heures du matin en Eglise du College des Ecossois, sossez S. Victor, Messieurs et
' dames s'y trouveront, s'il leur plaist.
     ' Un de profundis.'

 As her husband died *v.p.* he was never *Lord* Caryll, but Lady Mary appeared to have always used in France the title of *Comtesse de* Caryll. In Dennistoun's *Memoirs of Sir Robert Strange* he speaks of her son as *Earl of Caryll*; and says he was so created at the same time that his uncle was made *Marquis of Seaforth*, *i.e.* some twenty years before he was born.

CARYLL

8. *Hon.* Arabella Caryll, a nun (Dame Benedicta), O.S.B. at Dunkirk; professed, 1714; died there, 7th July 1759.
9. *Hon.* Fanny Caryll, 6th October 1794; a novice nun of the Holy Sepulchre at Liége; died during her novitiate.
10. *Hon.* Anne (Nanny) Caryll, born February 1699; a nun at Liége.

III. JOHN BAPTIST (CARYLL), third *Baron Caryll of Durford*, grandson and heir of the preceding, born and baptized at Harting, 13th December 1713; succeeded his grandfather, April 1736, and getting into difficulties, sold the West Grinstead estate about 1745, and in 1767 parted with the equity of redemption of the West Harting property to Mr. (afterwards Sir William) Burrell, the mortgagee of the estates. Proceeding to France he entered the Household of Charles III. He was deputed to meet the Princess Louisa of Stolberg at Loreto, and escort her to Nacerrata, where she was married, 17th April 1772, to the King. He, who had been made a *K.T.*, was, about 1768, appointed *Secretary of State*, which post he probably continued to hold until about 1777, when he appears to have returned to France and to have settled at Maisons-sur-Seine until 1783, when he retired to Dunkirk, where he died in the rue de Nieuport, 7th March 1788, aged seventy-four. He was buried there the 10th March following.[1] Will dated 11th April 1785.[2]

1736
—
1788

---

[1] 'Jean Baptiste Caryll. L'an de grace mil sept cent quatre-vingt-huit, le
'dixième jour de mars, Je, soussigné vicaire, aprés le service de la cloche ditte Marie,
'chanté par Monsieur Macquet curé de cette paroisse et doyen de la chrétienté, ai
'enterré au cimetière, le corps de Messir Jean Baptiste Caryll, homme veuf, âgé de
'74 ans, natif de Ladyholt, province de Sussex en Angleterre, Écuyer, grande croix
'de l'ordre de St. Andre, pair du Royaume d'Angleterre, décédé le sept de ce mois,
'dans son domicile, rue de Nieuport, administré des S.S. sacrements ordinaires. Ont
'été témoins le sieur, et Mr. Francois Bishop, prêtre et directeur des dames Anglaises
'et le sieur et Mr. Pierre de Marseman qui ont signé un double avec moi, jour, mois et
'an que dessus.
'Signé François Bishop, prêtre V. de Marseman, Pbter. Z.P. Renier, vicaire.'

[2] See *West Grinstead et les Caryll*, by Max de Trenqualion, two vols., Paris, 1893; Elwes' *Castles, Mansions, and Manors of West Sussex*, p. 253; and the Rev. H. D. Gordon's *History of Harting*, 1877. A good account of the first *Lord Caryll* is in the *Dictionary of National Biography*. It will be observed that Gordon (p. 143) says that John Baptiste Frances, born 13th December 1713, the elder son of the *Hon.* John Caryll, died aged four, and that the third *Lord Caryll* was a posthumous child born in France. As, however, the latter was seventy-four at the time of death in 1788, he was evidently the child born at Harting in December 1713.

CASTELBIANCO

He married, first (marriage-settlement dated May), 1738, the Hon. Dorothy Frances, younger daughter of William (Molyneux), fourth Viscount Molyneux [I], by Bridget, daughter and heiress of Robert Lucy of Cherlecote, co. Warwick. She died *s.p.* November 1760. He married, secondly, Mary Scarisbrick of Lancashire, who died *s.p.* at Maisons-sur-Seine, 27th October 1783, aged about forty, and was buried there, 29th October following.[1]

CASTELBIANCO, Duke [S].

i.e. 'CASTELBIANCO AND ST. ANDREWS,' DUKEDOM OF (de Bozas), created 4th February 1717. See 'ST. ANDREWS.'

CASTLEINCH, Baron [I].

i.e. 'CASTLEINCH,' co. Tipperary, BARONY OF (MacCarty), created 1st May 1689, with '*MOUNTCASHELL*,' VISCOUNTY OF, which see.

CASTLE LYONS, Baron [I].

1726 I. DANIEL O'BRIEN or OBRYAN, son of Morough O'Brien, Colonel of an Irish regiment in the French service, was on 17th March 1726 created by James III and VIII BARON OF CASTLE LYONS [I]. On 11th October 1746 he was further created BARON OF [   ], VISCOUNT OF TALLOW, and EARL OF LISMORE [I]. See '*LISMORE*,' EARLDOM OF [I], created 1746.

CASTLEMAINS, Baron [S].

i.e. 'CASTLEMAINS,' BARONY OF (Drummond), created 17th April 1692, with '*MELFORT*,' DUKEDOM OF, which see.

---

[1] 'Le 29 octobre 1783, par nous prêtre curé de Mesnil le Roy, en présence de
'Monsieur le curé de Maisons, avec son authorisation, a été inhumée, dans un caveau,
'situé près la principale porte de l'église de cette paroisse, très haute et très puissante
'dame, Marie Swarbrick, native de la province de Lancastre en Angleterre, epousé de
'Lord Caryll, pair d'Angleterre, resident en cette paroisse depuis six ans.
'L'inhumation de la dite dame, âgée d'environ 40 ans et décédée le 27 octobre, où
'furent présents M. Franc, prêtre habitué de la paroisse de Saint Germains-en-Laye,
'M. Jean Gifford, écuyer, né en Angleterre, present au Mesnil-le-Roy et autres
'personnes de cette paroise que ont signé avec nous.
   'Flint, curé du Mesnil-le-Roy.
   'E. Flyse, conseiller, médecin du Roy.
   'Cassan, desservant de Carrière-Saint Denis.
   'Baron, curé de Maisons.'

CLANRANALD

CASTLEROSSE, Baron [I].

i.e. '*CASTLEROSSE,*' BARONY OF (Browne), created 20th April 1689, with '*KENMARE,*' VISCOUNTY OF, which see.

CHESTER, Earl of [E].

I. CHARLES EDWARD LEWIS PHILIP CASIMIR (STUART), PRINCE OF ENGLAND AND SCOTLAND, DUKE OF CORNWALL [E] and ROTHESAY [S], eldest son and heir-apparent of King James III and VIII, was born in Rome 31st December 1720, and was created or declared shortly after his birth *PRINCE OF WALES*, and (by consequence?)[1] *EARL OF CHESTER*. *K.G.* and *K.T.* before 1745. On 1st January 1766 he succeeded his father as *de jure* King of England, Scotland, France, and Ireland. He died *s.p.l.* 31st January 1788.

c. 1720
—
1766

CHEVELEY, Viscount of [E].

i.e. '*CHEVELEY*,' co. Cambridge, VISCOUNTY OF (Jermyn), created 9th July 1689, with '*DOVER*,' EARLDOM OF, which see.

CHIEFLY, Viscount of the [E].

See '*CHEVELEY*,' co. Cambridge, VISCOUNT OF.

CLANRANALD, Baroness [S].

I. PENELOPE LOUISA MACKENZIE, widow of Allan Macdonald, fourteenth Chief of Clanranald, and daughter of Colonel Alexander Mackenzie, Governor of Tangiers under Charles II, by Louisa Bouvinot, was on 28th September 1716 created by James III and VIII *BARONESS CLANRANALD* [S]. Her husband (to whom she was married at St. Germains 9th October 1694) had been one of the most devoted and faithful of the adherents of the House of Stuart. He had been with Dundee at Killiecrankie, and afterwards, refusing to take the oaths of allegiance to William of Orange, had retired to France. He resided for some time at the Court of St. Germains, and afterwards served under the Duke of Berwick. On the Peace of

1716
—
1743

---

[1] See *The Complete Peerage*, ii. p. 230, for a similar case—that of Charles II.

CLANRANALD

Ryswick, 10th September 1697, he returned to Scotland, and fixed his residence at Ormiclate House in South Uist. In 1715 he joined Mar at the head of his clan, and was mortally wounded leading the right wing of the Jacobite army at the battle of Sheriffmuir, 13th November 1715, and died at Drummond Castle the day following, aged forty, and was buried at Innerpeffray, near Crieff, in the Perth family burial-place.[1] She died *s.p.* in Edinburgh 1743, and was buried there.

CLANRANALD, Baron [S].

1716 – 1725

I. RANALD MACDONALD OF CLANRANALD, younger son of Donald Macdonald of Clanranald, by Marion, daughter of John MacLeod of MacLeod, was born at Castle Tirrim about 1677; succeeded his elder brother, Allan (above named), in the Chiefship of his clan 14th November 1705, and was created by James III and VIII, 28th September 1716, BARON CLANRANALD [S], with remainder to his heirs-male. He did not return to Scotland after his brother's death, and died, unmarried, in the Faubourg St. Germains, Paris, 13th June 1725, and was buried in the Church of St. Sulpice there.

1725 – 1730

II. DONALD MACDONALD, second BARON CLANRANALD, second cousin and heir-male of the preceding, son and heir of Ranald Oig Macdonald of Benbecula, by his first wife, [   ], daughter of M'Neill of Barra, which Ranald Oig was the elder son of Ranald Macdonald of Benbecula, third but second surviving son of Allan Macdonald of Clanranald, the great-great-grandfather (by his eldest son) of the first BARON CLANRANALD. He was born at Borve Castle, Benbecula; succeeded his second cousin once removed in the BARONY and Chiefship of Clanranald, 13th June 1725, and died at Nunton, Benbecula, 1730, and was buried there in St. Mary's churchyard. He married, first, Janet, sister of the first LORD, only daughter of Donald Macdonald of Clanranald, by Marion, daughter of John MacLeod of MacLeod. She was born at Castle Tirrim aforesaid, and died at Nunton, and was buried there with her husband. He married, secondly, Margaret, daughter

---

[1] For particulars as to the dates and places of birth, death, and burial of the Chiefs of Clanranald and of their wives, the Editor is indebted to the Rev. A. J. Macdonald of Killearnan, author of *A History of Clan Donald.*

CLANRANALD

of George Mackenzie of Kildun. She was born at Kildun, and died at Nunton, and was buried there. He had issue by his first wife an only son, and by his second a son and daughter.
1. Ranald, MASTER OF CLANRANALD, his heir.
2. *Hon.* Alexander Macdonald of Boisdale.
3. *Hon.* Anne Macdonald, married Lochlan M'Kinnen of Strathuradale.

III. RANALD (MACDONALD), third BARON CLAN- 1730
RANALD, son and heir of the preceding, born at Nunton 1692; –
succeeded his father 1730. In 1745 he was the first chief to 1766
whom Prince Charles appealed, but he declined to join him and prevented his island clansmen from rising, although his son and the clansmen of the mainland did so. He continued to reside quietly on Benbecula during the war, but after Culloden he and his wife gave most active assistance to the Prince, and it was by their means that their kinswoman Flora was enabled to effect the Prince's escape. He was afterwards arrested, but nothing being proved against him, he was released. In 1753 he resigned the greatly impoverished estates to his son, and died at Nunton, 6th March 1766, and was buried there. He married Margaret, daughter of William MacLeod of Bernera. She was born at Bernera, and died at Ormiclate, Uist, 20th September 1780, and was buried at Nunton. He had issue:—
1. Ranald, MASTER OF CLANRANALD, his heir.
2. *Hon.* Donald Macdonald, an officer in the army, killed at Quebec, 13th September 1759.
3. *Hon.* Margaret Macdonald, died unmarried.

IV. RANALD (MACDONALD), fourth BARON CLAN- 1766
RANALD, elder son and heir of the preceding; born at Nunton 1722; –
educated at St. Germains. On the arrival of Prince Charles 1776
in Loch nan Uamh he went on board the *Doutelle*, and finding the Prince had come without arms or funds, he endeavoured to dissuade him from the enterprise; but finding Charles resolved, he immediately raised the clan and joined the Prince with two hundred and fifty men, being the first chief that did so. After the raising of the Standard at Glenfinnan, 19th August 1745, he was sent to Dundee with five hundred men, and proclaimed King James there, 8th September. He led the clan at the battle of Prestonpans, 31st September, gave a large bond to enable the

33

CLANRANALD

army to leave Edinburgh, took part in the advance to Derby, was present at Clifton, 17th December 1745, at Falkirk, 16th January, and at Culloden, 16th April 1746, where he was severely wounded. After that fatal defeat he escaped first to Inverness and then to Moidart, where he remained in hiding for some time. From thence he proceeded to Brahan Castle, where he was married, and afterwards embarked with his wife as 'Mr. and 'Mrs. Black' at Cromarty for London, whence they passed to France. He entered the French army as Lieutenant of the Scottish infantry regiment of Ogilvy, 28th February 1747, and served through the campaigns of 1747 and 1748 in Flanders as Aide-de-camp to Marshal Saxe, and was charged with conveying the news of the Marshal's death to Louis xv. In 1753, taking advantage of the fact that in the Act of Attainder he was called by mistake Donald instead of Ranald, he quitted the French army, 26th July, claimed the benefit of the indemnity, and returned home, where he lived quietly for the rest of his days. He succeeded his father, 6th March 1766, and died at Nunton, 2nd October 1776, and was buried there. He married, first, at Brahan, 1746, Mary, daughter of Basil Hamilton, M.P., by his wife, Isabella, daughter of *Lord* Alexander Mackenzie. She died 11th May 1750, aged thirty. He married, secondly, Flora, daughter of [   ] Mackinnon of Mackinnon, who died at Edinburgh, 1820, and was buried at Holyrood. He had issue by his first wife an only son, and by his second two sons and three daughters :—

1. Charles James Somerled, *Master of Clanranald*, born in France, May 1750; died there, 1756, aged five.
2. John, *Master of Clanranald*, his heir.
3. *Hon.* James Macdonald, an officer in the army.
4. *Hon.* Margaret Macdonald, died unmarried.
5. *Hon.* Mary Macdonald, died unmarried.
6. *Hon.* Penelope Macdonald, married at Edinburgh, 2nd March 1789, William (Hamilton), seventh Lord Belhaven and Stenton [S], who died 29th October 1814. She died 5th May 1816, leaving issue.

1776 – 1794

V. JOHN (MACDONALD), fifth *Baron Clanranald*, second but elder surviving son and heir of the preceding, born at Nunton 30th December 1761; succeeded his father, 2nd October 1776. He entered the army, and became Captain in

CLANRANALD

the 22nd dragoons. He retired, and afterwards lived quietly on his estates, and died at Edinburgh, 18th November 1794, and was buried at Holyrood. He married, first, Katherine, daughter of the Right Honourable Robert Macqueen of Braxfield, Lord Justice-Clerk of Scotland. She, who was divorced, died at Hartlepool 1844. He married, secondly, Jean, daughter of Colin Macdonald of Boisdale. She was born at Boisdale, South Uist, and died *s.p.* at Edinburgh, 2nd June 1847, and was buried at Holyrood. He had issue :—
1. Reginald George, *MASTER OF CLANRANALD*, his heir.
2. *HON.* Robert Johnstone Macdonald.
3. *HON.* Donald Macdonald.

VI. REGINALD (RANALD) GEORGE (MACDONALD), sixth *BARON CLANRANALD*, eldest son and heir of the preceding, born at Edinburgh 29th August 1788; educated at Eton and abroad; succeeded his father, 18th November 1794; J.P. and D.L., co. Inverness; M.P. for Plympton, 1812-1824; from 1816-1825 he was engaged in the celebrated controversy with Colonel Alaisdair Macdonald of Glengarry as to the Chiefship of the clan Donald. Before 1837 he sold most of the family estates, retaining only the ruins of Castle Tirrim and the island of Riska in Loch Moidart. He died in Clarendon Road, London, 11th March 1873, and was buried in Brompton Cemetery. He married first, 13th February 1812, Lady Caroline Anne, second daughter of Richard (Edgcumbe), second Earl of Mount-Edgcumbe [G B], by his wife, Lady Sophia, third daughter and co-heir of John (Hobart), second Earl of Buckinghamshire [G B]. She was born 22nd October 1792, and died in Edinburgh, 10th April 1824, and was buried at Holyrood. He married, secondly, Anne Selby, Dowager-Baroness Ashburton [G B], daughter of William Cunningham of Lainshaw, by his wife, Margaret Nicholson, daughter of the Hon. George Cranstoun. She died 8th July 1835, and he married thirdly, November 1855, Elizabeth Rebecca, daughter of [   ] Newman. He had issue only by his first wife, viz. :—
1. Reginald John, *MASTER OF CLANRANALD*, his heir.
2. *HON.* Caroline Sophia Macdonald, married, 8th September 1842, the Hon. Charles Henry Cust, M.P., who died 23rd May 1875. She died 16th October 1887, leaving issue.

1794 - 1873

CLANRANALD

3. *Hon.* Emma Hamilla Macdonald, married, 21st April 1840, Rev. the Hon. Alfred Wodehouse, who died 6th September 1848. She died 5th April 1852, leaving issue.
4. *Hon.* Louisa Emily Macdonald, married first, 13th April 1841, Charles William Marsham of Stratton Strawless, who died *v.p.* 13th December 1852, leaving issue. She married secondly, as second wife, 4th December 1856, Colonel Hugh Fitzroy, and died 13th February 1897, leaving issue.
5. Hon. Flora Clementina Isabel Macdonald, sometime Maid of Honour and Woman of the Bedchamber to Queen Victoria, died 25th December 1899.
6. *Hon.* Annie Sarah Macdonald, married first, 2nd April 1848, Alfredo Salvatore Ruggioro Andrea (di Sant' Andrea), Baron Porcelli di Sant' Andrea [Sicily], who died 18th January 1884. She married secondly, Major Woolhouse, and died 18th August 1897, leaving issue.

1873 – 1899

VII. REGINALD JOHN (MACDONALD), seventh *Baron Clanranald*, K.C.B., K.C.S.I., etc., only son and heir of the preceding, born 7th October 1819; entered the Royal Navy, 1833; served in the Carlist War, 1837-1838; promoted to be Post-Captain, 1854, for services on the West Coast of Africa; Rear-Admiral, 1870; Vice-Admiral, 1877; Commander-in-Chief in East Indies, 1875-1878, and at the Nore, 1881-1884; raised a force of one thousand Royal Naval Coast Volunteers at Greenock, 1859, for which he was thanked by the Government; commanded the squadron of honour sent to Alexandria to invest the Khedive with the G.C.B., and was attached to the Duke of Abercorn's special mission to the King of Italy in 1878. He died in London, 15th December 1899, and was buried there. He married, 12th June 1855, the Hon. Adelaide Louisa, second daughter of George John (Vernon), fifth Baron Vernon [G B], by his first wife, Isabella Caroline, daughter of Cuthbert Ellison of Hebburn, co. Durham, M.P. She, who was born 6th September 1831, survives. He had issue :—

1. Allan Douglas, *Master of Clanranald*, his heir.
2. *Hon.* Angus Roderick Macdonald, born April 1858; married 1884 Leucoline Helen, daughter of the Rev. Henry Clarke, M.A.

CONNOCK

3. *Hon.* Adelaide Effrida Macdonald.
4. *Hon.* Maud Macdonald.

VIII. ALLAN DOUGLAS (MACDONALD), eighth BARON CLANRANALD and twenty-seventh Captain and Chief of his clan, *late* Captain R.A., born April 1856; succeeded his father, 15th December 1899.

1899

CLERMONT, Viscount [E].

i.e. 'CLERMONT,' VISCOUNTY OF (Middleton), created before 17th October 1701, with 'MONMOUTH,' EARLDOM OF, which see.

CLEWORTH, Baron [E].

I. JOHN (DRUMMOND), first EARL, and afterwards DUKE OF MELFORT [S], was by patent, dated at Dublin,[1] 7th August 1689, created by James II and VII (after the revolution in England) BARON CLEWORTH (*i.e.* Clewer, near Windsor), co. Berks [E], with like special remainder as that with which the Scottish Earldom had been conferred. See '*MELFORT*,' *DUKE OF*.

1689 -

CONCRAIG, Baron [S].

i.e. '*CONCRAIG*,' BARONY OF (Drummond), created 1701, with '*PERTH*,' DUKEDOM OF, which see.

CONNOCK, Baronet [E].

I. WILLIAM CONNOCK, ESQ., grandson of George Connock, born 1575, a younger son of the family of Connock of Treworgy, co. Cornwall,[2] was on 22nd February 1732 created by King James III and VIII a KNIGHT and BARONET [E], with remainder to his grandson, Joseph Connock, son of the deceased Sir Timon Connock, Knight, 'as a mark of the Royal favour for ' Sir Timon's loyal services.' He had issue, at least, one son, viz. :—

1732 - 17

    1. Sir Timon Connock, Knight, a gentleman in the Spanish service and Aide-de-camp to Philip V, dead before

---

[1] *The Complete Peerage*, ii. p. 288.
[2] See C. S. Gilbert's *Historical Survey of Cornwall*, 1817.

CONSTABLE

22nd February 1732, married shortly before 21st March 1707 [?   , younger daughter of Sir Ignatius White, first Baronet [E], Marquis of Albeville and Count of Alby [H R E], Secretary of State [I] to James II and VII]. She was before 1707 Maid of Honour to Queen Mary of Modena, and, 21st March that year, had promises from King James III and VIII and Queen Mary to pay her £2000 and £1000 respectively within one year of the Restoration. They had issue, at least, one son.

(1) Joseph Connock, heir to the BARONETCY.

II. SIR JOSEPH CONNOCK, second BARONET, grandson and heir of the preceding. He is said to have derived the title of Count of Alby [H R E] from his mother and to have been created Marquis of Albeville.[1] He appears to have married and had issue.[2]

CONSTABLE, Baronet [E].

I. JOHN CONSTABLE, ESQ.,[3] was on 17th September 1753 created by King James III and VIII, for his services to Henry, Duke of York, a KNIGHT and BARONET [E], with remainder to the heirs-male of his body. He was for long Major-Domo of the Household to King James, and was living January 1766, when he was one of those dismissed by Charles III.[4]

COTTINGTON OF FONTHILL GIFFORD, Baron [E].

I. FRANCIS COTTINGTON of Fonthill Gifford, Esquire, eldest son and heir of Charles Cottington of the same, by his first wife Alithea, daughter of [   ] [   ], born before 14th October 1687 (when his mother died), and was a minor, 22nd December 1697, when he succeeded his father. On April 1716 he was

---

[1] See C. S. Gilbert's *Historical Survey of Cornwall*, 1817.

[2] 'In the late commotions in Spain the representative of the family, Don Joseph Connock, who is said to have been preceptor to Ferdinand VII, is noticed as pursuing that course of political conduct which did not sully his English extraction' (*Ibid.*).

[3] A John Constable was appointed by James II and VII to be his agent and receiver of the tenth of prizes at Dunkirk, June 1694; another was Clerk of the Kitchen in Ordinary, 27th June 1695 to 1st February 1697; and a third was appointed First Physician in Ordinary to James III and VIII, 24th October 1701.

[4] Dennistoun, ii. p. 102.

DARTFORD

created by King James III and VIII *BARON COTTINGTON OF FONT-HILL GIFFORD*, co. Wilts [E],[1] with remainder to his heirs-male, whom failing to his brother, John Cottington, and the heirs-male of his body. He died at West Wycombe, co. Bucks, 8th September 1728. Administration of his effects was granted 9th December following to Dame Winifred Golding, curatrix of Francis Cottington, a minor. He married [   ], daughter of [   ] [   ]. She died 2nd September 1728. He had issue at least one son :—

1. *HON.* Francis Cottington, his heir.

II. FRANCIS (COTTINGTON), second *BARON COTTINGTON OF FONTHILL GIFFORD*, son and heir of the preceding; a minor, 8th September 1728, when he succeeded his father. He is presumed to have alienated Fonthill Gifford to William Beckford, Alderman of London, and to have died March 1758.[2]

1728
—
1758 ?

CROMLIX, Baron [S].

i.e. '*CROMLIX,*' *BARONY OF* (Hay), created 5th October 1718, with '*INVERNESS,*' *EARLDOM OF*, which see.

CRONE, Baron [I].

I. MATTHEW CRONE had on 14th March 1697 a certificate, dated at St. Germains, from King James II and VII, declaring that he was a gentleman, descended from a good family in Ireland, and as 'Brigadier-General in the service of his 'Catholic Majesty, and Governor of Lerida,' he was on 16th February 1728 created by King James III and VIII *BARON CRONE* [I], with remainder to the heirs-male of his body.

1728
—
17

DARTFORD, Viscount [E].

i.e. '*DARTFORD,*' *VISCOUNTY OF* (Villiers), created April 1716, with '*JERSEY,*' *EARLDOM OF*, which see.

---

[1] He was a great-grandnephew to Francis (Cottington), first Baron Cottington [E], so created 10th July 1631, who died *s.p.* at Valladolid 19th June 1652.
[2] Hoare's *Wilts*, IV. i. 21.

39

DAVIA

DAVIA, Baron [S].

i.e. '*DAVIA*,' BARONY OF (Davia), created 12th April 1698, with '*ALMOND*,' EARLDOM OF, which see.

[DILLON], Viscount [I].

1717 — I. HON. ARTHUR DILLON, Lieutenant-General of his Majesty's armies, was on 1st February 1717 created by King James III and VIII BARON OF [   ] and VISCOUNT OF [?*DILLON*] [I], with remainder to the heirs-male of his body. On 24th June 1721 he was further created (by the same King) an Earl and Peer of Parliament, as EARL OF [*DILLON*], VISCOUNT OF [   ], and LORD OF [   ] [S]. See '*DILLON*,' EARLDOM OF.

[? DILLON], Earl of [S].

1721 — 1733 I. HON. ARTHUR DILLON, VISCOUNT and BARON [?*DILLON*] [I], was on 24th June 1721 created by King James III and VIII a Lord and Peer of Parliament, as EARL OF DILLON, VISCOUNT OF [   ], and LORD OF [   ] [S], with remainder to his heirs-male. He was the third but second surviving son of Theobald (Dillon), seventh Viscount Dillon [I], by his wife Mary, daughter of Sir Henry Talbot of Templeoge, co. Dublin, and Mount Talbot, co. Roscommon, was born in Roscommon 1670, accompanied the regiment raised by his father to France in May 1690, and became its Colonel 1st June following. He served in Spain 1693-1697, in Germany 1701, and Italy 1702; Brigadier 1702, and Brigadier-General (Maréchal de camp) 1705. In 1707 he commanded the left wing of the French army under Tessé in Provence, was Commander-in-Chief at the siege of Kaiserslautern, 1713, and was Lieutenant-General under the Duke of Berwick at the siege of Barcelona, 1714. The following year he returned to France, and on the 1st February 1717 he was appointed by King James his Ambassador at the French court, being the same day created BARON OF [   ], and VISCOUNT OF [?*DILLON*] [I]. On 24th June 1721 he was further created a Lord and Peer of Parliament as EARL OF [?*DILLON*], VISCOUNT OF [   ], and BARON OF [   ] [S], and two days afterwards he had a commission from King James as

DILLON

General and Commander-in-Chief of all the forces [I], and the next year, 26th May, he was made a *K.T.*, and he was also made a Knight-Commander of St. Louis. In 1728 he resigned the command of the celebrated Dillon regiment to his eldest son, and died at Paris 5th February 1733, leaving behind him the reputation of 'a brave soldier, a good officer, and most estimable ' man.' He married Christina, daughter of Ralph Sheldon, Equerry to James II and VII. She was born about 1680, was Maid of Honour to Queen Mary of Modena, and after her husband's death took lodgings in the English Austin Nunnery in Paris, where she died, 5th August 1757, and was buried in the cloister.[1]

II. CHARLES (DILLON), second *EARL*, *VISCOUNT*, and *BARON* [*DILLON*] [S], and *BARON* and *VISCOUNT* [*DILLON*] [I], eldest son and heir; Colonel of the Dillon regiment, 1728-1741; succeeded his father, 5th February 1733, and his cousin, as tenth VISCOUNT DILLON OF COSTELLO GALLEN, CO. Mayo [I], Feb. 1637. He died *s.p.s.*, 24th October 1741, in London, and was buried the 27th of that month at St. Pancras, Middlesex.[2]

1733
–
1741

III. HENRY (DILLON), third *EARL*, *VISCOUNT*, and *BARON* [*DILLON*] [S], eleventh VISCOUNT DILLON OF COSTELLO GALLEN (1621/2), and third *VISCOUNT* and *BARON* [*DILLON*] (1717) [I], brother and heir, born 1705; succeeded his brother, 24th October 1741; Colonel of the Dillon regiment, 1741-1744 and 1747-1772. He died 3rd September, and was buried 25th September 1787 at St. Pancras.

1741
–
1787

IV. CHARLES (DILLON, afterwards DILLON-LEE), fourth *EARL*, *VISCOUNT*, and *BARON* [*DILLON*] [S], twelfth VISCOUNT DILLON (1621/2), and fourth *VISCOUNT* and *BARON* [*DILLON*] (1717) [I], K.P., F.R.S., eldest son and heir, born 6th November 1745 in London; succeeded his father, 3rd September 1787; conformed to the Established Church, 1767; and claimed and was allowed the Viscounty of 1621/2 by the House of Lords [I] in 1778; K.P., 19th November 1798. He died 9th November 1813.

1787
–
1813

---

[1] *Dictionary of National Biography.*
[2] For a fuller account of the *Earls Dillon* see the extant peerages under Dillon, Viscount.

DIVRON

1813 — 1832
V. HENRY AUGUSTUS (LEE-DILLON), fifth *EARL*, *VISCOUNT*, and *BARON* [*DILLON*] [S], thirteenth VISCOUNT DILLON (1621/2), and fifth *VISCOUNT* and *BARON* [*DILLON*] (1717) [I], eldest son and heir, born 28th October 1777, died 24th July 1832.

1832 — 1865
VI. CHARLES HENRY (LEE-DILLON), sixth *EARL*, *VISCOUNT*, and *BARON* [*DILLON*] [S], fourteenth VISCOUNT DILLON (1621/2) and fifth *VISCOUNT* and *BARON* [*DILLON*] (1717) [I], eldest son and heir, born 20th April 1810 in Ely Place, Dublin, died *s.p.m.* 18th November 1865 at Ditchley, Oxon.

1865 — 1879
VII. THEOBALD DOMINICK GEOFFREY (LEE-DILLON), seventh *EARL*, *VISCOUNT*, and *BARON* [*DILLON*] [S], fifteenth VISCOUNT DILLON (1621/2), and seventh *VISCOUNT* [*DILLON*] (1717) [I], brother and heir, born 5th April 1811, died *s.p.* 30th November 1879.

1879 — 1892
VIII. ARTHUR EDMUND (LEE-DILLON), eighth *EARL*, *VISCOUNT*, and *BARON* [*DILLON*] [S], sixteenth VISCOUNT DILLON (1621/2), and eighth *VISCOUNT* and *BARON* [*DILLON*] (1717) [I], brother and heir, born 10th April 1812, died 12th January 1892.

1892
IX. HAROLD ARTHUR (LEE-DILLON), ninth *EARL*, *VISCOUNT*, and *BARON* [*DILLON*] [S], seventeenth VISCOUNT DILLON (1621/2), and ninth *VISCOUNT* and *BARON* [*DILLON*] (1717) [I], M.A., President of the Society of Antiquaries, Trustee of the British Museum and of the National Portrait Gallery, etc., son and heir, born 24th January 1844, succeeded his father 12th January 1892.

DIVRON, Lord [S].

i.e. '*DIVRON*,' BARONY OF (de Bozas), created 4th February 1717, with '*ST. ANDREWS*,' DUKEDOM OF, which see.

DOVER, Earl of [E].

1689 — 1708
I. HENRY JERMYN, second son of Thomas Jermyn of Rushbrooke, co. Suffolk, by Rebecca, daughter of [   ]

DRUMMOND

Rodway, born about 1636; Master of the Horse to the Duke of York, 1660-1675; was created 13th May 1685, by James II and VII, BARON DOVER OF DOVER, co. Kent [E]; Colonel of the 4th Horse Guards, 1686-1688, and of the Royal Body Guards; P.C., 17th August 1686; one of the Lords of the Treasury, 1687-1688; and Gentleman of the Bedchamber to King James, to whom he remained faithful, accompanying him to France and Ireland. He was attainted 20th June 1689, and on the 9th July following he was further created by James (after his alleged abdication) LORD GERMAIN (*i.e.* JERMYN) OF REYSTOWNE (*i.e.* ROYSTON), and BARON OF IPSWICH, co. Suffolk, VISCOUNT OF THE CHIEFLY (*i.e.* CHEVELEY), co. Cambridge, and EARL OF DOVER [E], with remainder to the heirs-male of his body. One of the Commissioners of the Treasury [I], 1st July 1698, but after the battle of the Boyne he submitted to the government of William. On 1st April 1703 he succeeded his elder brother as third BARON JERMYN of St. Edmundsbury [E], but owing to his attainder he was not recognised as such by the government. He died *s.v.p.* 6th April 1708, at his house at Cheveley, and was buried, at his own request, in the church of the Carmelites at Bruges, in Flanders. He married Judith, daughter of Sir Edmond Poley of Bradley, co. Suffolk, by Hester, daughter of Sir Henry Crofts of Little Saxham. She died about 1726; her will, dated 17th September 1725, was proved November 1726.[1]

DRUMCAIRN, Viscount of [S].

i.e. '*DRUMCAIRN*,' VISCOUNTY OF (Murray), created 2nd February 1721, with '*DUNBAR*,' EARLDOM OF, which see.

DRUMMOND, Marquis of [S].

i.e. '*DRUMMOND*,' MARQUISATE OF (Drummond), created 1701, with '*PERTH*,' DUKEDOM OF, which see.

---

[1] *The Complete Peerage; Dictionary of National Biography*. He is said to have been privately married to the Dowager-Princess of Orange, just as his father is said to have been to Queen Henrietta Maria.

DUNBAR

DUNBAR, Earl of [S].

1721 – 1770

I. HON. JAMES MURRAY, second son of David (Murray), fifth Viscount Stormont [S], by Marjory, only daughter of David Scott of Scotstarvit, Fife, born about 1690; Advocate 1710; M.P. for Dumfries 9th November 1710 to 8th August 1713, and for Elgin Burghs 17th September 1713 to 7th April 1715, on which date there was an order of the House of Commons for amending the return 'by erasing the name of James Murray, Esq.';[1] was, with his father and elder brother, one of those who were summoned to surrender themselves on the breaking out of the '15, but did not do so, and served through that campaign, afterwards retiring to France. In June 1718 he was appointed one of the plenipotentiaries for negotiating King James's marriage with the Princess Mary Clementina. On 2nd February 1721 he was created by King James III and VIII an Earl and Peer of Parliament as *EARL OF DUNBAR*, in the shire of East Lothian, *VISCOUNT OF DRUMCAIRN*, in the shire of Fife, and *LORD OF HADYKES*,[2] in the shire of Dumfries [S], with remainder to the heirs-male of his body, whom failing, to his brother David, Viscount of Stormont, and the heirs-male of his body lawfully begotten; *K.T.*, 31st December 1725; Governor to the Prince of Wales, 4th June 1727; empowered to open all letters addressed to the King or to Sir John Græme, 4th July 1727; and some time afterwards appointed *SECRETARY OF STATE*, in succession to the latter, which post he appears to have held for some twenty years. In October 1747, however, Prince Charles considering him responsible for the decision of the Duke of York to enter the Church, King James directed him to retire to Avignon in the expectation that Charles would then return to reside in Rome.[3] He died *s.p.* at Avignon, August 1770.[4]

1770 – 1796

II. DAVID (MURRAY), second *EARL OF DUNBAR*, *VISCOUNT DRUMCAIRN* and *LORD HADYKES* (1721) [S], also seventh VISCOUNT STORMONT (1621), and LORD SCONE (1605),

---

[1] *Return of Members of Parliament* [G B], pt. 11, p. 48.
[2] Now Halldykes (pronounced Ha'dykes), near Lockerbie. *Ex inform.* Lord Mansfield.
[3] Dennistoun, i. p. 177.
[4] The *Hist. Reg.* for 1728, vol. xiii. p. 54, has the following erroneous announcement:—'6 Oct. Died at Naples, James Murray, Esq., commonly called Lord Dunbar, ' Governor to the eldest son of the Pretender.'

DUNBAR

and fifth LORD BALVAIRD (1641) [S], and second EARL OF MANSFIELD, of Caen Wood, Middlesex (1792) [G B], nephew and heir, being the only surviving son and heir of David (Murray), sixth Viscount Stormont and Lord Scone, and fourth Lord Balvaird [S], by Anne, only daughter and heir of John Stewart of Innernytie, which David was elder brother to the first *EARL*. He was born 9th October 1727, succeeded his father as Viscount Stormont, etc., 23rd July 1748, his elder uncle as *EARL OF DUNBAR*, August 1770, and his younger uncle as Earl of Mansfield, co. Middlesex, 20th March 1793. K.T. (by George III), 30th November 1768. He died at Brighton, 1st, and was buried in Westminster Abbey, 9th September 1796.[1]

III. DAVID WILLIAM (MURRAY), third *EARL OF DUNBAR* [S], etc., also third EARL OF MANSFIELD [G B], son and heir, born in Paris 7th March 1777; K.T., 4th March 1835; died at Leamington, 18th February 1840. Will proved March following.   1796 – 1840

IV. WILLIAM DAVID (MURRAY), fourth *EARL OF DUNBAR* [S], etc., also fourth EARL OF MANSFIELD, co. Middlesex, and third EARL OF MANSFIELD, co. Notts [G B], born 21st February 1806, in Portland Place, Marylebone; succeeded his father, 18th February 1840, and his grandmother Louisa, *suo jure* Countess of Mansfield, co. Notts, 11th July 1843; K.T., 13th June 1843. He died 2nd August 1898, being at that time the 'Father of the House of Lords.'   1840 – 1898

V. WILLIAM DAVID (MURRAY), fifth *EARL OF DUNBAR*, *VISCOUNT DRUMCAIRN*, and *LORD HADYKES* (1721) [S], third EARL OF MANSFIELD, of Mansfield, co. Notts (1776), and fifth EARL OF MANSFIELD, of Caen Wood, Middlesex (1792) [G B], tenth VISCOUNT STORMONT (1621), and LORD SCONE (1605), and eighth LORD BALVAIRD (1641) [S], grandson and heir, being the eldest son and heir of William David Murray, styled Viscount Stormont, who died *v.p.* 12th October 1893; born 20th July 1860, and succeeded his grandfather, 2nd August 1898.   1898

---

[1] For a fuller account of this peer and his successors see the extant peerages under Mansfield.

DUNDEE

DUNDEE, Earldom of [S].

1705 — 1740

I. JOHN BAPTIST GUALTERIO, son of [ ] Count Gualterio, was shortly before the 12th November 1705 created by King James III and VIII, in recognition of the services of his brother, Cardinal Gualterio,[1] Papal Nuncio to the Court of Paris, EARL OF DUNDEE [S], 'for himself and his successors.' On 10th May 1708 he was created a K.T. He died shortly before the 14th August 1740.[2] He married, probably about 1706/7, [ ], daughter of [ ] [ ]. She died shortly before the 14th May 1709.[3] He had issue:—

1. [ ], [? VISCOUNT GUALTERIO], his heir.
2. LADY [ ] Gualterio, born shortly before the 7th May 1708;[4] presented for baptism by Cardinal Gualterio and the Countess Gualterio, as proxies for King James and Queen Mary; died before the 22nd October 1708.[5]

1740 — 17

II. [ ] (GUALTERIO), second EARL OF DUNDEE, only son and heir of the preceding, born shortly before the 14th May 1709,[3] and presented for baptism before the 31st December 1709 by Cardinal Gualterio, as proxy for King James. He succeeded his father shortly before the 16th August 1740, being at that time an Inquisitor of the Order of Malta.[2]

ERNE, Lord [S].

i.e. 'ERNE,' BARONY OF (Hay), created 5th October 1718, with 'INVERNESS,' EARLDOM OF, which see.

---

[1] This Philip Anthony, Cardinal Gualterio, was born 24th March 1660 at St. Quirice de Ferma in the March of Ancona, of a very ancient family of German origin, and died at Rome 21st April 1728, aged sixty-nine, leaving everything to his brother Count Gualterio (Migne's *Encyclopédie Théologique*, 1857, vol. xxxi.).

[2] On which day James writes to mon cousin, le comte de Dundee, Inquisiteur de 'Malte,' acknowledging his letter of the 16th August, saying that the Count Dandini has handed him the cross of St. Andrew of Scotland, with which he had invested the late *Earl of Dundee*, and commiserating with him on his loss.

[3] Letter from James to the Cardinal Gualterio of that date. There is also one to the *Earl of Dundee* to the same effect on the 31st July (*Calendar of Stuart Papers*, i. p. 232).

[4] Queen Mary to Cardinal Gualterio (*Ibid.* i. p. 223).

[5] Queen Mary to the Countess Gualterio (*Ibid.* i. p. 228).

ESK

ERSKINE, Marquis [S].

i.e. '*ERSKINE,*' *MARQUISATE OF* (Erskine), created 22nd October 1715, with '*MAR*,' *DUKEDOM OF*, which see.

ESK, Baron of [E].

I. SIR RICHARD GRAHAM, third BARONET [S], of Esk and Netherby, co. Cumberland, was born 24th September 1648, at Netherby; succeeded his father in the Baronetcy, 1657; educated at Westminster and at Christ Church, Oxford; matriculated 20th June 1664, aged fifteen; M.A., 4th February 1666/7; student of the Inner Temple, 1664; M.P. for Cockermouth, 1675-1681, and for co. Cumberland, 1685-1687;[1] having been created, 12/21 May 1681, VISCOUNT OF PRESTON, co. Haddington, and LORD GRAHAM OF ESK [S];[2] Ambassador to France, May 1682-1685; P.C., 21st October 1685; Chancellor to the Queen-Dowager, 26th October 1685; Lord President of the Council and Secretary of State, October 1688; was one of the committee of five appointed by the King to represent him in London during his absence at Salisbury, November 1688; and remaining faithful to James, was created by him, by patent dated at St. Germains,[3] 21st January 1689, *BARON OF ESK* [E]. He was arrested, May 1689, brought to London and committed to the Tower, and not admitted to bail until 25th October. On 11th November he appeared before the House of Lords in connection with a suit brought against him by the Earl of Montague, when he claimed the privilege of a peer of the realm [E] and his writ of summons; but the patent being found to be dated after the alleged abdication of King James was declared void, and he was returned to the Tower, and the Attorney-General instructed to prosecute him for a high misdemeanour. He was, however, released on withdrawing his claim, 27th November. He had all this time retained his seals of office

1688/9
—
1695

---

[1] Though a Protestant, he zealously maintained the right of the Duke of York and Albany to the throne, and he moved in the Commons on behalf of the Duke against the Exclusion Bill, 2nd November 1680.

[2] The preamble recites that Charles I in 1635 had given the warrant to Sir Richard Graham, the patentee's grandfather, and that it had been afterwards destroyed by the rebels.

[3] *Dictionary of National Biography.*

47

ESK

from James, and was regarded by the Jacobites as the real Secretary of State. He was again arrested, at midnight, 1st January 1691, on board a vessel bound for Calais, and was committed to the Tower, 3rd January. On 16th January he was indicted as an English Baronet at the Old Bailey, and on 17th found guilty and condemned to death two days afterwards. He was, however, subsequently pardoned. He died at Nunnington, Yorks, 22nd December 1695, and was buried in the chancel of the church there, aged forty-seven.[1] He married, 2nd August 1670, Lady Anne, second daughter of Charles (Howard), first Earl of Carlisle [E], by the Hon. Anne, daughter of Edward (Howard), first Baron Howard of Escrick [E]. He had issue :—

1. Charles, Lord Graham of Esk, born 1672; died *v.p.* and was buried at Westminster Abbey, 17th June 1785.
2. Edward, Lord Graham of Esk, his heir.
3. Hon. Catherine Graham, married, as second wife, William (Widdrington), fourth Baron Widdrington [E], but died *s.p.*
4. Hon. Mary Susan Graham.

1695 — 1710

II. EDWARD (GRAHAM), second VISCOUNT PRESTON and LORD GRAHAM OF ESK [S], and *BARON OF ESK* [E], fourth BARONET [S], second but first surviving son and heir, born about 1678; succeeded his father, 22nd November 1695; matriculated University College, Oxford, 24th November 1693; and died at Nunnington, and was buried there, 1710, aged about thirty-one. Will, dated 5th February 1706/7, was proved 4th November 1734. He married, 5th January 1702/3, at York Minster, Mary, daughter and eventually sole heiress of Sir Marmaduke Dalton of Hawskell, co. Yorks, by Barbara, daughter of the Hon. Henry Belasyse. She was living 1st September 1757. Will, dated 17th June 1751, was proved 18th January 1759. He had issue :—

1. Charles, Lord Graham.
2. Hon. Anne Graham, died unmarried.

1710 — 1738/9

III. CHARLES (GRAHAM), third VISCOUNT PRESTON and LORD GRAHAM OF ESK [S], and *BARON OF ESK* [E],

---
[1] *The Complete Peerage*, vi. p. 302.

FALKLAND

fifth BARONET [S], only son and heir, born 25th March 1706, died s.p. 22nd February 1738/9, aged thirty-two, and was buried at Nunnington, when his peerages became extinct, while the Baronetcy passed to his heir-male. He married Anne, daughter of Thomas Cox of London. She died 11th February 1744/5. Will proved 20th February 1744/5.[1]

EVERARD, Viscount [I].

I. SIR REDMOND EVERARD, fourth BARONET of Fethard, co. Tipperary [I], first surviving son and heir of Sir John Everard,[2] third Baronet of Fethard aforesaid, succeeded to the Baronetcy 12th July 1690; was M.P. [I] for co. Tipperary, 1703; for Kilkenny city, 1709-13; and for Fethard, 1713-14; D.C.L. (Oxford), 22nd September 1715. He was a Jacobite, residing principally abroad, and was witness to the will, 31st December 1725, of Bishop Atterbury, who speaks of him as 'the 'Knight of Chanton.' On 20th June 1723 he was created by James III and VIII VISCOUNT [EVERARD] [I], with apparently remainder to the heirs-male of his body. He died s.p. in France about 1740, when both the VISCOUNTY and Baronetcy became extinct. Will, dated 10th March 1739/40, proved in the Prerogative Court [I], 15th April 1746, after the death of his widow. He married, 15th June 1721, at Westminster Abbey, Mary, only daughter of Montagu Drake of Shardeloes, Bucks, by Jane, daughter and heiress of Sir John Garrard, third Baronet of Lamer [E]. She, who was born 15th and baptized 25th June 1694, at Amersham, Bucks, died intestate before April 1746.[3]

1723
-
1740 ?

FALKIRK, Viscount [S].

i.e. '*FALKIRK*,' VISCOUNTY OF (Græme), created 20th January 1760, with '*ALFORD*,' EARLDOM OF, which see.

FALKLAND, Earl of [E].

I. LUCIUS HENRY (CARY), sixth VISCOUNT OF FALKLAND, and LORD CARYE [S], only son and heir of Edward Cary

1722
-
1730

---
[1] *The Complete Peerage*, vi. p. 302.
[2] Who was killed at the battle of Aughrim on the side of King James.
[3] *The Complete Baronetage*, i. p. 240.

FALKLAND

of Caldicotte, co. Monmouth, by Anne, daughter and co-heir of Charles (Lucas), second Baron Lucas of Shenfield [E], born 27th August and baptized 7th September 1687, at St. James's, Westminster, succeeded his father 1692, and his cousin in the peerage, 24th May 1694. He was a faithful and devoted adherent of the exiled family, and on the 13th December 17?2 was created by James III and VIII EARL OF FALKLAND [E]. He died in Paris 31st December 1730, and was buried in the Chapel of St. Sulpice there. Will, dated in Paris 27th November 1730, proved 3rd February 1730/1. He married, first, at Chiswick, Middlesex, 5th October 1704, Dorothy, daughter of Francis Molyneux of St. Gregory's, London, woollen draper, by Mary, daughter of Charles Tancred of Whixley, co. Yorks. She died 26th June 1722, and was buried, 2nd July, at Stanwell. He married, secondly, LADY Laura, daughter of Arthur (Dillon), first EARL OF DILLON [S], by Catherine, daughter of Ralph Sheldon. She died at St. Germains-en-Laye, 12th July 1741.[1]

1730 – 1785   II. LUCIUS CHARLES (CARY), second EARL OF FALKLAND, etc., son and heir by first wife, born about 1707, died 27th February 1785. Will, dated 26th November 1784, proved 5th March 1785.

1785 – 1796   III. HENRY THOMAS (CARY), third EARL OF FALKLAND, grandson and heir, being the elder son of the Hon. Lucius Ferdinand Cary, *styled* VISCOUNT FALKLAND, Commander-in-Chief of the British forces in Tobago, who died *v.p.* 20th August 1780, was born 27th February 1726, and died unmarried at the White Lion Inn, Bath, being buried, 28th May 1796, in the Abbey there, aged thirty-one.

1796 – 1809   IV. CHARLES JOHN (CARY), fourth EARL OF FALKLAND, brother and next heir, born November 1768, died 2nd March 1809, aged forty, having been mortally wounded in a duel by A. Powell two days previously.

1809 – 1884   V. LUCIUS BENTINCK (CARY), fifth EARL OF FALKLAND, son and heir, born 5th November 1803; created, 15th May 1832, BARON HUNSDON of Scutterskelfe, co. Yorks [U K]; a

---

[1] *The Complete Peerage*, which see for a fuller account of his successors.

FITTON

Representative Peer [S], 1831-32; P.C., 1837; Governor of Nova Scotia 1840-46, and of Bombay 1848-53. He died *s.p.s.* 12th March 1884, aged eighty-one, at Montpelier, France.

VI. PLANTAGENET PIERREPOINT (CARY), sixth EARL OF FALKLAND, brother and heir, born 8th September 1806; Admiral R.N., 1876; died *s.p.* at South Norwood, 1st February 1886; buried at All Saints, Lower Norwood. Will proved 29th March following. 1884 – 1886

VII. BYRON PLANTAGENET (CARY), seventh EARL (1722) [E] and twelfth VISCOUNT (1620) [S] OF FALKLAND, and LORD CARYE [S], nephew and heir, being the only surviving son of the Hon. Byron Charles Ferdinand Plantagenet Cary, Captain R.N., who was younger brother to the two last named. He was born 3rd April 1845, and was elected a Representative Peer [S]. 1886

FERRITON, Baron [S].

i.e. '*FERRITON,*' *BARONY OF* (Erskine), created 22nd October 1715, with '*MAR,*' *DUKEDOM OF,* which see.

FITTON OF GOSWORTH, Baron [I].

I. SIR ALEXANDER FITTON of Gawsworth, co. Chester, second but first surviving son and heir of William Fitton of Awrice, co. Limerick and of Gawsworth aforesaid, by Eva, daughter of Sir Edward Trevor of Brynkynalt; student of the Inner Temple, 1655; called to the Bar, 12th May 1662, about which time he was dispossessed of the Gawsworth estate by the heir-general, and was imprisoned for the fines and expenses in connection with the legal proceedings. He, however, subsequently obtained his release, was knighted, and 12th February 1686/7 was appointed by James II and VII Lord Chancellor [I]; on 1st April 1689 he was created[1] by that King (some four months after the Revolution in England, while still *de facto,* as well as *de jure,* King of Ireland) BARON FYTTON OF GOSWORTH, co. Limerick [I], with remainder to the heirs-male of his body. On the departure of James after the battle of the Boyne he was 1689 – 1698

---

[1] See Preface, p. xii.

FITZHEMON

constituted one of the Lord Justices [I], but being attainted he retired to France, and died *s.p.m.* at St. Germains, November 1698, when the Barony became extinct. He married about 1655 Anne, daughter of Thomas Joliffe of Crofton, co. Worcester. She died 7th October 1687, and was buried in St. Patrick's Cathedral, Dublin.[1]

FITZHEMON, Marquis of [E].

i.e. '*FITZHEMON*,' *MARQUISATE OF* (Granville), created 3rd November 1721, with '*ALBEMARLE*,' *DUKEDOM OF*, which see.

FORDAN, Earl of [S].

i.e. '*FORDAN*,' *EARLDOM OF* (de Bozas), created 4th February 1717, with '*ST. ANDREWS*,' *DUKEDOM OF*, which see.

ffORESTER, Baronet [S].

1729   I. SIR JOHN ffORESTER, KNIGHT, was on 31st March 1729 created a *KNIGHT* and *BARONET* [S], with remainder to the heirs-male of his body.[2]

FORREST, Baron of [S].

i.e. '*FORREST*, *BARONY OF* (Erskine), created 22nd April 1715, with '*MAR*,' *DUKEDOM OF*.

FORSTAL, Baronet [I].

1734   I. SIR MARK FORSTAL was, 22nd January 1734, created by James III and VIII a *KNIGHT* and *BARONET* [I].[3]

---

[1] *Dictionary of National Biography.*

[2] He was doubtless the Sir John Forester who (under the cipher name of M. Fisher) is so frequently mentioned as a trusted agent in the *Stuart Papers*, 1714-1716. A Charles Forestier was appointed Page of the Bedchamber to King James II and VII, 1st June 1689. A Sir Mark Forester writes to the Duke of Mar from Calais, 24th February 1716. [Query if not the Sir Mark Forstal who was made a Baronet [I] 22nd January 1734.]

[3] See Note 2 above.

FRASER

FORTH, Marquis of [S].

i.e. '*FORTH,*' *MARQUISATE OF* (Drummond), created 17th April 1692, with '*MELFORT,*' *DUKEDOM OF,* which see.

FORTROSE, Earl or Viscount of [S].

i.e. '*FORTROSE,*' *EARLDOM* or *VISCOUNTY OF* (Mackenzie), created about 1690 with '*SEAFORTH,*' *MARQUISATE OF*, which see.

FRASER OF MUCHALLS, Baron [S].

I. CHARLES FRASER of Inverallochy, third son of Simon Fraser of Inverallochy, and grandson of Simon Fraser of the same, by Lady Margaret, first daughter of James (Erskine), seventh Earl of Buchan [S], which lady married, secondly, Charles (Fraser), fourth Lord Fraser [S], who died *s.p.* 12th October 1720.[1] He succeeded to the estates of the said Charles, Lord Fraser, 12th October 1720, and on the 20th July 1723 was created by James III and VIII a Lord and Peer of Parliament as *LORD FRASER OF MUSHALL* [Muchalls] [S], with remainder to his heirs-male.[2] He served himself heir to his brother-german, William Fraser of Inverallochy,[3] 30th August 1749, and was living 16th April 1746, but was dead before 13th February 1789.[4] He married Anne, only daughter of John Udny of Udny, M.P., by Lady Martha, daughter of George (Gordon), first Earl of Aberdeen [S], and sister, and in her issue

1723 - 17

---

[1] This Charles, Lord Fraser, was tried for high treason, 29th March 1693, at Edinburgh, and fined £200 for drinking the health of King James. He took part in the '15, but afterwards remaining in hiding, he managed to escape attainder. On his death *s.p.* the title, which had been conferred on his great-grandfather, Andrew Fraser of Kinmundie, by Charles I, 29th June 1633, with remainder to his heirs-male for ever, became dormant, and has since so remained. He devised his estates to the grandson of his wife by her first husband, Charles Fraser above named. See also following note.

[2] The preamble sets out that the title is conferred in recognition of his services, and particularly those of 'his father, who died bravely asserting our cause, and in considera- ' tion of the earnest desire of the late Lord Fraser, when we were last in Scotland, to ' resign his titles of honour in favour of the said Charles' father.' The patent is endorsed ' taken by Glenderule.'

[3] Who had previously served himself heir to *his* elder brother, Alexander Fraser of Inverallochy, 23rd November 1698.

[4] Some account of this family is in J. Anderson's *Historical Account of the Family of Fraser.*

FRASER

(1789) sole heir, of Alexander Udny of the same. She was born about 1704, and died 24th August 1753, aged forty-nine. He had issue:—

1. Charles, MASTER OF FRASER, younger of Inverallochy, who was slain *s.p.*, *v.p.* on the side of the Stuarts, at the battle of Culloden, 16th April 1746.
2. William, MASTER OF FRASER, his heir.
3. HON. Martha Fraser of Inverallochy, married 1747 Colin Mackenzie of Kilcoy, Ross-shire, and was ancestress of the families of Burton-Mackenzie of Kilcoy and of Fraser of Castle Fraser. On 6th February 1793 she and her sister served themselves heirs to their brother, William Fraser Udny of Castle Fraser and Inverallochy.
4. HON. Eliza Fraser of Castle Fraser, died unmarried 1814.

17
-
1792

II. WILLIAM (FRASER, afterwards FRASER-UDNY), second LORD FRASER OF MUCHALLS, second but only surviving son and heir, succeeded to the Peerage on the death of his father, to whom he served himself heir, 1789. He inherited the estate of Udny, Aberdeenshire, on the death of his uncle, Alexander Udny, 1789, when he assumed that name, and was served heir of entail and provision-general to him, 2nd December 1789, and heir-general, 15th January 1790. He died *s.p.* 13th December 1792.

1792
-
1815

III. ARCHIBALD CAMPBELL (FRASER), third DUKE OF FRASER, etc., thirteenth LORD LOVAT and third LORD FRASER OF MUCHALLS, cousin and next heir-male, being the third but then (1792) only surviving son and heir of Simon, first DUKE OF FRASER, who was son and heir of Thomas, tenth Lord Lovat, which Thomas was the third but only son, whose male issue then survived, of Hugh, seventh Lord Lovat, son and heir of Simon, sixth Lord Lovat, which last Simon was, through his third son (Sir Simon Fraser of Inverallochy), the great-great-grandfather of the first LORD FRASER OF MUCHALLS. He died *s.p.s.* 8th December 1815.

1815
-
1875

IV. THOMAS ALEXANDER (FRASER), fourteenth or twelfth LORD LOVAT, fourth LORD FRASER OF MUCHALLS, cousin

FRASER

and next heir-male being son and heir of Captain Alexander Fraser, who was son and heir of Alexander Fraser, son and heir of Alexander Fraser (a lord of session, 1730-1735), second son· but eventual heir of Alexander Fraser, son and heir of Thomas Fraser, son and heir of Thomas Fraser, son and heir-apparent of Thomas Fraser, son and heir of the Hon. Thomas Fraser, all of Strichen, Aberdeenshire, which Thomas was next brother to Hugh, fifth Lord Lovat, and second son of Alexander, fourth Lord Lovat. He was born at Strichen 17th June 1802; and became on the death of his cousin, 8th December 1815, *de jure* fourteenth LORD LOVAT and fourth *LORD FRASER OF MUCHALLS*. On 28th January 1807 he was created by William IV BARON LOVAT OF LOVAT, Inverness-shire [U K], and 10th July 1854 he became *de facto* Lord Lovat [S] by the reversal of the attainder of the eleventh Lord Lovat; K.T. 1865. He died at Beaufort Castle, Inverness-shire, 28th June 1875.

V. SIMON (FRASER), fifteenth [S] and second [U K] LORD LOVAT, fifth *LORD FRASER OF MUCHALLS*, son and heir, born at Beaufort Castle aforesaid, 21st December 1828. He died suddenly on Moy Hall Moor, Inverness, 6th September 1887, and was buried in Eskdale Chapel.   1875 – 1887

VI. SIMON JOSEPH (FRASER), sixteenth LORD LOVAT [S], and sixth *LORD FRASER OF MUCHALLS* [S], and third BARON LOVAT [U K], second but first surviving son and heir, born 25th November 1871, succeeded his father 6th September 1887.   1887

FRASER, Duke of [S].

I. SIMON (FRASER), eleventh LORD LOVAT [S], second but first surviving son and heir of Thomas (Fraser), tenth Lord Lovat,[1] by Sybella, fourth daughter of John MacLeod of MacLeod, born about 1667, probably at Tanich in Ross; educated at Aberdeen University, M.A. 1683. On the death of his cousin, the ninth Lord, 1696, he endeavoured to secure his daughter and heir of line, Amelia (then considered *suo jure* Baroness Lovat), in marriage, but having failed, he forcibly compelled her mother to marry him. He was (with his father) found guilty of high   1740 – 1747

---
[1] This Thomas Fraser was with Dundee at Killiecrankie, and was attainted 6th September 1698 for attempting to surprise Edinburgh Castle in 1696.

FRASER

treason, 1698, and outlawed 17th February 1701, when he retired to France. In 1715 he returned to Scotland, changed sides, and as a reward obtained a pardon, 10th March 1716, from the Government, together with the grant of the Lovat estates, forfeited by the husband of his aforesaid cousin for his share in the '15. On the 30th July 1730 he was declared entitled to the Lovat Peerage. He had previously, 28th September 1721, received a pardon from King James under the Great Seals [E and S] 'upon his returning to his duty,' and 10th March 1722 a commission as Major-General. On 30th July 1723, in expectation of a fresh rising, he was appointed by James Lord-Lieutenant of Inverness, Nairn, and Sutherland, and was ordered to seize Inverness, and act as Governor thereof. He was one of the first to join the association formed in 1737 for the restoration of the House of Stuart, and on 14th March 1740 he was created by King James DUKE OF FRASER, MARQUIS OF BEAUFORT, EARL OF STRATH-THERRICK [*i.e.* Stratherrick] AND UPPER TARF [*i.e.* Abertarf], VISCOUNT OF THE AIRD AND STRATH-GLASS, LORD LOVAT AND BEAULIEU [*i.e.* Beauly] [S], with remainder to the heirs-male of his body.[1] He now became suspected by the Government, who deprived him of all his posts. On 23rd December 1743 he was appointed by James Lord-Lieutenant north of the Spey, and by the head of the Spey to the north side of Loch Lochy. After the battle of Prestonpans, 21st September 1745, he raised his clan and sent them under his son to join Prince Charles, but being upwards of seventy-eight, he did not himself join. He was, however, arrested, 11th December 1745, but escaped 2nd January. After Culloden he exhorted the Prince to make one more effort, reminding him that his ancestor, Robert the Bruce, had won Scotland after losing seven battles. He was finally captured on Loch Morar, was sent to the Tower, and 18th March 1746/7 found guilty of high treason, whereby his honours were considered as forfeited, and his estates were seized by the Crown. He was beheaded at the age of eighty on Tower Hill, 9th April 1747, and was buried in St. Peter's ad Vincula in the Tower. He married, first, Amelia, Dowager Baroness Lovat, daughter of John (Murray), first Marquis of Atholl [S], K.T., by Lady

---

[1] The patent is endorsed : '*N.B.*—This warrant was sent sealed down to Lochyel and writ on the cover in the King's hand—A paper relating to Lord Lovat, to be left with Lochyel at Boulogne-sur-Mer, to be carefully kept by him till my further orders.'

FRASER

Amelia Sophia, daughter, and in her issue heir, of James (Stanley), seventh Earl of Derby [E], which marriage, however, was held invalid. He married, secondly, 1717, Margaret, daughter of Ludovick Grant of Grant, by his first wife, Janet, daughter of Alexander Brodie of Lethen. She was living 1729. He married, thirdly, 1st July 1733, Primrose, sister to John (Campbell), fourth Duke of Argyll [S], fifth daughter of the Hon. John Campbell of Mamore, by the Hon. Elizabeth, daughter of John (Elphinstone), eighth Lord Elphinstone [S]. She died at Edinburgh 23rd May 1796, aged eighty-six. He had issue by his second wife two sons and two daughters, and by his third wife one son, viz. :—

1. Simon, *MARQUIS OF BEAUFORT*, his heir.
2. *LORD* Alexander Fraser, Brigadier-General in the Dutch service, baptized at Kiltarity, 1st July 1729; died unmarried, 7th August 1762, at Dumnaglass, near Farraline, buried at Kirkhill.
3. *LORD* Archibald Campbell Fraser, heir to his eldest brother.
4. *LADY* Janet Fraser, married Euan Macpherson of Cluny, and died 14th April 1765, leaving issue.
5. *LADY* Sybella Fraser, died unmarried 9th February 1755.

II. SIMON (FRASER), second *DUKE OF FRASER*, etc., twelfth LORD LOVAT, eldest son and heir, born at Kiltarity 19th and baptized 30th October 1726; educated at University of St. Andrews; joined (it is said unwillingly) Prince Charles after the battle of Prestonpans at the head of his clan. Was attainted 4th June 1746, and imprisoned in Edinburgh Castle, November 1746 to August 1747; pardoned, April 1750. He joined the Scottish Bar, passing as Advocate 25th July 1750. He became Advocate-Depute, and assisted in the prosecution of James Stewart of Aucharn in Appin, who was executed for the murder of Colin Campbell of Glenure in 1752.[1] He was permitted to join the British army and to raise a Highland regiment, which was embodied in 1757, his commission as Colonel being dated 5th January of that year. He greatly distinguished himself in America with Wolfe, and afterwards in Portugal in 1762-63. He

1747 -
1782

---

[1] This murder is the principal subject of R. L. Stevenson's romances *Kidnapped* and *Catriona*.

GALSTON

became Major-General in 1771, and was rewarded by having the family estates restored to him in 1774, by Act of Parliament, on payment of £20,983. He raised two additional battalions of Highlanders in 1775, for service in the war with the American colonies, but he did not accompany them. M.P. for Inverness 1761 to his death *s.p.* in Downing Street, 1782. He married [   ], daughter of [   ] Bristow of England. She was living, a widow, 1825.

1782 — 1815

III. ARCHIBALD CAMPBELL (FRASER), third DUKE OF FRASER, etc., thirteenth LORD LOVAT, next surviving brother and heir, born 16th August 1736; Consul-General at Algiers, 1766; M.P. co. Inverness, 1782. He died *s.p.s.* 8th December 1815, when the DUKEDOM OF FRASER and the minor honours conferred with it became extinct, while the Barony of Fraser passed to his heir-male. He married, 1763, Jane, sister of Sir William Fraser, first Baronet [U K], only daughter of William Fraser of Ledeclune, by his second wife, Helen, daughter of William Ross of Monquieth. He had issue, five sons, viz.:—

1. John Simon, MARQUIS OF BEAUFORT, born about 1765; M.P. for co. Inverness, 1796; Colonel of the Fraser Fencibles; died unmarried at Lisbon, 6th April 1803, aged thirty-eight.
2. LORD Archibald Fraser, born in Edinburgh, died young, 1792.
3. LORD Henry Emo Fraser, born in Algiers, died unmarried at Edinburgh, 25th August 1782.
4. LORD George Fraser, died in infancy, 1781.
5. LORD William Henry Fraser, died unmarried in Edinburgh, 25th February 1801.

GALSTON, Baron [S].

i.e. 'GALSTON,' BARONY OF (Drummond), created 17th April 1692, with 'MELFORT,' DUKEDOM OF, which see.

GARIOCH, Viscount [S].

i.e. 'GARIOCH,' VISCOUNTY OF (Erskine), created 22nd October 1715, with 'MAR,' DUKEDOM OF, which see.

GAYDON, Baronet [I].

1743 — 17

I. RICHARD GAYDON, one of the four gallant Irishmen who effected the escape of the Princess Mary Clementina

GORING

from the Castle of Innspruck, 27th April 1719, where she had been imprisoned by the Emperor on her way to be married to King James, for which service he was, together with his three companions, knighted. On 29th July 1743 he was, as ' Sir ' Richard Gaydon, Knight, Major-General of our forces, and ' at present Lieutenant-Colonel of Dillon's regiment in the service ' of his most H.M.C.M.,' created by James III and VIII a *KNIGHT* and *BARONET* [I], with remainder to the heirs-male of his body.[1]

GERALDINE, Baronet [I].

I. THOMAS GERALDINE is said to have been created by James III and VIII a *BARONET* [I].

17

GERMAIN OF ROYSTON, Baron [E].

See Jermyn of Royston.

GLENSHIE, Viscount of [S].

i.e. '*GLENSHIE*,' *VISCOUNTY OF* (Murray), created 1st February 1717, with '*RANNOCH*,' *DUKEDOM OF*, which see.

GLEN TILT, Earl of [S].

i.e. '*GLEN TILT*,' *EARLDOM OF* (Murray), created 1st February 1717, with '*RANNOCH*,' *DUKEDOM OF*, which see.

GORING, Viscount [E].

I. SIR HARRY GORING, fourth BARONET [E], fourth son of Henry Goring of Wappingthorn in Steyning, son and heir-apparent of Sir Henry Goring, second Baronet, who died *v.p.* 1687, by his second wife, Mary, youngest daughter and co-heir of Sir John Covert of Stonyham, Sussex, Baronet [E], born 1679, succeeded his elder brother, Sir Charles, January 1713. On 2nd January 1722 he was created by James III and VIII *BARON BULLINGHEL* and *VISCOUNT GORING* [E], with remainder to the heirs-male of his body, and on 24th March following had a commission as Major-General, and was appointed

1722
—
1732

---

[1] A John Gaydon was appointed 1st Ensign of the 2nd Troop of Guards, commanded by Lord Lucan, January 1692.

GORING

governor of Bristol, both of which appointments were renewed September 1728; M.P. for Horsham 4th April 1707-1708, for Steyning Borough 1st February 1708/9-5th January 1714/15; and again for Horsham 29th January 1714/15, but unseated by an order of the House of Commons dated 17th March following. He died 12th November 1732. He married Elizabeth, eldest daughter and co-heir of Admiral Sir George Matthew, Knight, of Twickenham, Middlesex. She died 28th July 1768, aged nearly one hundred.

1732 - 1769
II. CHARLES MATTHEW (GORING), second VISCOUNT GORING and BARON BULLINGHEL, fifth BARONET, eldest son and heir, died August 1769.

1769 - 1824
III. HARRY (GORING), third VISCOUNT GORING and BARON BULLINGHEL, sixth BARONET, elder son and heir, born 26th April 1739, died 1st December 1824.

1824 - 1844
IV. CHARLES FORSTER (GORING), fourth VISCOUNT GORING and BARON BULLINGHEL, seventh BARONET, elder son and heir, born 11th July 1768, died 26th March 1844.

1844 - 1859
V. HARRY DENT (GORING), fifth VISCOUNT GORING and BARON BULLINGHEL, eighth BARONET, eldest son and heir, born 30th December 1801, died 19th April 1859.

1859 - 1884
VI. CHARLES (GORING), sixth VISCOUNT GORING and BARON BULLINGHEL, ninth BARONET, only son and heir, born 2nd June 1828, died s.p. 3rd November 1884.

1884 - 1897
VII. CRAVEN, CHARLES (GORING), seventh VISCOUNT GORING and BARON BULLINGHEL, tenth BARONET, cousin and heir-male, being the elder son and heir of Rev. THE HON. Charles Goring, next younger brother of the fifth VISCOUNT, born 24th October 1841, died s.p.m. 16th March 1897.

1897
VIII. HARRY YELVERTON (GORING), eighth VISCOUNT GORING and BARON BULLINGHEL, eleventh BARONET, cousin and heir-male, being the eldest son of the HON. Forster Goring, fourth son of the fourth VISCOUNT, born 19th July 1840;

GRANT

married 19th July 1875 Sarah Anne, daughter of John Hickin, and has with other issue a son :—
  1. Forster Gurney, LORD BULLINGHEL, born 19th June 1876.

GOSWORTH, Baron [I].

See Fitton of Gosworth.

GRANT, Baron [S].

I. JAMES GRANT OF GRANT, third son of Ludovick Grant of Grant by his first wife Janet, only daughter of Alexander Brodie of Lethen, born 28th July 1679; he succeeded his father-in-law, Sir Humphrey Colquhoun of Luss, as sixth Baronet [S] 1718, when he assumed the name of Colquhoun, and his elder brother, Alexander, as Chief of Grant 1719, when he resumed the name of Grant. On 24th June 1721 he was created by James III and VIII a Lord and Peer of Parliament as LORD [GRANT], with remainder to his heirs-male; M.P. for co. Inverness, 12th April 1722-1741, and for Elgin Burghs, 28th May 1741-16th January 1747. On the arrival of Prince Charles in 1745 he was in Scotland, but after an interview at Castle Grant with his son he hurried up to London and returned no answer to the letter addressed to him by the Prince. He died in London 16th January 1747. He married, 29th January 1702, Anne, only daughter of Sir Humphrey Colquhoun of Luss, fifth Baronet [S], by Margaret, daughter of Sir Patrick Houstoun of that Ilk. She was born 1685, and died at Castle Grant 25th June 1724.[1]

1721
–
1747

II. LUDOVICK (GRANT, sometime (1718-1732) COLQUHOUN), second *BARON GRANT* and seventh BARONET, second but elder surviving son and heir, born on Monday, 13th January 1707; advocate, 1728; became heir-apparent to the Grant estates on the death, unmarried *v.p.*, of his elder brother Humphrey, in September 1732, when he resumed the name of Grant, the Colquhoun estates, which he had till then held, passing under the entail to his next younger brother. During the '45 he exerted himself in opposition to the Jacobites and served under the Duke of Cumberland. M.P. for Moray, 1741 to 1761. He succeeded

1747
–
1772

---

[1] *The Chiefs of Grant,* by William Fraser, LL.D., Edinburgh, 1883.

GRANT

his father 16th January 1747, and died at Castle Grant 21st March 1773. He married first, at Edinburgh 6th July 1727, Marion, daughter of the Hon. Sir Hew Dalrymple, first Baronet [S], by his first wife, Marion, daughter of Sir Robert Hamilton of Pressmanen. She died January 1735, and was buried on the 18th in the Chapel Royal, Holyrood. He married secondly, 31st October 1735, Lady Margaret, daughter of James (Ogilvie), fifth Earl of Findlater and second Earl of Seafield [S] She died 20th February 1757.

1772 – 1811   III. JAMES (GRANT), third BARON GRANT, eighth BARONET, only son and heir, born 19th May 1738, died 18th February 1811.[1]

1811 – 1840   IV. LEWIS ALEXANDER (GRANT), fourth BARON GRANT, ninth BARONET, son and heir, born at Moy 22nd May 1767; succeeded his cousin, 5th October 1811, as fifth EARL OF SEAFIELD, VISCOUNT REIDHAVEN, and LORD OGILVIE OF DESKFORD AND CULLEN [S]. He died unmarried 26th October 1840.

1840 – 1853   V. FRANCIS WILLIAM (GRANT, afterwards (1840) OGILVIE-GRANT), sixth EARL OF SEAFIELD, etc., fifth BARON GRANT, tenth BARONET, brother and heir, born 6th March 1778, died 30th July 1853.

1853 – 1881   VI. JOHN CHARLES (OGILVIE-GRANT), seventh EARL OF SEAFIELD, etc., sixth BARON GRANT, eleventh BARONET, son and heir, born 4th September 1815. On the 14th August 1858 he was created BARON STRATHSPEY OF STRATHSPEY [U K]. He died 18th February 1881.

1881 – 1884   VII. IAN CHARLES (OGILVIE-GRANT), eighth EARL OF SEAFIELD, etc., seventh BARON GRANT, twelfth BARONET, only son and heir, born 7th October 1851, died unmarried 31st March 1884, when the Barony of Strathspey [U K] became extinct.

1884 – 1888   VIII. JAMES (OGILVIE-GRANT), ninth EARL OF SEAFIELD, etc., eighth BARON GRANT, thirteenth BARONET, uncle and heir, born 27th December 1817; created BARON STRATHSPEY OF STRATHSPEY [U K], 17th June 1884; died 5th June 1888.

---

[1] For a fuller account of the *Lords Grant* see the extant peerages under Seafield.

HAY

IX. FRANCIS WILLIAM (OGILVIE-GRANT), tenth EARL OF SEAFIELD, etc., ninth BARON GRANT, second BARON STRATHSPEY, fourteenth BARONET, son and heir, born 9th March 1847, died 3rd December 1888. — 1888

X. JAMES (OGILVIE-GRANT), eleventh EARL OF SEAFIELD, VISCOUNT REIDHAVEN, and BARON OGILVIE, tenth BARON GRANT [S], third BARON STRATHSPEY [U K], and fifteenth BARONET [S], eldest son and heir, born 18th April 1876. — 1888

GRÆME, Baronet [S].

I. JOHN GRÆME was on 6th September 1726 created by James III and VIII a KNIGHT and BARONET [S] for his services at the Court of Vienna. On the 20th June 1760 he was further created by the same King EARL OF ALFORD, etc. See ALFORD, EARLDOM OF. — 1726

HADYKES, Baron [S].

i.e. 'HADYKES,' BARONY OF (Murray), created 2nd February 1721, with 'DUNBAR,' EARLDOM OF, which see.

HALES OF EMLEY, Baron [E].

i.e. 'HALES OF EMLEY,' co. Kent, BARONY OF (Hales), created 3rd May 1692, with 'TENTERDEN,' EARLDOM OF, which see.

HAY, Baron [E].

I. JOHN (HAY), first EARL OF INVERNESS [S], was on 3rd April 1727 created by James III and VIII BARON [HAY] [E], with remainder to the heirs-male of his body. The next day he was further created DUKE OF [INVERNESS] [S]. See INVERNESS, DUKEDOM OF. — 1727

HAY, Baronet [S].

I. COLONEL WILLIAM HAY was on 31st January 1747 created by James III and VIII a KNIGHT and BARONET [S]. — 1747 17

HAY

HAY, Baronet [S].

1766 – 1784

I. JOHN HAY, Portioner of Restalrig, near Edinburgh, brother of Thomas Hay, a Senator of the College of Justice by the title of Lord Huntingdon, and second son of Alexander Hay of Huntingdon and East Lothian, Advocate and Sheriff-Deputy of Haddington, by Mary, daughter of [   ] Gordon of Lismore; was apprenticed to Hew Crauford, Edinburgh, W.S., and was admitted a W.S. 1st March 1726.[1] He was Fiscal, 1732-1734; Treasurer, 1736-1746; and Substitute-Keeper of the Signet,[2] 1725-1741 and 1742-1744.[3] On the arrival of Prince Charles in 1745 he joined him, and was for some time Treasurer and afterwards (1746) Secretary. He served through the campaign, and was blamed by Lord George Murray for grossly neglecting his duties as Quartermaster on the eve of the battle of Culloden. He was attainted 1746, and escaped to France with Prince Charles, in whose personal service he continued. He was one of the British attendants[4] whom Charles took with him in January 1766 when he went to Rome on his father's death, and he was by him appointed Major-Domo of the Household in place of Sir John Constable. On 31st December 1766 he was created by King Charles III a *KNIGHT* and *BARONET* [S], with remainder to his heirs-male. He remained with Charles until 8th December 1768, when, together with Andrew Lumisden and Captain Urquhart, he was dismissed. He returned to Scotland in 1771, and died there 6th December 1784. He married, December 1727, Anne, daughter and heiress of James Elphinstone of Restalrig aforesaid, by whom he had, with possibly other issue, a son.

1. *SIR* Alexander, his heir.

---

[1] *A History of the Society of Writers to H.M.'s Signet*, Edinburgh, 1890, 4to, p. 96.

[2] Mr. W. B. Blaikie, to whom the Editor is indebted for many of the particulars concerning this John Hay, writes: 'It will be noticed that John Hay became Substitute-'Keeper of the Signet in 1725, while he was not a W.S. until 1726, unless this is a 'mistake caused by Old and New Styles. It must be remembered, however, that this 'is unlikely. In Scotland the year began on 1st January from 1600 onwards.'

[3] Misprinted '46' on p. 96 of *A History of the Society of Writers*, etc.; see p. 228 of that work.

[4] The others were: Colonel Lauchlan Macintosh, attainted 1745; Captain Adam Urquhart of Bythe, a cadet of Meldrum; John Roy Stuart, his valet-de-chambre; and the Rev. Mr. Wagstaffe, who died 1770. See *Dennistoun*, ii. p. 102.

HOO

II. SIR ALEXANDER HAY, second *BARONET*, son and heir of the preceding, died *s.p.* 1791.[1]

1784 - 1791

III. SIR THOMAS HAY, third *BARONET*, cousin and next heir-male, being the eldest son of Alexander Hay of Mordington, Advocate, by his first wife, Jane Douglas, daughter of Alexander Hamilton of Ballincrief and Inverwick, which Alexander was the son and heir of Thomas Hay, Lord Huntingdon aforesaid, the elder brother of the first *BARONET*. He succeeded his kinsman, Sir Henry Hay-Macdougall, as fifth BARONET [S] (1703), and died 1832.[2]

1791 - 1832

IV. SIR JAMES DOUGLAS HAMILTON HAY, *fourth* (1766) and sixth (1703) BARONET [S], son and heir of the preceding, born 28th December 1800, died 30th July 1873.

1832 - 1873

V. SIR HECTOR MACLEAN HAY, *fifth* (1766) and seventh (1703) BARONET [S], son and heir of the preceding, born 28th March 1821, succeeded his father 30th July 1873.

1873

HELY, Baronet [I].

I. SIR JOHN HELY, KNIGHT, was on 28th June 1728 created by James III and VIII a *KNIGHT* and *BARONET* [I], with remainder to the heirs-male of his body.

1728 -

HIGGINS, Baronet [I].

I. DR. [   ] HIGGINS, first Physician to the King of Spain, was on 6th May 1724 created by James III and VIII a *KNIGHT* and *BARONET* [I].[3]

1724 -

HOO, Baron [E].

i.e. HOO,' co. Kent, *BARONY OF* (Villiers), created April 1716, with '*JERSEY,*' *EARLDOM OF*, which see.

---

[1] Burke's *Peerage and Baronetage*, 1902, Hay of Alderston.
[2] For a fuller account of this family see the extant peerages under Hay of Alderston.
[3] A Thomas Higgins was appointed a Gentleman Usher of the Privy Chamber, 27th October 1701.

HOOKE

HOOKE OF HOOKE CASTLE, Baron [I].

1708
—
1738

I. NATHANIEL HOOKE, third but second surviving son of John Hooke of Drogheda, merchant, by Margaret, daughter of Christopher Hooke of Alway, Gloucestershire; born about 1663; entered Trinity College, Dublin, July 1679, but left almost immediately and proceeded, 1680, to Glasgow University. He removed the next year to Cambridge, and was admitted to Sidney Sussex College, as a sizer, 6th July 1681. He was a Puritan, and joined the Earl of Argyll in Holland, and in 1685 landed at Lyme Regis with the Duke of Monmouth, acting as his Independent Chaplain. He was sent secretly to London with one Danvers[1] to raise an insurrection in the City, and was exempted from the general pardon, 10th March 1685/6. After remaining for some time in hiding, he, in 1688, only four months before the Revolution, surrendered,[2] threw himself on the King's mercy, was pardoned, and from thenceforth remained a faithful servant of King James and of his son. He became a Catholic, joined Lord Dundee in Scotland, but in May 1689 was taken at Chester and committed to the Tower of London. He was released 12th February 1689/90, when he immediately proceeded to Ireland, and was present at the battle of the Boyne. On the surrender of Limerick, 3rd October 1691, he retired to France, and was appointed Colonel *reformé* of the regiment of Galmoye. On 8th January 1703 he was transferred with the same rank to the regiment of Sparre, with which he served in Flanders and on the Moselle, and was present at the battle of Ramillies, 23rd May 1705. The following August he went on a special mission to Scotland, and on his return he obtained letters of naturalisation dated January 1706, which were confirmed and registered 1st January 1720.[3] In April 1707 he was again in Scotland with Lieutenant-Colonel John Murray, to confer with the Jacobite party. On 19th February 1708 he was created by James III

---

[1] He is said to have proposed a plan to assassinate King James, but Hooke refused to have anything to do with it.

[2] And 'gave himself into the hands of him who had been told by one of Hooke's old 'comrades, Col. Ayloffe, that though he had the power, yet he had not the nature 'to pardon : and as by kindness to Penn, so now also by mercy to Hooke, James, out 'of a nonconformest adversary, won a staunch friend.' See the Rev. W. D. Macray's *Correspondence of Colonel Hooke*, vol. ii.

[3] These are printed in full in Macray's work, ii. p. x. *et seq.*, and contain many interesting genealogical details.

HOOKE

and VIII *BARON HOOKE OF HOOKE CASTLE* [I], co. Waterford, with remainder to the heirs-male of his body;[1] made Brigadier 3rd March 1708, and was one of the General officers selected to accompany his young Sovereign in the expedition which sailed from Dunkirk 17th March following; the next year he was again serving with the French army, and was present at the battles of Oudenarde, 11th July, and Malplaquet, 11th September. In 1710 he was sent to Gertruydenberg as James's Envoy to the general peace negotiations, and in 1711 was sent as French Ambassador by Louis XIV to the court of Dresden. Brigadier-General (Maréchal-de-camp), 18th March 1718; Knight-Commander of the Order of St. Louis, 27th February 1721. He died in France 25th October 1738.[2] He married, first, April 1708, Eleanor Susan, sometime Maid of Honour to Queen Mary of Modena, daughter of Donogh or Denis MacCarthy of the Carbery family, by Catherine Douvns,[3] and secondly[4] Helen de St. Jean, widow respectively of the Sieur O'Brien, who died 1708, and of the Sieur MacCarthy, who died 1724.

II. JAMES NATHANIEL (HOOKE), second *BARON HOOKE*, only son and heir, born 14th December 1705, and presented for baptism by King James, who gave him his own name; succeeded his father 25th October 1738. He entered the French army, Captain *réformé* of the cavalry regiment of Rottenburg 1st June 1719, and Captain of the Rattsky Hussars 1st July 1734; received permission to enter the service of the Emperor Charles VII 16th November 1743, and was killed, near Strasburg, 20th August 1744, when his honours became extinct.[5] He married Helen de Coulanges.[6]

1738 - 1744

---

[1] The patent was among the MSS. of Sir William Betham, and formed one of the articles in lot 53 at the sale of his library, 10th May 1860, when it was purchased by Sir Thomas Phillipps. In the catalogue of the latter's collection it was numbered 15,339, but had been mislaid when Mr. Macray tried to find it.
[2] Macray's *Correspondence of Colonel Hooke*, *Dictionary of National Biography*.
[3] A pedigree of the MacCarthys is given in Lainé's *Archives généalogiques de la Noblesse de France*, vol. v. Therein the wife of this Donogh is given as Margaret de Coucy, but in the certificate of *Lord Hooke's* naturalisation the name of his wife's mother is given as in the text.
[4] Statement of services supplied by French Minister of War.
[5] A Baron de Hooke was living at Gatterville, in Normandy, in 1814, but he was descended from another branch of the family, who had left Ireland in Cromwell's time, and settled in the French West Indies. See O'Callaghan's *Irish Brigade*, p. 330.
[6] Statement of service supplied by French Minister of War.

INNERPAPHRIE

INNERPAPHRIE, Viscount of [S].

i.e. '*INNERPAPHRIE*,' VISCOUNTY OF (Hay), created 5th October 1718, with '*INVERNESS*,' EARLDOM OF, which see.

INNISKILLEN, Baron [I].

See Maguire of Enniskillen.

INVERNESS, Earl and Duke of [S].

1718 – 1740

I. COLONEL THE HON. JOHN HAY of Cromlix, third son of Thomas (Hay), sixth Earl of Kinnoull [S], by the Hon. Elizabeth, only daughter of William (Drummond), first Viscount Strathallan [S], born 1691 ; accompanied his brother-in-law, the Earl of Mar, when he set out in disguise in a coal ship from Gravesend, and took an active part in the '15. He was sent on a mission from Mar to offer the Duke of Atholl the command under Berwick ; took possession of Perth for King James 14th September 1715 ; Governor of that city 18th September ; was sent to France on a mission to James, and, on his return with the King, was made Brigadier-General and Master of the Horse. On the collapse of the rising he retired to St. Germains, and was attainted, 1716. A Groom of the Bedchamber, 2nd February 1718, and on 5th October (N.S.) following he was created[1] by James III and VIII an Earl and Peer of Parliament as EARL OF INVERNESS, VISCOUNT OF INNERPAPHRIE [*i.e.* Innerpeffray], and LORD CROMLIX AND ERNE [S], with remainder to the heirs-male of his body. In 1723 he was sent on a special mission to Brussels, where he had an interview with Bishop Atterbury. In 1724 he succeeded the Duke of Mar, with whom he had quarrelled, as temporary SECRETARY OF STATE, and on 5th March 1725 was confirmed in that position; *K.T.*, 31st December 1725. Owing to the hostility of the Queen, instigated, it is said, by Mar, he was dismissed from the Secretaryship, 3rd April 1727, but was the same day created by King James BARON HAY [E], and the day following (4th April) DUKE OF INVERNESS [S]. He died *s.p.* 1740, when all his honours became extinct. He married

---

[1] The patent is endorsed : 'This warrant is all writ in the King's own hand.'

JERSEY

the Hon Marjory, third but first surviving daughter of David (Murray) fifth Viscount Stormont [S], by Marjory, only daughter of David Scott of Scotstarvit, Fifeshire.

IPSWICH, Baron [E].

i.e. '*IPSWICH*,' BARONY OF (Jermyn), created 9th July 1689, with '*DOVER*,' EARLDOM OF, which see.

ISLA, Earl of [S].

i.e. '*ISLA*,' EARL OF (Drummond), created 17th April 1692, with '*MELFORT*,' DUKEDOM OF, which see.

JAMAICA, Marquis of [E].

JAMES FRANCIS FITZ-JAMES, styled Earl of Tinmouth, son and heir-apparent of James (Fitz-James), first Duke of Berwick [E], K.G., is sometimes, but apparently erroneously, stated to have been in or about 1720 created by his uncle, James III and VIII, MARQUIS OF JAMAICA. He had married, 31st December 1716, Catherine Ventura, *suo jure* Duchess of Veraguas and La Verga, Marchioness of Jamaica [Spain], sister and sole heir of Peter, and only daughter of Peter Emmanuel Nuno (de Portugal-Colomb), Dukes of Veraguas and La Verga, Marquises of Jamaica, etc. [Spain], which probably caused the confusion.

JERMYN OF ROYSTON, Baron [E].

i.e. '*JERMYN OF ROYSTON*,' BARONY OF (Jermyn), created 9th July 1689, with '*DOVER*,' EARLDOM OF, which see.

JERSEY, Countess and Earl of [E].

I. BARBARA VILLIERS, widow of Sir Edward (Villiers), Baron Villiers of Hoo, and Viscount Villiers of Dartford, co. Kent [E] (so created by William of Orange, 20th March 1690/1), and Earl of the Island of Jersey (so created by the same King, 13th October 1697), who died 25th August 1711; was, April 1716, granted the title and precedency of a Countess, 1716 — 1735?

JERSEY

as COUNTESS OF JERSEY [E], by James III and VIII. She, who was an active Jacobite, was the daughter of William Chiffinch of Fibbers, in Bray, Berks, Keeper of the Royal Closet, and was born about 1663, being aged eighteen at the time of her marriage (Lic. Fac. 8th, and Articles 17th December), 1681. She died in Paris about 1735. Admon. 13th December 1735. Will, dated 12th October 1711, proved 26th February 1735/6.[1]

1716 — 1721

II. WILLIAM (VILLIERS), second EARL OF JERSEY, etc. (by creation of William of Orange), son and heir of Edward, first Earl of Jersey, by Barbara, afterwards (1716) *suo jure* COUNTESS OF JERSEY, as above, born about 1682; educated at Queen's College, Cambridge; M.A., 1700; M.P. for Kent, 1705-1708; succeeded his father, 26th August 1711. On April 1716 he was, as William Villiers, Esq.,[2] created by King James III and VIII BARON OF HOO, co. Kent, VISCOUNT OF DARTFORD, co. Kent, and EARL OF JERSEY [E],[3] with remainder to the heirs-male of his body. He died at Castlethorpe, Bucks, 13th July 1721, and was buried 23rd, at Westerham, Kent. He married, 22nd March 1704/5, at Hampstead, Middlesex, Judith, only daughter and heir of Frederick Herne of London, by [   ], daughter of [   ] Lile, of co. Northampton. She, who was a great heiress, was buried, 31st July 1735, at St. Bride's, London.

1721 — 1769

III. WILLIAM (VILLIERS), *second* (1716) and third (1697) EARL OF JERSEY, son and heir; he succeeded his cousin, John (Fitzgerald, *alias* Villiers), fifth Viscount and first Earl of Grandison [I], 14th March 1766, as sixth VISCOUNT GRANDISON OF LIMERICK. He died 28th August 1769, and was buried, 7th September, at Middleton Stoney, Oxford.[4]

1769 — 1805

IV. GEORGE BUSSY (VILLIERS), *third* (1716) and fourth (1697) EARL OF JERSEY, second but only surviving son and heir, born 9th June, and baptized 6th July 1735 at St. George's, Hanover Square; died 22nd August 1805.

---

[1] *The Complete Peerage*, iv. p. 329.
[2] His Williamite earldom was of course not recognised by James.
[3] Almost the identical titles which had been conferred on his father by William of Orange.
[4] For a fuller account of this earl and his successors see the extant peerages.

KENMARE

V. GEORGE (VILLIERS, afterwards (1819) CHILD-VILLIERS), *fourth* (1716), and fifth (1697) EARL OF JERSEY, etc., son and heir, born 19th August 1773; died 3rd October 1859 at 38 Berkeley Square, Middlesex, and was buried at Middleton Stoney.

1805
–
1859

VI. GEORGE AUGUSTUS FREDERICK (CHILD-VILLIERS), *fifth* (1716) and sixth (1697) EARL OF JERSEY, etc., son and heir, born 4th April 1808 in Berkeley Square; died 24th October 1859 at Brighton, and was buried at Middleton Stoney.

1859
–
1859

VII. VICTOR ALBERT GEORGE (CHILD-VILLIERS), sixth EARL OF JERSEY, VISCOUNT DARTFORD, and BARON HOO (1716), seventh EARL OF THE ISLAND OF JERSEY (1697), VISCOUNT VILLIERS OF DARTFORD, and BARON VILLIERS OF HOO (1691) [E], also tenth VISCOUNT GRANDISON OF LIMERICK (1621) [I], son and heir, born 20th March 1843, succeeded his father 24th October 1859.

1859

KENMARE, Viscount of [I].

I. SIR VALENTINE BROWNE, third BARONET [I], of Killarney, co. Kerry, son and heir of Sir Valentine Browne, Baronet, by the Lady Mary, daughter of Charles (Macarty), first Viscount Muskerry [I], was born 1638, succeeded his father, aged two, in 1640; Commissioner of Oyer and Terminer for co. Kerry; P.C. [I]; Colonel of a regiment of foot in the army of King James, by whom he was, 20th April 1689 (after the Revolution in England, but while still *de facto* as well as *de jure* King of Ireland),[1] created BARON OF CASTLEROSS and VISCOUNT KENMARE, co. Kerry [I], with remainder to the heirs-male of his body. He appears to have been among those taken prisoners at the battle of Aughrim, 12th July 1691, and to have been attainted. He died 1694. Will, dated 7th June 1690, proved in Dublin, 22nd June 1694. He married Jane, daughter and heir of the Hon. Sir Nicholas Plunkett of Balrath, co. Meath, by his first wife, daughter and co-heir of William Turner, Alderman of Dublin.[2]

1689
–
1694

---

[1] See Preface, p. xii.
[2] See *The Complete Peerage*, from which the particulars here given are taken. In that work, however, the month of the creation of the title is given as 'May,' whereas it should be 'April.'

KENMARE

1694 – 1720   II. NICHOLAS (BROWNE), second *Viscount Kenmare*, son and heir, was also a Colonel in the service of King James, whom he followed to St. Germains. He was attainted by William of Orange, and his vast estates forfeited. He died 1720. He married, 1684, his cousin Helen, eldest daughter and co-heir of Thomas Browne of Hospital, co. Limerick, by Elizabeth, daughter and heir of Sir John Browne of Hospital aforesaid. She died at St. James's, Westminster. Her admon. as 'Dame Helen Browne, *alias* Viscountess Kenmare,' 22nd July 1700.

1720 – 1736   III. VALENTINE (BROWNE), third *Viscount Kenmare*, son and heir, born 1695; he appears to have recovered possession of the family estates. He died 30th June 1736. He married, first, November 1720, Honoria, second daughter of Colonel Thomas Butler of Kilcash, by Margaret, Dowager-Viscountess Magennis [I], daughter of William (Bourke), seventh Earl of Clanricarde [I]. She died 1730. He married, secondly, October 1735, Mary, Dowager-Countess of Fingall [I], daughter of Maurice FitzGerald of Castle Ishen, co. Cork. She married, thirdly, as his second wife, John (Bellew), fourth Baron Bellew of Duleek [I]. She died in London 1742.

1736 – 1790 or 1795   IV. THOMAS (BROWNE), fourth *Viscount Kenmare*, etc., second but only surviving son and heir by first wife, born 1726. He died 9th September 1790 or 1795. He married, December 1750, Anne, daughter of Thomas Cooke of Painstown, co. Carlow, by Helen, daughter of Nicholas Purcell.

1790 or 1795 – 1812   V. VALENTINE (BROWNE), fifth *Viscount Kenmare*, etc., only son and heir, born January 1754. He was, as 'Sir 'Valentine Browne, Baronet of Killarney, co. Kerry' (the creation of 1689 being ignored), created by George III, 12th February 1798, Baron of Castlerosse and Viscount Kenmare [I],[1] and some three years later, 3rd January 1801, Viscount Castlerosse and Earl of Kenmare [I]. He died at Castlerosse 3rd October 1812.[2]

---

[1] The same titles conferred on his ancestor one hundred and eight years before by King James II and VII.

[2] For a fuller account of this peer and his successors see the extant peerages.

LALLY

VI. VALENTINE (BROWNE), second EARL OF KEN- 1812
MARE, sixth VISCOUNT KENMARE, born 15th January 1788. On
the 14th August 1841 he was created by Queen Victoria BARON 1853
KENMARE OF CASTLEROSSE, co. Kerry [U K]. He died *s.p.* 31st
October 1853, at Great Malvern, co. Worcester, when the
Barony of Kenmare of Castlerosse [U K] became extinct.

VII. THOMAS (BROWNE), third EARL OF KENMARE, 1853
seventh VISCOUNT KENMARE, next brother and heir, born 15th –
January 1789, and was created, 12th March 1856, BARON KEN- 1871
MARE OF KILLARNEY, co. Kerry [U K]. He died 26th December
1871, at 54 Eton Place, Middlesex.

VIII. VALENTINE AUGUSTUS (BROWNE), fourth 1871
EARL OF KENMARE and VISCOUNT CASTLEROSSE (1801), and
VISCOUNT KENMARE and BARON CASTLEROSSE (1798), eighth
VISCOUNT KENMARE and BARON CASTLEROSSE (1689) [I], second
BARON KENMARE OF CASTLEROSSE (1856) [U K], and tenth
BARONET (1622) [I], only son and heir, born 16th May 1825;
succeeded his father, 26th December 1871; K.P. 3rd June
1872.

KILDRUMMIE, Earl of [S].

i.e. '*KILDRUMMIE*,' EARLDOM OF (Erskine), created 22nd
October 1715, with '*MAR*,' DUKEDOM OF, which see.

KILPEE, Baron [E].

I. WALTER PYE is said to have been created *BARON* 169?
KILPEE [E] by King James II and VII.

LALLY, Baronet [I].

I. GERARD LALLY, second son of Thomas Lally or 1707
O'Mullally, of Tullaghnadaly, co. Galway, by Jane, sister of 1737
Theobald (Dillon), seventh Viscount Dillon [I]. He was an
officer in the army, and after the surrender of Limerick, 3rd
October 1691, he retired to France, and became Lieutenant-
Colonel of the regiment commanded by his cousin General (after-
wards *EARL*) Dillon, 28th July 1708. On 7th July 1707 he was
created by King James III and VIII, by letters patent dated at

73

LANSDOWN

St. Germains-en-Laye, a *BARONET* [I],[1] with presumably remainder to the heirs-male of his body; appointed Brigadier-General in the French army, 20th February 1734, with the promise of being made at the next promotion a Maréchal-de-camp, with precedency of 1719. He died at Arras November 1737. He married, 18th April 1701, at Romans, diocese of Vienne, Anne Mary, daughter of Charles James de Bressac, Seigneur de la Vache.

1737 — II. SIR THOMAS ARTHUR LALLY, second *BARONET*, only son and heir, was in 1746, on his return from Scotland, created by James III and VIII *BARON OF TOLLENDALLY, VISCOUNT OF BALLYMOLE*, and *EARL OF MOENMOYNE* [I]. See *MOENMOYNE, EARL OF*.

LANSDOWN, Baron [E].

i.e. '*LANSDOWN*,' *BARONY OF* (Granville), created 6th October 1721, with '*BATH*,' *EARLDOM OF*, which see.

LANSDOWN OF BIDEFORD, Baron [E].

i.e. '*LANSDOWN OF BIDEFORD*,' co. Devon, *BARONY OF* (Granville), created 3rd November 1721, with '*ALBEMARLE*,' *DUKEDOM OF*, which see.

LISMORE, Earl of [I].

1746 — 1759 I. DANIEL O'BRIEN or OBRYAN, son[2] of Major-General Morough O'Brien of Carrisgogunnell, co. Limerick, an

---

[1] See a letter signed 'G. D. B.' in *N. and Q.*, 9th series, x. p. 453.

[2] The Duke of Luynes says that he was a man of low birth, not an O'Brien at all. According to him, his grandfather was a groom in the service of one of the Clancarty family, who came to France after the Revolution, entered one of the Scottish or Irish infantry regiments, served with distinction, and was advanced from the rank of Sergeant to that of Lieutenant-Colonel. See an article by A[lice] S[hield] in *The Royalist*, xi. pp. (*sic*) 32-36. This, however, is obviously incorrect. His father, Murrough O'Brien, for many years Colonel of the O'Brien regiment, was an officer of bravery and ability; in proof of which his gallantry at Ramelles, and the fine manœuvre at Pallicë, are particularly cited. 'That brave old soldier, Major-General Morough O'Brien,' observes an English contemporary, an adherent of the House of Hanover, 'has left a son behind him that joins all the abilities of the statesman, with the politeness of the courtier, to 'the martial spirit of the father.' See O'Callaghan's *History of the Irish Brigade*. The official record of his services, supplied by the French Minister of War, is as follows: Volunteer, Hamilton's English infantry regiment, 30th April 1671, with

LISMORE

officer in the French service, and (1706-1720) Colonel of the regiment afterwards commanded by Lord Clare; born at Perpignan 1683; entered the French army as a cadet, 1694; Ensign in the Irish infantry regiment of Talbot (afterwards known as that of O'Brien or Clare), March 1695; Captain *réformé*, June 1697;[1] obtained a company, September 1706; and attained the rank of Colonel, 20th June 1719. He was a faithful and one of the most trusted of the servants of King James III and VIII, whom he served long and well at the French Court. On 17th March 1726 he was created[2] *BARON OF CASTLE LYONS* [I], with remainder to the heirs-male of his body, and (having been for several years previously his agent there)[3] was, 26th September 1745, appointed King James's *AMBASSADOR* at the Court of Paris; on 7th February 1747 he received full powers to treat with the Court of Madrid, and continued to represent James at these Courts until May 1747, when he was recalled to Rome, and from November 1747 to his death was *SECRETARY OF STATE*. He had previously, 11th October 1746, as 'Daniel Obryan, *BARON OF* [   ], Our Minister at 'the Court of France,' been created *BARON OF* [   ], *VISCOUNT OF TALLOW*, and *EARL OF LISMORE* [I], with remainder to the heirs-male of his body, but he does not appear to have

---

which he passed into France. Ensign, 1673; passed (by incorporation) into the German infantry regiment of Furstemberg, 10th March 1678; Captain *réformé*, 1688; Captain of foot, 1689; passed into the Irish infantry regiment of O'Brien, afterwards Clare's, 1691; Major, 12th March 1694; Lieutenant-Colonel, 25th January 1705; Colonel, 11th August 1706; Brigadier of infantry, 29th March 1710; Maréchal-de-camp, 1st February 1719; died, July 1720. Campaigns in Bar and Westphalia, 1672-1673; Germany, 1674, 1675, 1676, 1677, and 1678; Catalonia, 1684; Roussillon, 1690-1691; Italy, 1693-1696; on the Meuse, 1697; Germany, 1701, 1702, 1703, and 1704; with the army of the Moselle, 1705; in Flanders, 1706, 1707, 1708, 1709, 1710, 1711, and 1712; and on the Rhine, 1713.

[1] Daniel O'Brien, 'now serving with the troops in France,' and the son of gentle parents in co. Cork, had a declaration of his noblesse from King James, 31st October 1702.

[2] He is in the patent described as 'Daniel Obryan, Esq., son of the deceased '[   ] Obryan.' The name of the title is left blank, but his credentials to the Court of Paris are endorsed: 'The date blank in all but the year, viz. 1745. But they were 'signed by the King, 15 Nov. 1745'; and in another handwriting, 'Col. Obryan filled 'up the date of these full powers at Albano, 26 Sept. 1745, in the 45th year of the 'King's reign, and also filled up the blank of Baron with the title of Castel Lyons.'

[3] Miss A[lice] S[hield], in her article in *The Royalist* above referred to, says that from the early thirties to 1747 he represented the King at the French Court as *chargé d'affaires*, but there appears to be some confusion between this Colonel Daniel O'Brien and Colonel John O'Brien (created a Baronet [I] 19th January 1723), who was the Colonel O'Brien appointed King James's Minister at the French Court, 21st July 1733.

75

LISMORE

assumed the title[1] until his appointment as Secretary of State, upon which occasion he was made a *K.G.* In May 1749 he undertook a mission to Madrid, and on his return to Rome, the December following, was nominated by King James for the GRAND CROSS OF ST. LOUIS, which he received 1750. He died at Rome, 5th November 1759, aged seventy-six. LORD LISMORE married, before 1736, Margaret Josepha O'Brien, who claimed to be of the family of Lord Clare. She had held before her marriage a small post at the Spanish Court,[2] which would seem to establish her gentility, and she was probably the daughter of a Jacobite refugee. She was much mixed up in all the intrigues of the time, and on her husband's departure for Rome she remained in Paris, and continued as a sort of semi-accredited ambassadress, recognised, if not trusted, by King James. In January 1749 she was banished from Paris, being accused by her enemy de Maurepas of being concerned in the manufacture of lampoons, but was recalled on his disgrace the October following. In April 1757, however, she was sent to Caen by a *lettre de cachet*, but was back in Paris shortly afterwards, and in conjunction with her son continued to manage the King's affairs until November 1763, when his health having failed, the Duke of York assumed the direction of affairs, and immediately took management out of their hands, and warned them if they complained they would be deprived of the pension allowed them by the King. He had issue an only son :—

1. James Daniel, VISCOUNT TALLOW, his heir.[3]

1759 – I

II. JAMES DANIEL (O'BRIEN), second EARL OF LISMORE, VISCOUNT TALLOW, and BARON CASTLE LYONS, only son and heir of the preceding, born in Paris, 18th August 1736; entered as an Ensign in the Guard of the King of Spain, 1744; admitted into the first company of the musketeers of the ordi-

---

[1] King James did not like the titles he conferred used. On *Lord Lismore's* creation Prince Charles immediately demanded that Lochiel should be allowed to call himself a Baron. King James refused. He could not, he said, declare Lochiel's title unless he were to declare all the letters patent, which were in great number, and it would be highly improper to do so. *Lord Lismore* was not a precedent, for his title would not have been declared if he had not gone to fill so high a position near his (the King's) person. 'Lochiel's interest and reputation in his own country, and being at the head 'of a regiment in France, will make him more considered than any empty title I could 'give him.'

[2] See the article in *The Royalist*, xi. p. (*sic*) 35, above mentioned.

[3] D'Argenson speaks of him as 'Lord Talon.'

LOCHIEL

nary Guard of the King of France, 29th May 1750; Captain *réformé* of the Irish infantry regiment of Clare, 10th September 1751; Colonel *réformé* of the regiment of Rothe, 18th August 1754, and Knight of St. Louis; succeeded his father, 5th November 1759; acted for some time, till November 1763, in conjunction with his mother, as the King's agent in Paris. On 25th November 1766 he was authorised to enter the service of the Elector of Bavaria.[1] He is said to have died unmarried before 1789.

LOCHIEL, Baron [S].

I. JOHN CAMERON OF LOCHIEL, eldest son and heir of the celebrated Sir Ewen Cameron of Lochiel,[2] by his second wife, Isabel, daughter of Sir Lauchlan Maclean of Duart, first Baronet [S]. He joined[3] the Earl of Mar in 1715 at the head of his clan, his father being then upwards of eighty-six and too old to lead it in person. He was present at Prestonpans, and being attainted, retired to France, where he lived for over thirty years in exile. On 27th January 1717 he was, as 'John Cameron, eldest lawful 'son of Sir Ewen Cameron of Lochiel,' created by King James a Lord and Peer of Parliament as LORD LOCHIEL [S], with remainder to his lawful heirs-male. He died at Nieuport in Flanders 1748.[4] He married Isabel, daughter of Alexander Campbell, sixth of Lochnell, by Margaret, only child of Duncan Stewart, seventh of Appin. He had issue:—

1717
–
1748

1. Donald, MASTER OF LOCHIEL.
2. HON. John Cameron of Fassifern, Argyllshire. He took no active part in the '45, but was nevertheless arrested, 28th April 1753, on the charge of corresponding with attainted persons and exiled. He settled in the West Indies, where he became a merchant; he afterwards returned to Scotland and died

---

[1] Information supplied by the French Minister of War.
[2] Sir Ewen was a noted Royalist. He fought under Montrose, was one of the first to join the rising of 1652 in favour of the King, and the last who held out against Cromwell. Although past seventy, in 1689 he led the clan at Killiecrankie, and greatly distinguished himself at that battle.
[3] Before doing so, however, he made over the estates to his son Donald, thereby saving them for the time from forfeiture.
[4] Other accounts say at Boulogne, 1747.

LOCHIEL

at Fassifern. He married Jean, daughter of John Campbell of Achallader, and had issue.
3. HON. Archibald Cameron, M.D. He took an active part in the '45, was attainted 1746, but escaped to France. Returning, however, to Scotland in 1753, he was arrested and imprisoned in Edinburgh Castle, 26th March, from thence transferred to the Tower, and on 17th May arraigned before the Court of the King's Bench upon the Act of Attainder of 1746, and in spite of the Act of Indemnity of 1747 executed on Tower Hill, on Thursday, 7th June 1753. He was buried beneath the altar of the Chapel Royal of the Savoy. He married Jean, daughter of Archibald Cameron of Dungallon, and left issue.
4. HON. Alexander Cameron, a priest, died a prisoner on board a ship in the Thames.
5. HON. Ewen Cameron, emigrated to Jamaica, and became a sugar-planter there, where he died.

1748
-
1748

II. DONALD (CAMERON), second LORD LOCHIEL, 'the 'gentle Lochiel,' born 1695, succeeded his grandfather, Sir Ewen Cameron, February 1719, as actual chief of clan Cameron, his father being then in exile. On the arrival of Prince Charles in 1745, in consequence of having long prepared for another attempt to restore the Stuarts, he was able to put a regiment of eight hundred well-armed and well-disciplined men in the field, at the head of which he served throughout the campaign. He was desperately wounded at Culloden, 16th April 1746, but managed to escape, and remained in hiding until 29th September, when in attendance on the Prince he sailed for France. He was made Colonel of the regiment of Albany by Louis XIV, 20th October 1747. He succeeded his father 1748, but died 26th October the same year at Borgue, of an attack of brain fever. He had been attainted 1746 and his estates confiscated. He married Anne, only daughter of Sir James Campbell of Auchinbreck, M.P., fifth Baronet [S], by his first wife, Janet, daughter of Norman MacLeod of MacLeod. He had issue :—
1. John, MASTER OF LOCHIEL, his heir.
2. HON. James Cameron, Captain of the Royal Scots regiment, commanded by LORD Lewis Drummond, died unmarried 1759.

LOCHIEL

3. *Hon.* Charles Cameron, succeeded his eldest brother.
4. *Hon.* Isabel Cameron, married Colonel Mores of the French army.
5. *Hon.* Janet Cameron, a nun in Paris.
6. *Hon.* Henrietta Cameron, married Captain Portin of the French army.
7. *Hon.* Donalda Cameron died unmarried.

III. JOHN (CAMERON), third *Lord Lochiel*, eldest son and heir, Captain in the regiment of Albany, succeeded his father 26th October 1748, returned to Scotland in 1759, and died unmarried at Edinburgh, 10th November 1762.[1]

1748 – 1762

IV. CHARLES (CAMERON), fourth *Lord Lochiel*, only surviving brother and heir. He was permitted to return to Scotland, and assisted in raising the second regiment of Fraser's Highlanders in 1775. He died in Glasgow in 1776. He married, 1767 [   ], daughter of [   ] Marshall, and had, with other issue, a son :—

1762 – 1776

1. Donald, *Master of Lochiel*, his heir.

V. DONALD (CAMERON), fifth *Lord Lochiel*, son and heir, born 1769; he obtained the restoration of his estates under the General Act of Amnesty of 1784. He died 1832. He married at Edinburgh, 23rd April[2] 1795, the Hon. Anne, eldest daughter of General Sir Ralph Abercromby, K.C.B., by Mary Anne, *suo jure* Baroness Abercromby [U K], second daughter and co-heir of John Menzies of Fernton, Perth. She died 17th September 1844. He had issue :—

1776 – 1832

1. Donald, *Master of Lochiel*, his heir.
2. Rev. the *Hon.* Alexander Cameron, married, 1st September 1835, Charlotte, daughter of Very Rev. the Hon. Edward Rice, D.D., and had issue.
3. *Hon.* Mary Anne Cameron, married, 2nd September 1846, Rear-Admiral Lord John Hay, who died *s.p.* 26th August 1851. She died 30th November 1850.
4. *Hon.* Matilda Cameron, died unmarried 1894.

---

[1] *Scots Magazine*, 1762, p. 623.   [2] *Ibid.* 1795, p. 275.

LOCHIEL

1832 — 1858

VI. DONALD (CAMERON), sixth LORD LOCHIEL, D.L., co. Inverness, etc., elder son and heir, born 25th September 1796; entered the army, 1814, and served with the Grenadier Guards at the battle of Waterloo. He died 2nd December 1858. He married, 31st July 1832, Lady Vere Catherine Louisa, sister of George Robert (Hobart), fifth Earl of Buckinghamshire [G B], daughter of the Hon. George Vere Hobart, by his second wife, Janet, daughter of Colonel Alexander Maclean. She died 15th November 1888. He had issue :—

1. Donald, MASTER OF LOCHIEL, his heir.
2. HON. George Hampden Cameron, assumed the additional surname of Hampden, born October 1840, died, unmarried, 23rd June 1874.
3. HON. Anne Louisa Cameron, died unmarried 24th June 1864.
4. HON. Julia Vere Cameron, married, 15th June 1870, Major-General Hugh Mackenzie, and has issue.
5. HON. Sibella Matilda Cameron, married as first wife, 12th December 1865, the Rev. Henry George John Veitch of Eliock, co. Dumfries, and died 7th April 1890, leaving issue.
6. HON. Albinia Mary Cameron, died unmarried January 1861.

1858

VII. DONALD (CAMERON), seventh LORD LOCHIEL, twenty-fourth CAPTAIN OF CLAN CAMERON, Lord-Lieutenant co. Inverness, J.P. co. Bucks, and J.P., D.L., Argyll; M.P. for co. Inverness, 1868-1875; born 5th April 1835; succeeded his father, 2nd December 1858. He married, 9th December 1875, Lady Margaret Elizabeth, second daughter of Walter Francis (Montagu-Douglas-Scott), fifth Duke of Buccleuch and seventh Duke of Queensberry [S], by his wife, the Lady Charlotte Anne, daughter of Thomas (Thynne), second Marquis of Bath [G B]. She was born 10th October 1846. He has issue :—

1. Donald Walter, MASTER OF LOCHIEL, Lieutenant Grenadier Guards, born 4th November 1876.
2. HON. Ewen Charles Cameron, born 18th February 1878.
3. HON. Allan George Cameron, 2nd Lieutenant Cameron Highlanders, born 27th July 1880.
4. HON. Archibald Cameron, born 5th January 1886.

LUCAN

LOVAT, Baron [S].

i.e. '*LOVAT*,' BARONY OF (Fraser), created 14th March 1740, with '*FRASER*,' DUKEDOM OF, which see.

LOUGHMORE, Baron [I].

I. NICHOLAS PURCELL, Lord of the Barony of Lough-   1689
mow, co. Tipperary, was a Colonel of a regiment of horse in   –
King James's army in 1689. He was probably the [   ]
Purcell said to have been created in 1689 or 1690 by King
James BARON LOUGHMORE [I].[1]

LUCAN, Earl of [I].

I. PATRICK SARSFIELD, of Lucan, co. Dublin, second   1690/1
son of Patrick Sarsfield of Lucan, by Anne, daughter of Rory   –
O'More, born at Lucan near Dublin, educated at a French   1693
Military College; succeeded his elder brother William in the
family estates, 1688; Captain in Colonel Dongan's regiment of
foot, 9th February 1678; Captain in Hamilton's Dragoons, 20th
June 1685; and Lieutenant-Colonel of Dover's Horse, 18th
October following; Colonel, 22nd May 1686. In 1688 he raised
a troop of horse in Ireland for King James, of which he was
made Colonel with the rank of Brigadier-General, and also P.C.
[I]; M.P. co. Dublin, 7th May 1689. He greatly distinguished
himself at the first siege of Limerick, August 1690, and in reward
was created by King James, January 1690/1, *BARON ROSBERRY,
VISCOUNT OF TULLY,* and *EARL OF LUCAN,* co. Dublin [I], with
presumably remainder to the heirs-male of his body; appointed
Colonel of the Life Guards and Commander-in-Chief of the
forces in Ireland, January to May, and again July to October
1691. The favourable terms of the capitulation of Limerick,
3rd October 1691, were mainly owing to his skill.[2] After the
surrender he retired to France and was appointed Captain of
the second troop of the Irish Horse Guards, January 1692. He
was killed, at the head of a French division, at the battle of
Landen in the attack on the village of Nerwinden, in Flanders,
29th July 1693.[3] He married Lady Honora, second daughter of

---
[1] *King James' Irish Army List,* 1689, by J. D'Alton, 1855, pp. 239-245.
[2] *The Complete Peerage.*
[3] *The Dict. of Nat. Biog.* says he was wounded, and died a few days later, 19th August, but the commission to Lord Clancarty to succeed him is dated 14th August.

LUCAN

William (Bourke), seventh Earl of Clanricarde [I], by his second wife, Lady Ellen, daughter of Donough (MacCarty), first Earl of Clancarty [I]. She married, secondly, as first wife, 26th March 1695, in the Chapel Royal, St. Germains, James (FitzJames), first Duke of Berwick [E], K.G. She died at Pezenas in Languedoc, 16th January 1698, in her twenty-third year, and was buried in the English convent at Pontoise. He had issue :—

1. James, *Viscount Tully*, his heir.
2. *Lady* [   ] Sarsfield, married, about 1718, Baron Theodore de Neuhof, sometime King of Corsica.

1693 – 1719

II. JAMES FRANCIS EDWARD (SARSFIELD), second *Earl of Lucan, Viscount Tully, Baron of Rosberry*, only son and heir, born 30th March 1693, and baptized at St. Germains 12th May following, the Prince of Wales being sponsor; succeeded his father, 29th July 1693. He had an annual pension of 3000 *livres* granted him by Louis XIV before 30th November 1698;[1] was at first brought up under the care of his paternal relations, the Misses Sarsfield (generally styled the Ladies Kilmallock);[2] and in 1703 was sent with his step-brother, Lord Tinmouth, by the Duke of Berwick, to the College at Plessis. He afterwards entered the Spanish army, and greatly distinguished himself at the reduction of Barcelona, being wounded in the last assault; became Captain of the Bodyguard to King Philip V and Knight of the Golden Fleece. In 1715 he was in Ireland 'on the King's business.'[3] He died *s.p.* at St. Omer in Flanders, 12th May 1719, when all his titles became extinct.[4]

---

[1] See warrants from James II and VII, 20th November 1698, and from Mary of Modena, 8th February 1703, to Henry Conquest, empowering him to receive the pension granted by Louis XIV to the young Earl of Lucan.—*Calendar of Stuart Papers*, i. pp. 134, 181.

[2] See *The Royalist*, xi. pp. 11, 12.

[3] The following proclamation was issued April 1715, 'That the Government having ' certain intelligence that Sarsfield, otherwise called Earl of Lucan, and several officers, ' who had lately landed and dispersed themselves in several parts of the Kingdom, had ' held conferences with divers Papists of distinction, with design to ferment a rebellion ' in favour of the Pretender; and that they had certainly concerted a general insurrec- ' tion, which was to be in all parts of the kingdom the same night and hour, having to ' this end their emissaries in each province, therefore it was thought fit to give notice ' thereof to all the inhabitants, that they might take the necessary measures to appre- ' hend the said Sarsfield, and all the officers who were come into the Kingdom with that ' design, etc.,' and a reward of £1000 was promised for securing any one of the said persons within three months. See O'Callaghan's *History of the Irish Brigade*, p. 320, which work contains a good account of the two Earls of Lucan.

[4] His death is thus noticed in the *London Gazette*, May 1719: 'Sarsfield, called Lord ' Lucan, who had lately been in Ireland, died at St. Omers, on the 12th instant.'

MACCLESFIELD

LUMISDEN, Baronet [S].

I. JOHN LUMISDEN, eldest son of Andrew Lumisden, sometime Rector of Duddingston and afterwards (1727-1733) Bishop of Edinburgh and Primus of Scotland, by Catharine Craig of Riccarton, and cousin of Andrew Lumisden, for many years the faithful Secretary of Kings James III and VIII and Charles III. On 5th January 1740 he was created by King James a *KNIGHT* and *BARONET* [S].[1] He died *s.p.* in France 1751.[2] He married (having been tutor to her son) Mary, Dowager-Viscountess Kenmure [S] (widow of William (Gordon), sixth Viscount Kenmure [S], executed on Tower Hill, 24th February 1715/16, for his loyalty), sister of Robert (Dalzell), fifth Earl of Carnwath [S], and daughter of Sir John Dalzell, by Harriet, daughter of Sir William Murray, Baronet [S]. She died, 16th August 1776, at Terregles.

1740
—
1751

MACCLESFIELD, Earl of [E].

I. WILLIAM DORINGTON, Lieutenant-Colonel of the King's Royal Irish regiment of Foot Guards, an Englishman, was made a P.C. [I], April 1689,[3] a few days after King

17
—
1718

---

[1] The patent is endorsed: 'Sent to my Lady Kenmare.'
[2] Of his two uncles the elder, Charles, was a surgeon in Edinburgh, and had an only son, John, who died *s.p.*, and the younger, William, born 15th June 1688, was engaged in the '15, and refusing to take the oaths, could not pass the Scottish Bar, but became a Writer in Edinburgh, where he died 1757. He married Mary, third daughter of Robert Bruce, third son of Robert Bruce of Kennet, and by her, who died 1756, had issue :—
    1. Andrew Lumisden, attainted 1746; Assistant Secretary to James III and VIII, 1751-1763; sole Secretary, 1763-1766, and to Charles III, 1766-1768. He died in Edinburgh 25th December 1801.
    2. Isabella, born 17th October 1719; died 28th February 1806; married 1747, the well-known Sir Robert Strange, and had issue.
See *Memoirs of the Family of Lumisden or Lumsden*, by H. W. Lumsden, 1889.
[3] Together with William (Herbert), first *Duke of Powis* [E].
    James (FitzJames), first Duke of Berwick [E].
    Richard (Bourke), eighth Earl of Clanricarde [I].
    Claud (Hamilton), fourth Earl of Abercorn [S]; second Lord Strabane [I].
    Nicholas (Taaffe), third Earl of Carhampton [I].
    John (Drummond), first Earl of Melfort [S].
    David (Sarsfield), third Viscount Sarsfield of Kilmallock [I].
    Daniel (O'Brien), third Viscount Clare [I].
    [   ] Meryon.
    Valentine (Browne), first *Viscount Kenmare* [I].
    Ignatius (White), first Marquis of Albeville [H R E], first Baronet [E].
    Sir Edward Herbert, Lord Chief-Justice [E].
    Colonel Patrick Sarsfield, *afterwards* Earl of Lucan [I].

MACCLESFIELD

James's arrival in Dublin, and shortly afterwards Colonel of the Foot Guards in succession to the Duke of Ormond. He served with distinction at the blockade of Derry, 1689, and at the battle of the Boyne, July 1690; Governor of the city and county of Limerick; was captured at the battle of Aughrim, 12th July 1691, and was imprisoned in Dublin, Chester, and the Tower,[1] but being afterwards exchanged, he returned to Ireland and was attainted as 'of Dublin.' After the Treaty of Limerick he went with his regiment to France, with which he was in Normandy in 1692 as part of the force designed to restore King James. He was at the battle of Landen, July 1693, and at the capture of Charleroi; Brigadier [F] by brevit, 28th April 1694; served with the army of Flanders, 1695-1697. The Royal Irish Foot Guards being broken up after the Peace of Ryswick, by order 27th February 1698, he was the same day appointed Colonel of the new regiment formed out of it, which henceforth bore his name, and of which he continued Colonel to his death; served with the army of Germany, 1701/2; appointed Major-General by brevit, 23rd December 1702; with the army of Bavaria, 1703, being present at the battles of Hochstadt and Blenheim, 13th August 1704; Lieutenant-General, 26th October 1704; with the army of the Rhine, 1705/6; and with the army of Germany, 1709/10. He accompanied King James to Scotland in 1715, and is said to have been created *EARL OF MACCLESFIELD*, etc. [E].[2] He died in Paris, 11th December 1718.[3]

[1] There was an order, in September, for Major-General Dorington 'to have the 'liberty of the Tower, and for his friends and relations to visit him.' Yet, among other matters for which, in 1694, Lord Lucas, as 'Governor of the Tower,' was 'several times 'called before the Council,' is mentioned 'the ill-usage of Major-General Dorington.' See O'Callaghan's *History of the Irish Brigade*, p. 89.

[2] *La Quotidienne* of Paris for 22nd March 1841 has the following: 'À Abbeville, 'viennent de mourir, à quelques jours de distance deux frères, le comte et le chevalier 'Macclesfield Dorrington, âgés, l'un de 85, l'autre de 74 ans, et issus d'un comte 'William Dorrington, colonel d'un régiment anglais de son nom, qui émigra avec 'Jacques II, et qui fut créé, mais dans l'exil, pair l'Angleterre, par le monarque dont il 'avait servi et suivi la triste fortune avec la plus courageuse fidélité.

'En ces deux frères s'est éteinte la branche des Dorrington, établi en France de 'puis l'expulsion des Stuarts.

'La branche anglaise, après être tout-à-fait tombée, s'est relevée, et le chef de cette 'branche occupe aujourd'hui, à Londres, un emploi très-lucratif et très-important près 'de la chambre des communes. C'est un homme fort distingué par l'élégance de ces 'manières et de son esprit.'

[3] O'Callaghan's *Irish Brigade*, p. 90. Statement of services supplied by French Minister of War. A William Dorington was appointed Registrar of the Court of Chancery [I], 23rd July 1689, and an Andrew Dorington was captain in the Earl of Clancarty's regiment of infantry.

MACDONELL

MACDONALD, Baronet [I or S].

I. JOHN MACDONALD or MACDONELL, stated to have been 'brother's son to the Earl of Antrim,'[1] is said to have been created in 1745 a *BARONET* [? I or S] by the Prince Regent. He was one of the seven who accompanied Prince Charles to Scotland in 1745 and served under him down to Culloden.

1745 -

MACDONELL, Baron [S].

I. ALASTAIR MACDONELL or MACDONALD of Glengarry, son and heir of Ranald Macdonell of Scotus, and afterwards (1682) of Glengarry,[2] by Flora, daughter of Alexander MacLeod of MacLeod; succeeded his father between 1682 and 1689, was a devoted Royalist and joined Dundee. At the battle of Killiecrankie he carried the Royal Standard, and was attainted by the Government in 1690, but appears to have managed to retain possession of his estates. In 1715 he joined Mar, and at Sheriffmuir with some three thousand of his clan fought on the right wing, and when the fall of Alan of Clanranald had momentarily caused dismay he stepped forward and led the final charge. He was again attainted in 1716, and in recognition of his great services he was, 9th December 1716, created by James III and VIII a Lord and Peer of Parliament as *LORD MACDONALD* or *MACDONELL* [S], with remainder to his heirs-male.[3] He died 1724. He married, first, the Hon. Anne, second daughter of Hugh (Fraser), eighth Lord Lovat [S], by Anne, daughter of Sir John Mackenzie of Tarbat, first Baronet [S], by whom he had one daughter, Anne. He married, secondly, Lady Mary, fourth daughter of Kenneth (Mackenzie), third Earl of Seaforth

1716 - 1724

---

[1] *Report of Proceedings on the Conduct of* . . . *Sir John Cope* (London, 1749), p. 156. It must be noted, however, that the first Earl of Antrim died in 1636, leaving two sons, Randal, second Earl and first Marquis, died *s.p.* 1682, and Alexander, third Earl (attainted for adhering to James II and VII), who died 1699, leaving an only son Randal, fourth Earl, who died 1721, himself leaving an only son. The Chevalier Johnstone refers to him contemptuously as 'Macdonell an Irishman.'

[2] Ranald was the nephew and heir of Æneas (Macdonell), first Baron Macdonell and Arrass [S], so created by Charles II, 20th December 1660, in recognition of his services against Cromwell. He died *s.p.* (see *The Complete Peerage*, v. p. 197, note c) 1680.

[3] The patent is endorsed: 'Young Glengarry, grandchild to Glengarry in this ' warrant, Representing that the original was destroyed, and begging a duplicate of it, ' the duplicate signed by the King was sent to him by Edgar, the 24th Dec. 1748.'

MACDONELL

[S], by Isabella, daughter of Sir John Mackenzie of Tarbat, first Baronet [S]. He had issue :—
1. Donald, younger of Glengarry, killed at Killiecrankie, 17/27 July 1689.
2. John, *Master of Macdonell*, his heir.
3. *Hon.* Randulph Macdonell of Kylles.
4. *Hon.* Alexander Macdonell.

1724 — 1754

II. JOHN (MACDONELL), second *Lord Macdonell*, second but eldest surviving son and heir, succeeded his father 1724. On the arrival of Prince Charles in 1745 he allowed his clan, under the command of his second son, Angus or Æneas, to join him. The Prince halted at his castle of Invergarry on Lochness on his advance from Glenfinnan, and again the morning after Culloden, but on both occasions the chief was absent. The castle was plundered and burned by Cumberland. He died 1754. He married, first, [   ], only daughter of Colin Mackenzie of the Hilton family, by Isabella, daughter of Donald Simpson of Ferintosh, by whom he had two sons. He married, secondly, [   ], daughter of John Gordon of Glenbucket. He had issue :—
1. Alastair, *Master of Macdonell*, his heir.
2. *Hon.* Æneas Macdonell. He commanded the clan during the '45, was present at Prestonpans, formed part of the rearguard in the retreat from Derby, and was accidentally shot after the battle of Falkirk by one of Clanranald's regiment. He married Margaret, daughter of Alexander Robertson of Struan, and had, with a daughter, Augusta, one son :—
    (1) Duncan, fourth *Lord Macdonell*.
3. *Hon.* James Macdonell, married and had issue.
4. *Hon.* Charles Macdonell, a Major in the army.
5. *Hon.* Helen Macdonell, married Ranald Macdonell of Scotus.

1754 — 1761

III. ALASTAIR (MACDONELL), third *Lord Macdonell*, eldest son and heir, succeeded his father 1754. He had been sent to France early in 1745 with a message to Prince Charles from the Scots Jacobites, but he missed him, and returning to Scotland was captured in a French transport on 25th November 1745, and confined in the Tower for twenty-two months. He died *s.p.* 23rd December 1761.

MACDONELL

IV. DUNCAN (MACDONELL), fourth LORD MACDONELL, nephew and heir, succeeded his uncle, 23rd December 1761. He died, 11th July 1788, at Elgin.¹ He married, 1772, Marjory, second daughter of Sir Ludovick Grant of Dalvey, sixth Baronet [S], by Margaret, daughter of Sir James Innes, fifth Baronet [S]. He had issue :—

1761
–
1788

1. Alastair, MASTER OF MACDONELL, his heir.
2. HON. Lewis Macdonell, a Captain in the army. Died unmarried, aged nineteen.
3. HON. Sir James Macdonell, K.C.B., a Lieutenant-General in the army, greatly distinguished himself at Waterloo. Died unmarried 1857.
4. HON. Angus Macdonell, died an infant.
5. HON. Somerled Macdonell, R.N., died unmarried at Curaçoa in the West Indies.
6. HON. Elizabeth Macdonell, married first, at Invergarry House, 1795, before 1st April,² William Chisholm of that Ilk, and had issue. She married, secondly, 1819, Colonel Sir Alexander Ramsay of Balmain, seventh Baronet [S], who died s.p. 1830.
7. HON. Margaret Macdonell, married Major James Downing. She died 7th October 1859, aged eighty-two.
8. HON. Sibella Macdonell, unmarried.

V. ALASTAIR (MACDONELL), fifth LORD MACDONELL, eldest son and heir, born 15th September 1771, succeeded his father 11th July 1788, and died at Corran on Loch Linnhe, 17th January 1828, from an attack of brain fever, as the result of an accident whilst escaping from a steamer which had gone ashore.³ He married at Edinburgh, 20th January 1802,⁴ Rebecca, daughter of Sir William Forbes of Pitsligo, sixth Baronet [S], by Elizabeth, daughter of Sir James Hay of Hayston, sixth Baronet [S]. She died 1840. He had issue one son and seven daughters :—

1788
–
1828

1. Æneas, MASTER OF MACDONELL, his heir.
2. HON. Elizabeth Macdonell, married Roderick C. Mac-

---

¹ *Scots Magazine*, 1788, p. 362. ² *Ibid.*, 1795, p. 275.
³ As to his character, see an article in Blackwood's by his daughter, and also *The Royalist*, iv. p. 141. ⁴ *Scots Magazine*, 1802, p. 181.

MACDONELL

donald of Castletinin, Prince Edward's Island, and had issue :—
   (1) John Alastair Macdonald, a monk in Canada.
   (2) Emma Macdonald, now deceased.
   (3) Elizabeth Macdonald, a nun.
3. HON. Marsali Macdonell, married, 22nd October 1833, Andrew Bonnar, fourth son of Andrew Bonnar of Kimmerghame, Berwick, and had issue two sons and two daughters.
4. HON. Jemima Rebecca Macdonell, married, 5th July 1833, Charles Hay Forbes of Canaan Park, Edinburgh, and by him, who died 5th November 1859, had, with other issue, an elder son, Sir William Stuart Forbes of Pitsligo, ninth Baronet [S].
5. HON. Louisa Christian Macdonell, born 1814, died unmarried at Rothesay, Bute, 26th February 1900, and was buried there.
6. HON. Caroline Hester Macdonell, died unmarried at Rothesay, June or July 1885, and was buried there.
7. HON. Guilelmina Macdonell, married, 12th April 1853, Hugh H. Brown of Newhall and Carlops, and had issue two sons, Horatio and Allan Brown, who died in Australia 10th January 1902. She still survives.
8. HON. Euphemia Macdonell, who died, aged twelve.

1828 – 1852

VI. ÆNEAS RANALDSON (MACDONELL), sixth LORD MACDONELL and sixteenth CHIEF OF GLENGARRY, only son and heir, born 19th July 1818, succeeded his father 17th January 1828. On coming of age he sold the Glengarry portion of the estates to Lord Ward, afterwards Earl of Dudley, for £91,000, and some time afterwards the Knoydart portion, with the two splendid forests of Ladhar Bheinn and Barrisdale, was disposed of to a Mr. Baird. He died at Invergarry, 19th June 1852, and was buried in the family burial-ground at Kilfinnan. He married, 18th December 1833, Josephine, eldest daughter of William Bennett, and grandniece of the Right Rev. William Bennett, Bishop of Cloyne. She died at Edinburgh, 5th July 1857, and was buried in the Inverleith Cemetery. He had issue :—
   1. Alexander Ranaldson, MASTER OF MACDONELL, his heir.

MACDONELL

2. *Hon.* Æneas Robert Macdonell, a distinguished student, born 1835, drowned 15th December 1855.
3. *Hon.* Charles Ranaldson Macdonell, afterwards eighth LORD MACDONELL.
4. *Hon.* Marsali Macdonell, married 1869 Hector Frederick Maclean of Edinburgh, and died *s.p.* 11th February 1887.
5. *Hon.* Eliza Macdonell, born 1840, died unmarried in 1857.
6. *Hon.* Helen Rebecca Macdonell, eventual (1887) sole heir of her father, married, 7th August 1865, Captain John Cuninghame of Balgownie House, Fifeshire, J.P., who died 23rd September 1879. She died 29th May 1888, leaving issue :—
   (1) John Alastair Erskine Cuninghame of Balgownie House, heir-of-line of the Macdonells of Glengarry, born 10th November 1869, married, 6th June 1901, Margaret Jean, youngest daughter of William Carstares Dunlop of Gairbraid, and has issue a daughter, Margaret Helen Erskine, born 23rd August 1903.

VII. ALEXANDER RANALDSON (MACDONELL), seventh LORD MACDONELL and seventeenth CHIEF OF GLENGARRY, eldest son and heir, born 5th October 1834, succeeded his father 19th June 1852, and emigrated to Australia. He died unmarried in Dunedin, New Zealand, 2nd June 1862, and was buried in the Church of England burial-ground in the Southern Cemetery there.

1852 – 1862

VIII. CHARLES RANALDSON (MACDONELL), eighth LORD MACDONELL and eighteenth CHIEF OF GLENGARRY, next surviving brother and heir, born 1838, succeeded his brother 2nd June 1862, and died *s.p.* at sea on his way home from New Zealand, June 1868. He married, 1865, Agnes Campbell, eldest daughter of Alexander Cassels, W.S.

1862 – 1868

IX. ÆNEAS RANALD (MACDONELL), ninth LORD MACDONELL, cousin and next heir-male, being son and heir of Æneas Macdonell of Scotus, by Anne, daughter of William

1868 – 1868

MACDONELL

Fraser of Culbockie, which Æneas was the eldest son and heir of Ranald Macdonell, son and heir of Donald Macdonell (who was slain on the Jacobite side at Culloden), son and heir of Angus Macdonell, all of Scotus, who was the next younger brother to the first LORD MACDONELL. He was born 1790, and entered, when young, the Madras Civil Service, and in June 1868 became, by the death of his relation, LORD MACDONELL and nineteenth CHIEF. He died at Cheltenham, October following, aged seventy-eight. He married in Bombay, 1819, Julianna Charlotte, daughter of Archdeacon Wade, of Bombay. She was born in 1803, and died at St. Heliers, Jersey, 1882, aged seventy-nine. He had issue, with several others who died in infancy :—

1. Æneas Ranald Macdonell, of the Madras Civil Service, born 1825, died *v.p.* February 1867. He married first, at St. Mary's Church, Cheltenham, 18th September 1845, Emma, daughter of General Briggs, H.E.I.C.S. He married secondly, 1866, Mary, daughter of [   ] Johnstone. He had issue :—
    (1) Æneas Ranald Westrop Macdonell, tenth LORD MACDONELL.
    (2) John Bird Macdonell, Captain 12th (Suffolk) regiment, born 1858, died unmarried at Netley Hospital, 1886.
    (3) Angus Macdonell, born (posthumous) June 1867, now in India, married 1898 Elsie, daughter of [   ] Murdoch, and has issue one daughter.
    (4) Emma Jane Macdonell, married first, at St. Mary's, Bryanston Square, London, 23rd November 1880, Patrick Henderson Chalmers of Aberdeen, who died February 1889; and secondly, James Sinclair of Bearwell, Ceylon. She had issue by her first husband :—
        (1) Charles Hugh Lindsay Henderson Chalmers, born at Aberdeen 1st June 1882.
        (2) James William Douglas (Hamish) Chalmers, born at Aberdeen, April 1884, died 1886.
        (3) Ian Patrick Honyman Chalmers, born

MACDONELL

    30th August 1888 at Aberdeen; now at Eton.

   (5) Charlotte Lindsay Macdonell, born at Trichinopoly, India, married 1887 the Rev. Herbert Cooper, rector of St. Andrews, near Bridgewater, *s.p.*

2. *Hon.* William Fraser Macdonell, V.C., sometime Magistrate of Sarum, and afterwards a Judge of the High Court of Calcutta; received the V.C. (being one of the few civilians who ever did so) for his gallantry in the attempted relief of Arrah, 29th July 1857; born December 1829, died at Cheltenham, 1894. He married in the Cathedral, Calcutta, August 1851, Anne Louisa, daughter of Captain Duff, H.E.I.C.S., and had issue.
3. *Hon.* Thomas Munro Macdonell, Captain in the Indian army, married 1866 Minnie, daughter of [   ] Clowes, and died 1880.
4. *Hon.* Alexander Kyle Macdonell, born 1843.
5. *Hon.* Anna Macdonell, born 1820, died *s.p.* 17th October 1900; married first, 19th July 1842, Charles Basil Lindsay, Captain Madras Cavalry, who died 31st August 1848; secondly, 17th February 1852, Hugh Hamilton Lindsay, who died 29th May 1881.
6. *Hon.* Juliana Charlotte Macdonell, born 1821, died September 1902; married 1845 John Bird, Madras Civil Service, and had issue.

X. ÆNEAS RANALD WESTROP (MACDONELL), tenth L*ord* M*acdonell* and twentieth C*hief of* G*lengarry*, grandson and heir, born at Cuddalore, India, 5th December 1847; educated at Eton; succeeded his grandfather, October 1868, and died at London, 2nd January 1901. He married at the Parish Church, Hove, near Brighton, 29th October 1874, Catherine Frances Creed, daughter of Henry Herries Creed, and had issue:—

1868 – 1901

1. Æneas Ranald, M*aster of* M*acdonell*, his heir.
2. *Hon.* Hugh Herries Macdonell, born 16th March 1878, died 18th March following.
3. *Hon.* Alastair Somerled Macdonell, born 13th February 1881, died 20th July 1900.

MACDONELL

4. *Hon.* Marion Lindsay Macdonell, born 4th October 1876, married 12th July 1902 Walter E. Tower, and has issue :—
   (1) Anthony Pascel Tower, born April 1903.
5. *Hon.* Elsie Catherine Macdonell, born 26th January 1883, died 1st October 1900.
6. *Hon.* Dorothy Frances Macdonell, born 27th October 1884.

1901

XI. ÆNEAS RANALD (MACDONELL), eleventh LORD MACDONELL [S], and twenty-first CHIEF OF GLENGARRY, only surviving son and heir, born at Sevenoaks, Kent, 8th August 1875; educated at St. Paul's School, London; succeeded his father, 2nd January 1901; sometime with the banking firm of Herries, Farquhar, and Company, afterwards (1896) emigrated to Ceylon, and is now of the firm of Messrs. Schebaieff and Company, of Baku.[1]

MACDONELL OF KEPPOCH, Baronet [S].[2]

1743
–
1746

I. ALEXANDER (ALASTAIR) MACDONELL, sixteenth CHIEF OF KEPPOCH, eldest son and heir of Coll Macdonell, fifteenth Chief of Keppoch, by Barbara, daughter of Sir Donald MacDonald of Sleat and Lady Mary, daughter of Robert (Douglas), third Earl of Morton [S], born about 1694 to 1698; was for ten years in the French army, and succeeded his father between 1730-1736. In 1743 he was sent on a mission to King James III and VIII from the Scottish Jacobites, and was by that monarch, 6th June 1743, created a *KNIGHT* and *BARONET* [S], with remainder to his heirs-male. On hearing of Prince Charles's arrival in Scotland in 1745, he called a council at Keppoch, and gave it as his opinion that their duty was to raise men instantly for the protection of his person, whatever might be the consequence, and he was himself one of the first to join the Prince at Glenfinnan. He died 16th April 1746, being slain fighting for

---

[1] The dates relating to the fifth, sixth, and seventh Lords Macdonell are taken from the Glengarry family Bible now in possession of J. A. E. Cuninghame of Balgownie House, who has most kindly extracted them for the above article; and for similar information regarding the succeeding *Lords Macdonell* the Editor is indebted to Mrs. Sinclair, *née* Macdonell, to both of whom his best thanks are due for the assistance they have given him.

[2] For much of the information in this article the writer has to thank Miss Josephine M. Macdonell of Keppoch.

MACDONELL

his King at the battle of Culloden. He married, about 1722/3, Jessie, sister of Dugald (Stewart), first BARON APPIN [S], daughter of Robert Stewart, eighth of Appin, by his second wife, Ann, daughter of Sir Duncan Campbell of Lochnell. She died after 1757. He had issue :—

1. SIR Ranald, younger of Keppoch, his heir.
2. SIR Alexander Macdonell, heir to his nephew.
3. Anna Macdonell, born about 1724/5; married Dr. Abraham Gordon, and died, 31st August 1818, aged eighty-five; buried in the cemetery of the Grey Friars Church at Stirling.[1]
4. Clementina Macdonell, married, first, [ ] MacDonald of Dalness, and secondly, [ ] Buchanan, but died s.p.
5. Barbara Macdonell, born at Keppoch 1727, married there, 1757, the Rev. Patrick MacDonald of Kilmore. She died at Kilmore, Argyll, 18th July 1804, aged seventy-seven, leaving issue ten children.[2] He died 1824.
6. Katherine Macdonell, born about 1733, married John M'Donald of Killichonate, and died 1829, aged ninety-six, leaving issue one son and four daughters; buried at Cille Chaorill in Lochaber.
7. Jessie Macdonell, married Alexander M'Donald of Tullochcrom, and had issue one son and four daughters. She was buried in the churchyard of St. Kenneth at Laggan.
8. Charlotte Macdonell, born at Keppoch (the night Prince Charles slept there, before the attempt to surprise him at Moy Hall), February 1746; married, about 1776/7, Alexander Macdonell of Garvabeg in Badenoch; and died about 1781, leaving issue a son, who died unmarried, and two daughters.[3]

---

[1] She had issue two children, (1) Abraham, who died unmarried, and (2) Mary Jane, who married [ ] Masterton of Braco Castle, and died s.p.

[2] Anne, the eldest daughter and co-heir, married her cousin, Donald Macdonell, and was mother of Angus, who succeeded Sir Chichester Macdonell as Chief of Keppoch.

[3] The elder (and only one who left issue), Jessie, was born at Garvabeg in the parish of Laggan, 1779, and died at Gogar, near Stirling, 27th May 1859, having married at Laggan, 1801, John MacNab of Shenaghart in Kintyre, and of Sherrobeg in Badenoch, by whom, who was born 1765, and died at Sherrobeg, 10th April 1847, she had with five sons an only daughter, Christina, wife of Angus Macdonell, twenty-second Chief of Keppoch.

MACDONELL

1746
–
1788

II. SIR RANALD MACDONELL, second *Baronet*, elder son and heir, born about 1735/6, succeeded his father, 16th April 1746, under the tutorship of his illegitimate brother Angus.[1] He entered the 1st battalion of the 78th or Fraser Highlanders as Lieutenant when that regiment was raised in 1759, serving in

---

[1] This Angus was born in Skye, 21st July 1726, and on his father's death at Culloden assumed the leadership of the clan, and was one of the eight chiefs who on the 8th May 1746 entered into a mutual bond never to lay down their arms without the consent of the whole, and meanwhile to raise as many men as possible for the Prince, and assemble on Thursday, 15th May, at Ach-na-carry, in Lochaber. Not one of the chiefs, however, was able to meet on the appointed day. Angus remained in hiding for some time near Loch Treig, and afterwards accompanied Prince Charles through some of his perilous wanderings. He was attainted and died after 1813. He married at Kilmonivaig in Lochaber, 31st March 1752, Christina, daughter of Archibald Macdonell of Achnancoichean, in Lochaber, and had issue seven sons, of whom the eldest, Alexander, died young; the second, Archibald, was Lieutenant-Colonel 92nd (Gordon) Highlanders, and died 1813, leaving three sons; and the third, Donald, was born 1st May 1761, and died at Torgulbin 1834. He married at Kilmore, Argyll, 1797, his cousin-german, Anne, eldest daughter and co-heir of the Rev. Patrick MacDonald of Kilmore, by Barbara, third daughter and in her issue (1838) senior co-heir of *Sir* Alexander Macdonell of Keppoch, first *Baronet*, and by her, who was born at Kilmore 20th March 1764, and died at Torgulbin 23rd April 1838, he had issue:—
1. Angus Macdonell, his heir.
2. Ranald Macdonell, died unmarried.
3. Barbara Macdonell, married Donald MacDonald, and had issue one son John, who died unmarried.

Angus Macdonell, born at Torgulbin 5th July 1801, succeeded his cousin, *Sir* Chichester Macdonell, sixth *Baronet*, as twenty-second CHIEF OF KEPPOCH, 1838, and died at Keppoch 28th February 1855. He married at Sherrobeg, 17th August 1835, Christina, only daughter of John MacNab of Shenaghart in Kintyre, and of Sherrobeg in Badenoch, by Jessie, elder daughter and eventual heiress of Alexander Macdonell of Garvabeg, and Charlotte, youngest daughter and in her issue (1838) co-heir of *Sir* Alexander Macdonell of Keppoch, first *Baronet*, and by this lady, who was born at Sherrobeg 9th November 1816, and now (1904) survives, he had issue:—
1. Donald Macdonell, twenty-third CHIEF OF KEPPOCH, born at Keppoch 3rd July 1839; died unmarried at Melbourne, Australia, 28th February 1889.
2. John Macdonell, born at Keppoch 3rd March 1850; died 21st April 1851.
3. Joseph Macdonell, born at Keppoch 1853, and died there, 1853.
4. Charlotte Macdonell, died unmarried 2nd December 1855.
5. Anne Margaret Macdonell, married in Australia about 1869, and died November 1876, leaving issue.
6. Jessie Macdonell, married at Keppoch, May 1867, Keith M'Lellan of Melfort, and has issue a daughter.
7. Maria Macdonell, married at Keppoch, 18th January 1866, Alexander Macdonald Ord, and has issue three sons and three daughters.
8. Theresa Macdonell, married at Keppoch, 1877, George Keith Maitland, who died 1896, leaving issue three sons and two daughters.
9. Frances Macdonell, Mother-Superior of the Order of the Assumption in Paris, born at Keppoch 26th August 1848.
10. Josephine Mary Macdonell, born at Keppoch 20th May 1852.
11. Alice Claire Macdonell, born at Keppoch 31st January 1855.

MACDONELL

Jamaica and America, and retiring with the rank of Major. In or about 1759 he obtained from the Duke of Gordon a lease of the family estates, which had been forfeited in 1746. He died 1788. He married in Jamaica, about 1770/1, Sarah, daughter of [   ] Cargill of Jamaica. He had issue :—

1. SIR Alexander, his heir.
2. SIR Richard, heir to his brother.
3. Jessie Macdonell, married Duncan Stewart, W.S., cadet of Fasnacloich, and had issue, who all died *s.p.*
4. Clementina Macdonell, died unmarried.

III. SIR ALEXANDER MACDONELL, third BARONET, eighteenth CHIEF OF KEPPOCH, elder son and heir, born in Jamaica 29th October 1772; succeeded his father in 1788; Major, 1st Royals, now Royal Scots. He died unmarried in Barbados, 25th June 1808.[1]

1788 – 1808

IV. SIR RICHARD MACDONELL, fourth BARONET, nineteenth CHIEF OF KEPPOCH, brother and next heir, born at Keppoch 29th November 1780; Lieutenant, 92nd or Gordon Highlanders; succeeded his brother 1808. He died unmarried of yellow fever at Up Park Camp, Jamaica, 14th August 1819.[2]

1808 – 1819

V. SIR ALEXANDER MACDONELL, fifth BARONET, twentieth CHIEF OF KEPPOCH, uncle and next heir-male, born at Keppoch about 1742/3; sometime Major in the Glengarry Fencibles; emigrated to Canada, and finally settled in Prince Edward's Island. He succeeded his nephew in 1819, and died in Prince Edward's Island, 1820. He married, in Lochaber, his second cousin, Sarah, daughter of Major Donald Macdonell of Tirnadris, by his second wife, Mary, daughter of James Macdonell. She survived him. He had issue :—

1819 – 1820

1. SIR Chichester, his heir.
2. John Macdonell, died of cholera in Montreal, 1832, unmarried.[3]

---

[1] *Scots Magazine*, 1808, p. 638.   [2] *Ibid.*, 1819, p. 581.
[3] In *The Macdonalds, Lords of the Isles*, by A. Mackenzie, this John is erroneously said to have died in Baltimore, U.S.A., in 1824, leaving issue. Miss Josephine Macdonell writes: 'I have had an infinity of trouble getting all the documents and 'dates from Canada to disprove this, and fortunately have been able to do so to the full, 'and I had the whole refutation published in Scotland and in Canada, and have a letter 'from the husband of the Marchioness d'Oyley (a grand-daughter of John Macdonell 'of Baltimore), in which he acknowledges that his wife has long known that her 'ancestor and the son of my great-granduncle were two different persons.'

MACGREGOR

3. Janet Macdonell, a nun, died 1832.
4. [   ] Macdonell, died young *v.p.*
5. [   ] Macdonell, died young *v.p.*

1820 — 1838   VI. SIR CHICHESTER MACDONELL, sixth *BARONET*, twenty-first CHIEF OF KEPPOCH, elder son and heir, born 18 , succeeded his father 1820, and died in Greenock 1838. He married [   ], daughter of [   ], and had issue two sons :—
    1. [   ] Macdonell, died *v.p.* } being both killed in
    2. [   ] Macdonell, died *v.p.* }   Canada.
On his death *s.p.s.* the *BARONETCY* became dormant, while the Chiefship of Keppoch devolved on his cousin, Angus Macdonell.[1]

MACGREGOR, Baronet [S].

1740 — 1749   I. ALEXANDER MACGREGOR, otherwise DRUMMOND, of Balhaldies, son of Duncan MacGregor or Drummond of the same, born about 1660; succeeded his father as head of a junior branch of the clan Gregor, with the Gaelic patronymic of *Mac Iain Mhalich* (son of John of the shaggy eyebrows); descended from the house of Roro, and, in consequence of his own name being proscribed by the Government, he assumed with many of the clan the name of Drummond. In 1704, on the death of the last chief of clan Gregor without issue, he was for political reasons elected to the Chiefship, but the fact was kept secret.[2] He was a distinguished Jacobite, and was engaged in most of the plots of the time for the restoration of the House of Stuart. On the 14th March 1740 he was created by King James III and VIII a *KNIGHT* and *BARONET* [S], with remainder to the heirs-male of his body.[3] He died at Dunblane 1st March 1749, aged eighty-nine. He married, 1686, Margaret, sister of John (Cameron), first *LORD LOCHIEL* [S], eldest daughter of Sir Ewen

---

[1] It is not known whether any male issue survives of either of the two brothers of the first *Baronet*. Major Donald, the elder, was slain at Culloden, and the younger, Captain Archibald, fell at Falkirk. Donald, the son of one of them, was taken prisoner at Carlisle, and executed at Kennington, 22nd August 1746.

[2] 'When a great-grandson attempted to revive this claim, the opinion of counsel was ' to the effect that he had no right to it.' *Ex inform.*, Miss A. G. Murray MacGregor.

[3] The preamble specially mentions William MacGregor, his eldest son, 'to whom we ' hope the title will descend.'

MACGREGOR

Cameron of Lochiel, by his second wife, Isabel, daughter of Sir Lauchlan MacLean. He had issue :—[1]

1. SIR William MacGregor, otherwise Drummond, his heir.
2. Ewen MacGregor, otherwise Drummond, died *s.p.*
3. John MacGregor, otherwise Drummond, author of the memoir of his grandfather, Sir Ewen Cameron of Lochiel.
4. Duncan MacGregor, otherwise Drummond, died *s.p.*
5. Alexander MacGregor, otherwise Drummond, died *s.p.*
6. Donald MacGregor, otherwise Drummond, a sailor, went to Nova Scotia; married Ann, daughter of [   ] Grosbeck of New York, and had one son who died unmarried, and five daughters, of whom the third, Mary, married in 1781, as below, her cousin-german, SIR Alexander MacGregor, third BARONET.

II. SIR WILLIAM MACGREGOR, otherwise DRUMMOND, of Balhaldies, second BARONET, eldest son and heir, born 1698; succeeded his father before 1749, and was, like him, a noted Jacobite. He took an active part in the '15, afterwards retiring to France, where he was much in the company of Bishop Atterbury, LORD SEMPILL, and other active Jacobites. In 1740 he was in Scotland, and early in 1741 was despatched to Rome as the agent of the Association of Scottish Jacobites formed that year for the purpose of restoring the House of Stuart. The same year he was sent by James on a mission to Cardinal Fleury in Paris, and, 23rd December 1743, had a commission as Colonel. He took no part in the '45, but was attainted, and exempted by name from the Act of Indemnity of 1747. He died near Paris, 1765. He married, in the Swedish Chapel at Paris, 1st January 1758, the HON. Janet, second daughter of Laurence (Oliphant), first LORD OLIPHANT OF GASK [S], by the Hon. Amelia Anne Sophia, second daughter of William (Murray), second Lord Nairne [S]. She died Friday, 8th December 1758, and was buried, 11th December, in the Protestant burial-ground in Paris, near the Fort de St. Martin.[2] He had issue an only son.

1749
–
1765

---

[1] For much of this information as to the descendants of *Sir* Alexander MacGregor, the writer has to thank Miss Murray MacGregor of MacGregor, author of the *History of Clan Gregor*.

[2] Kington-Oliphant's *Jacobite Lairds of Gask*, p. 296.

MACKINTOSH

1765 – 1794

III. *Sir* ALEXANDER JOHN WILLIAM OLIPHANT MACGREGOR, otherwise DRUMMOND, third *Baronet*, only son and heir, born in Paris 26th September / 7th October 1758; succeeded his father, 1765. He returned to England, entered the British army, was Captain in 65th regiment of foot, and died 1794. He married, 1781, his cousin-german, Mary, third daughter of Donald MacGregor, otherwise Drummond, of New York, by Anne, daughter of [   ] Grosbeck. He had issue five sons and five daughters :—

1. *Sir* William Oliphant, fourth *Baronet*, his heir.
2. *Sir* Donald, heir to his brother.
3. [   ] MacGregor, otherwise Drummond, Assistant-Commissary-General in the West Indies; married, 1815, Charlotte, daughter of [   ] Houston of Tobago.
4. James MacGregor, otherwise Drummond, died young.
5. Keith MacGregor, otherwise Drummond,
6. Anne MacGregor, otherwise Drummond, married, 1844, [   ] Murray, writer in Stirling;

And four other daughters.

1794 – 1810

IV. *Sir* WILLIAM OLIPHANT MACGREGOR, otherwise DRUMMOND, fourth *Baronet*, eldest son and heir, born 1782; succeeded his father at Balhaldies, 1794; an officer in the army—Major, 77th regiment. He died *s.p.* 1810.

1810 – 18

V. *Sir* DONALD MACGREGOR, otherwise DRUMMOND, fifth *Baronet*, next brother and heir, succeeded to Balhaldies, 1810.[1]

MACKINTOSH, Baron [S].

1717 – 1731

I. LAUCHLAN MACKINTOSH, twentieth Chief of Clan Chattan, son and heir of Lauchlan Mackintosh, nineteenth Chief of Clan Chattan, by his first wife, Magdalene, only daughter of [   ] Lindsey of Edzell, succeeded his father, 9th December 1704. He joined Lord Mar in 1715, and for his services in that rising was on 21st January 1717 created by James III and VIII a Lord and Peer of Parliament as *Lord*

---

[1] The estate of Balhaldies was sold 16th September 1885.

MACKINTOSH

MACKINTOSH [S], with remainder to his heirs-male. He died *s.p.* 1731. He married Anna, eldest daughter of Alexander Duff, Provost of Inverness, M.P. [S and G B], by Katharine, daughter of Adam Duff of Drummuir.

II. WILLIAM (MACKINTOSH), second *LORD MACK-* 1731 *INTOSH*, cousin and next heir-male, being the eldest son and heir – of Lauchlan Mackintosh of Daviot, by Anne, daughter of Colin 1741 Mackenzie of Redcastle, which Lauchlan was the eldest son and heir of Angus Mackintosh of Daviot, who was the third son (but the only one whose male issue then survived) of Sir Lauchlan Mackintosh of Mackintosh, Heritable Steward of Lochaber, which Sir Lauchlan was (through his eldest son and heir, William Mackintosh of Mackintosh) the great-grandfather of the first *LORD MACKINTOSH*. He succeeded his cousin in 1731, and died *s.p.* 1741. He married Christian, daughter of Sir Alexander Menzies, second Baronet [S], by Christian, daughter of Lord Neil Campbell.

III. ANGUS (or ÆNEAS) (MACKINTOSH), third *LORD* 1741 *MACKINTOSH*, brother and next heir. He was a captain in the – Black Watch in 1745, and refused to join Prince Charles. He 17 died . He married Anne, elder daughter of John Farquharson of Invercauld, by his third wife, Margaret, daughter of Lord James Murray. She, who was commonly called 'Colonel 'Anne,' raised the Mackintoshes and the Macgillivrays for Prince Charles shortly before the battle of Falkirk, and joined Lord Strathallan at Perth. She was taken prisoner by the Hanoverians after Culloden, but was shortly afterwards released through her husband's influence.

IV. ANGUS (or ÆNEAS) (MACKINTOSH), fourth 17 *LORD MACKINTOSH*, only son and heir. On the 30th December – 1812 he was created by George III a BARONET. He died *s.p.* 21st 1820 January 1820.

V. ALEXANDER (MACKINTOSH), fifth *LORD MACK-* 1820 *INTOSH*, cousin and next heir-male, being the elder son and heir – of Duncan Mackintosh of Daviot, by Anne, daughter of [ ] 1827 Dallas of Cantray, who was son and heir of Alexander Mackintosh of the same, younger brother of the second and third *LORDS MACKINTOSH*. He died *s.p.* 1827.

MACKINTOSH

1827 – 1833

VI. ANGUS (MACKINTOSH), sixth LORD MACKINTOSH, brother and heir, was a Member of the Legislative Council of Upper Canada. He died 25th January 1833. He married, 1784, Archange, daughter of [   ] St. Martin, and niece of Major-General [   ] Macomb, Commander-in-Chief of the army of America. She died 11th July 1827. He had issue :—
1. Duncan Mackintosh, died unmarried *v.p.* 1824.
2. Alexander, MASTER OF MACKINTOSH, his heir.
3. HON. Æneas Mackintosh of Daviot, Inverness, J.P., D.L., born 12th June 1812; married first, 1843, Mary, daughter of Alexander MacLeod of Dalvey, who died 1848; secondly, 11th March 1851, Louisa Fanny Sybella, daughter of Major Alexander MacLeod, and died 1882, leaving issue.
4. HON. James St. Martin Mackintosh, married, and died December 1897, leaving issue.
5. HON. Anne Mackintosh, married Colonel H. J. Hunt.
6. HON. Archange Mackintosh, married, 1817, Colonel Claudius Shaw, and had issue.
7. HON. Isabella Mackintosh, married Lieutenant Felix Troughton, R.A.
8. HON. Jane Mackintosh.
9. HON. Catherine Mackintosh.
10. HON. Margaret Mackintosh, married Major Angus M'Intyre.
11. HON. Eliza Mackintosh.
12. HON. Sara Mackintosh, married Alexander Colvin.
13. HON. Christiana Mackintosh.

1833 – 1861

VII. ALEXANDER (MACKINTOSH), seventh LORD MACKINTOSH, second but eldest surviving son and heir, born 23rd August 1787, succeeded his father 25th January 1833, and died 1861. He married first, 29th December 1812, Mary, sixth daughter of John Glass of Minorca. She died *s.p.* 1840. He married secondly, 18th October 1842, Charlotte, fifth daughter of Alexander MacLeod of Dalvey. He had issue :—
1. Alexander Æneas, MASTER OF MACKINTOSH, his heir.
2. HON. Alfred Donald Mackintosh, heir to his brother.
3. HON. Æneas Norman Mackintosh, Captain 3rd (Militia) Battalion Cameron Highlanders, born 18th May 1854, died 5th March 1900.

MACLEAN

4. *Hon.* Marion Charles Mackintosh.
5. *Hon.* Mary Archange Mackintosh.
6. *Hon.* Isabella Anne Mackintosh, married Charles T. Part of Aldenham Lodge, St. Albans.

VIII. ALEXANDER ÆNEAS (MACKINTOSH), eighth LORD MACKINTOSH, J.P., D.L., Captain of the Mackintosh Company of Rifle Volunteers, born 7th August 1847, succeeded his father 1861, and died *s.p.m.* 17th December 1875. He married, 4th May 1875, Margaret Frances, eldest daughter of Sir Frederick Ulric Graham, third Baronet [G B], by Lady Jane Hermione, eldest daughter of Edward Adolphus (St. Maur), twelfth Duke of Somerset [E], K.G. She married secondly, 30th April 1878, James Walter (Grimston), third Earl of Verulam [U K]. He had issue :— 1861 – 1875

1. *Hon.* Eva Hermione Mackintosh, born May 1876, married, 26th January 1898, Godfrey Baring, and has issue.

IX. ALFRED DONALD (MACKINTOSH), ninth LORD MACKINTOSH of Mackintosh, twenty-eighth Captain of Clan Chattan, J.P., D.L., Inverness, Colonel commanding 3rd battalion Cameron Highlanders, late Lieutenant 71st Highland Light Infantry, born 24th June 1851; succeeded his brother, 27th December 1875; married 1880 Ella, only daughter and heiress of Edward Priest Richards of Plas Newydd, co. Glamorgan, and has issue:— 1875

1. Angus Alexander, MASTER OF MACKINTOSH, his heir.
2. *Hon.* Violet Charlotte Mackintosh, born February 1881, died April 1883.[1]

MACLEAN, Baron [S].

I. SIR HECTOR MACLEAN, fifth BARONET [S], son and heir of Sir John Maclean,[2] fourth Baronet, by Mary, daughter of Sir Æneas Macpherson of Invereshie, succeeded his father 1716 – 1751

---

[1] Burke's *Landed Gentry*, 1900.
[2] This Sir John Maclean commanded the right wing of the Jacobite army at Killiecrankie, and held out in the island of Kernburgh until 1692, when he made his peace with William of Orange. He afterwards went to France and remained at St. Germains until the Act of Indemnity of 1703, when he returned to Scotland. He joined Lord Mar in 1715, and after Sheriffmuir retired to Gordon Castle, where he died in March 1716. The Castle of Duart and most of his other lands were seized by Argyll, and never afterwards recovered. In the '45 the Macleans were led by Charles Maclean of Drimnin. See *The Royalist*, iv. p. 38.

MACLEAN

March 1716, and was on 17th December 1716 created by James III and VIII a Lord and Peer of Parliament as LORD MACLEAN, with remainder to his heirs-male. In June 1745 he was in Edinburgh, and he was immediately arrested, together with his servant, on the charge of being in the French service and of enlisting men for it. He was sent to the Tower of London, where he remained until liberated by the Act of Indemnity of 1747. He died unmarried in Paris, January or February 1751.[1]

1751 — 1783

II. ALLAN (MACLEAN), second LORD MACLEAN, sixth BARONET, cousin and next heir-male, being the only son and heir of Donald Maclean of Brolas, by Isabella, daughter of Allan Maclean of Ardgour, which Donald was the only son and heir of Lauchlan Maclean, son and heir of Donald Maclean, both of Brolas, who was the second son of Hector Og Maclean of Duart, which Hector Og was, through his eldest son, Sir Lauchlan Maclean, first Baronet [S], the great-great-grandfather of the first LORD MACLEAN. In 1745 he joined the Argyleshire Militia, and fought against Prince Charles. He died *s.p.m.* 10th December 1783. He married Anne, daughter of Hector Maclean of Coll. He had issue:—

1. *Hon.* Maria Maclean, married Charles Maclean of Kinlochaline.
2. *Hon.* Sibella Maclean, married John Maclean of Inverscadell.
3. *Hon.* Ann Maclean, married Dr. Mackenzie Grieve of Edinburgh.

1783 — 1818

III. HECTOR (MACLEAN), third LORD MACLEAN, seventh BARONET, cousin and next heir-male, being the only son and heir of Donald Maclean by his first wife, Mary, daughter of John Dickson of Glasgow, which Donald was the son and heir of John Maclean, son and heir of Hector Og Maclean, second son of Donald Maclean, who was the second son of Hector Og Maclean of Duart above named. He was an officer in the army, and died *s.p.* at Halfield, co. York, 2nd November 1818.

---

[1] Macfarlane's *Genealogical Collections.* In Douglas's *Baronage* he is said to have died in Rome in October 1750.

MACLEAN

IV. FITZROY GEOFFRIES GRAFTON (MAC- LEAN), fourth LORD MACLEAN, eighth BARONET, half-brother and next heir, being the only son of Donald Maclean above named, by his second wife, Margaret, daughter of James Wall of Clonea Castle, co. Waterford. He was a General in the army and Colonel of the 45th regiment; served in the West Indies, at the capture of Tobago, attack on Martinique, etc.; Governor of St. Thomas and St. John. He died 5th July 1847. He married, first, Elizabeth, widow of John Bishop of Barbados, only child of Charles Kidd. She died 1832. He married secondly, 17th September 1838, Frances, widow of Henry Campion of Malling Deanery, Sussex, daughter of [   ]. She died s.p. 12th July 1843. He had issue:—
1818 - 1847

1. Charles Fitzroy, MASTER OF MACLEAN, his heir.
2. HON. Donald Maclean, Barrister-at-Law, M.P. Oxford City 1833-1847; born 1800; married, 7th September 1827, Harriet, daughter of General Frederick Maitland, who died 20th September 1850. He died 21st March 1874.

V. CHARLES FITZROY (MACLEAN), fifth LORD MACLEAN, ninth BARONET, elder son and heir, born 14th October 1798; Colonel of the 81st regiment 1831-1839, afterwards Military Secretary at Gibraltar. He died 27th January 1883. He married, 10th May 1831, Emily Eleanor, fourth daughter of Rev. the Hon. Jacob Marsham, D.D., Canon of Windsor, by Amelia Frances, only daughter and heir of Joseph Bullock of Caversfield, Oxon. She, who was born January 1803, died 12th April 1838.
1847 - 1883

VI. FITZROY DONALD (MACLEAN), sixth LORD MACLEAN [S], tenth BARONET (1632) [S], twenty-sixth CHIEF OF THE MACLEANS, born 18th May 1835; succeeded his father 27th January 1883; sometime Lieutenant-Colonel 13th Hussars and Colonel West Kent Yeomanry Cavalry; served in the Crimea 1854-1855 (medal with two clasps and Turkish medal); J.P. co. Kent, President of the Clan Gillean Association and of the Highland Society of London; C.B. (civil) 1897. He married, 17th January 1872, Constance Marianne, younger daughter of George Holland Ackers of Moreton Hall, Cheshire, by Harriott Susan, second daughter of Henry William Hutton of Beverley, co. York.[1]
1883

---
[1] For a fuller account of this family see the extant baronetcies.

MACLEOD

MACLEOD, Baron [S].[1]

1716 — 1772

I. NORMAN MACLEOD, nineteenth CHIEF OF MACLEOD, only and posthumous son and heir of Norman MacLeod, eighteenth Chief of MacLeod, by the Hon. Anne, second daughter of Hugh (Fraser), eleventh Lord Lovat [S], born 1706, and was infeft in the family estates as heir to his father and grandfather, November 1731 and May 1732; M.P. for co. Inverness 1741-1754. On the 8th December 1716, although then only ten years of age, he was, in recognition of the loyal services of the tutor of MacLeod, created by James III and VIII a Lord and Peer of Parliament as *BARON MACLEOD* [S], with remainder to his heirs-male. He was one of those who was in correspondence with Prince Charles before 1745, but upon his arrival he, mainly by the influence of President Forbes of Culloden, refused to join him, and sent information to the Government of the Prince's arrival, this being the first intimation they received of it. He raised his clan for the Government, marched through Ross and Inverness to Aberdeenshire, but was completely defeated by Lord Lewis Gordon at the battle of Inverurie (23rd December 1745), and forced back to the Highlands. He died 27th July 1772 and was buried at St. Andrews. He married first, about 1726, the *HON.* Janet, fourth and youngest daughter of Donald (MacDonald), first *BARON SLEAT* [S], by Mary, daughter of Donald MacDonald of Castletoun. He married, secondly, Anne, daughter of William Martin of Inch Fure. He had issue by his first wife a son and daughter, and by his second three daughters:—

1. John, *MASTER OF MACLEOD*, married, 1753, Emilia, only daughter of Alexander Brodie of Brodie, Lyon King of Arms. She died 1803. He died *v.p.* at Beverley, co. York, 11th January 1766, and was buried in the Minster there. He had issue:—
   (1) Norman, second *BARON MACLEOD*.
   (2) Alexandra MacLeod, married Charles Mackinnon of Mackinnon, and had issue. She survived her husband, and becoming a Roman Catholic, entered a convent in Italy, where she died.

---

[1] For many of the dates in this article the Editor has to thank MacLeod of MacLeod and his brother, the Rev. R. C. MacLeod.

MACLEOD

    (3) Mary MacLeod, married Captain Ramsay, R.N., and had issue.
    (4) Isabella MacLeod, married [   ] Spence, and died *s.p.*
    (5) Anne MacLeod, died unmarried 1826.
    (6) [   ] MacLeod, of whom nothing is known.
2. *Hon.* Emilia MacLeod, married Captain Augustus Moore of Salston, Ireland.
3. *Hon.* Elizabeth MacLeod, born 1748, married Sir James Pringle, fourth Baronet [S], of Stichill, and had issue.
4. *Hon.* Anne MacLeod, married Professor Hill of St. Andrews, and had issue.
5. *Hon.* Rich Mary MacLeod, died 14th September 1787; married 1st September 1777 Thomas Shairp of Houstoun, co. Linlithgow, and had issue.

II. NORMAN (MACLEOD), second *Baron MacLeod*, etc., grandson and heir of the preceding, born at Brodie House, Nairnshire, 4th March 1754; succeeded his grandfather 1772; educated at St. Andrews and at University College, Oxford. In 1775 he raised a company for the new 71st (Fraser Highlanders) regiment, of which he was appointed Captain. He served in the American War, was 21st March 1780 made Lieutenant-Colonel of the second Battalion 42nd Highlanders, raised by himself, and continued at the head of the battalion until, in 1786, it was formed into a separate regiment designated the 73rd, when he became its Lieutenant-Colonel. Served in India, promoted to the rank of Brigadier-General, May 1783, and appointed Commander-in-Chief of the Malabar army; M.P. for Inverness co., 1790-1796. He died at Guernsey, 16th August 1801, and was buried in Edinburgh. He married first, about 1775, Mary, eldest daughter of Kenneth Mackenzie, third of Suddie. She died 1782 in France. He married secondly, 1784, Sarah, daughter of Nathaniel Stackhouse, Second Member of Council at Bombay (she being then aged seventeen). He had issue by his first wife a son and daughter, and by his second a son and three daughters, viz. :—

    1. Norman, *Master of MacLeod*, Lieutenant R.N., drowned *v.p.* in the *Queen Charlotte*.
    2. John Norman, *Master of MacLeod*, his heir.

1772 – 1801

MACLEOD

3. *Hon.* Mary MacLeod, married her cousin-german, Colonel Norman Ramsay, and died *s.p.* shortly afterwards. He fell at Waterloo.
4. *Hon.* Sarah MacLeod, born 1st August 1785, married 1807 her cousin-german, Robert Pringle, and died *s.p.* shortly afterwards.
5. *Hon.* Emilia Anne MacLeod, born 17th October 1786, married 1809, as first wife, her cousin-german, Sir John Pringle, 5th Baronet [S], and had issue.
6. *Hon.* Anne Eliza MacLeod, born 14th June 1797, married 3rd July 1821 Spencer Perceval, eldest son of the Right Hon. Spencer Perceval, Prime Minister of Great Britain. She died 2nd October 1889, aged ninety-two, leaving issue.

1801–1835

III. JOHN NORMAN (MACLEOD), third *Baron MacLeod*, etc., only surviving son and heir of the preceding, born 3rd August 1788; succeeded his father August 1801; M.P. for Sudbury, 1828-1832; died at Altyne 25th March 1835, and was buried at Dunvegan. He married 16th November 1809 Anne, daughter of John Stephenson of Merstham, Kent. She, who was born 1790, died 9th January 1861. He had issue:—

1. Norman, *Master of MacLeod*, his heir.
2. *Hon.* Torquil James MacLeod, born 1815, died unmarried 28th April 1821.
3. *Hon.* Harold John MacLeod, born 12th January 1821, died unmarried 1846.
4. *Hon.* Emily Sarah MacLeod, born 14th November 1810, died unmarried 7th August 1896.
5. *Hon.* Anna Eliza MacLeod, born 1813; died 9th September 1843; married 2nd June 1840 James Ogilvie Fairlie of Williamfield, Ayrshire, and had issue.
6. *Hon.* Harriette Maria MacLeod, born 11th January 1817 (twin); died 14th January 1877; married November 1844 John Campbell of Glensaddel, Argyleshire, and had issue.
7. *Hon.* Eleanor Anna MacLeod, born 11th January 1817 (twin), died 3rd December 1830.
8. *Hon.* Mary Lowther MacLeod, born 13th August 1819; died 1st August 1884; married, August 1846,

MACLEOD

Robert Fergusson, M.D., F.R.S., Physician to the Queen, and had issue.
9. HON. Elizabeth Roma MacLeod, born 18th February 1823, died unmarried 9th March 1845.

IV. NORMAN (MACLEOD), fourth *BARON MACLEOD*, etc., eldest son and heir of the preceding, born 18th July 1812; educated at Harrow, member of the Inner Temple, 1834; succeeded his father, 25th March 1835; Junior Clerk in the Prisons Department of the Home Office, 1849-1852; Registrar or Assistant-Secretary in the Science and Art Department 1852-1874, and chief of that department 1874-1881; Lieutenant-Colonel of the volunteer Engineer Corps of the Science and Art Department employees, 1861-1871; and Hon. Colonel, 1871-1895; Sergeant-at-arms in the Royal Household, 1853-1895, J.P., D.L. co. Inverness. He died in Paris 5th February 1895, and was buried at Dunvegan. He married first, 15th July 1837, the Hon. Louisa Barbara, only and posthumous daughter of St. Andrew (St. John), thirteenth Baron St. John of Bletsoe [E], by his wife Louisa, daughter of Sir Charles William Rouse-Boughton, ninth [E] and first [G B] Baronet. She, who was born 14th January 1818, died 27th October 1880. He married secondly, 14th July 1881, the Baroness Hanna, eldest daughter of Baron Ettingshausen [Austria]. She, who was born 1854, survives. He had issue :—

1835
—
1895

1. Norman Magnus, *MASTER OF MACLEOD*, his heir.
2. HON. Torquil Olave MacLeod, born 10th August 1841, died 3rd September 1857.
3. HON. Reginald MacLeod, C.B., Registrar-General for England, 1900-1902; Under-Secretary for Scotland, 1902; born 1st February 1847; married, 17th April 1877, the Lady Agnes Mary Cecilia, eldest daughter of Stafford Henry (Northcote), first Earl of Iddesleigh [U K], and has issue :—
   (1) Flora Louisa Cecilia MacLeod, born 3rd February 1878, married 5th June 1901 Hubert, son of John Walter of Bearwood, and has issue.
   (2) Olive Susan Miranda MacLeod, born 17th February 1880.
4. Rev. THE HON. Roderic Charles MacLeod, M.A. Trinity College, Cambridge, J.P. Hunts; Rector of

MACLEOD

Conington, Peterborough, 1884-1886; Vicar of Bolney, Sussex, 1886-1897; Vicar of Mitford Morpeth, 1897; born 18th April 1852; married, 10th February 1885, Katherine Louisa, daughter of the Rev. W. E. Jelf of Caerdeon, Dolgelly, and has issue :—
  (1) Ian Breac MacLeod, born 4th September 1893.
  (2) Brenda Katharine MacLeod, born 12th October 1887.
  (3) Eila St. John MacLeod, born 3rd May 1891.
5. *Hon.* Louisa Cecilia MacLeod, born 19th May 1838, married 18th December 1860 John Moyer Heathcote of Conington Castle, Hunts, and has issue.

1895   V. NORMAN MAGNUS (MACLEOD), fifth *Baron Macleod*, twenty-third chief of his clan, C.M.G., eldest son and heir of the preceding, J.P., D.L. co. Inverness; born 27th July 1839; succeeded his father, 5th February 1895; entered the army, 1858; Aide-de-camp to General Sir Hope Grant, Commander-in-Chief of the Presidency of Madras, 1862-1865; retired as Captain 74th Highlanders, 1872; Protector of Immigrants in Natal, with a seat in the Legislative and Executive Councils, 1874-1875; political agent on the Transvaal border during Zulu war, 1878; commanded in the attack on Sekukuni under Sir Garnet Wolseley in 1879; received Zulu war medal and made C.M.G., 1880. He married 27th April 1881 Emily Caroline, second daughter of Sir Charles Isham, tenth Baronet [E], by his wife, Emily, youngest daughter of the Right Hon. Sir John Vaughan, and has issue :—
  1. *Hon.* Emily Pauline MacLeod, born 3rd June 1882.
  2. *Hon.* Margaret Louisa MacLeod, born 3rd August 1884.

MACLEOD, Baronet [S].

1723   I. JOHN MACLEOD of Glendale and Meidle, Skye,
  I   eldest son and heir of Alexander MacLeod[1] of the same, by his second wife, Christina, daughter of John MacLeod, fifth of Drynoch, was brought up at the Court of St. Germains, and

---

[1] This Alexander, being engaged in one of the plots to restore the Stuarts, was obliged to retire to France with his son. He afterwards returned, and died at a great age at Ebost in the Isle of Skye. See A. Mackenzie's *History of the MacLeods*, p. 210.

MACLEOD

was for some time page to King James III and VIII, by whom he was on 5th September 1723 created a *KNIGHT* and *BARONET* [S], with remainder to his heirs-male. He is said by some to have taken part in the '45, and after Culloden to have remained in hiding in Skye for some time, when he escaped to France. He afterwards obtained a pardon and returned to Scotland, where he lived on a tack of the Chief of the Mackinnons. In 1770 he emigrated to America and died, [   ] aged seventy-five, in North Carolina. He married Margaret, daughter of Lachlan Macqueen of Totorome in Skye, and had issue :—

1. Æneas MacLeod, married [   ], daughter of [   ] Cathcart, and had a son, Donald MacLeod, who died *s.p.v.p.*
2. *SIR* William, his heir.
3. Kenneth MacLeod, Captain in the army, killed in the American War.

II. *SIR* WILLIAM MACLEOD, second *BARONET*, second but eldest surviving son and heir, born about 1750, educated at the University of Edinburgh, where he remained when his father went to America. M.D. (Edinburgh). He died at Borline in Skye, 10th August 1811, aged sixty-one. He married Isabella, eldest daughter of Alexander Macleod of Luskintyre, and had issue :—

1. Alexander MacLeod, married Eliza, daughter of Major Macdonald of Kishorn, and died *s.p.v.p.*
2. Sir John, his heir.
3. Sir Bannatyne William, heir to his brother.
4. Donald Macleod, an officer of the 1st Royal Scots, killed 1817 while leading a grenadier company at the battle of Mahidpore. He married Mary, daughter of John Stuart, and had issue.
5. Evan MacLeod, H.E.I.C.S., died in India.
6. Margaret MacLeod, married, first, the Rev. Alexander Campbell, and secondly, Alexander MacLeod.

1811

III. *SIR* JOHN MACLEOD, third *BARONET*, second but elder surviving son and heir, was appointed physician to the forces in Spain when only twenty-one, and died *s.p.* at Portsmouth on his way home, 1814.

1811 – 1814

MACLEOD

1814 – 1856
IV. SIR BANNATYNE WILLIAM MACLEOD, fourth BARONET, next brother and heir, M.D., C.B., Indian Medical Service, Inspector-General of Army Hospitals in Bengal, died 1856. He married, 1822, Louisa, daughter of Henry Taylor, B.C.S., and had issue :—
1. SIR Harry John Bannatyne, his heir.
2. Caroline MacLeod, married Edward Henry Morland, of West Ilsley, Berks, B.C.S., and died s.p.
3. Frances MacLeod, married Colonel Stuart Frederick Graham, B.C.S., and has issue.

1856 – 1877
V. SIR HARRY JOHN BANNATYNE MACLEOD, fifth BARONET, only son and heir, born 1824, Colonel R.A., died at Edinburgh 1877. He married Christiana, eldest daughter of Edward Cox of Fernhill, Mulgoa, New South Wales, and had issue :—
1. SIR Bannatyne, his heir.
2. Edward Cox MacLeod, born 1863, died 1864.
3. Harry John MacLeod, Lieutenant 24th regiment, born 1865, died at Trichinopoly 1893.
4. William Bernera MacLeod, Surgeon R.N., born 1868, married Isabella, daughter of [   ] Cuthbert.
5. Christiana MacLeod.
6. Jane MacLeod.

1877
VI. SIR BANNATYNE MACLEOD, sixth BARONET, eldest son and heir, born at Hobart, Tasmania, 1860, educated at Edinburgh Collegiate School, Edinburgh University, and Clare College, Cambridge; M.A.; entered Indian Civil Service, and appointed after examination of 1878; arrived 13th December 1880, and served in Madras as assistant-collector and magistrate and forest settlement officer; head assistant, January 1889; sub-collector and joint-magistrate, September 1894; Barrister-at-Law, Inner Temple, 1894; collector and district magistrate, May 1897. He married at Bangalore, 25th July 1882, Morgiana Lilian, eldest daughter of Colonel William Nesbitt Wroughton, M.S.C., and has issue :—
1. William Bannatyne MacLeod, Lieutenant Indian army, born 1883, educated at Bedford Grammar School.

MAGUIRE

2. Roland Theodore Wroughton MacLeod, born 1900.
3. Marguereta Lilian Chamier MacLeod.
4. Meriel Clare Wroughton MacLeod.[1]

MACMAHON, Baron [I].

I. COLONEL DONALD MACMAHON, was on the 19th January 1723 created BARON MACMAHON [I].

1723 –

MAGUIRE OF ENNISKILLEN, Baron [I].

I. ROGER MAGUIRE, who, but for the attainder of 1641, would have been fifth LORD MAGUIRE and BARON OF ENNISKILLEN [I], elder son and heir of the Hon. Rory or (Roger) Maguire,[2] by his wife Deborah, widow of Sir Leonard Blennerhassett, daughter of Sir Henry Mervyn, was born about 1641, succeeded his father 13th November 1648, and had summons to the parliament [I] which met in Dublin on 7th May 1689 as LORD ENNISKILLEN, or possibly LORD MAGUIRE OF ENNISKILLEN, and took his seat accordingly.[3] Lord-Lieutenant of Fermanagh, 4th July 1689; Colonel of an infantry regiment raised by himself, with which he was present at the battle of Aughrim, 12th July 1691. He was attainted, and after the capitulation of Limerick he accompanied the Irish refugee army to France, but having no regiment assigned him, he retired to St. Germains, where

1689 – 1708

---

[1] Particulars relating to the first, second, and third Baronets are taken from Mackenzie's *History of the MacLeods*.

[2] This Rory Maguire was a son of SIR BRYAN MAGUIRE, who on the 3rd March 1627/8 was created LORD MAGUIRE, BARON OF ENNISKILLEN [I], with remainder to the heirs-male of his body, and whose eldest son, CONNOR (MAGUIRE), second LORD MAGUIRE, having taken the principal lead in the Irish rebellion of 1641, was attainted and hung at Tyburn, 10th February 1644.

[3] This is not strictly a Jacobite creation—'the writ and sitting in the Irish House 'of Peers does *not* as in England constitute a Peerage. The writ in Ireland is not 'from the Crown itself, but from the Crown's deputy, *e.g.* the Lord Lieut., Lord 'Deputy, etc. The only case *per contra* was one which is generally admitted to have 'been wrongly decided, viz. that of the Barony of De la Poer allowed in 1767 (owing 'to the great influence of the parties) to the Beresford family, now Marquesses of 'Waterford'—*ex inform.* G. E. Cokayne, Clarenceux King-of-Arms, who adds: 'The 'Irish attainders seem often to have been invalid of themselves—and I think there 'are one or two cases of the heir of an attainted [Irish] Peerage sitting, whether 'lawfully or otherwise, in the [Irish] House of Peers.' As, however, the Lords Enniskillen are frequently mentioned in the Stuart correspondence, an account of them has been here inserted.

MAGUIRE

he died October 1708, aged sixty-seven. He married Mary, daughter of Philip MacHugh O'Reilly, and had issue :[1]—
   1. Alexander, second or sixth LORD MAGUIRE OF ENNISKILLEN.
   2. HON. Bryan Oge Maguire, a Captain of foot, died s.p. 1719.
   3. HON. Rose Maguire.
   4. HON. Marion Maguire.
   5. HON. Catherine Maguire.

II. ALEXANDER (MAGUIRE), second or sixth LORD MAGUIRE OF ENNISKILLEN, elder son and heir, Lieutenant-Colonel in Cuconaght Maguire's regiment, retired to France, where he died s.p. after 1719, when the male issue of his father became extinct. The title, however, continued to be assumed, as under.

III. PHILIP (MAGUIRE), (but for the attainder of 1641) seventh LORD MAGUIRE, BARON OF ENNISKILLEN, uncle and heir-male, married Mary, sister of Brigadier-General Gordon O'Neill, daughter of Sir Phelim O'Neill.

IV. THEOPHILUS or THOMAS (MAGUIRE), (but for the attainder of 1641) eighth LORD MAGUIRE, BARON OF ENNISKILLEN, son and heir, married Margaret, daughter of [   ] O'Donnell of Tyrconnel.

V. ALEXANDER (MAGUIRE), (but for the attainder of 1641) ninth LORD MAGUIRE, BARON OF ENNISKILLEN, son and heir, born at Newport in Ireland, 25th December 1721 ; entered the French army as Lieutenant *réformé* in the Irish infantry regiment of Berwick, 5th May 1740 ; Ensign, 10th June 1743 ; Foot Lieutenant, 13th December 1743 ; transferred to the Lalley regiment, 6th October 1744 ; Captain *réformé*, 17th October 1746 ; given command of a company, 1st August 1756 ; retired on half-pay, 23rd March 1763, when he had a grant of 1000 livres ; Knight of St. Louis, 1763. He served in Flanders 1742, on the Rhine 1743, again in Flanders 1744-1748, and in India 1758-1761.[2]

---

[1] Lodge's MSS., ii. p. 121. Additional MSS. British Museum, 23694.
[2] Statement of services supplied by French Minister of War. Dalton, *King James's Irish Army List*, says he was pensioned as a *réformé* Captain of Lally's regiment at the commencement of the French Revolution in 1789.

MAR

MALMESBURY, Earl of [E].

i.e. '*MALMESBURY*,' co. Wilts, *EARLDOM OF* (Wharton), created 22nd December 1716, with '*NORTHUMBERLAND*,' *DUKEDOM OF*, which see.

MAR, Duke of [S].

I. JOHN (ERSKINE), twenty-third (1115) and sixth (1565) EARL OF MAR and eleventh LORD ERSKINE [S], son and heir of Charles (Erskine), twenty-second and fifth Earl of Mar, by Lady Mary, daughter of George (Maule), second Earl of Panmure [S], born at Alloa February 1675; succeeded his father 23rd April 1689, and took his seat in Parliament [S] 8th September 1696, when he protested 'against the calling of any ' Earl before him in the Roll'; P.C. [S], 1697; one of the Commissioners for the Union, 1705; K.T. (by Anne), 1706; Secretary of State [S], 1706-1707; Keeper of the Signet [S], with a pension, 1707; a Representative Peer [S], 1707-1713; P.C. [G B], 1708; one of the Secretaries of State [G B], 1713-1714. He signed the proclamation of King George, August 1714, but being known for a strong Jacobite, he was immediately dismissed from office by that Prince. He escaped from London in disguise on board a coal-ship, embarking from Gravesend, with Major-General Hamilton and Colonel Hay. On his arrival in Scotland he summoned a great council of the chief Scottish nobles and gentry, known as the 'Hunting of Braemar,' 26th August, and on 6th September following he raised the royal standard at Aboyne, and publicly proclaimed James III and VIII as King. Commander-in-Chief of that King's forces in Scotland, 7th September 1715 to 4th/15th February 1716. On 22nd October 1715 he was created by King James, by patent dated at Commercy, *DUKE OF MAR, MARQUIS ERSKINE, EARL OF KILDRUMMIE, VISCOUNT GARIOCH, LORD ALLOA, FERRITON, AND FORREST* [S], with remainder to his heirs in tail general. He accompanied King James to France, 4th February 1716, and was attainted by Act of Parliament, 17th February 1715/16, as from 19th January, whereby all his honours and estates were forfeited. By King James he was appointed, 21st February 1716,

1715
–
1732

MAR

a Gentleman of the Bedchamber, and, 8th April following, a *K.G.*, and (on the dismissal of the Earl of Bolingbroke), March 1716, SECRETARY OF STATE. On 10th November 1717 he was further created by the same King BARON OF [   ] and EARL OF MAR, co. York [E], with remainder to the heirs-male of his body, and on 13th December 1722 DUKE OF [MAR] [I]. Lord-Lieutenant and High Commissioner [S], 28th June 1721. The following year, after a long series of intrigues, he resigned the Secretaryship, and retired from public life. He died at Aix-la-Chapelle, May 1732. He married first, at Twickenham, Middlesex, 6th April 1703, Lady Margaret, eldest daughter of Thomas (Hay), sixth Earl of Kinnoull [S], by the Hon. Elizabeth, daughter of William (Drummond), first Viscount Strathallan [S]. She, who was born 30th September 1686, died at Dupplin, 25th April 1707, and was buried, 3rd May, at Alloa. He married secondly, 26th July 1714, at Acton, Middlesex, Lady Frances, daughter of Evelyn (Pierrepont), first Duke of Kingston-upon-Hull [G B], by his first wife, Lady Mary, daughter of William (Fielding), third Earl of Denbigh [E] and second Earl of Desmond [I]. She was declared a lunatic, March 1730, and died 4th, and was buried 9th, March 1761, at Marylebone, aged above eighty.

1732 — 1766

II. THOMAS (ERSKINE), second DUKE (1715) and twenty-fourth (1115) and seventh (1565) EARL OF MAR, second MARQUIS ERSKINE, EARL OF KILDRUMMIE, VISCOUNT GARIOCH, LORD ALLOA, FERRITON, AND FORREST (all 1715), and twelfth LORD ERSKINE (1429) [S], also second BARON [   ] and EARL OF MAR, co. York (1717) [E], and DUKE OF [MAR] (1722) [I], only son and heir by first wife, born about 1705; M.P. for Stirling Burghs 1728-1734, for co. Stirling 1747, and for co. Clackmannan 1747-1754; succeeded his father, May 1732, but owing to the attainder of 1716 he was not recognised as a Peer by the Government. In 1739 the family estates were conveyed to him by his uncle, Thomas Erskine, Lord Grange, who had purchased them in 1725. He died at Gayfield *s.p.* 16th March 1766, when the BARONY OF [   ] and EARLDOM OF MAR, co. York [E], became extinct, as did also, presumably, the DUKEDOM OF MAR [I], while the DUKEDOM OF MAR [S], and the minor titles conferred with it, together with the Earldom of Mar (1115) and Lordship of Garioch, passed to his sister, and the Earldom of

MAR

Mar (1565)[1] and the Barony of Erskine (1429) devolved, *de jure*, on his cousin-german and next heir-male, Charles Erskine. He married, 1st October 1741, at Hopetoun House, Lady Charlotte, eighth daughter of Charles (Hope), first Earl of Hopetoun [S], by Lady Henrietta, only daughter of William (Johnstone), first Marquis of Annandale [S]. She, who was born 4th March 1720, died 24th November 1788 at Edinburgh.

III. FRANCES (ERSKINE), DUCHESS and COUNTESS OF MAR, etc., only sister and heir, being the only child of the first *DUKE* by his second wife. She died 20th June 1776. She married, October 1740, her cousin-german, James Erskine, Knight-Marischal [S], who became on the death *s.p.* of his elder brother Charles (above named), 1774, *de jure* ninth Earl of Mar (1565) and fourteenth Lord Erskine (1429). He died at the Abbey-mill[2] 27th February 1785, aged seventy-one.

1766
-
1776

IV. JOHN FRANCIS (ERSKINE), fourth *DUKE OF MAR*, etc., elder son and heir, born 1741; an officer in the army, 1757-1770. He succeeded his mother as *DUKE OF MAR* and as twenty-sixth Earl (1115) of Mar, 20th June 1776, and his father as tenth Earl of Mar (1565) and fifteenth Lord Erskine (1429), February 1785. On 17th June 1824 he was, in his eighty-third year, restored by Act of Parliament 'to the dignity and title to Earl 'of Mar.' He died 20th August 1825. He married, 17th March 1770, at Upway, Dorset, Frances, daughter of Charles Floyer, Governor of Madras, by Mary, daughter of [   ] Berriman. She died 20th December 1798 at Alloa.

1776
-
1825

V. JOHN THOMAS (ERSKINE), fifth *DUKE* and twenty-seventh EARL (1115) and eleventh EARL (1565) OF MAR, etc., son and heir, born 1772. He died 20th September 1828 at Alloa House.

1825
-
1828

VI. JOHN FRANCIS MILLER (ERSKINE), sixth *DUKE* and twenty-eighth EARL (1115) and twelfth EARL (1565) OF MAR,

1828
-
1866

---

[1] As to this Earldom of Mar, whose existence was not then, nor till long afterwards, suspected, but which, 'according to the decision of the House of Lords, on '25th February 1875, was supposed to have been created (*de novo*) by patent in 1565, 'in tail male,' see *The Complete Peerage*, v. pp. 238, 239, and also a correspondence in the *Genealogist*.

[2] *Scots Magazine*, 1785, p. 154.

MAR

and seventeenth LORD ERSKINE (1429), only son and heir, born 28th December 1795. He succeeded his distant cousin, Methven (Erskine), Earl of Kellie, etc. [S], in 1828 or 1829 as eleventh Earl of Kellie (1619), Viscount Fentoun (1606 and 1619), and Lord Erskine of Dirletoun (1604). He died *s.p.* 19th June 1866 at Alloa House, when the Earldom of Kellie and the other honours inherited therewith, as did also the Earldom of Mar (1565) and the Barony of Erskine (1429), devolved on his cousin and next heir-male, while his other honours passed to his nephew and heir of line.

1866

VII. JOHN FRANCIS ERSKINE (GOODEVE, afterwards (1866) GOODEVE-ERSKINE), seventh DUKE OF MAR, MARQUIS ERSKINE, EARL OF KILDRUMMIE, VISCOUNT GARIOCH, LORD ALLOA, FERRITON, AND FORREST (1715), twenty-ninth EARL OF MAR (1115) [S], nephew and heir of line, being son and heir of William James Goodeve of Clifton, co. Somerset, by the Lady Frances Jemima, daughter of John Thomas (Erskine), fifth DUKE OF MAR, born at Clifton 29th March 1836; succeeded his uncle, 19th June 1866; and had the Earldom of Mar (1115, 1395, or 1404) confirmed to him by Act of Parliament, 6th August 1885.[1]

MAR, Earldom of [E].

1717 -

I. JOHN (ERSKINE), first DUKE OF MAR, etc. [S], was on 10th November 1717 created by James III and VIII BARON OF [ ] and EARL OF MAR, co. York [E], with remainder to the heirs-male of his body. See '*MAR,*' DUKE OF [S].

[MAR], Duke of [I].

1722 -

I. JOHN (ERSKINE), first DUKE OF MAR, etc. [S], EARL OF MAR [E], was on the 13th December 1722 created by James III and VIII DUKE OF [MAR] [I], with presumably remainder to the heirs-male of his body. See '*MAR,*' DUKE OF [S].

MELFORT, Duke of [S].

1692 -
1714/15

I. HON. JOHN DRUMMOND, second son of James, third Earl of Perth [S], by Anne, eldest daughter of George (Gordon), second Marquis of Huntly [S], born about 1650; Secretary of State [S], 1684-1688; was on 14th April 1685 created by James

---

[1] For a fuller account of this family see the extant peerages under Mar, Earl of.

MELFORT

II and VII VISCOUNT OF MELFORT and LORD DRUMMOND OF GILSTOUN [S], with a special remainder to the heirs-male of his body by his second wife, whom failing to the heirs-male of his body whatsoever. On 12th August 1686 he was further created by the same King, EARL OF MELFORT, VISCOUNT OF FORTH, LORD DRUMMOND OF RICCARTOUN, CASTLEMAINS, AND GILSTOUN [S], with like special remainder; K.T., 6th June 1687, being one of the eight original knights of that order. In 1687 he is said to have resigned all his lands and honours into the hands of the King at Whitehall, who in 1688 erected and united all the honours so resigned into a new Earldom of Melfort and Lordship of the Regality of Forth in favour of Euphemia, Countess of Melfort for life, and of John, Viscount Forth and the heirs-male of his body, whom failing to the heirs-female of his body, whom failing to his heirs whatsoever.[1] On 7th August 1689 he was created *BARON CLEWORTH* [E], with the same remainder as the Scottish Earldom. On the revolution he fled to France, 16th December 1688, afterwards accompanying King James to Ireland, whence, 25th August 1689, he was sent on a mission to the Court of Paris, and, 31st July 1690, to that of Rome. He was made *K.G.*, 19th April 1693; PRINCIPAL SECRETARY OF STATE and PRIME MINISTER, 1689-1693; and one of the SECRETARIES OF STATE, 1693-1694; on 17th April 1692 he was created DUKE OF MELFORT, MARQUIS OF FORTH, EARL OF ISLA AND BURNTISLAND, VISCOUNT OF RICKERTON, LORD CASTLEMAINS AND GALSTON [S], with the like special remainder as in the previous creations. He was outlawed 23rd July 1694, and attainted[2] by Act of Parliament 2nd July 1695, whereby all his honours were considered as forfeited. In 1701 he was created by Louis XIV a French Peer and DUKE OF MELFORT [F], with the same remainder as aforesaid. He died 25th January 1714/15, and was buried at St. Sulpice, Paris. He married first, 30th September 1670, Sophia, daughter and eventual heir of line of the Hon. Robert Maitland of Lundin, Fife, by Margaret, daughter and heir of John Lundin of Lundin aforesaid. He married secondly, 1680, Euphemia, daughter of Sir Thomas Wallace of Craigie, a Lord of Session (1671-1680), by Euphemia, daughter and heir of William Gemmill of Templelands, Ayr. She, who was 'a great beauty in her time,' died in 1743 at St. Germains, aged ninety.

---

[1] Burke's *Peerage*, article 'Perth.'   [2] 'For having been seen at St. Germains.'

MITCHELL

1714/15
1754

II. JOHN (DRUMMOND), second *DUKE OF MELFORT*, etc., younger son, but eldest son by the second wife, and heir under the special remainder. He was born 26th May 1682, and retired with his father to France. He served as Aide-de-camp to the Duke of Vendôme, Grand Prior of France, in 1705, was a Major-General under Lord Mar in the '15, and after the collapse of that movement accompanied King James to France, 4th February 1716. He died 29th January 1754, and was buried at St. Nicholas des Champs, Paris. He married, 25th May 1707, at St. Eustache's, Paris, Marie Gabrielle, *DOWAGER-DUCHESS OF ALBEMARLE* [E], *suo jure* Countess of Lussan [F], only daughter and heir of John (d'Audibert), second Count of Lussan, by Marie Frances Raymond. She was born about 1675, and died at the Chateau of St. Germains-en-Laye, 15th May 1741, aged about sixty-six.

1754
1766

III. JAMES (DRUMMOND), third *DUKE OF MELFORT*, also fourth COUNT OF LUSSAN [F],[1] son and heir born, 13th May 1708, at St. Germains; succeeded his father 29th January 1754, and his mother, as Count of Lussan, 15th May 1741. He died 25th December 1766.

1766

IV. JAMES LEWIS (DRUMMOND), fourth *DUKE OF MELFORT*, etc., son and heir, a General in the French service. On 2nd July 1800 he succeeded his distant cousin James (Drummond), eighth *DUKE* and eleventh Earl of Perth [S], as *DUKE* and Earl of Perth.[2] See '*PERTH,*' *DUKEDOM OF.*

MITCHELL, Baron [E].

1
—
1709

I. HUMPHREY BORLASE or BORLACE of Treludro, co. Cornwall, eldest son and heir of Nicholas Borlase, a Colonel of horse under Charles II, by Catherine, daughter of [   ] Bury of Devon; succeeded his father, 1677; M.P. for Mitchell, co. Cornwall, 1660-1662, and again 1679-1680; High Sheriff of Cornwall, 1687-1688. He is said to have followed King James to France after the Revolution of 1688,

---

[1] His younger brother, Lord Lewis Drummond, a Lieutenant-General in the French service, and a Knight Grand Cross of St. Louis, was second in command of the Scots Royal at Culloden, where he was taken prisoner. He was afterwards Governor of Normandy, and was still alive in 1792.

[2] For a fuller account of this family see the extant peerages under Perth, Earl of.

MOENMOYNE

and to have been created by that King LORD BORLASE OF BORLASE and BARON OF MITCHELL, co. Cornwall [E]. He died *s.p.s.* 1709; buried at Newlyn. Will, dated 20th January 1704, proved 1st December 1709. He married (settlement dated 3rd June), 1663, Anne, daughter of Sir John Winter of Lydney, co. Gloucester, who was Maid of Honour to Queen Henrietta Maria. He had issue :—

1. Nicholas Borlase, died in infancy.
2. Trese Borlase, buried at Newlyn 1679.[1]

MOENMOYNE, Earl of [I].

I. SIR THOMAS ARTHUR LALLY, second *BARONET* (1707) [I], only son and heir of Sir Gerard Lally, first *BARONET*, by Anne Mary, daughter of Charles James de Bressac, Seigneur de la Vache, born at Romano, in Dauphiny, and baptized there, 15th January 1702. He had a commission given him, 1st January 1707, in the famous Dillon regiment commanded by his cousin, Lieutenant-General *EARL DILLON*; was present before Gerona, September 1709, and at Barcelona, 1714; Captain in the same regiment, 15th February 1728; Aide-Major, 26th January 1732; served in 1733 at the reduction of Kehl, and 'was as much dis- 'tinguished by his brilliant valour there as by his uncommon ' military knowledge '; present with his father at Etlingen, where the former, being 'grievously wounded, was on the point of ' falling into the enemy's hands, when his son threw himself ' between them and his father, covered him with his own body, ' and, by prodigies of valour, succeeded in rescuing him.' He made a tour of the three kingdoms in 1737 for the purpose of making observations as to suitable places for landing an army and of establishing communications with the different Jacobite centres. On his return he undertook a mission to Russia. Captain of Grenadiers, 6th February 1738; Major of the Dillon regiment, 15th November 1741; Aide-Major to Marshal de Noailles, 1743; Colonel of infantry, 19th February 1744; Colonel of the new Irish infantry regiment afterwards called after him, 1st October 1744, at the head of which he was present at Fontenoy, 30th April 1745. He served through the '45, being Aide-de-camp to the Prince Regent at the battle

1746 — 1766

---

[1] See the *Genealogist*, N.S., ii., pedigree facing p. 288, also *The Complete Peerage*, viii. p. 315. Hals in his *Cornwall* says (*c.* 1750), 'by letters patent, yet extant.'

MOENMOYNE

of Falkirk, 16th January 1746, and on his return to France was created by King James III and VIII *EARL OF MOENMOYNE, VISCOUNT OF BALLYMOLE*, and *BARON OF TOLLENDALLY* [I].[1] He was Quartermaster-General to Count de Lowendahl's army in the Bergen-op-Zoom expedition, and was promoted to be Major-General, 31st December 1755. Either about this time or shortly before he appears to have been created or recognised by Louis XV as COUNT OF LALLY and BARON OF TOLLENDAL [F]. On the 19th November 1756 he was appointed Lieutenant-General of the force designed to assist the French East India Company, and at the same time Commissioner for the King, Syndic of the Company, and Commander-in-Chief of all the French establishments in the East Indies;[2] Commander of St. Louis, 5th February 1757; Honorary Grand Cross, 16th December following; and Knight Grand Cross, 15th January 1761.[3] After obtaining many successes against the British, he was, owing to the jealousy of his subordinates, defeated and taken prisoner at Pondicherry, 15th January 1761. He was sent to England, but released on parole, October, and allowed to return to France. He was arrested and imprisoned, 5th November 1761, in the Bastille, where he remained till May 1766, when he was brought to trial, condemned to death by *arrêt* of the *Parlement de Paris*, 6th, and executed in Paris, 9th May 1766. This sentence was afterwards, 21st May 1778, cancelled by the King in Council, and

---

[1] See O'Callaghan's *History of the Irish Brigade*, 1870, which contains a good account of him; see also *Nouvelle Biographie Générale*, Paris, 1859.

[2] When the deputation from the secret committee of the Company applied to the French Minister, the Count of Argenson, for 3000 of the King's troops, to be joined with its own and commanded by the Marquis of Lally, the equally sagacious and well intentioned Minister, who disapproved of Lally's accepting that post, said to the applicants: 'You do not see your way, I am better acquainted than you are with the 'worth of M. de Lally, and moreover, he is my friend; but he should be left with us in 'Europe. He is on fire with activity. He makes no compromise with respect to dis- 'cipline, has a horror of every proceeding that is not straightforward, is vexed with 'everything that does not go on rapidly, is silent upon nothing that he knows, and 'expresses himself in terms not to be forgotten. All that is excellent among us; but 'what is the prospect of it for you, among your factories in Asia. At the first act of 'negligence that will clash with the service of the King, at the first appearance of 'insubordination or knavery, M. de Lally will thunder forth if he does not resort to 'rough measures. They will cause his operations to fail, in order to be revenged upon 'him. Pondicherry will have civil war within its walls, as well as foreign war without its 'gates. I believe the plans of my friend to be excellent; but, in India, a person 'different from what he is ought to be charged with the execution of them. Leave me, 'in order to deliberate on all that, and come and see me again,' and it was only with great reluctance that he was ultimately induced to propose Lally's name to the King.

[3] Statement of services supplied by French Minister of War.

MONMOUTH

his innocence formally declared. He married Felicite, daughter of [ ] Crafton,

II. TROPHIME GERARD (LALLY), second EARL OF MOENMOYNE, VISCOUNT OF BALLYMOLE, and BARON OF TOLLENDALLY [I], first MARQUIS and second COUNT OF LALLY-TOLLENDAL, etc. [F], only son and heir, born in Paris 5th March 1751; educated at the College of Harcourt under the name of Trophime; succeeded his father, 9th May 1766; Deputy of the *noblesse* of Paris to the States-General, 1789; retired from France on the Revolution, and was for some time in England. He was living at Bordeaux in 1805. P.C. and Minister of Public Instruction, 1815, to Louis XVIII, by whom, on 19th August 1815, he was created MARQUIS OF LALLY-TOLLENDAL and a Peer of France; Member of the French Royal Academy, 21st March 1816; Grand Cross of the Legion of Honour, Knight-Commander and Grand Treasurer of the Order of the Holy Ghost. He died in Paris 11th March 1830.[1] He married [ ], daughter of [ ] [ ]. He had issue an only daughter, viz. :— 1766 - 1830

    1. LADY Elizabeth Felicite Claude de Lally, Marchioness of Lally, married [ ], Count of Aux.

MONEYDIE, Viscount of [S].

i.e. 'MONEYDIE,' VISCOUNTY OF (Davia), created 12th April 1698, with 'ALMOND,' EARLDOM OF, which see.

MONK, Marquis [E].

i.e. 'MONK,' MARQUISATE OF (Granville), created 3rd November 1721, with 'ALBEMARLE,' DUKEDOM OF, which see.

MONMOUTH, Earl of [E].

I. CHARLES MIDDLETON, second EARL OF MIDDLETON, LORD CLERMONT AND FETTERCAIRN [S], son and heir of John (Middleton), first Earl of Middleton, by his first wife, 1701 - 1719

---

[1] *Nouvelle Biographie Générale*, Paris, 1859.

MONMOUTH

Grizel, widow respectively of Sir Alexander Fotheringham and of Sir Gilbert Ramsay of Balmain, and daughter of James Durham of Pitkerrow; born about 1640; was with his father in the Highlands in 1654 fighting against Cromwell with the rank of Captain, though then but fourteen years of age. He succeeded his father, 1673; was Ambassador to the Court of Vienna, and afterwards (1682) Secretary of State [S]. In August 1684 he was appointed one of the principal Secretaries of State [E]. Though a strong Protestant, he remained faithful to King James. With Lord Dundee he followed the King to Rochester, and entreated him to remain in England. In 1692 he was arrested and committed to the Tower, but after a few months' detention was released on bail, and finally, November, discharged. In February 1693 he went on a mission to St. Germains; was outlawed by the Court of Justiciary, 23rd July 1694, and attainted by Act of Parliament, 2nd July 1695, whereby all his honours were forfeited; SECRETARY OF STATE, 1693-1702 and 1703-1713, with the 'chief control of affairs at the exile Court at St.
' Germains, his conversion to the Roman Catholic faith[1] (which
' was the cause of his retirement, 1702-1703) not being till *after* the
' death of King James, under whose will he was made one of the
' Council to assist the young Prince ... and the Queen-Dowager,
' his mother.' Shortly after the death of James II and VII, and before the 17th October 1701, he was created by the young King EARL OF MONMOUTH[2] and VISCOUNT CLERMONT[3] [E], with presumably remainder to the heirs-male of his body. In 1703 he was offered but declined the Garter.[4] On the 24th December 1713 he resigned his seals of office, and was early the next year appointed Great Chamberlain to the Queen-Dowager, which office he continued to hold until her death at St. Germains-en-

---

[1] 'He came into the Catholic Church under remarkable circumstances. Even on ' his deathbed James II had earnestly, but vainly, endeavoured to convert him to ' Catholicism. A few months after the King's death he told the Queen that his old ' master had appeared to him during the night, and informed him that by his prayers ' he had obtained his friend's salvation. The vision, the literally undying care of the ' King for his soul, made so deep an impression upon the obstinate, but practical ' Minister, no morbid visionary, but a cheery soul, that he professed himself a Catholic, ' resigned his office, went into retreat, and then made his adjuration' (*The Royalist*, x. p. 35).

[2] His father's second wife was Martha, fifth daughter and co-heir of Henry (Carey), second Earl of Monmouth, who died *s.p.m.s.* 13th June 1661, when that Earldom became extinct.

[3] His son was styled 'Viscount Clermont.'

[4] Out of modesty, says St. Simon.

MONMOUTH

Laye, 8th May 1719. He died at the same place, 1719, aged about seventy-nine.[1] Will, dated 7th July 1719 (N.S.), was proved 4th March 1726/7 and again 3rd March 1812. He married, about 1670, Lady Catharine, daughter of Robert (Brudenell), second Earl of Cardigan [E], by his second wife, the Hon. Anne, daughter of Thomas (Savage), first Viscount Savage [E]. She, who was governess to the Princess Louisa, 25th November 1701 till the latter's death, 18th April 1712, died at St. Germains, 11th March 1743, in her ninety-fifth year. Her will was dated 26th October 1740, and proved 25th May 1749. He had issue :—

1. John, VISCOUNT CLERMONT, his heir.
2. Hon. Charles Middleton, who appears to have died unmarried before October 1740.
3. Lady Elizabeth Middleton married Edward, sixth DUKE OF PERTH, and was living in Paris at a great age in 1773.
4. Lady Catherine Middleton married first, in or shortly after June 1706, Sir John Giffard, Knight (by whom she had a daughter Mary, living 1740), and secondly Michael, Count de Rothe.

II. JOHN (MIDDLETON), second EARL OF MONMOUTH [E], third EARL OF MIDDLETON, etc. [S], elder son and heir. On 24th February/17th March 1708 he, being then a Colonel, and his brother, Captain Charles Middleton, accompanied King James in the attempted expedition to Scotland, but were captured on board the *Salisbury* by Admiral Byng, and were sent prisoners to the Tower, but were afterwards released on parole, and in June 1713, as the result of the Peace of Utrecht, were allowed

1719
-
1747

---

[1] Macky, in his 'Characters,' writes of him [1702?] when towards sixty years old : ' He was against the violent measures of King James's reign, and for that reason made ' no great figure at Court while that Prince was upon the throne; yet was proof ' against all the offers made him by King William, and, after being frequently im- ' prisoned in England, followed King James to France, when he had the chief ' administration given him. He is one of the politest gentlemen in Europe, has a ' great deal of wit, mixed with a sound judgment and a very clear understanding ; of ' an easy indifferent address, but a careless way of living. He is a black man, of a ' middle stature, with a sanguine complexion, and one of the pleasantest companions ' in the world.' To which Dean Swift adds : '*Sir William Temple told me he was a* ' *very valuable man and a good scholar. I once saw him.*' Quoted in *The Complete Peerage*, v. p. 310, from which the above account is largely taken. See also an account of him in *The Royalist*, x. p. 65, above the well-known initials, A. S., *i.e.* Alice Shield.

MONTGOMERY

to return to France. Gentleman of the Bedchamber, 15th December 1713. He succeeded his father 1719, and appears to have died unmarried in or shortly before February 1746/7, when the EARLDOM OF MONMOUTH [E] presumably became extinct, while the Earldom of Middleton, Baronies of Clermont and Fettercairn [S], which were under attainder, remained dormant.

MONTGOMERY, Marquis of [E].

i.e. '*MONTGOMERY*,' *MARQUISATE OF* (Herbert), created 12th January 1689, with '*POWIS*,' *DUKEDOM OF*, which see.

MOUNTCASHELL, Viscount of [I].

1689 – 1694

I. HON. JUSTIN MACCARTY, third and youngest son of Donough, first Earl of Clancarty [I], by the Hon. Eleanor, sister of James, first Duke of Ormonde [E and I], daughter of Thomas Butler, styled Viscount Thurels, entered the French army while young, but was recalled to England in 1678. He was made a Lieutenant-General in the army, and held command in Munster, where, before the arrival of King James at Kinsale, 22nd March 1689, he had succeeded in suppressing the insurrection under Lord Inchiquin and Henry Boyle. M.P. [I], co. Cork, April 1689, and Master-General of the Ordnance [I], 14th May 1689, having on the 1st May[1] previously been created by King James (after the Revolution in England, but while still *de facto* as well as *de jure* King of Ireland[2]) BARON OF CASTLEINCH or CASTLE-INCHY[3] and VISCOUNT MOUNTCASHELL, co. Tipperary [I]. He was sent against the Enniskillen insurgents and laid siege to Crom Castle, but was defeated and taken prisoner, 31st July 1689, at

---

[1] *The Complete Peerage* gives the date as 23rd May, and other authorities as the 3rd June (the anniversary of his brother's glorious death on board the *Royal Charles* in the famous action between James, Duke of York, and the Dutch Admiral Opdom, 3rd June 1665, when the same cannon-ball is said to have killed Richard Boyle, Charles Berkeley, Lord Falmouth, and Charles Maccarty, Lord Muskerry), but the patent is dated 1st May. There appears no doubt, however, that it was not declared until after the opening of the Irish Parliament, 17th May. Dalton, in his *King James's Irish Army List*, 1689, says: 'Early in May 1689 he was created Lord Viscount Montcashel and Baron of Castleinchy, and was introduced with that title, on the second day of the meeting of the Parliament of Dublin, to the House of Peers.'

[2] The Preface, p. xii.

[3] The name of the Barony is blank in the warrant.

MOUNT LEINSTER

Newtown Butler. He escaped in December, and on 18th April 1690 was despatched to Brest in command of five infantry regiments; Lieutenant-General in the French army 30th May following. The same year he served under the Marquis of St. Ruth in Savoy, in 1691 under the Duke of Noailles in Catalonia, and in 1693 with the army of Germany. He died *s.p.* 1st July 1694 at the baths at Barèges, when all his honours became extinct.[1] He married Lady Arabella, second and youngest daughter of Thomas (Wentworth), first Earl of Strafford [E], by his second wife, Lady Arabella, daughter of John (Holles), first Earl of Clare [E].

MOUNT LEINSTER, Viscount of [I].

I. EDWARD CHEEVERS of Macetown, son and heir of John Cheevers of Macetown and Ballyhaly, by his first wife, Mary, daughter of Sir Henry Bealing (or by his second wife, Joan, daughter of Edward Sutton), succeeded his father about 1688, and joined his brother-in-law, the gallant Earl of Lucan, in supporting King James, by whom he was on 23rd August 1689 created (after the Revolution in England, but while he was still *de facto* as well as *de jure* King of Ireland[2]) *BARON OF BANO, i.e.* [*BANNOW*], co. Wexford, and *VISCOUNT MOUNT LEINSTER*, co. Carlow [I].[3] Aide-de-camp to King James at the battle of the Boyne; was included in the Articles of Limerick, 1691, but declined to accept the benefits of the capitulation, and accompanied his Sovereign to France, where he died unmarried 1709, when all his honours became extinct. He married Anne, sister of Patrick (Sarsfield), *EARL OF LUCAN* [I], elder daughter of Patrick Sarsfield of Lucan, co. Dublin, by Anne, daughter of Rory O'More.[4]

1689
–
1709

---

[1] *The French Gazette* contains the following announcement: 'My Lord Montcassel, 'Lieutenant-General of the Armies of the King, commander of three Irish regiments, 'died the 1st of this month at Barrege, of the wounds that he has received on several 'occasions, in which he was always extremely distinguished.' He is sometimes, but erroneously, said to have been created Duke of Mount Cashell. See a memoir of him in *The Royalist*, ii. p. 85.

[2] See Preface, p. xii.

[3] The patent is printed in full in *The Royalist*, v. p. 134.

[4] There is a good pedigree of this family in Burke's *Extinct Peerage*, 1883, pp. 116, 117.

MUNSTER

MUNSTER, Duke of [I].

John O'Sullivan is sometimes, but apparently erroneously, said to have been created by King James III and VIII, in or about 1746, DUKE OF MUNSTER [I]. In 1753 he was created, 'as Sir John O'Sullivan, Knt.,' a BARONET [I]. See O'SULLIVAN, BARONET [I].

MURRAY.

i.e. EARL (or COUNT) MURRAY was the title generally used after 1759 by the Hon. Alexander Murray, who on the 12th August that year was created by King James EARL OF WESTMINSTER. See 'WESTMINSTER,' EARL OF.

NAIRNE, Earl of [S].

1721 – 1726

I. WILLIAM (MURRAY), second LORD NAIRNE [S], fourth son of John (Murray), first Marquis of Atholl [S], by Lady Amelia Sophia, daughter of James (Stanley), seventh Earl of Derby [E], was born about 1665, and on 30th May 1683 succeeded his father-in-law, Robert (Nairne), first Lord Nairne [S] (under the special remainder with which that dignity had been, 27th January 1680/1, created), as LORD NAIRNE. He took his seat in Parliament [S], 22nd October 1690, but never took the oaths to the Revolution Government. He was one of the first to join the rising in 1715; was taken prisoner, 14th November 1715, at Preston; sent to the Tower; and on 9th February 1716 tried and condemned to death for high treason, when his honours were forfeited. He was however respited, and allowed the benefit of the Act of Indemnity of 6th December 1717. On 24th June 1721 he was created by James III and VIII LORD OF [   ], VISCOUNT OF STANLEY,[1] and EARL OF NAIRNE [S], with remainder to his heirs-male. He died 3rd February 1726, aged about sixty. He married, February 1690, the Hon. Margaret, only daughter and heir of Robert (Nairne), first Lord Nairne [S], by Margaret, daughter of Patrick Graham

---

[1] Doubtless in consequence of his mother (of whom, however, he was not the representative) having been heiress of the Stanleys, Earls of Derby [E]. See *The Complete Peerage*, vi. p. 2.

NAIRNE

of Inchbraco. She, who was born 16th December 1669, died 14th November 1747.

II. JOHN (NAIRNE), second *EARL OF NAIRNE*, etc., eldest son and heir,[1] born about 1691. Lieutenant-Colonel in Lord Charles Murray's regiment; was taken prisoner with his father, 13th November 1715, at Preston; was found guilty of high treason and attainted, 4th March 1716. He succeeded his father, 3rd February 1726, but was of course not recognised by the Government. He obtained in 1737-1738 an Act of Parliament to enable him to inherit property, etc. In 1745 he again took part in the rising on behalf of the House of Stuart, and the following year was again attainted. He died at Sancerre in France, 11th July 1770. He married his cousin-german, Lady Catherine, third and youngest daughter of Charles (Murray), first Earl of Dunmore [S], by Catherine, daughter of Robert Watts. She died at Versailles, 9th May 1754, and was buried as 'Countess of Nairne' 12th, at Port St. Martin, near Paris.[2]

1726
–
1770

III. JOHN (NAIRNE), third *EARL OF NAIRNE*, etc., second but eldest surviving son and heir. He succeeded his father, 11th July 1770, but never assumed the title. He was a Lieutenant-Colonel in the army, and died 7th November 1782. He married about 1756 Brabazon, daughter of Richard Wheeler of Leyrath, co. Kilkenny, who died 22nd April 1801.

1770
–
1782

IV. WILLIAM (NAIRNE), fourth *EARL OF NAIRNE*, etc., second but only surviving son and heir, born 1756; succeeded his father, 7th November 1782, but did not assume the title. He was also an officer in the army, being for some time Assistant-Inspector-General of Barracks in Scotland. By Act of Parliament, 17th June 1824, the attainder of the second Lord Nairne in 1716 was repealed, when he became *de facto* as well as *de jure* Lord Nairne. He died 9th July 1830. He married, June 1806, the *HON.* Caroline, third daughter of Laurence (Oliphant), second *LORD OLIPHANT OF GASK* [S], by Margaret, eldest daughter of

1782
–
1830

---

[1] In *The Complete Peerage* it is this Lord Nairne who is said to have been created Earl of Nairne by King James; but though the Christian name is left blank in the warrant, it is made out to Lord Nairne, which this John did not become till some five years later than the date of the patent.
[2] Kington-Oliphant's *Jacobite Lairds of Gask*, p. 287.

NEWCASTLE

Duncan Robertson of Struan. She, the well-known Lady Nairne, was born at Gask, 16th August 1766, and named after the King (Charles III), and died there, 27th October 1845.

1830 — 1837

V. WILLIAM (NAIRNE), fifth EARL OF NAIRNE and VISCOUNT STANLEY (1721), sixth LORD NAIRNE (1681) [S], only son and heir, born 1808; succeeded his father, 9th July 1830, and died unmarried, 7th December 1837, when the Barony of Nairne passed to his heir-of-line, Margaret, *suo jure* Baroness Keith [I and U K], while the EARLDOM OF NAIRNE devolved upon his heir-male, as under.

1837 — 1845

VI. ALEXANDER EDWARD (MURRAY), sixth EARL OF NAIRNE, also sixth EARL OF DUNMORE [S], and second BARON DUNMORE [U K], cousin and next heir-male, being the eldest son of George, fifth Earl of Dunmore, son and heir of John, fourth Earl, son and heir of William, third Earl, brother and next heir of John, second Earl, who was son and heir of Charles, first Earl of Dunmore, which Charles was the next elder brother (whose male issue then survived[1]) of the first Earl of Nairne. He was born 1st June 1804, and died 15th July 1845.

1845

VII. CHARLES ADOLPHUS (MURRAY), seventh EARL OF NAIRNE and VISCOUNT STANLEY (1721), also seventh EARL OF DUNMORE, VISCOUNT FINCASTLE, and LORD MURRAY (1686) [S], and third BARON DUNMORE (1831) [U K], only son and heir, born 24th March 1841.

NEWCASTLE, Earl of [I].

c. 1692 — 1740

I. PIERS (BUTLER), third VISCOUNT OF GALMOYE [I], son and heir of Edward (Butler), second Viscount Galmoye, by Eleanor, widow of Sir Arthur Aston, daughter of Sir Nicholas

---

[1] Lyon King writes: 'As to your query, a Scots peerage with remainder to heirs-male whatsoever goes in the case you mention to the heirs of the next younger brother; in case of the failure of all younger brothers and their issue it would go to the immediate elder brother. Failing all collateral succession, the title would then ascend to the father and his collaterals, and so on.'

The first Earl of Nairne had three elder brothers and four younger: of the latter Henry and George died young, Mungo was killed, unmarried, in the Darien expedition, 1700, and Edward's only son, John, died (apparently unmarried) in 1748, while his immediate elder brother, James, had only daughters.

NORTH

White of Leixlip, born 21st March 1652;[1] succeeded his father in 1667; D.C.L. of Oxford, 6th August 1677; P.C. [I], 1686. He remained faithful to King James, and was in command of a regiment of horse at the battle of the Boyne, 1st July 1690; was outlawed by King William, 11th May 1691; and was taken prisoner at the battle of Aughrim, 12th July 1691. He was afterwards exchanged, and was one of the parties on the Irish side to the Treaty of Limerick, 3rd October 1691, in which he was included. He however elected to follow his King into exile. He accordingly retired into France, and in 1692 was created by King James *EARL OF NEWCASTLE*, co. Limerick [I], in consequence of which he was, 1697, attainted by the *de facto* Government. He afterwards entered the French army and was made a Major-General. Gentleman of the Bedchamber to James III and VIII, 14th February 1703. He died *s.p.m.s.* 18th June 1740, when the *EARLDOM OF NEWCASTLE* presumably became extinct, and the Viscounty of Galmoye devolved on his heir-male. He married Elizabeth, daughter of Theobald Mathew of Thurles, co. Tipperary. He had issue an only son :—

1. Edward, *VISCOUNT GALMOYE*, Colonel in the French army, was slain *v.p.* 11th September 1709, at the battle of Malplaquet.

NEWTON, Baron [S].

i.e. '*NEWTON*,' *BARONY OF* (Græme), created 20th January 1760, with '*ALFORD*,' *EARLDOM OF*, which see.

[NORTH], Earl of [E].

I. WILLIAM (NORTH), sixth LORD NORTH DE KIRTLING (1554) and second LORD GREY DE ROLLESTON (1673), eldest son and heir of Charles (North), Lord North and Grey, by the Hon. Katharine, widow of Sir Edward Moseley of Hough, co. Lancaster, and Rolleston, co. Stafford, second Baronet [E], daughter of William (Grey), first Baron Grey of Werke; born 22nd December 1673, succeeded his father 1690; a Lieutenant-General in the army, distinguished himself at the battle of Blenheim, 13th August 1704, where he had his right hand shot off. P.C. to

1722 - 1734

---

[1] Statement of services supplied by French Minister of War.

NORTHUMBERLAND

Anne. He subsequently devoted himself to the Jacobite cause, and was much mixed up in all the plots to restore the House of Stuart. On 2nd January 1722 he had a commission[1] as Lieutenant-General from King James, and on 5th of the same month, as 'William North,'[2] was appointed Commander-in-Chief in and about the City of London and Westminster, being the following day created[3] by the same King EARL OF [NORTH], VISCOUNT OF [   ], and BARON OF [   ] [E], with remainder to the heirs-male of his body. He was also appointed, 26th May 1722, one cf the nine LORDS REGENT [E][4] during the King's absence. He died *s.p.* at Madrid, 1734, when the EARLDOM OF NORTH, together with the minor titles conferred with it, as also the Barony of Grey de Rolleston, became extinct, while the Barony of North de Kirtling devolved on his next heir-male. He married Maria Margaretta, daughter of Cornelius de Yong, Lord of Elmeet [Holland], Receiver-General of the United Provinces. She remarried in 1735 Patrick (Murray), seventh Lord Elibank [S], and died 6th June 1762, and was buried at Aberlady.

NORTHUMBERLAND, Duke of [E].

1716 – 1731

I. PHILIP (WHARTON), sixth BARON WHARTON (1544), also second MARQUIS OF WHARTON AND MALMESBURY (by George I, 1715), EARL OF WHARTON and VISCOUNT WINCHENDON (by Anne, 1706) [E], and BARON TRIM, EARL OF RATHFARNHAM, and MARQUIS OF CATHERLOUGH (by George I, 1715) [I], only son and heir of Thomas (Wharton), fifth Baron and first Marquis of Wharton, etc., by his second wife, the Hon. Lucy, daughter and heir of Adam (Loftus), first Viscount Lisburne [I]; born on or shortly before 21st December 1698, at Adderbury, or Ditchley, Oxon., and baptized 5th January 1698/9, William of Orange, the Princess Anne, and the Duke of Shrewsbury being his sponsors; succeeded his father, 12th April 1715. The following September

---

[1] This is endorsed: 'Renewed of the same date, and given to him 17 June '1727.'

[2] For some reason King James does not appear to have recognised either of his peerages, though both were of pre-Revolution origin.

[3] The patent is endorsed: 'Renewed of the same date, and given to him 17 June '1727. The titles of Earl, Viscount, and Baron "blank."'

[4] See under 'Albemarle, Duke of,' p. 4.

NORTHUMBERLAND

he visited King James at Avignon, by whom of course his post-Revolution peerages were not recognised, but by whom he was, 22nd December 1716, created *Viscount Winchendon*, co. Bucks, *Earl of Malmesbury*, co. Wilts, *Marquis of Woburn*, co. Bucks, and *Duke of Northumberland* [E].[1] So desirous, however, were the Government of obtaining his support, that he was allowed to take his seat, 12th August 1717, in the Irish House of Lords, and on 28th January 1718, being then not twenty, he was created by George I Duke of Wharton, co. Westmoreland.[2] Notwithstanding this, he continued to oppose the Government, and made a famous speech in the House of Lords in defence of Bishop Atterbury. In 1726 he left England and openly declared

---

[1] On the 17th November 1724 Mar writes to him in Paris : 'I scarce believe the story
' you heard from England of many &hsk [dukes] to be made, but that is nothing as to Mr.
' Worsly [Wharton], for as soon as I spoke of it to Ross [the King] he ordered me to let
' you know that as soon [as] he is able to write the warrant shall be past of the same date
' when he was with him and be put into Mr. Clark's hands, where Worsly may be sure
' it shall be safe from harm, and safer and better there for some time than in his own.
' You will easily see for many reasons the importance of keeping this an absolute
' secrety, nobody here knows of it nor else where. You see how ready Mr. Ross is to
' oblige you, and I am persuaded he will never have cause to repent it.' Across the
letter is written, 'Tell Worsly to send me the names and places necessary to be put
' in this warrant.' To this Wharton replies on the 26th November, and after thanking
Mar for his good offices continues : 'I have thanked the King for it by the inclos'd and
' will never depart from the assurances I have giv'n his Majesty. I shall endeavour to
' correspond constantly with Yr. Grace from England by cypher. Your letters for
' me must be adres'd as usual to Gordon. As to the names and places necessary to
' be put in the warrants, I hope the King will let it be fil'd up as is mentioned on the
' other side. The title of Northumberland being extinct and having an estate in the
' county, I think (if the King has no objection to it) it will be most proper. If his
' Majesty has, I hope he will let me know it, and I shall change it.' On the other side
are written the titles : 'Philip Wharton, Baron Wharton of Wharton, in the county of
' Westmoreland (an honour given to Sir Tho. Wharton, then Ld. Warden of the
· Marshes, by Henry ye 8th), Viscount Winchendon in the county of Buckingham, Earl
' of Malmesbury in the county of Wilts, Marquess of Woburn in the county of Bucks,
' Duke of Northumberland.' This letter is endorsed 'recd. at Avignon 21 Dec.,' and on
the 22nd Mar writes to him that the warrant has been made out according to his wish
and handed to Mr. Clark.

[2] ' The hope of attracting this rich and influential young profligate from the Jacobite
' to the Whig party by the extraordinary mark of favour singularly failed. The pre-
' amble supplements the (feeble) claim of the grantee thereto (1) as being of noble
' descent, and (2) as having "chosen to distinguish himself by his personal merit," by
' recounting how much the "invincible King William III" owed to the grantee's father,
' "that constant and courageous assertor of the public liberty and Protestant religion,"
' and how "the same extraordinary person deserved so well of us in having supported
' "our interests by the weight of his counsels, the force of his wit, and the firmness of his
' "mind at a time when our title to the succession of this realm was endangered." As,
' however, this "patriot" had himself been rewarded with a Viscounty, two Earldoms,
' and two Marquessates for such his services, the reason for conferring a Dukedom on
· his infant son is not very convincing." See *The Complete Peerage*, viii. p. 129, note a.

NUGENT

for King James, by whom he was created K.G., 5th March 1726, and declared Prime Minister. He was afterwards sent on a mission to the Court of Madrid, to assist the Duke of Ormond in pressing for a new expedition to Scotland; and having joined the Spanish army as a volunteer in the attack on Gibraltar, May 1727, was by resolution of the House of Lords outlawed, 'tho' 'informally and irregularly,' for high treason, 3rd April 1729. Having, 'after a career of singular extravagance, become a ruined ' man,' he ultimately died in great poverty at the Monastery of the Franciscans at Pobled, in Catalonia, 31st May 1731, and was buried the next day in the church there,[1] when all his honours became extinct, except perhaps the Barony of Wharton.[2] He married first, 2nd March 1715, Martha, daughter of Major-General Richard Holmes. She died in Gerrard Street 14th, and was buried 22nd April 1726, at St. Anne's, Soho. He married secondly, 23rd or 26th July 1726, at Madrid, Maria Theresa O'Neill, said to have been daughter of Henry O'Brien, an Irish Colonel in the Spanish service, by Henrietta, daughter of Henry O'Neill. She died in Golden Square, London, 13th, and was buried at St. Pancras 20th February 1777.

NUGENT OF RIVERSTON, Baron [I].

1689
–
1715

I. THE HON. THOMAS NUGENT of Pallas, co. Galway, second son of Richard (Nugent), second Earl of Westmeath [I], by Mary, daughter of Sir Thomas Nugent of Moyrath, Baronet [I]; K.C. [I], 12th September 1685; third Puisne Justice of the King's Bench [I], 23rd April 1686, and Chief Justice thereof, 15th October 1687. By writ of summons, 3rd April 1689, to the Parliament of Dublin on 7th May following, he was created by King James II and VII (after the Revolution in England, but while he was still *de facto* as well as *de jure* King of Ireland[3])

---

[1] His epitaph is in *N. and Q.*, 9th series, i. p. 91.

[2] As to which see *The Complete Peerage*, from which many of the particulars given above are taken.

[3] The validity of this Peerage, created 3rd April 1689, depends on the fact as to whether or no at that date James II was legally King of Ireland. By the English Parliament his throne was declared to have been vacated on 11th December 1688; such declaration, however, was not made in Scotland till 4th April 1689, while in Ireland that King was in full possession of royal authority, the Government being solely carried on in his name, until the landing of General Schomberg in Ulster in August 1689, some four months after this creation. Indeed, James II appears to have been the

NUGENT

Baron Nugent of Riverston, co. Westmeath [I], with remainder to the heirs-male of his body. Lord Chief-Justice [I], 28th June 1689, and subsequently one of the Commissioners of the Treasury [I]. He remained faithful to King James, and was outlawed by the Parliament of William of Orange. He served in the army of King James throughout campaigns of 1690 and 1691, but subsequently under the provisions of the Treaty of Limerick, 3rd October 1691, he recovered his estates. He died May 1715. He married, 1680, the Hon. Mariana, daughter of Henry (Barnewall), second Viscount Barnewall of Kingsland [I], by his first wife, the Hon. Mary, eldest daughter of John (Netterville), second Viscount Netterville of Douth [I]. She was born 26th March 1662, and died 16th September 1735, at Pallas aforesaid.

II. HYACINTH RICHARD (NUGENT), second *Baron Nugent of Riverston*, son and heir, born about 1687. He was attainted for high treason 1694, when under seven years of age, but after having conformed to the established church [I], and having served in the army, he obtained an Act of Parliament in 1727 for his relief, whereby he recovered his estates some ten years later. He died *s.p.* 6th March 1737/8, in London, and was buried at Howth.

1715 – 1738

III. WILLIAM (NUGENT), third *Baron Nugent of Riverston*, brother and heir, succeeded 6th March 1737/8, and died 11th May 1756.

1738 – 1756

---

de facto King of Ireland even as late as the battle of Boyne in July 1690. It is to be noted that Charles II on 2nd July 1650, when he was King of Ireland alone (monarchy in England having been abolished on the deposition of Charles I), created Thomas Preston Viscount Tara [I], a dignity which was always fully recognised. Peerages made by a sovereign in possession have always been recognised by his successor, as by Edward IV in the case of those made by Henry VI, etc. The Peerage granted to Nugent was recognised not only by James II (who by patent 28th June 1689 styles the grantee 'Lord Baron Nugent of Riverston,' and subsequently LORD BARON OF RIVERSTON), but by General de Ginkell, Commander-in-Chief of King William's forces, who, in his letter of protection, 5th October 1691, styles him 'The Right Hon. ' Thomas, LORD RIVERSTON'; and also by the Commissioners of Irish forfeiture, who, in an order dated 5th July 1701, style him 'THE LORD RIVERSTON.' See 'Case of ' William Thomas Nugent of Pallas, co. Galway, Esq., claiming to be Baron Nugent ' of Riverston [I],' 1839? signed by 'W. W. Follet,' Solicitor-General 1834-1835, 1841-1844, Attorney-General 1844-1845, and 'J. Fleming' (*The Complete Peerage*, vi. pp. 108, 109).

133

O'BRIEN

1756 – 1814
IV. ANTHONY (NUGENT), fourth *Baron Nugent of Riverston*, third but only surviving son and heir, died 1814; will proved 10th February 1815 at Dublin.

1814 – 1851
V. WILLIAM THOMAS (NUGENT), fifth *Baron Nugent of Riverston*, son and heir, born 29th September 1773. About the year 1839 he claimed that peerage, but the case does not appear to have been legally referred. He died 6th September 1851.

1851 – 1879
VI. ANTHONY FRANCIS (NUGENT), sixth *Baron Nugent of Riverston*, son and heir, born 1st November 1805. On 1st May 1871 he succeeded his distant cousin, George Thomas John (Nugent), first Marquis of Westmeath [I], as ninth Earl of Westmeath (1621) and twenty-third Baron Delvin (1175 or 1486) [I], and established his right thereto in the House of Lords on 7th July following. He died 12th May 1879.

1879 – 1883
VII. WILLIAM ST. GEORGE (NUGENT), tenth Earl of Westmeath, twenty-fourth Baron Delvin, and seventh *Baron Nugent of Riverston*, eldest son and heir, born 28th November 1832, died 31st May 1883.

1883
VIII. ANTHONY FRANCIS (NUGENT), eleventh Earl of Westmeath, twenty-fifth Baron Delvin, and eighth *Baron Nugent of Riverston* [I], born 11th January 1870, succeeded his father 31st May 1883.

O'BRIEN, Baronet [I].

1723 – 17
I. JOHN O'BRIEN or OBRYAN was appointed by James III and VIII, on 13th October 1717, a Colonel of foot, and on 19th January 1723 he was created by the same King a *Knight* and *Baronet* [I]. On 21st July 1733 he was appointed Minister at the Court of Paris.

O'CALLAGHAN, Earl of [I].

17 –
I. [   ] O'CALLAGHAN is sometimes said to have been created by James III and VIII *Earl O'Callaghan*.

O'GARA

O'GARA, Baronet [I].

I. LIEUTENANT-COLONEL OLIVER O'GARA, M.P. for co. Sligo, 1689, was Colonel of a regiment of infantry with which he was present at the battle of Aughrim, 12th July 1691. He was afterwards appointed to be one of the hostages on the part of the Irish for the safe return from France of the Williamite ships by which the Irish troops were conveyed there pursuant to the Treaty of Limerick. He was released March 1692 and proceeded to France, where he was appointed Lieutenant-Colonel of the King's regiment of Foot Guards under Colonel William Dorington and afterwards Colonel of the Queen's dragoons. On 2nd May 1727 he was created by James III and VIII a *KNIGHT* and *BARONET* [I], with remainder to the heirs-male of his body. He married the Hon. Mary, widow of Richard Fleming of Staholmock and daughter of Randall (Fleming), twenty-first Baron of Slane [I], and only child by his first wife Eleanor, daughter of Sir Richard Barnewall, second Baronet [I]. He had issue :—[1]

1727 -

1. John Patrick O'Gara, baptized at St. Germains 25th October 1692, entered the Spanish service and died with the rank of Brigadier.
2. James Oliver O'Gara, baptized at St. Germains 15th December 1694, Colonel of the regiment of Hibernia in Spain.
3. [   ] O'Gara, Lieutenant-Colonel of the regiment of Irlandia in Spain, greatly distinguished himself at the battle of Veletri in Italy 1743, for which he was made a Commander of the Spanish Order of Calatrava.[1]
4. Charles O'Gara, baptized at St. Germains 16th July 1699,[2] having for godfather King James II and VII. He entered the service of Leopold, Duke of Lorraine,

---

[1] See O'Callaghan's *History of the Irish Brigade*, first edition, i. pp. 163-165.

[2] 'Ce jourd'hui, sixième juillet, 1699, a été baptisé dans la Chapelle du Château-Viel 'de ce lieu, par M. l'Abbé Ronchy, Aumônier du Roi et de la Reine d'Angleterre, 'Charles, né en legitime mariage, le quatrième du present mois, fils d'Olivier O'Gara, 'Colonel Irlandois et de Marie Flaming, ses père et mère, le parrain très-haut et très 'puissant Prince, Jacques second Roi d'Angleterre, qui a signé, en-presence et du 'consentement de Maître Michel Trinité, Prêtre Vicaire de cette Paroisse, lequel a 'apporté les saintes huiles, revêtu d'étole et de surplus, signé J. R., P. Ronchy, S. B. 'Telkeley, Trinité, Vicaire' (*Ibid.*).

OGLETHORPE

by whom he was appointed First Equerry to his two sons; and when the eldest was elected emperor, 13th September 1745, he was created by him an Imperial Councillor of State and Chamberlain and Grand Master of the Household to his sister the Princess Elizabeth Theresa. He was afterwards created a COUNT OF THE HOLY ROMAN EMPIRE and KNIGHT OF THE GOLDEN FLEECE, and died *s.p.* in opulent circumstances in Brussels, the end of 1775 or the beginning of 1776.[1]

5. Marie O'Gara, baptized at St. Germains 24th October 1696.

OGLETHORPE OF OGLETHORPE, Baron [E].

1717 — 1737

I. THEOPHILUS OGLETHORPE, second son of Sir Theophilus Oglethorpe of Westbrook Place, Godalming, Knight,[2] M.P., Major-General and First Equerry to King James II and VII, by Eleanor Wall of Tipperary, was born about 1682; succeeded his elder brother Louis at Westbrook, 1704; M.P. for Haslemere, 1708-1713/4. Lost the election that year, and being unsuccessful in a petition, he retired to the Continent. After spending some time in Ghent and Bruges he retired to Messina in 1714. After that he went to Paris, and was, 20th December 1717, by King James III and VIII, probably in recognition of his father's services, created *BARON OGLETHORPE OF OGLETHORPE* [E], with remainder to the heirs-male of his body, whom failing to James Oglethorpe, his brother, and the heirs-male of his body. He died, unmarried, in France about 1737 and before 1738.

1737 — 1785

II. JAMES EDWARD (OGLETHORPE), second *BARON OGLETHORPE OF OGLETHORPE*, brother and heir of the preceding,

---

[1] In Burke's *Extinct Peerages*, 1883, p. 217, however, Mary Fleming is said to have had by her second husband a son, Charles, who died unmarried 1785.

[2] Sir Theophilus was the son of Sutton Oglethorpe, who was sequestered by the Parliament for his loyalty to King Charles, and fined £20,000. He remained loyal to King James and was engaged with Sir John Fenwick in the North. In 1692 a warrant was issued for his arrest, but he managed to escape to France. After the Peace of Ryswick, however, he returned, and was M.P. for Haslemere 1698-1702. He had nine children, five sons and four daughters, who were all devoted Jacobites. See an article entitled 'The Loyal Oglethorpes' by A[lice] S[hield] in *The Royalist*, ix. pp. 41-45.

OGLETHORPE

born in London 22nd December 1696, and baptized the next day at St. Martin's in the Field; matriculated at Corpus Christi College, Oxford, 8th July 1714; entered the British army, 1710; was Aide-de-Camp to Lord Peterborough and on his staff of Embassy to Italy in 1717; succeeded his elder brother, Theophilus, then in exile, at Westbrook, 1718. One of the most distinguished of English philanthropists, M.P. for Haslemere, 1722-1754. He acted with the Jacobite Tories who supported Bishop Atterbury, and made his maiden speech in the House against the attainder of Bishop Atterbury, 1723;[1] exerted himself in the crusade against the horrible English gaols, 1728-1729. He founded the colony of Georgia, 1732, and governed it, 1732-1743, retaining, however, his seat in Parliament, passing backwards and forwards on several occasions. In 1736 he took the Wesleys up, 'whom he loved for their enthusiasm, though their ' intolerant temper led to ructions and parting.' In 1744 he was appointed, under Lord Stair, to oppose the expected French invasion. In 1745 he served in Wade's army, but fell under suspicion of corresponding with the Prince and of lingering on the road when ordered to pursue the retreating army from Derby. He was arrested at Godalming, tried by court-martial, and acquitted. He married, 15th September 1743, Elizabeth, only surviving daughter of Sir Nathan Wright, second Baronet [G B], by his fourth wife, Abigail, daughter of Samuel Trist of Culworth, Northampton, with whom he acquired the estate of Cranham, co. Essex. He died at Cranham, 1st July 1785, when his honours became extinct. His widow, who raised a handsome monument to his memory in Cranham Church, died 26th October 1787, and was buried with him.

[? OGLETHORPE], Countess of [I].

I. ANNE HENRIETTA OGLETHORPE, eldest daughter of Sir Theophilus Oglethorpe of Westbrook Place, Godalming, Knight, by Eleanor Wall, and sister of the first *BARON OGLETHORPE* [E], was born between 1680/1 and 1684, and was on the Revolution sent with her sister Eleanor (afterwards wife of Eugene Maurice de Béthesy, Marquis of Mezieres [F]) to France to be brought up at St. Germains as a Catholic. In 1704 she returned to England without a pass, and was consequently

1722 -
c. 1776

---

[1] *Dictionary of National Biography.*

OLIPHANT

arrested, which led to her connection with Harley. On 1st May 1707 she appeared at the Court of the Queen's Bench, charged with high treason, for trepanning Frances Shaftoe into France and trying to force her into the Catholic Church. She was 'continued upon her recognisances' and appeared again, 27th May, but was discharged by Anne's order, 14th June. On Harley's fall she returned to Paris, and appears to have been attached to the household of the Duchess of Portsmouth. On 6th October 1722 she was, by James III and VIII, created COUNTESS OF [? OGLETHORPE] [I], 'as a special mark of his Royal favour.' She returned to England some time before 1736, and lived at the town house and at Godalming, deep in the plots that went on so busily, until 1754, at least. In 1752 she is said to have concealed the Prince at Westbrook for some time. She was living in 1774, an old lady of ninety-one. There is no register of her death at Godalming or at St. James's, Piccadilly, where other members of the family were buried.

OLIPHANT, Baron [S].

1760 – 1767

I. LAURENCE OLIPHANT, Laird of Gask, Perthshire, son and heir of James Oliphant of the same, by Janet, daughter of the Rev. Anthony Murray of Woodend, Perthshire, born about 1692; was sent by his father in 1715 to join Lord Mar, and received a commission as Lieutenant in the Perthshire (Lord Rollo's) regiment of horse, 2nd October 1715. He was present at the battle of Sheriffmuir, 13th November 1715, and was one of the adjutants to the garrison of Scone during the residence there of King James III and VIII. He succeeded his father 1732, and continued to reside at Gask until the arrival of Prince Charles in 1745, when he joined him at Blair Athole. His tenants, however, refused to take up arms, and he laid an inhibition on their cornfields, which was removed by the Prince Regent on his arrival at Gask. On the advance into England he was sent back to Perth to undertake, with Lord Strathallan, the civil and military government of the North. He was present with his son at Falkirk and Culloden, and after remaining in hiding for some six months he succeeded in obtaining a passage to Sweden, where he landed, 10th October 1746, passing from thence to France. He was attainted, and Gask was seized and sold by the Government, but in 1753 was purchased

OLIPHANT

by some friends and presented to him. On the death of Francis (Oliphant), seventh Lord Oliphant [S], 19th September 1748, he laid claim to that title,[1] which, however, was assumed by Charles Oliphant of Langton. This Charles Oliphant died *s.p.* 3rd June 1751, when he appears to have become, if not before, *de jure* eleventh or twelfth BARON OLIPHANT [S]. On 14th July 1760 he was, by James III and VIII, created [2] *BARON OLIPHANT* [S],

[1] In May 1751 he appears to have petitioned King James for formal recognition as Lord Oliphant, as on 8th June of that year Edgar wrote to him from Albano as follows :—
  'I have received the letter you are pleased to write to me of the 3rd May, and have done myself the honour to lay it before the King. In return to which H.M. Commands me to tell you that as he does full justice to you and your Family's merits and sufferings, and has a particular value and esteem for yourself, it would be a pleasure to him to enter into what you propose, and do what would be agreeable to you, in relation to the Tittle you claim of Lord Oliphant. H.M. does not doubt from what you say on that head but that you may have a good right to that Tittle, But still as that may happen to be disputeable, if H.M. were to acknowledge you as Lord Oliphant, it could not be but in conformity to the Laws and Customs of our Country, *Salvo jure cujus-libet*, and if contraverted, a Parliament could only determine that matter. H.M. however under this restriction, will not oppose, if you should have a great mind for it, your assuming the Tittle of Lord Oliphant. But H.M. thinks the present not a proper time for anybody to assume Tittles of Honor, and therefore he is of opinion it would be proper to delay doing it, unless you have strong motives to the contrary, and such as may tend to your real advantages. You will see by this how much H.M. is inclined to favor you, and in writing it to you he directs me to make you a kind compliment in his name.
  'As to the Priority of Resignation of the Honors you have in your custody, it is a strong evidence in your behalf, but I do not see it can be of any use to you at present, for I don't find that there has ever been any such Resignation made in H.M.'s hands, or in those of the King his Father's, since the Revolution, and without a presedent one would not know how to go about an affair of that kind. Besides that, all Resignations before the Revolution must by Law have been made in the Resigner's lifetime, for the Act of Parliament (and a good one it is) for Resignations being made after the Resigner's death was, I think, in the Prince of Orange's time, and until that Act be confirmed by lawfull authority, which no doubt it will be, H.M. cannot receive such a Resignation.'—See Kington-Oliphant's *Jacobite Lairds of Gask,* p. 256.
[2] The preamble sets forth :—
  'Whereas we are fully sensible of the constant duty and attachment of our trusty and well-beloved Laurence Oliphant of Gask and of his family towards us, of which they have given us many and distinguished proofs, and in consequence of which the said Laurence and his son are both attainted by the present usurpation : And on this occasion it having been represented to us, that the title of Lord Oliphant was originally conferred on the representative of that family by King James the third of our ancient kingdom of Scotland, which continued in it till the time of our royal grandfather, King Charles the first, when the only daughter and child of the then Lord Oliphant married Mr. Douglas, a son of the Earl of Angus, who was thereupon created Lord Mordington ; with the precedency due to the Lord Oliphant ; and at the same time our royal grandfather created Patrick Oliphant, the heir-male of that family, Lord Oliphant, and to the heirs-male of his body, which are all now extinct, whose grandson Patrick Oliphant, Lord Oliphant, made a procuratory of resignation of that title and honour in favor of the late James Oliphant of Gask, father of the said Laurence, which procuratory never having been completed, the said title and honor is

OLIPHANT

with remainder to the heirs-male of his body, whom failing to the heirs-male of the body of James Oliphant, his father, and with precedency of the Barony of Oliphant, granted by Charles I in 1633 to Patrick Oliphant, and resigned in 1711 by his grandson in favour of the said James Oliphant, father of the said Laurence. He was permitted to return to Scotland in 1763, and died at Gask early in 1767, being buried in the kirkyard there. He married, 26th September 1719, the LADY Amelia Anne Sophia, second daughter of William (Murray), first EARL and second Baron Nairne [S]. She was born about 1699 and died at Gask 18th March 1774. He had issue :—

1. Laurence Oliphant, MASTER OF OLIPHANT, his heir.
2. HON. Margaret Oliphant, married in Perth, June 1748, Peter Græme of Inchbraikie, Captain of the Scots Brigade in the Dutch service.
3. HON. Janet Oliphant, married in the Swedish Chapel at Paris, 1st January 1758, SIR William Macgregor Drummond of Balhaldies, second BARONET [S], Chief of the Macgregors, and had issue. She died Friday, 8th December 1758, and was buried 11th December in the Protestant burial-ground in Paris, near the Port de St. Martin.

1767
—
1792

II. LAURENCE (OLIPHANT), second BARON OLIPHANT, son and heir of the preceding, born at Williamstoun 25th May 1724; joined the Jacobite forces with his father, and was Aide-de-Camp to Prince Charles at the battle of Prestonpans. He was with his father at Falkirk and Culloden, and escaped with him, October 1746. He refused to apply for a pardon, and continued to reside abroad until 1763, when he returned with his father, whom he succeeded four years later. He remained loyal to the Stuarts to the end, and never accepted nor recognised the Hanoverian Government. He died at Gask, 1st January 1792, and was buried there. He had married at Versailles, 29th May/ 9th June 1755, Margaret, only daughter of SIR Duncan Robertson

' now at our disposition : And we being very desirous to give the said Laurence Oliphant,
' descended from a second son of the first Lord Oliphant, a special mark of our royal
' favor for his distinguished merit, and for his sufferings in our cause and service,
' have therefore thought it proper to confer and bestow on him, and the heirs-male
' of his family after mentioned, the title of honor of Lord Oliphant, with the precedency
' from the date of the patent given by our royal grandfather, King Charles the first, to
' Patrick then made Lord Oliphant.' The patent is printed in full in Kington-Oliphant's
Jacobite Lairds of Gask, p. 310.

OLIPHANT

of Struan, second *BARONET*, by the *LADY* May, fourth daughter of William (Nairne), first *EARL* and second Lord Nairne [S], she being then aged fifteen years and a half and he thirty-one. She died at Gask, 4th November 1774. They had issue:—

1. Laurence Oliphant, *MASTER OF OLIPHANT*, born in London 27th September 1756, died young.
2. Laurence Oliphant, *MASTER OF OLIPHANT*, his heir.
3. *HON.* Charles Oliphant, born at Gask, and baptized 9th June 1772; died 1797.
4. *HON.* Marjory Ann Mary Oliphant, born at Gask 22nd October 1762, baptized at Muthil; married Dr. Alexander Stewart of Bonskied.
5. *HON.* Amelia Oliphant, born at Gask 1765; married Charles Stewart of Dalguise, and had issue.
6. *HON.* Carolina Oliphant, born at Gask 16th August 1766, and named after the King;[1] the poetess, 'the ' noblest Oliphant of them all.' She married, June 1806, William (Nairne), third *EARL* of and fifth Baron Nairne [S], and died at Gask, 27th October 1845, aged seventy-nine, leaving issue.
7. *HON.* Margaret Oliphant, born at Gask 1770; married Alexander Keith of Ravelston.

III. LAURENCE (OLIPHANT), third *BARON OLIPHANT*, son and heir of the preceding, born at Gask June 1768; succeeded his father, 1st January 1792. In 1794 he joined the Perthshire Light Dragoons, and the following year (29th May) was appointed Captain in the Perthshire regiment of Fencibles. He died at Paris, 3rd July 1819,[2] and was buried in Père la Chaise. He married Christian Robertson, heiress of Ardblair in Perthshire, daughter of Dr. Robertson, sometime surgeon in the Scottish Brigade in the Dutch service. He had issue:—

1. Laurence Oliphant, *MASTER OF OLIPHANT*, his heir.
2. *HON.* James Blair Oliphant, successor to his brother.
3. *HON.* Rachel Oliphant, born at Edinburgh, 27th January 1797;[3] died unmarried 1864.

1792
-
1819

---

[1] Her birth is set down in a list of births and deaths, reaching from 1668 to 1774, in her father's hand: 'Carolina, after the King, at Gask, Aug. 16th, 1766' (*Jacobite Lairds of Gask*). [2] *Scots Magazine*, N.S., v. p. 200.
[3] For the dates relating to the children of the 3rd *Lord Oliphant*, which are taken from the family Bible at Gask, the Editor is indebted to Mrs. Gregson-Ellis, *née* Kington-Oliphant.

O'ROURKE

4. *Hon.* Margaret Oliphant, born at Gask 21st August 1799; married, 26th May 1830, Thomas Kington, Esq., of Charlton House, Somerset, who died 1857. She died 1839, having had a family of three sons and one daughter, of whom the eldest was the late Thomas Laurence Kington-Oliphant of Gask, J.P., D.L.
5. *Hon.* Christian Oliphant, born at Gask, 12th October 1800; died unmarried, 28th June 1830.
6. *Hon.* Harriet Oliphant, born at Gask, 20th November 1801; died there, August 1822.
7. *Hon.* Amelia Oliphant, born at Gask, 22nd December 1802; died there, October 1820.
8. *Hon.* Caroline Oliphant, born at Gask, 16th January 1807; died unmarried, 9th February 1831; buried at Clifton.

1819 — 1824

IV. LAURENCE (OLIPHANT), fourth BARON OLIPHANT, elder son and heir of the preceding, born at Gask 6th May 1798; succeeded his father 3rd July 1819, and died unmarried 31st December 1824.

1824 — 1847

V. JAMES BLAIR (OLIPHANT), fifth BARON OLIPHANT, brother and next heir of the preceding, was born at Christian Bank, near Edinburgh, 3rd March 1804; succeeded his brother, 31st December 1824; was a J.P. and D.L. for co. Perth, and was, 18th August 1839, served heir-male of Francis, tenth Lord Oliphant [S]. He married, 20th October 1840, Henrietta, daughter and heir of James Gillespie Graham of Orchill, co. Perth. She died December 1886. He died *s.p.* at Leamington, 7th December 1847, and was buried in the chapel at Gask, when the whole of the male issue of James Oliphant of Gask, father of the first BARON OLIPHANT of the 1760 creation, became extinct, as did the BARONY.

O'ROURKE, Baron[1] [I].

1727 —

I. OWEN O'ROURKE of Carha, co. Leitrim, was on 24th May 1727 created by King James III and VIII BARON O'ROURKE

---

[1] In the warrant appointing Le Sieur Smidt agent to the Tribunal of the Council of Bohemia, dated 6th May 1741, mention is made of 'EARL O'ROURKE,' our Minister and Plenipotentiary at the Court of Vienna, but as no mention of his having been created an Earl occurs in the new patent of the Viscounty of Breffney, given him July 1742, this is probably a mistake.

O'SULLIVAN

OF *CARHA*, co. Leitrim. On 31st July 1731 he was further created VISCOUNT OF BREFFNEY in Connaught [I]. See '*BREFFNEY*,' VISCOUNT.

O'SULLIVAN, Baronet [I].

I. JOHN WILLIAM O'SULLIVAN, of the O'Sullivans of Munster, born in co. Kerry 1700; educated in Paris for the Catholic priesthood, and entered the French army under Marshal Maillabois, with whom he served in Corsica, 1739, and afterwards in Italy on the Rhine; and about 1744 was admitted to the Household of the young Prince of Wales, to whom he was appointed Adjutant-General. He landed with him at Lochnanuagh, 5th August 1745, and through the whole campaign he remained his chief adviser in both civil and military affairs. He commanded with Cameron of Lochiel the nine hundred Highlanders who captured Edinburgh, 16th September, and became the leader of what was known as the Irish Party. He was Quartermaster-General of the Prince's army, and the mutual jealousy between him and Lord George Murray led to constant recriminations. After Culloden he was one of the small retinue whom the Prince chose to accompany him in his wanderings, and he remained with him until the Prince's escape with Flora MacDonald. He then managed to escape, 1st October 1746, to France in a French cutter under Captain Dumont, and he immediately proceeded to Versailles, to urge forward means for the Prince's safety. He was KNIGHTED by King James between 19th December 1746 and 17th April 1747.[1] He is said to have previously been created by the Prince Regent Duke of Munster [I].[2] On 9th May 1753 he was, as 'Sir John O'Sullivan, knighted 'some years ago for his attachment to us and his services to 'Charles, Prince of Wales,' created by James III and VIII a

1753 – 17

---

[1] On 19th December 1746 Prince Charles writes to his father at Rome: 'O'Sullivan 'showed me the letter Your Majesty did him the honour to write him. I cannot let 'slip this occasion to do him justice, by saying I really think he deserves Your 'Majesty's favour'; to which the King replies, 17th April 1747, saying that he had made him a Knight at H.R.H.'s request and against his 'present rule,' adding that for the present he has desired O'Sullivan not to mention his Knighthood.

[2] Mr. O'Sullivan [*i.e. Sir* John Louis, fifth and last *Baronet*] writes: 'I have been 'told by an Irish gentleman' (he afterwards gave his name as Samuel Daly Lauktree, his brother-in-law), 'who claimed to know, that Charles Edward (who was Regent for 'his father James) conferred on General O'Sullivan the title of DUKE OF MUNSTER.' *Ex inform.* R. T. Nichol, to whom and to Mrs. John Louis Sullivan the Author is indebted for the account given above of *Sir* John O'Sullivan's descendants.

O'SULLIVAN

Knight and *Baronet* [I], with remainder to the heirs-male of his body. He married Louisa, daughter of Thomas FitzGerald by Louisa O'Connor.

17
–
1824

II. *Sir* THOMAS HERBERT O'SULLIVAN, second *Baronet*, only son and heir. He was an officer in the Irish Brigade in the French service, but having horsewhipped his superior officer, the notorious Paul Jones, he fled to America and entered the British service under Sir Henry Clinton at New York. He served through the American War until the conclusion of peace in 1783, when he entered the Dutch service, in which he continued till his death in Holland, 1824. He married first, in New York, Mary, daughter of Thomas M'Cready, by his wife, Barbara, daughter of [   ] Miller. He married secondly, about 1818 or 1820, Mademoiselle Adriane des Portes, who died *s.p.* about 1833. He had issue a son and daughter :—
  1. *Sir* John William Thomas Gerald, his heir.
  2. Barbara O'Sullivan.

1824
–
1825

III. *Sir* JOHN WILLIAM THOMAS GERALD O'SULLIVAN, third *Baronet*, only son and heir. He was educated at Montreal and settled in the United States, becoming a naturalised American citizen. He was U.S. Consul-General to the Barbary States, and perished in a shipwreck in May 1825. He married Mary, daughter of the Rev. Samuel Rowley of Bower End and Fenton Vivian, co. Salop, and had issue :—
  1. *Sir* William, his heir.
  2. *Sir* John Louis, successor to his brother.
  3. Thomas Samuel O'Sullivan, married 1844 Mary Lamed, daughter of [   ] Allen, and had issue two sons, Herbert and Lewis, who died in infancy. He died *s.p.* November 1855.
  4. Charles Herbert FitzGerald O'Sullivan, died unmarried May 1846.
  5. Mary Juana O'Sullivan, married Cristoval Madan, died April 1867.
  6. Adelaide O'Sullivan, sometime Superior of the House of Discalced Carmelites in Guatemala as Mother Adelaide, whence she and her nuns were expelled in 1872 by President Barrios. They finally settled at Leon in Spain, where she died, 1893.

PERTH

IV. *Sir* WILLIAM O'SULLIVAN, fourth *Baronet*, eldest son and heir, succeeded his father 1825. A Lieutenant in the U.S. navy. He died unmarried, the man-of-war on which he sailed from New York never being heard of again.

1825
-
18

V. *Sir* JOHN LOUIS O'SULLIVAN, fifth *Baronet*, brother and heir, born at Gibraltar November 1813; educated at Sorize, France, and Westminster School; was for some time (1854-1858) American Minister at Lisbon. He died *s.p.* in New York, 24th March 1895, when the *Baronetcy*, together with any other title which may have been conferred on his ancestor, the first *Baronet*, became extinct. He married, 21st October 1846, Susan, daughter of Dr. John Kearny Rodgers of New York, by his wife, Mary Ridgeley, daughter of Captain John Ridgeley Nicholson of Baltimore. *Lady O'Sullivan* still survives.

18
-
1895

PERTH, Duke of [S].

I. JAMES (DRUMMOND), fourth EARL OF PERTH (1605), seventh LORD DRUMMOND (1488) [S], eldest son and heir of James (Drummond), third Earl of Perth, by Lady Anne, daughter of George (Gordon), second Marquis of Huntly [S], born 1648; educated at St. Andrews; succeeded his father 2nd June, and was served heir to him 1st October 1675; P.C. 1678; Justice-General and an extra Lord of Session, 16th November 1682; High Chancellor [S], 1684-1688; K.T. (being one of the eight original Knights of that Order), 29th May 1687. He is said to have had a *novodamus*, 17th December 1687, (on resignation) of his dignities, creating him EARL OF PERTH, LORD DRUMMOND, STOBHALL, and MONTEFEX [S], with remainder, failing heirs-male of his and of his brother's body, to the heirs-male of the second Earl. On the Revolution he was imprisoned for four years at Kirkcaldy and Stirling, but was released on warrant, 4th August 1693, on condition of leaving the kingdom under a penalty of £5000. He joined the exiled King at St. Germains, by whom he was, on 19th August 1696, appointed Governor to the young Prince of Wales, and by whose testamentary directions[1] he was,

1701
-
1716

---

[1] See *The Complete Peerage*, vi. p. 236. Other dates given for this creation are 1692, 1695, and 1696.

PERTH

before 17th October 1701,[1] created by James III and VIII *DUKE OF PERTH, MARQUIS OF DRUMMOND, EARL OF STOBHALL, VISCOUNT CARGILL*, and *BARON CONCRAIG* [S], with remainder to his heirs-male whatsoever. He was confirmed in his appointment as Governor of the King by the Queen-Regent, 17th October 1701, and on 14th February 1703 he was made a Gentleman of the Bedchamber; *K.G.*, 21st June 1706. In 1701 he was recognised as a Duke in France by Louis XIV. He was afterwards Chamberlain to Queen Mary of Modena, and is said to have been created a Knight of the Golden Fleece by the King of Spain. He died at St. Germains, 11th May 1716, aged sixty-eight, and was buried in the Scots Chapel at Paris.[2] He married first, 18th January 1670, Lady Jane, daughter of William (Douglas), first Marquis of Douglas [S], by his second wife, Lady Mary, daughter of George (Gordon), first Marquis of Huntly [S]. He married, secondly, Lilias, Dowager-Countess of Tullibardine [S], daughter of Sir James Drummond of Machany. She died about 1685. He married thirdly, the same year, Lady Mary, widow of Adam Urquhart, daughter of Lewis (Gordon), third Marquis of Huntly [S], by Mary, daughter of Sir John Grant of Freuchie. She, who was made a Lady of the Bedchamber in Ordinary to Queen Mary of Modena, 30th October 1701, died 13th March 1726, in her eightieth year, her heart being buried with her husband.

1716
–
1720

II. JAMES (DRUMMOND), second *DUKE OF PERTH*, son and heir by first wife, born about 1674; educated at the Scots College in Paris. He accompanied King James to Ireland in 1689, and afterwards joined Lord Mar in 1715. He escaped to France with King James, 6th February, and was attainted 17th February 1716. *K.T.*, 'as Marquis of Drummond,' March 1705, and Master of the Horse. He succeeded his father 11th May 1716, but in consequence of his attainder he was not recognised by the Government. He died at Paris, 17th April 1720, aged forty-six, and was buried in the Scots College aforesaid. He married (contract dated 5th August 1706) Lady Jean, daughter of George (Gordon), first Duke of Gordon [S], by Lady Elizabeth, daughter of Henry (Howard), sixth Duke of Norfolk [E]. She, who was imprisoned in Edinburgh Castle from February to

---

[1] A warrant of this date is addressed to him as Duke of Perth.
[2] See *Coll. Top. et Gen.*, vii. pp. 32-42, for inscriptions in the Scots College at Paris.

PERTH

November 1746 for her part in the '45, died at Stobhall, 30th January 1773, aged about ninety.

III. JAMES (DRUMMOND), third *DUKE OF PERTH*, elder son and heir, born at Drummond Castle 11th May 1713; educated at the Scots College at Douay, and afterwards at Paris. He succeeded his father, 17th April 1720, having previously, under a disposition executed by his father, 28th August 1713, become possessed of the family estates. He was one of the seven who in 1740 formed the Association for the Restoration of the House of Stuart, and he took a prominent part in the '45. He was badly wounded at the battle of Culloden, and died unmarried on board the French frigate *La Bellone*, 13th May 1746, on his thirty-third birthday, and was buried at sea. He was attainted, under the name of 'James Drummond, taking upon himself the 'title of Duke of Perth,' by Act of Parliament 1745, unless he surrendered on or before 12th July 1746, but died before the latter date as aforesaid.

1720 — 1746

IV. JOHN (DRUMMOND), fourth *DUKE OF PERTH*, etc., only brother and heir, born about 1716; educated at Douay; was Colonel of the Scots Royal Regiment in the French service. He brought his regiment to Scotland in 1745, and served with it throughout the campaign. After Culloden he made his escape to France. He was attainted 12th July 1746. He afterwards served under Marshal Saxe, and died unmarried of a fever contracted at the siege of Bergen-op-Zoom in 1747, and was buried in the Chapel of the English Nuns at Antwerp.

1746 — 1747

V. JOHN (DRUMMOND), fifth *DUKE OF PERTH*, etc., uncle of the half-blood and heir-male, being son of the first *DUKE* by his second wife. He was born about 1680, and died *s.p.* at Edinburgh, 27th October 1757, being buried in Holyrood Chapel.

1747 — 1757

VI. EDWARD (DRUMMOND), sixth *DUKE OF PERTH*, etc., brother of the half-blood and heir-male, being son of the first *DUKE* by his third wife. He was born about 1690, and died *s.p.* at Paris, 7th February 1760, when the whole of the male issue of the first *DUKE* and fourth Earl became extinct.

1757 — 1760

PERTH

1760 – 1781

VII. JAMES (LUNDIN, afterwards (1760) DRUMMOND), seventh *Duke* and tenth Earl of Perth, cousin and heir-male, being son and heir of Robert Lundin of Lundin, Fife, by Anne, daughter of Sir James Inglis of Cramond, which Robert was the eldest son of John (Drummond), first *Duke of Melfort*, K.G., K.T. (by his first wife), who was younger brother to the first *Duke of Perth*. He was born 6th November 1707; succeeded his elder brother, John Lundin, 9th October 1735, in the estate of Lundin, and his second cousin, Edward, sixth *Duke of Perth*, as *Duke* and Earl of Perth, but only assumed the latter title. He died at Stobhall, 18th July 1781, aged seventy-four, and was buried at Innerpeffray.

1781 – 1800

VIII. JAMES (DRUMMOND, formerly LUNDIN), eighth *Duke* and eleventh Earl of Perth, but did not assume either title, third and youngest, but only surviving son and heir, was born at Lundin House 12th February 1744; obtained the restoration of the estates forfeited in 1745, in 1783, and on 26th October 1797; was created by George III Lord Perth, Baron Drummond of Stobhall, co. Perth [G B]. He died *s.p.m.s.* at Drummond Castle, 2nd July 1800, when his Barony [G B] became extinct. He was buried at Innerpeffray.

1800 – 1800

IX. JAMES LEWIS (DRUMMOND), ninth *Duke* and twelfth Earl of Perth, also fourth *Duke of Melfort*, cousin and heir-male, being son and heir of James, third *Duke of Melfort*, who was son and heir of John, second *Duke of Melfort*, younger son (by his second wife) of John, first *Duke of Melfort*, which John was only brother to James; first *Duke of Perth*. He was born about 1750, and succeeded his cousin as above, 2nd July 1800. He died *s.p.* at Lepe in Spain, September 1800.

1800 – 1840

X. CHARLES EDWARD (DRUMMOND), tenth *Duke of Perth* and fifth *Duke of Melfort*, next brother and heir. He was born 1st January 1752, and died unmarried at Rome, 9th April 1840.

1840 – 1902

XI. GEORGE (DRUMMOND), eleventh *Duke of Perth*, Marquis of Drummond, Earl of Stobhall, Viscount Cargill, and Baron Concraig (1701), fourteenth Earl of Perth (1605),

PERTH

sixth DUKE OF MELFORT, MARQUIS OF FORTH, EARL OF ISLA AND BURNTISLAND, VISCOUNT OF RICKERTON, LORD CASTLEMAINS AND GALSTON (1694), EARL OF MELFORT, VISCOUNT OF FORTH, LORD DRUMMOND OF RICCARTOUN, CASTLEMAINS, and GILSTOUN (1686 and 1688), and VISCOUNT OF MELFORT and LORD DRUMMOND OF GILSTOUN (1685), seventeenth LORD DRUMMOND (1488) [all S], and sixth BARON CLEWORTH (1689) [E], also sixth DUKE OF MELFORT (1701), seventh COUNT OF LUSSAN (*c.* 1628), and BARON OF VALROSE (?) [all F], nephew and heir-male, being only surviving son and heir of LORD Leon Maurice Drummond, by Marie Elizabeth Luce de Longuemarre, which LORD Leon was fourth and youngest son of James, third DUKE OF MELFORT abovenamed. He was born 6th May 1807, and baptized at St. Marylebone; succeeded his uncle 9th April 1840; established his right to his French titles in 1841; and, having obtained the reversal of the attainders of his ancestor, 28th June 1853, was on 19th July following declared to be entitled to all the pre-Revolution peerages of his family. He died *s.p.s.m.* 28th February 1902, when the Earldom of Melfort and minor titles conferred with it [S], and the County of Lussan [F], devolved on his only surviving daughter; the DUKEDOM OF MELFORT and its minor titles [S], and the Dukedom of Melfort [F], and the BARONY OF CLEWORTH [E], became extinct; and the DUKEDOM OF PERTH (1701), the Earldom of Perth (1605) (together with their minor titles), and the Barony of Drummond, passed to his heir-male as below.

XII. WILLIAM HUNTLY (DRUMMOND), twelfth DUKE OF PERTH, MARQUIS OF DRUMMOND, EARL OF STOBHALL, VISCOUNT CARGILL, and BARON CONCRAIG (1701), fourteenth EARL OF PERTH (1605), eighteenth LORD DRUMMOND (1488), also eleventh VISCOUNT STRATHALLAN (1686), and BARON DRUMMOND OF CROMLIX (1686), and fourteenth LORD MADERTY (1609) [all S], cousin and heir-male, being the elder son and heir of James David (Drummond), tenth Viscount Strathallan, who was the heir-male of James (Drummond), first Lord Maderty, the second son (but the only one whose issue then survived) of David, second Lord Drummond, which David was, through his elder son, Patrick, third Lord Drummond, the grandfather of the first Earl of Perth. He was born 5th August 1871, succeeded his father as Viscount Strathallan, etc., 5th December 1893, and his

1902

PORTLAND

cousin as Earl and *Duke* of Perth, etc., but has not assumed either of those latter titles.

PORTLAND, Earl of [E].

1689?
–
1698

I. Sir EDWARD HERBERT, third and youngest son of Sir Edward Herbert, Lord Keeper of the Great Seal to Charles II (1653-1654), by Margaret, widow of the Hon. Thomas Carey, daughter of Sir Thomas Smith, Master of the Requests, born about 1648; scholar of Winchester aged thirteen, 1661; Probationer fellow of New College, Oxford, August 1665; B.A., 21st April 1669; entered the Middle Temple and called to the Bar, K.C. [I], 31st July 1677; Chief-Justice of Chester, 25th October 1683; knighted at Whitehall, 10th February 1684; Attorney-General to the Duke of York and Albany, January 1684/5, and on the latter's accession, 6th February following, to the Queen; M.P. for Ludlow, 15th April 1685; P.C. [E], 16th October 1685; Chief-Justice of the King's Bench [E], 23rd October 1685, and of the Common Pleas, April 1687. On the Revolution he remained loyal to his King, whom he accompanied to France and afterwards to Ireland; P.C. [I], April 1689. He was included in the Bill of Attainder, which however lapsed, owing to the early prorogation of Parliament; but his estates were confiscated and given to his brother Arthur, who, having espoused the opposite side, had been created Earl of Torrington by William of Orange. On the King's return to St. Germains he was created EARL OF PORTLAND [E], and appointed Lord Chancellor [E]. He died *s.p.* at St. Germains, November 1698.[1]

POWIS, Duke of [E].

1689
–
1696

I. WILLIAM (HERBERT), third BARON POWIS OF POWIS, co. Montgomery (1629), and second BARONET (1622) [E], only son and heir of Percy (Herbert), second Baron Powis, by Elizabeth, sister (and in her issue co-heir) of William (Craven), first Earl of Craven [E], eldest surviving daughter of Sir William Craven, Lord Mayor of London; born 1617; succeeded his father 19th January 1667; and on 4th April 1674 was created by Charles II

---

[1] *Dictionary of National Biography.*

POWIS

EARL OF POWIS, co. Montgomery [E]. He was arrested (25th October), together with his wife, on suspicion of being concerned in the alleged Popish Plot, and was imprisoned in the Tower, 1679-1684. By James II and VII he was, 17th July 1686, made a P. C., and on 24th March 1687 created VISCOUNT MONTGOMERY and MARQUIS OF POWIS [E]. On the Revolution he remained loyal to King James; was outlawed 9th October 1689, and was one of those exempted from the Act of Indemnity of 1690. He had previously, 12th January 1689,[1] been created by James *MARQUIS OF MONTGOMERY* and *DUKE OF POWIS* [E], by whom he was also made a P. C. [I], and in 1690 Lord Chamberlain of the Household, K.G. 19th April 1692, and a Commissioner of the Household 24th December 1694 and 24th December 1695. He died at St. Germains-en-Laye 2nd June 1696, and was buried there.[2] He married, 2nd August 1654, at St. Giles'-in-the-Field, Lady Elizabeth, younger daughter of Edward (Somerset), second Marquis of Worcester [E], by his first wife, Elizabeth, daughter of Sir William Dormer. She was governess to the children of King James, June 1688-March 1691. She died at St. Germains-en-Laye, 11th March 1691, and was buried there.

II. WILLIAM (HERBERT), second *DUKE OF POWIS*, only son and heir, born about 1666; styled, after 1689 to 1696, *MARQUIS OF MONTGOMERY*; Colonel of a regiment of foot, 1687. After the Revolution he was imprisoned in the Tower from May to November 1689, and on his release he followed King James to France, rewards being offered for his apprehension in 1690 and 1696. Colonel of a regiment of horse, 'to be raised in 'England,' 10th March 1692. He succeeded his father 2nd June 1696, and was outlawed December following; and being arrested, was again imprisoned in the Tower till June 1697. He was again arrested in 1715, but after the failure of that rising he made his peace with the Government, and was allowed to take

1696 - 1745

---

[1] This is the date given in the memoir of him in the *Dictionary of National Biography*, but the patent is not among the *Stuart Papers*. There is, however, a warrant to him as Lord Chamberlain of the Household on the 1st June 1689, in which he is styled *Duke of Powis*.

[2] Macaulay says of him that he was 'a sincere Roman Catholic, and yet generally 'allowed by candid Protestants to be an honest man and a good Englishman,' and that he 'was an eminent member of the British aristocracy, and his countrymen 'disliked him as little as they disliked any conspicuous Papist.' Quoted in *The Complete Peerage*, vi. p. 296.

RAMSAY

his seat in the House of Lords as Marquis of Powis, 8th October 1722. He died at Hendon, Middlesex, 22nd October 1745, and was buried there on 28th of that month. He married, about 1695, Mary, eldest surviving daughter and co-heir of Sir Thomas Preston of Furness, third Baronet [E], by the Hon. Mary, daughter of Caryll (Molyneux), third Viscount Molyneux of Maryborough [I]. She died 8th January 1724, and was buried at Hendon on the 11th.

1745 — 1748

III. WILLIAM (HERBERT), third DUKE OF POWIS, etc., elder son and heir, born about 1698; succeeded his father 22nd October 1745; and died unmarried 8th March 1748, aged about fifty, when all his honours became extinct. He was buried at Hendon 15th March following.[1]

RAMSAY, Baronet [S].

1735 — 17

I. ANDREW MICHAEL RAMSAY, Knight of the Military Order of St. Lazarus in France, and Governor of the King's nephew, the Prince of Turenne, was on the 23rd March 1735 created by King James III and VIII a KNIGHT and BARONET [S], with remainder to the heirs-male of his body.

RANNOCH, Duke of [S].

1717 — 1746

I. WILLIAM (MURRAY), third MARQUIS OF ATHOLL, EARL OF TULLIBARDINE, VISCOUNT OF BALQUHIDDER, LORD MURRAY, BALVANY, and GASK (1676), fourth EARL OF ATHOLL (1629), seventh EARL OF TULLIBARDINE (1606), and LORD MURRAY OF TULLIBARDINE (1604), also (possibly) second DUKE OF ATHOLL, MARQUIS OF TULLIBARDINE, EARL OF STRATHTAY and STRATHARDLE, VISCOUNT OF BALWHIDDER, GLENALMOND, and GLENLYON, and LORD MURRAY, BALVENIE, and GASK, all in Perthshire (1703) [S], generally styled Marquis of Tullibardine, second but elder surviving son and heir of John (Murray), first Duke (1703) and second Marquis (1676) of Atholl, by his first

---

[1] His only brother, Lord Edward Herbert, married, 7th July 1734, Lady Henrietta Waldegrave, and died the November following, leaving a posthumous daughter, Barbara, who married, 30th March 1751, Henry Arthur (Herbert), (who had some three years previously, viz. 27th May 1748, been created) Earl of Powis [G B].

RANNOCH

wife, Lady Katharine, daughter of William (Douglas, afterwards Hamilton), first Duke of Hamilton [S], born about 1688, and was for some time in the navy. He was one of the first to join Lord Mar in 1715, and he was consequently attainted the following year, but managed to escape to France. On 1st February 1717 he was, as 'William, Marquis of Tullybardin,'[1] created by James III and VIII a Duke and Peer of Parliament as[2] *DUKE OF RANNOCH, MARQUIS OF BLAIR, EARL OF GLEN TILT, VISCOUNT OF GLENSHIE*, and *LORD STRATHBRAN* [S], with remainder to his heirs-male. In 1719 he landed in the north of Scotland with a Spanish force, but after the battle of Glenshiel, 18th June 1719, he was again obliged to retire to France, a reward of £2000 being offered for his capture. On 26th June 1721 he was made by King James Lord High Admiral of Scotland. On the death of his father, 14th November 1724, he assumed the title of Duke of Atholl, and (though this was a creation of Anne's) was acknowledged as such by King James.[3] The family titles were, however, also assumed, in accordance with an Act of Parliament of 1715, by his next younger brother, Lord James Murray. On the 1st February 1736 he also became *de jure* Sovereign of the Isle of Man and fifth Baron Strange (1628) [E], though these titles and estates were also taken possession of by his brother. After remaining in exile for upwards of twenty-six years he was one of the seven who accompanied Prince Charles to Scotland in July 1745, and it was he who, 'tottering with age and infirmities and supported by an attendant 'on each side,' unfurled the royal standard at Glenfinnan on 19th August 1745. After the battle of Culloden he surrendered himself, 27th April 1746, and was committed a prisoner to the Tower on 21st June, being then very ill. He died unmarried there 9th July following, aged fifty-eight, and was buried in the chapel of the Tower. On his death all his honours devolved on his next brother, as under.

II. JAMES (MURRAY), second *DUKE OF RANNOCH*, etc. 1746 (1717), also second or third DUKE OF ATHOLL (1703), etc., next – 1764

---

[1] It will be observed that on this occasion James, contrary to his invariable custom, recognises a post-Revolution creation.

[2] The titles which are left blank in the Warrant Book are taken from the Duke of Atholl's privately printed *Atholl Chronicles*.

[3] See note 1. Is it possible that the first Duke obtained a confirmation of his Dukedom from King James?

RANNOCH

brother and heir, born about 1690, and on his father's death, 14th November 1724, assumed the family honours, to which, however, he did not become *de jure* entitled until the death of his elder brother, 9th July 1746, when he also became second DUKE OF RANNOCH, etc. He died *s.p.m.* 8th January 1764, at Dunkeld, when the Barony of Strange (1628) [E] devolved on his only daughter, and his other honours passed to his nephew.

1764 – 1774
III. JOHN (MURRAY), third DUKE OF RANNOCH, DUKE OF ATHOLL, etc., nephew and heir-male, being son and heir of Lord George Murray (Lieutenant-General of the forces under the Prince Regent in 1745-1746), by Amelia, only surviving daughter and heir of James Murray of Glencarse, was born 6th May 1729, and died at Dunkeld 5th November 1774.

1774 – 1830
IV. JOHN (MURRAY), fourth DUKE OF RANNOCH, DUKE OF ATHOLL, etc., eldest son and heir, born 30th June 1755, succeeded his father 5th November 1774, and his mother, as Baron Strange [E], 13th October 1805. On 18th August 1786 he was created by George III BARON MURRAY OF STANLEY, co. Gloucester, and EARL STRANGE [G B]. K.T., 4th April 1800. He died 29th September 1830.

1830 – 1846
V. JOHN (MURRAY), fifth DUKE OF RANNOCH, DUKE OF ATHOLL, etc., son and heir, born 26th June 1778, and died unmarried 14th September 1846.

1846 – 1864
VI. GEORGE AUGUSTUS FREDERICK JOHN (MURRAY), sixth DUKE OF RANNOCH, DUKE OF ATHOLL, etc., nephew and heir, being son and heir of James (Murray), first Lord Glenlyon (1821) [U K], who was second son of the fourth Duke of Atholl, was born 20th September 1814, and died at Blair Castle 16th January 1864, and was buried in the church there on the 25th.

1864
VII. JOHN JAMES HUGH HENRY (MURRAY, afterwards (1865) STEWART-MURRAY), seventh DUKE OF RANNOCH, MARQUIS OF BLAIR, EARL OF GLEN TILT, VISCOUNT OF GLENSHIE, and LORD STRATHBRAN (1717), seventh or eighth DUKE OF ATHOLL, MARQUIS OF TULLIBARDINE, EARL OF STRATHTAY and STRATHARDLE, VISCOUNT OF BALWHIDDER, GLENALMOND,

REDMOND

and GLENLYON, and LORD MURRAY, BALVENIE, and GASK (1703), ninth MARQUIS OF ATHOLL, EARL OF TULLIBARDINE, VISCOUNT OF BALQUHIDDER, LORD MURRAY, BALVANY, and GASK (1676), tenth EARL OF ATHOLL (1629), thirteenth EARL OF TULLIBARDINE (1606), and LORD MURRAY OF TULLIBARDINE (1604) [S], fourth EARL STRANGE and BARON MURRAY OF STANLEY (1786) [G B], eleventh BARON STRANGE (1628) [E], sixth BARON PERCY (1722) [G B], and second BARON GLENLYON (1821) [U K], only son and heir, born 6th August 1840; succeeded his father 16th January 1864, and his maternal uncle, Algernon (Percy), fourth Duke of Northumberland [G B], as Lord Percy, 12th February 1865.

REDMOND, Baronet [E].

I. SIR PETER REDMOND, Knight of the Order of Christ, was on 20th December 1717 created a *KNIGHT* and *BARONET* [E], with remainder to the heirs-male of his body. On 15th December 1721 he was further created *BARON* [*REDMOND*] [I]. See that title.

1717

[REDMOND], Baron [I].

I. SIR PETER REDMOND, Knight of the Order of Christ, was on 20th December 1717 created by James III and VIII a *KNIGHT* and *BARONET* [E]. By the same King he was, 1st January 1718,[1] appointed Consul-General for Portugal, and on 15th December 1721 created *BARON* [*REDMOND*] [I], with remainder to the heirs-male of his body. He was probably dead *s.p.m.* before 26th March 1732. He married Anne, daughter of [   ] Parker, and had issue:—

1. Elizabeth Bridget Redmond,
2. Francis Catharine Julia Redmond,
3. Anne Marie Xaviere Redmond,
4. Josepha Marie de Jesus Redmond,

all living 26th March 1732, when they had a declaration of their noblesse.

1721
17

---

[1] On 2nd November 1718 James wrote of him to Ormonde as follows: 'I find that one Sr Peter Redmond hath a great vocation to be my man in those parts (Spain). I am sure I never promised him he should be so, and tho' I think few people more honest I know few more unfitt, all things considered, for such a nice business.'

RICKERTON

RICKERTON, Viscount of [S].

i.e. '*RICKERTON,*' *VISCOUNTY OF* (Drummond), created 17th April 1692, with '*MELFORT,*' *DUKEDOM OF*, which see.

RIVERSTON, Baron [I].

i.e. '*NUGENT OF RIVERSTON,*' which see.

ROBERTSON, Baronet [S].

1725 — 1749

I. ALEXANDER ROBERTSON of Struan, thirteenth Chief of Clan Robertson, second but eldest surviving son and heir of Alexander Robertson of the same, by his second wife, Marion, daughter of General Baillie of Letham, born about 1670, educated at St. Andrews University, and succeeded his father 1687. On the Revolution he left St. Andrews University,[1] and joined Dundee, for which he was attainted 1690, and his estates confiscated. He escaped to France, where he remained till the accession of Anne, from whom in 1703 he obtained a pardon, when he returned to Scotland.[2] He joined Lord Mar with his clan in 1715, and was taken prisoner at the battle of Sheriffmuir, 16th September 1715, but escaped on the way to Edinburgh by the assistance of his sister, and once more fled to France, being again attainted by Act of Parliament in 1716. In 1725 he is said to have been created[3] by James III and VIII a *KNIGHT* and

---

[1] This was much against the wish of his mother, who, in order to deter him from carrying out his purpose, wrote as follows in a letter to the Robertsons dated from Carie, 25th May 1689 : ' Gentlemen, tho' you have no kindness for my son,' the clan had some doubts as to her share in the death of her step-son, the heir of Struan, 'yet for God's sake have it for the laird of Strowan. He is going to Badenoch just now ; for Christ's sake come in all haste and stop him, for he will not be advised by me' (*Hist. MSS. Com.* 12th *Rep.* part viii. p. 37).

[2] The Duke of Perth wrote of him in 1705 : ' He has ever been scrupulously loyal to the Jacobite cause, and since his return to his own country, would never take any oath or meddle with those that now govern ' (*Hooke's Correspondence*, p. 228).

[3] See an article on Jacobite creations by F. A. Lumbye, in *The Whirlwind*, 27th December 1890, ii. p. 205, etc. There appears, however, to be no record of this creation among the *Stuart Papers*, but on the 10th May 1725 there is a warrant creating *Alexander Robertson of Fascally* a Baronet [S]. This appears remarkable, for while Struan was one of the most trusted and devoted of James's adherents, the name of Fascally appears quite unknown. It is of course possible that both Struan and Fascally were created Baronets, the omission of Struan's Baronetcy from the Warrant Books having no significance, several other titles, of the creation of which there is abundant evidence, being similarly omitted.

ROBERTSON

Baronet [S], with remainder to his heirs-male. He returned to Scotland in 1731, and in 1745 he for a third time took up arms for the House of Stuart, and joined Prince Charles, being present (as a spectator) at the battle of Prestonpans. In consequence of his age, being then upwards of seventy-five, he did not join in the advance into England, but returned home, and thus escaped fresh attainder. He died at Carie in Rannoch, 18th April 1749, aged eighty-one, and was buried in the family tomb at Struan. He was a poet of some note.[1]

II. *Sir* DUNCAN ROBERTSON [second *Baronet*], cousin and next heir-male, being the elder son of Alexander Robertson, son and heir of John Robertson, son and heir of Duncan Robertson, all of Drumachine, which Duncan was the third son (but the eldest whose issue then survived) of Robert Robertson, tenth Baron of Struan, who through his eldest son and heir was the great-grandfather of the first *Baronet*. He succeeded his cousin as above 18th April 1749, but on the pretext that he had not been included by name in the last Act of Indemnity he was dispossessed and his estates seized by the Crown, 1752. He died . He married the *Lady* May, fourth daughter of William (Nairne), first *Earl of Nairne* [S], by the Hon. Margaret, only daughter and heir of Robert (Nairne), first Lord Nairne [S]. He had issue :—

1. *Sir* Alexander, his heir.
2. Walter Philip Collyer Robertson, died unmarried 1818.
3. Margaret Robertson, married at Versailles, 29th May/9th June 1755, Laurence (Oliphant), second *Lord Oliphant* [S], and died at Gask 4th November 1774, aged thirty-four, leaving issue.

1749 - 17

III. *Sir* ALEXANDER ROBERTSON [third *Baronet*], elder son and heir, a Colonel in the army. He obtained the restoration of his estates in 1784, and died unmarried 1822.

17 - 1822

IV. *Sir* ALEXANDER ROBERTSON [fourth *Baronet*], cousin and next heir-male, being the son and heir of Duncan Robertson, second son of Robert Bane Robertson, son and heir of Donald Robertson, who was second son (but the elder

1822 - 1830

---
[1] *Dictionary of National Biography.*

ROBERTSON

whose male issue then, 1822, survived) of Duncan Robertson of Drumachine, third son of Robert Robertson, tenth Baron of Struan above named. He succeeded his cousin as above, 1822, and was infeft in the barony of Struan by Crown Charter, 23rd June 1824. He died 20th March 1830. He married, first, Mary, daughter of William Best of Mansfield, co. York, by whom he had issue two sons. He married, secondly, Jean, daughter of Gilbert Stewart of Fincastle, by whom he had further issue :—
1. S*IR* George Duncan, his heir.
2. Francis Robertson, lost at sea, unmarried.
3. S*IR* Alexander Gilbert [seventh *BARONET*].
4. Robert Joseph Robertson.

1830 — 1842

V. S*IR* GEORGE DUNCAN ROBERTSON [fifth *BARONET*], eldest son and heir, born 29th April 1766; a Major-General in the army, C.B., Knight of the Austrian Order of Leopold; died 1st July 1842. He married, 31st May 1799, Anne, daughter of James Outhwaite of Richmond, co. York. She died 2nd December 1868. He had issue :—
1. S*IR* George Duncan, his heir.
2. Mary Anne Robertson, married William Jenkins of Struan Grove, and died 1849, leaving issue three daughters.
3. Frances Robertson, died unmarried 1851.

1842 — 1864

VI. S*IR* GEORGE DUNCAN ROBERTSON [sixth *BARONET*], only son and heir, born 26th July 1816; J.P. co. Perth, Lieutenant 42nd Highlanders; died *s.p.* 3rd April 1864. He married, 3rd April 1839, Mary Stuart, daughter of Major Archibald Mensies of Avondale, Stirlingshire.

1864 — 1884

VII. S*IR* ALEXANDER GILBERT ROBERTSON [seventh *BARONET*], uncle and next heir-male, born 6th March 1805, succeeded his nephew 3rd April 1864, and died 16th October 1884. He married, January 1863, Charlotte Wilhelmina, daughter of [   ] Hoffman. He had issue :—
1. S*IR* Alexander Stewart, his heir.
2. Duncan Robertson, born 11th September 1867, died 1869.
3. Jean Rosine Robertson, born 7th September 1865.

ROBERTSON

VIII. SIR ALEXANDER (ALASDAIR) STEWART ROBERTSON [eighth BARONET], twentieth BARON OF STRUAN, Perthshire, and Chief of Clan Robertson, styled 'Struan Robert-'son,' Captain West of Scotland Artillery, born 6th November 1863, succeeded his father 16th October 1884.[1]   1884

ROBERTSON OF FASCALLY, Baronet [S].

I. ALEXANDER ROBERTSON of Fascally, co. Perth, son and heir of Alexander Robertson of the same,[2] succeeded his father March 1712, and was on the 10th May 1725 created[3] by James III and VIII a KNIGHT and BARONET [S], with remainder to his heirs-male. He died in 1732.   1725 – 1732

II. SIR GEORGE ROBERTSON of Fascally, second BARONET, son and heir, succeeded his father in 1732. On the retreat of the Jacobite army from Stirling in February 1746 he and his kinsman, James Robertson of Blairfetty, raised one hundred and forty men, and with 'seven pieces of brass cannon 'and four covered waggons' joined Prince Charles at Perth. He served himself heir to his father in 1764, probably in order to make up his title to the estates with a view of selling, as they   1732 – 17

---

[1] Burke's *Landed Gentry*, 1900.

[2] Sir James Balfour Paul, Lyon King, has most kindly supplied the Editor with the following notes regarding this branch of the Robertsons, taken from the Register of the Great Seal and the Retours :—

ALEXANDER ROBERTSON OF STRUAN and Elizabeth Stewart had a charter of Fascally and other lands, 24th January 1504/5.

ALEXANDER ROBERTSON OF FASCALLY and Isobel Hay, his wife, had a charter of Fascally on his own resignation, 16th February 1533/4, and another of Dysart, 1st May 1543.

He was succeeded by GEORGE ROBERTSON, who in 1557 seems to have sold Fascally; he married Christian Oliphant.

His son, ALEXANDER, bought back, or more likely redeemed, Fascally, 8th November 1599; he married Egidia Oliphant.

GEORGE, their son, got a charter of Fascally, 6th February 1611, to himself and his wife, Elizabeth Lundy. He died *s.p.* and perhaps *v.p.*, and was succeeded by his brother.

DUNCAN, who was served heir to him, 6th December 1615. He had a son, or possibly a brother, who succeeded him.

ROBERT: he had a son.

ALEXANDER, who was served heir to his father in 1671, and recorded his arms in the Lyon Register in or about 1672. He died in March 1712, and was succeeded by his son Alexander, created a *Baronet* as above.

[3] See note 3, p. 156.

ROCHFORD

were disposed of about 1770 to the Duke of Atholl and Butter of Pitlochry. He is said to have been the last of the direct male line [1] of Fascally.

ROCHFORD, Earl of [E].

i.e. '*ROCHFORD*,' *EARLDOM OF* (Fitzjames), created 13th January 1696, with '*ALBEMARLE*,' *DUKEDOM OF*, which see.

ROMNEY, Baron of [E].

i.e. '*ROMNEY*,' *BARONY OF* (Fitzjames), created 13th January 1696, with '*ALBEMARLE*,' *DUKEDOM OF*, which see.

RONCHI, Baronet [E].

1715 — I. JOSEPH RONCHI, was on 24th July 1715 created [2] a *KNIGHT* and *BARONET* [E] by James III and VIII, with remainder to the heirs-male of his body.

RONCHI, Baronet [E].

1722 — I. JOSEPH RONCHI, was on 5th October 1722 created by James III and VIII a *KNIGHT* [3] [? and *BARONET*] [E], with remainder to the heirs-male of his body.

---

[1] J. A. Robertson, *The Earldom of Atholl*, p. 63.

[2] The patent is endorsed : 'Copy made 2 Aug. 1735, by Felix Ronchi, with attestation 'that it is a true copy by Louis Riva.' Several Ronchis are mentioned in the *Stuart Papers* : Don Giacomo Ronchi is mentioned, January 1694, as having been Almoner to Queen Mary since her arrival at St. Germains, and his brother Don Pellegrino with having served her for many years, when together with another brother, Don Pietro Ronchi, priest of St. Vincent and Anastasia, in the diocese of Bologna, they are recommended by her to Cardinal Cibo. In the same letter the Queen mentions that their family have been long attached to her service. A John Ronchi was appointed a Gentleman Usher of the Presence to King James, 17th October 1701.

[3] The words are : 'La dignité et le titre de Chevalier de notre royaume d'Angleterre 'pour s'en appropprier la qualité et pour enjouer par luy et par les hoirs males de son corps 'legitimement nés avec tous honeurs, priveleges et advantages y appartiennent.' The warrant is endorsed : 'This was copied from the original in June 1756. The Ronchis 'requesting a duplicate of it, and as it has not been entered in the Books that is now 'done.' See Warrant Book, iv. p. 149.

ST. ANDREWS

ROSBERRY, Baron [I].

i.e. '*ROSBERRY,*' *BARONY OF* (Sarsfield), created January 1691, with '*LUCAN,*' *EARLDOM OF*, which see.

RUTLEDGE, Baronet [I].

I. WALTER RUTLEDGE, 'armateur,' of Dunkirk, son of James Rutledge, Esq., of the family of Rutledge of the province of Connaught, by Juliana, daughter of Sir Thomas Blake, Knight Baronet [I], had on 5th July 1745 a declaration of his noblesse from King James III and VIII, and on 23rd December 1748 was created by the same King for his services to Charles, Prince of Wales, a *KNIGHT* and *BARONET* [I], with remainder to the heirs-male of his body.

1748
-

ST. ANDREWS, Duke of [S].

I. DON JOSEPH (DE BOZAS), COUNT OF CASTELBLANCO [Spain], Knight of the Order of Alcantara, an active Jacobite, who was much engaged in the attempts to restore the Stuarts in 1715-1716,[1] was on 4th February 1717 created by King James III and VIII a Duke and Peer of Parliament as *DUKE CASTELBLANCO* and *DUKE OF ST. ANDREWS, MARQUIS OF BORLAND, EARL OF FORDAN, VISCOUNT OF THE BASS,* and *LORD DIVRON* [S], with remainder to his heirs-male. He died   . He married, first, Lady Mary, second daughter of John (Drummond), first *DUKE OF MELFORT* [S and F], by his second wife, Euphemia, daughter of Sir Thomas Wallace of Craigie, a Lord of Session (1671-1680). She died *s.p.* 1713. He married, secondly (by dispensation from the Pope), Lady Frances, third daughter of John, *DUKE OF MELFORT* above named, and sister to his first wife. She died 1726. He had issue :—

1. [   ], *MARQUIS OF BORLAND*, his heir.

1717
-

---

[1] Bolingbroke speaks of him as ' a Spaniard who married a daughter of Lord ' Melfort, and who under that title set up for a meddler in English business.' See Scottish History Society Publications, vol. xix. p. 145. According to Stair the money for the expedition to Scotland in 1719 was found by him (Stair to Craggs, 7th May 1719, *State Papers*, Foreign, France, 353).

SEAFORTH

2. LADY [   ] de Bozas, married, first, M. de Campillo, Prime Minister to Philip v, King of Spain; and secondly, Lord Peter FitzJames, Knight of Malta, Admiral of Spain.

3. LADY Margaret de Bozas, married a Spanish grandee.[1]

17 — II. [   ] (DE BOZAS), second DUKE CASTLEBLANCO and DUKE OF ST. ANDREWS, etc. [S], also COUNT OF CASTELBLANCO [Spain]. He married a Spanish heiress, and had issue.[1]

SEAFORTH, Marquis of [S].

1690?
—
1701

I. KENNETH (MACKENZIE), fourth EARL OF SEAFORTH (1623), and fifth LORD MACKENZIE OF KINTAIL (1609) [S], elder son and heir of Kenneth Mackenzie, third Earl of Seaforth, by Isabella, sister of George (Mackenzie), first Earl of Cromarty [S], third daughter of Sir John Mackenzie, first Baronet [S]; succeeded his father December 1678; P.C. [S], 1685; K.T. (being one of the eight original Knights of that Order), 29th May 1687. He remained loyal to King James, whom he followed to France. He took part in the campaign of 1689 in Ireland, and was created MARQUIS OF SEAFORTH and EARL (? VISCOUNT or LORD) FORTROSE [S],[2] about 1690. In 1690 he returned to Scotland and raised his clan, but after the defeat of Buchan at Cromdale, 1st May 1690, he submitted and surrendered to Hugh Mackay, alleging that he had merely taken up arms for the sake of appearances, and had never any real intention of joining Buchan.[3] He was, however, kept prisoner till 1st March 1697, when he was allowed to return to France. He died in Paris January 1701. He married Lady Frances, daughter of William (Herbert), first DUKE OF POWIS [E], by Lady Elizabeth, daughter of Edward (Somerset), second Marquis of Worcester [E]. She, who was styled[4] 'Duchess' of Seaforth, died in Paris 16th December 1732.

---

[1] Burke's *Extinct Peerage*, 1883, article Drummond, Duke of Melfort, p. 180.

[2] G. E. C., referring to the courtesy title used by his son, says: 'It is not known why the style of Fortrose was assumed instead of that of "Mackenzie" or "Kintail." There was apparently neither a Viscounty nor a Barony of the name of Fortrose or Mackenzie of Fortrose vested in his father.' It was, however, without doubt an Earldom or Viscounty conferred by King James with the Marquisate of Seaforth.

[3] *Dictionary of National Biography*.

[4] See *The Complete Peerage*, vii. p. 98.

SEAFORTH

II. WILLIAM (MACKENZIE), second *MARQUIS OF SEA-FORTH*, etc., elder son and heir, succeeded his father January 1701, and joined Lord Mar, at the head of over three thousand men, in August 1715. He was present at Sheriffmuir, 16th September 1715, and was afterwards appointed Lieutenant-General of the Northern Counties [S]. He made an attempt to capture Inverness, but being unsuccessful, he passed over to Lewis, and afterwards escaped to France, reaching St. Germains February 1716. He was attainted, 7th May 1716, whereby all his honours were considered as forfeited, and his estates were seized by the Crown. He returned to Scotland in 1719, and at the head of his clan joined the Spanish force landed that year under the Earl Marischal; but being desperately wounded at the battle of Glenshiels, 10th June 1719, he once more fled to France. In 1725 he made arrangements with his followers for paying their future rent to the Government, and on 12th July 1726 he was discharged from the penalties of execution or imprisonment, being by Act of Parliament 1736 further restored to personal immunities.[1] He returned to Scotland and died in the island of Lewis, 8th January 1740, and was buried in the chapel of Ui there. He married, 22nd April 1715, Mary, daughter and heiress of Nicholas Kennet of Coxhow, co. Northumberland. She died in Paris August 1739.

1701 - 1740

III. KENNETH (MACKENZIE), third *MARQUIS OF SEAFORTH*, etc., son and heir, born about 1718, styled *LORD FORTROSE*. In 1745 he declined to join the Prince Regent, and actively supported the existing Government. M.P. for Inverness, 1741-1747, and for Ross-shire, 1747-1761. He died in Grosvenor Square, 18th October 1761, and was buried on the 22nd in Westminster Abbey. He married, 11th September 1741, Lady Mary, eldest daughter of Alexander (Stewart), sixth Earl of Galloway [S], by Lady Anne, younger daughter of William (Keith), ninth Earl Marischal [S]. She died 10th April 1751, and was buried at Kensington on the 18th.

1740 - 1761

IV. KENNETH (MACKENZIE), fourth *MARQUIS OF SEAFORTH*, etc., only son and heir, born at Edinburgh 15th January 1744; succeeded his father 18th October 1761, and on

1761 - 1781

---
[1] *The Complete Peerage*, vii. p. 98.

SEMPILL

18th November 1766 was created by George III BARON ARDELVE and VISCOUNT FORTROSE, both in co. Wicklow [I], and subsequently, 3rd December 1771, EARL OF SEAFORTH [I]. He died *s.p.m.* on his passage with his regiment to the East Indies, August 1781, when his Irish honours became extinct.

1781
-
1783

V. THOMAS FREDERICK (MACKENZIE, afterwards MACKENZIE-HUMBERSTON), fifth *MARQUIS OF SEAFORTH*, etc., cousin and next heir-male, being elder son and heir of Major William Mackenzie, by Mary, only daughter of Matthew Humberston of Humberston, co. Lincoln, which William was only son to LORD Alexander Mackenzie, younger son of the first *MARQUIS OF SEAFORTH*. He succeeded his father, 12th March 1770, and his cousin as above, August 1781. He died unmarried in the East Indies, 30th April 1783, from the effect of a wound received in a naval engagement with the Mahrattas.

1783
-
1815

VI. FRANCIS HUMBERSTON (MACKENZIE), sixth *MARQUIS* (1690) and ninth EARL (1623) OF SEAFORTH, sixth EARL OF (?) *FORTROSE* (1690), and tenth LORD MACKENZIE OF KINTAIL (1609), only brother and heir, born 9th June 1754; succeeded his brother 30th April 1783, and was created, 26th October 1797, by George III, LORD SEAFORTH, BARON MACKENZIE OF KINTAIL, Ross-shire [G B]. He died *s.p.m.s.* 11th January 1815, when his peerage of Great Britain became extinct, as did possibly also the *MARQUISATE OF SEAFORTH*,[1] while the Earldom of Seaforth and the Barony of Mackenzie of Kintail [S] (both of which were under attainder) became dormant.

SEMPILL, Baron [S].

17
1737

I. ROBERT SEMPILL, son and heir of the Hon. Archibald Sempill, who was the fourth son (but the only one whose male issue in 1712 survived) of Hugh (Sempill), fifth Lord Sempill [S], was born 1672 at Sempill Castle,[2] and entered the French army as a cadet in the infantry regiment of Normandois before 1688, became Ensign in the Scottish Guards, June 1689,

---

[1] There being no record of this creation among the *Stuart Papers* the remainder is not known.
[2] Statement of services supplied by French Minister of War.

SHERIDAN

and Captain *réformé* in the Irish infantry regiment of Galmoye 29th June 1708, and was transferred to the Dillon regiment, 15th February 1715, in which he was still serving, 27th May 1726. On 11th May 1712, being then a Captain in Lord Galmoye's regiment, he had a declaration of his noblesse from King James III and VIII, in which he was declared to be the 'sole heir-
' male of the property and the very ancient title of the said Hugh,
' Lord Sempill, whose fourth son, Archibald, father of the said
' Robert, is the only one who left any living male child.'[1] On 16th July 1723 he appears as 'Mr. Robert Sempill, Captain of the
' regiment of Dillon,' but seems after that date to have been created by James III and VIII a Lord and Peer of Parliament as LORD SEMPILL [S]. He died at Paris intestate. Admon. as 'Robert, Lord Sempill, *alias* Robert Sempill,'[2] 11th November 1737. He married Elizabeth, daughter of [   ] [   ], who survived him. He had issue :—

1. *HON.* Francis Sempill.
2. *HON.* Hugh Sempill.
3. *HON.* George Sempill.
4. *HON.* Henrietta Sempill.

II. FRANCIS (SEMPILL), second LORD SEMPILL, eldest son and heir, being described as such in his father's Admon. He was an active Jacobite, 1740-1745. He died 9th December 1748, and was buried at St. Andrews, Chartres, in France. He was probably the Francis Sempill who married Lady Mary, widow of the *HON.* John Caryll, daughter of Kenneth (Mackenzie), first MARQUIS OF SEAFORTH [S], by Lady Frances, daughter of William (Herbert), first DUKE OF POWIS [E]. She was buried at Harting, co. Sussex, 16th April 1740.

1737
-
1748

SHERIDAN, Baronet [I].

I. THOMAS SHERIDAN, only son and heir of Thomas Sheridan,[3] sometime Private Secretary to James II and VII, by, it

1726
-
1746

---

[1] See p. 206.
[2] *The Complete Peerage*, vii. p. 113.
[3] This Thomas Sheridan, the elder, was brother to William Sheridan, Bishop of Kilmore and Ardagh 1681/2, deprived by William of Orange for not taking the oaths, both being sons of Denis Sheridan by daughter of [   ] Foster of England. Thomas, who was the fourth son, was born 1646 in the village of St. John's, near Trim, in Meath ; matriculated at Trinity College, Dublin, 17th January 1660/1 ; B.A. 1664 ; Fellow 1667 ;

SHERLOCK

is said, a natural daughter of that King. Was engaged in the '15, being sent 27th December 1715[1] on a mission from the Duke of Ormond to Lord Mar. On 17th March 1726 he was created by King James a KNIGHT and BARONET [I], and about 1739 was appointed Governor to the young Prince of Wales, being one of the seven who accompanied that Prince to Scotland in July 1745. After Culloden he escaped, 4th May 1746, from Arisaig on board a French man-of-war and hastened to Rome, where he died a few months later, when the BARONETCY became extinct.

SHERLOCK, Baronet [I].

1716 — I. SIR PETER SHERLOCK, KNIGHT, was on 9th December 1716 created by James III and VIII a KNIGHT and BARONET [I], with remainder to the heirs-male of his body.

SLEAT, Baron [S].

1716 – 1718

I. SIR DONALD MACDONALD, fourth BARONET [S], eldest son and heir of Sir Donald MacDonald, third Baronet, by Lady Mary, second daughter and in her issue sole heir of

---

entered the Middle Temple, 29th June 1670; Collector of Customs, Cork, 1671; Hon. D.C.L. Oxford, 6th August 1677; F.R.S. 6th February 1679. Having received some favour from the Duke of York, he to show his gratitude visited him when in retirement at Brussels in 1679, and on his return was accused of being concerned in the so-called Popish Plot and arrested, but being shown to be a Protestant, he was released on the dissolution of Parliament; Chief Secretary and Commissioner of the Revenue [I], 1687. He followed King James into exile and was appointed his private secretary; Commissioner of the Household, 17th October 1699, 14th August 1700, 6th December 1701, and 17th May 1708. There is a good account of him in the *Dictionary of National Biography*, where, however, the date of his death is said to be unknown. This, however, would appear from the *Stuart Papers* to have been shortly before 13th November 1712, when there was an agreement before a notary between George Magauly, an Irishman, captain of the regiment of Bourke, and Matthew Kennedy, LL.D., Judge of the Admiralty [I], as procurator for Thomas Sheridan, for himself, and his wards, his sisters Helen and Mary, concerning 1500 livres due from Thomas Sheridan deceased, the father of the said Thomas Sheridan, to the said Magauly or his wife, of which 500 livres were then repaid by Kennedy to Magauly. According to the *Dictionary of National Biography* he had one daughter, wife of Colonel Guillaume, Aide-de-camp to William of Orange, but this would appear to be a mistake.

[1] When the Duke of Ormond wrote to Lord Mar: 'I refer to the bearer Mr. Sheridene, who will have the honour to present this to you, he is a person that has been with me, zealous for the King's Service, and whom I must recommend to your Grace's protection. He has the care of arms and ammunition that I send your Grace, I thought to have made use of them in the West, but had not an opportunity, as the bearer will inform your Grace more particularly.'

SLEAT

Robert (Douglas), tenth Earl of Morton [S]. He joined Lord Mar with his clan and was present at the battle of Sheriffmuir, 16th September 1715, and was attainted 7th May following. On 23rd December 1716 he was created by James III and VIII a Lord and Peer of Parliament as LORD SLEAT (or SLATE) [S], with remainder to his lawful heirs-male. He died 1718. He married Mary, daughter of Donald MacDonald of Castletown.

II. DONALD (MACDONALD), second LORD SLEAT, only son and heir. He succeeded his father 1718, and died unmarried 1720.

1718 -
1720

III. JAMES (MACDONALD), third LORD SLEAT and sixth BARONET, uncle and next male heir, being the second son of Sir Donald MacDonald, third Baronet. He died 1723.

1720 -
1723

IV. ALEXANDER (MACDONALD), fourth LORD SLEAT and seventh BARONET, elder son and heir. He was one of those chiefs who held out promises of support to Prince Charles, but upon his arrival in 1745, he declined to join him. He and his neighbour, MacLeod of MacLeod, the principal personages of the Isle of Skye, both supported the Hanoverian dynasty, and it was the defection of these two powerful chiefs that largely contributed to the failure of the '45. He died at Bernera, on his way to London, 23rd November 1746, aged thirty-five. He married first, 5th April 1733, Anne, widow of James (Ogilvy), fourth (attainted) Earl of Airlie [S], daughter of David Erskine of Dun, co. Forfar. She died at Edinburgh, 27th November 1735, aged twenty-seven. He married secondly, at St. Paul's Church, Edinburgh, 24th April 1739, Lady Margaret, ninth daughter of Alexander (Montgomerie), ninth Earl of Eglinton [S], by his third wife Susanna, daughter of Sir Alexander Kennedy, first Baronet [S]. She, who was a devoted and active Jacobite, died in Welbeck Street, Marylebone, 30th March 1799.

1723 -
1746

V. JAMES (MACDONALD), fifth LORD SLEAT and eighth BARONET, elder son and heir. Died unmarried at Rome, 26th July 1766.

1746 -
1766

VI. ALEXANDER (MACDONALD), sixth LORD SLEAT and ninth BARONET, brother and next heir-male, was on the 17th

1766
1795

STANLEY

July 1766 created by George III BARON MACDONALD OF SLATE, co. Antrim [I]. He died 12th September 1795.

1795 – 1824   VII. ALEXANDER WENTWORTH (MACDONALD), seventh LORD SLEAT [S], second BARON MACDONALD [I], tenth BARONET [S], eldest son and heir, died unmarried 9th June 1824.

1824 – 1832   VIII. GODFREY (MACDONALD, sometime BOSVILLE), eighth LORD SLEAT [S], third BARON MACDONALD [I], eleventh BARONET [S], brother and heir, born 14th October 1775, died 13th October 1832.

1832 – 1863   IX. GODFREY WILLIAM WENTWORTH (MACDONALD), ninth LORD SLEAT [S], fourth BARON MACDONALD [I], twelfth BARONET [S], eldest son and heir, born 16th March 1809, died 25th July 1863.

1863 – 1874   X. SOMERLED JAMES BRUNDENELL (MACDONALD), tenth LORD SLEAT [S], fifth BARON MACDONALD [I], thirteenth BARONET [S], eldest son and heir, born 2nd October 1849, died December 1874.

1874   XI. RONALD ARCHIBALD (MACDONALD), eleventh LORD SLEAT [S], sixth BARON MACDONALD [I], fourteenth BARONET [S], brother and next heir-male, born 9th June 1853.[1]

STANLEY, Viscount [S].

i.e. '*STANLEY*,' VISCOUNTY OF (Nairne), created 24th June 1721, with '*NAIRNE*,' EARLDOM OF, which see.

STEWART, Baronet [S].

1784 – 1   I. COLONEL JOHN ROY STEWART, a distinguished poet and soldier,[2] son of Donald Stewart, by his second wife,

---

[1] For a fuller account of this family see the extant peerages under MacDonald of Slate.
[2] 'He was generally acknowledged to be one of the best swordsmen of his day.... 'His songs, some of which have been translated by Dr. Roger of Stirling, breathe the 'most deeply rooted hatred to the "Butcher Cumberland"; and he insinuates in

STIRLING

Barbara, daughter of John Shaw of Rothiemurchus, and grandson of John Stewart, last Baron of Kincardine,[1] was born at Knock, Kincardine, 1700, and was for some time Lieutenant and Quartermaster in the Scots Greys, but being engaged in a Jacobite plot, he fled to France and entered the French army. In 1745, however, he returned to Scotland and joined Prince Charles at Blair Atholl. He raised the Edinburgh regiment, of which he was given the command. At Culloden he was wounded in both ankles, and after being carried from hiding-place to hiding-place, finally escaped to France, where he became one of the household of the Prince of Wales, with whom he shared his imprisonment in Paris 1748. He afterwards left the Prince and retired to Holland, but eventually rejoined him at Ancona, and as his *valet-de-chambre* was one of the five British attendants who accompanied him to Rome in January 1766. He shortly afterwards was appointed to succeed Sir John Hay as Major-Domo of the Household, and after 1768 was the only British attendant left with the King. On 4th November 1784 he was created[2] a *BARONET* [G B][3] (*sic*), with remainder to the heirs-male of his body. As major-domo he had a legacy from King Charles of £750 a year, but this King Henry IX refused to pay, and the matter was finally compromised by payment of 1250 scudi per annum. He married an Italian lady and had issue.

II. SIR [ ] STEWART, second *BARONET*, son and heir, a Colonel in the Papal service, was in command of the Pope's artillery, 1848.[4]

STIRLING, Marquis of [S].

i.e. '*STIRLING*,' *MARQUISATE OF* (Erskine), created 22nd October 1715, with '*MAR*,' *DUKEDOM OF*, which see.

' the most direct terms motives of vile treachery on the part of Lord George Murray,
' while the brightest anticipations of the return of the Stuarts, and a just retaliation of
' every wrong, are set forth in the most glowing language.' See *Highland Legends,* Edinburgh, 1859.

[1] See *In the Shadow of Cairngorm,* by the Rev. W. Forsyth, M.A., D.D., Edinburgh, 1900.

[2] The patent is printed in Dennistoun's *Memoirs of Sir Robert Strange,* Appendix iv. p. 313. The Rev. John Grant in the *Old Statistical Account of Abernethy,* 1792, incorrectly says that he died in 1752.

[3] It is so in the patent, but must surely have been an oversight, since the Stuarts never recognised the Union.   [4] Dennistoun.

STOBHALL

STOBHALL, Earl of [S].

i.e. '*STOBHALL*,' *EARLDOM OF* (Drummond), created before 17th October 1701, with '*PERTH*,' *DUKEDOM OF*, which see.

STRAFFORD, Duke of [E].

1722 – 1739

I. THOMAS (WENTWORTH), third BARON RABY (1640 and 1641), and fourth BARONET (1611) [E], second but first surviving son and heir of Sir William Wentworth of Northgate Head, in Wakefield, co. York, by Isabella, daughter of Sir Allen Apsley. He was born at Standly Hall, and baptized at Wakefield 17th September 1672; Page of Honour to Queen Mary of Modena, 1685; Colonel of the royal regiment of dragoons, 1697-1715; Lieutenant-General, 1707; succeeded his cousin, William (Wentworth), second Earl of Strafford [E], as Baron Raby, etc., 16th October 1695; Ambassador to the Court of Berlin, 1701-1711, and to the Hague, 1711-1714; P.C. [G B], 1711. Was on the 29th June 1711 created by Anne VISCOUNT WENTWORTH OF WENTWORTH WOODHOUSE, AND OF STAINBOROUGH and EARL OF STRAFFORD, all in co. York [G B], with remainder to the heirs-male of his body, whom failing to his brother, Peter Wentworth, and the heirs-male of his body. British Plenipotentiary to the Congress of Utrecht, 23rd December 1711; K.G., 25th October 1712; one of the Lords Regent [E], 1st August to 18th September 1714. On the accession of George I he took no further part in public affairs, but entered into active correspondence with the Jacobite party. On the 4th January 1722 he was appointed by King James III and VIII Commander-in-Chief of all his forces north of the Humber, and on the following day was created by him *DUKE OF* [*STRAFFORD*] [E], with remainder to the heirs-male of his body. On the 26th May of the same year he was further appointed one of the nine *LORDS REGENT*[1] [E] during the King's absence. In the summer of 1725 he was engaged with the Duke of *NORTHUMBERLAND* and Wharton in negotiations for a fresh attempt on behalf of the House of Stuart. He died at Wentworth Castle, 15th November 1739, and was buried 2nd December following at Toddington, co. Beds.

---

[1] See p. 4.

TENTERDEN

He married, 6th September 1711, Anne, daughter and heir of Sir Henry Johnson of Bradenham, co. Bucks, and Toddington, co. Beds, by his first wife. She died 19th September 1754.

II. WILLIAM (WENTWORTH), second *DUKE OF* [*STRAFFORD*], also EARL OF STRAFFORD, etc., only son and heir, born shortly before 27th September 1722; succeeded his father 15th November 1739, and died *s.p.* at Wentworth Castle, 10th March 1791, and was buried at Toddington the 26th of that month, when the *DUKEDOM OF STRAFFORD* became extinct, while his other honours devolved on his cousin and heir-male.[1]

1739 — 1791

STRATHBRAN, Baron of [S].

i.e. '*STRATHBRAN*,' BARONY OF (Murray), created 1st February 1717, with '*RANNOCH*,' DUKEDOM OF, which see.

STRATH-GLASS, Viscount of [S].

i.e. '*STRATH-GLASS*,' VISCOUNTY OF (Fraser), created 14th March 1740, with '*FRASER*,' DUKEDOM OF, which see.

STRATHERRICK, Earl of [S].

i.e. '*STRATHERRICK*,' EARLDOM OF (Fraser), created 14th March 1740, with '*FRASER*,' DUKEDOM OF, which see.

TARBERT, Baron [I].

i.e. '*TARBERT*,' BARONY OF (Roche), created 1689 or 1690, with '*CAHIRAVAHILLA*,' VISCOUNTY OF, which see.

TENTERDEN, Earl of [E].

I. SIR EDWARD HALES, third Baronet (1611) [E], of Hackington, otherwise St. Stephen's, co. Kent, eldest son and

1692 — 1695

---

[1] *The Complete Peerage*, vii. p. 263.

TENTERDEN

heir of Sir Edward Hales,[1] second Baronet of Tunstall, Kent, by Anne, fourth daughter and co-heir of Thomas (Wotton), second Baron Wotton of Marley [E], by Mary, daughter and co-heir of Sir Arthur Throckmorton; educated at Oxford; succeeded his father about 1660 shortly after the Restoration, and was elected M.P. for Queenborough 1661, which he continued to represent through three Parliaments to 1681. In November 1673 he was appointed Colonel of a regiment of foot, and was one of the Lords of the Admiralty 1679-1685. On the accession of James II and VII, he declared himself a Catholic, and was formally received into that Church, 11th November 1685, being one of the Roman Catholic officers who, by the King's dispensary power (confirmed, in this case, by the Court of King's Bench), were enabled to refuse taking the oath of supremacy. He was sworn to the Privy Council, and appointed Deputy-Governor of the Cinque Ports and Lieutenant of Dover Castle, and in June 1687 Lieutenant of the Tower and Master of the Ordnance. He was dismissed from his post at the Tower November 1688, but continued devoted to King James and remained with him to the last, and was one of the three[2] who accompanied him, 11th December 1688, when the approach of the Dutch army compelled the King to leave London. The vessel in which they were, however, being discovered the next day at Faversham, Hales was recognised and confined in the courthouse there; and on the King's departure for London he was conveyed to Maidstone gaol and afterwards to the Tower, where he remained a prisoner for a year and a half. On 26th October 1689 he was brought up to the Bar of the House of Commons and ordered to be charged with high treason in being reconciled to the Church of Rome. On 31st January 1689/90 he and Obadiah Walker, of University College, his former tutor, were brought by Habeas Corpus from the Tower to the Bar of the King's Bench and were bailed on good security; but both were exempted out of the Act of Pardon issued by William of Orange 23rd May following. Eventually Hales obtained his discharge, 2nd June 1690. He proceeded to St. Germains the October following, and was by King James (when in exile), 3rd May 1692, created *BARON HALES OF EMLEY*, co. Kent, *VISCOUNT*

---

[1] A zealous Royalist who died in France about 1660.
[2] The other two were Mr. Sheldon and Mr. Abbadie, Page of the Backstairs (Rapin's *History of England*, ii. p. 781).

TENTERDEN

Tunstall, and *Earl of Tenterden* [E], with a *special remainder*, failing heirs-male of his body, to his brothers John and Charles, (both of whom died unmarried) in like manner. In 1694 he applied to the Earl of Shrewsbury for permission to return to England, but he did not obtain it, and died in France 1695, being buried in the Church of St. Sulpice in Paris. He 'was scru-'pulously just in his dealings, regular in his habits, and remark-'ably charitable to those in distress.' By his will, dated July 1695, proved April 1708, he bequeathed £5000 to be disposed of according to his instructions by Bishop Bonaventure Giffard and Dr. Thomas Witham. He had purchased the house and estate of St. Stephen near Canterbury in the reign of Charles II. *Lord Tenterden* married (Lic. Vic. Gen. 12th July 1669, he being about twenty-four and she about twenty-five) Frances, daughter of Sir Francis Windebank of Oxford, Secretary of State to Charles I, by whom, who died 1693, he had issue:—

1. Edward Hales, killed 1st July 1690 at the battle of the Boyne fighting for King James, unmarried *v.p.*
2. John, *Viscount Tunstall*, his heir.
3. *Hon.* Charles Hales, died unmarried.
4. *Hon.* Robert Hales, died unmarried.
5. *Hon.* James Hales, died unmarried.
6. *Lady* Anne Hales, died unmarried.
7. *Lady* Mary Hales, married [   ] Bauwens, Judge of the Admiralty at Ostend.
8. *Lady* Frances Hales, born about 1673; married first (settlement 7th September 1690), Peter (Plunkett), fourth Earl of Fingall [I], by whom, who died 24th January 1717/18, she had issue. She married secondly, July 1719, Stephen Taafe of Dowestown, co. Meath, who died soon afterwards; and thirdly, Patrick Bellew (eldest son of Sir John Bellew, second Baronet [I]), who died *s.p.v.p.* 12th June 1720. She died 6th August 1749, in her seventy-sixth year at Inchicore and was buried at Killeen.[1]
9. *Lady* Jane Hales, died unmarried.
10. *Lady* Elizabeth Hales, died unmarried.
11. *Lady* Catherine Hales, died unmarried.
12. *Lady* Clare Hales, married [   ] Hussey of Ireland.

---

[1] *The Complete Peerage*, iii. p. 354.

TENTERDEN

1695 – 1744

II. JOHN (HALES), second *EARL OF TENTERDEN*, second but eldest surviving son and heir of the preceding, succeeded his father in 1695, and lived quietly at St. Stephen's, taking no part in public affairs. He was offered a Peerage by King George I, but insisted on his right to the titles that had been conferred upon his father by King James, with precedence according to that creation.¹ He died at his house of St. Stephen's the latter part of December 1744.² He married first, Helen, daughter of Sir Richard Bealing of Ireland, Secretary to Katherine, Queen-Dowager of Charles II. He married secondly, Helen, daughter of Dudley Bagnal of Newry, Ireland. She died at Luckly, near Wokingham, Berks, November 1737. He had issue by his first wife two sons and a daughter, and by his second three sons :—

1. John, *VISCOUNT TUNSTALL*, died in infancy.
2. Edward, *VISCOUNT TUNSTALL*, died in gaol at Canterbury v.p. 1729, having married [   ], widow of [   ] Parker and granddaughter of Sir Richard Bulstode, by whom, who died in 1749 and was buried at Tunstall, he had issue :—
   (1) Edward, *VISCOUNT TUNSTALL*, successor to his grandfather.
3. *HON.* James Hales, an officer in the Imperial service, killed in Italy 1735, unmarried.
4. *HON.* Alexander Hales, died *s.p.*
5. *HON.* Philip Hales, died *s.p.*
6. *LADY* Frances Hales, born about 1698, married George Henry (Lee), third Earl of Lichfield [E], who died 15th February 1742/3. She died 25th February 1769, aged seventy-one, and was buried at St. Pancras, Middlesex, having issue.

1744 – 1802

III. EDWARD (HALES), third *EARL OF TENTERDEN*, grandson and heir of the preceding, born about 1730, succeeded December 1744, and died August 1802. Will proved 1803.

---

¹ Hasted's *History of Kent*, ii. p. 577.

² During the latter part of his life he is said to have lived in complete retirement at St. Stephen's, having his food brought to him by an old servant who lived near, to whom on certain days Sir John let down a basket from a window, with a note of what he would have, and the money in it; till at length, this not being repeated for more than a fortnight, the house was broken open, and Sir John found dead, lying in his clothes across the bed, and appeared to have been dead for some time.

TULLY

He married first, in or before 1758, Barbara Isabella, daughter and heir of John Webb (eldest son of Sir John Webb, third Baronet [E]), by Mabella, daughter and co-heir of Sir Harry Joseph Tichborne, fourth Baronet [E]. She died 1770. He married secondly, [   ], widow of [   ] Palmer of Ireland and daughter of [   ], who died *s.p.* He had issue :—

1. Edward, VISCOUNT TUNSTALL, his successor.
2. LADY Barbara Hales, married [   ] Jouchère, a French officer.
3. LADY Mary Hales, married [   ] Demorlaincourt, a French officer.

IV. EDWARD (HALES), fourth EARL OF TENTERDEN, only son and heir, born 1758; succeeded August 1802; married, 1789, Lucy, second daughter of Henry Darell of Calehill, Kent, by Elizabeth, daughter of Sir Thomas Gage, Baronet [E]. He died *s.p.* at Hales Place, in Hackington, 15th March 1829, aged seventy-two, when all his honours became extinct. Will proved June and May 1829. LADY TENTERDEN survived him.[1]

1802
-
1829

TRELESSICK, Marquis of [E].

I. JAMES PAYNTER of Trelisk (*sic*), co. Cornwall (possibly the James baptized at St. Erth 18th August 1666, fourth son of Arthur Paynter of Trelessick, by Mary, daughter of James Praed), proclaimed King James at St. Columb 7th October 1715, and is said to have been, 20th June 1715, created by that King MARQUIS OF TRELESSICK [E]. He died *s.p.*[2]

1715
-
17

TULLY, Viscount [I].

i.e. ' TULLY,' VISCOUNTY OF (Sarsfield), created January 1691, with '*LUCAN*,' EARLDOM OF, which see.

---

[1] *The Complete Baronetage*, i. pp. 76, 77; Hasted's *History of Kent*, ii. p. 577. See also an article on the first *Earl* in the *Dictionary of National Biography*, xxiv. pp. 27, 28.

[2] A fragment of a patent signed 'James Francis Stuart Rex' (a signature never used by that King) is in possession of the Paynter family.

TUNSTALL

TUNSTALL, Viscount of [E].

i.e. '*TUNSTALL,*' VISCOUNTY OF (Hales), created 3rd May 1692, with '*TENTERDEN,*' EARLDOM OF, which see.

TYRCONNELL, Duke of [I].

1689 — 1691

I. RICHARD TALBOT, fifth or eighth son of Sir William Talbot, first Baronet [I] (1622) of Carton, co. Kildare, by Alison, daughter of John Netterville of Castletown, co. Meath, born about 1625; obtained a commission in the Irish army 1641, serving afterwards as a volunteer under the Duke of York and Albany against the Dutch, by whom he was taken prisoner at Solebay in 1672. On the accession of James II and VII he was made a Lieutenant-General,[1] and created,[2] 20th June 1685, BARON OF TALBOTSTOWN, co. Wicklow, VISCOUNT BALTINGLASS, co. Wicklow, and EARL OF TYRCONNELL [I], with remainder to the heirs-male of his body, whom failing to his nephews, Sir William Talbot, .third Baronet, and William Talbot of Haggardstone, and their heirs-male respectively. Captain-General of the Irish army and Viceroy of Ireland, 1686, till the arrival of King James in Dublin, 24th March 1689. On 30th March following he was created by that King (some four months after the Revolution in England, but while still *de facto* as well as *de jure* King of Ireland) *MARQUIS* and *DUKE OF TYRCONNELL*, co. Tyrone [I]. One of the Commissioners to the Treasury [I], 1st July 1689. He was present at the battle of the Boyne, in command of a regiment of horse, and afterwards was sent on a mission to France to urge the immediate despatch of the supplies promised by Louis XIV. He returned to Ireland in January 1691, and died of apoplexy at Limerick, 14th August 1691, when the *DUKEDOM* and *MARQUISATE OF TYRCONNELL* became extinct, while his other honours, which had been attainted by William of Orange shortly

---

[1] As 'a man of great abilities and clear courage, and one who for many years had 'a true attachment to His Majesty's person and interest' (Dalton's *King James's Irish Army List*, 1689).

[2] The preamble to the patent recites 'his immaculate allegiance and his infinitely 'great services performed to the King and to Charles II in England, Ireland, and 'foreign parts, in which he suffered frequent imprisonments and many great wounds.'

TYRCONNELL

before, devolved on his nephew and heir-male.[1] He was buried in St. Minchin's Church, Limerick. He married first, Katharine Boyton. He married secondly, in Paris, 1679, Frances, Dowager-Countess Hamilton, widow of Sir George Hamilton, Count Hamilton [F], sister of the celebrated Sarah, Duchess of Marlborough, and daughter and co-heir of Richard Jennings of Sandridge, co. Herts, by Frances, daughter and co-heir of Sir Giffard Thornhurst, Baronet [E]. She, 'La Belle Jennings,' who was one of the Maids of Honour to Queen Catherine of Braganza, was for long a reigning beauty at the Court of Charles II. After 1691 she retired to St. Germains, and was a Lady of the Bedchamber to Queen Mary of Modena. She returned to Ireland, however, about 1720, and was permitted 'to 'erect a house, still standing, in King Street, Dublin, as a 'nunnery for poor Claires, and in this obscure retirement, burying 'all the attractions and graces which once so adorned the Court 'of England,' she died, from a fall from her bed, at Paradise Row or Arbour Hill, Dublin, 6th March 1731, and was buried on the 9th in St. Patrick's Cathedral there, aged eighty-two.[2]

---

[1] II. WILLIAM (TALBOT), second EARL OF TYRCONNELL, etc. [I], son and heir of Sir Garret or Griffith Talbot (who died 26th December 1724, aged eighty-two) by Margaret, daughter of Henry Gaydon of co. Louth, was attainted as 'William Talbot of Dundalk,' 1691, succeeded his uncle 14th August 1691 as Earl of Tyrconnell, which title he assumed. He is presumed to have died at St. Germains. He had issue a son and heir.

III. RICHARD FRANCIS (TALBOT), third EARL OF TYRCONNELL, etc. [I], who was born before 1710; entered the French army and was Maréchal-de-camp, 1748; and died as French Ambassador to the Court of Berlin, 1752 (*French Military Records*).

[2] *Dictionary of National Biography*, *Complete Peerage*. In Burke's *Extinct Peerage* is the following quotation from 'an eloquent writer': 'Of Richard Talbot, Duke of 'Tyrconnell, much ill has been written, and more believed; but his history, like that 'of his unfortunate country, has only been written by the pen of party, steeped in gall, 'and copied servilely from the pages of prejudice by the lame historians of modern 'times, more anxious for authority than authenticity. Two qualities he possessed in an 'eminent degree, wit and valour; and if to gifts so brilliant and so Irish he joined 'devotion to his country, and fidelity to the unfortunate and fated family with whose 'exile he began life, and with whose ruin he finished it, it cannot be denied that in his 'character the elements of evil were mixed with much great and striking good. Under 'happier circumstances the good might have predominated, and he whose deeds are 'held even by his own family in such right estimation might have shed a lustre on his 'race by those talents and heroism which gave force to his passions and celebrity to 'his errors.' To which G. E. C. in his *Complete Peerage*, vii. p. 445, adds: 'The 'most eminent of his vituperators is Lord Macaulay (in whose "History" he figures 'as "lying Dick Talbot"), who credits him with most if not all the vices which are 'incident to human nature, the epithets of "Sharper, Bully, Bravo, Pimp, Sycophant" 'and "Hypocrite" being but some out of those he applies to him. This view of his 'character may, however, be charitably and not inaptly coupled with the words of 'Mason [*History of St. Patrick's Cathedral*], "Whatever were his faults, he had the rare '"merit of sincere attachment to an unfortunate Master."'

UPPER TARF

UPPER TARF, Earl of [S].

i.e. '*UPPER TARF*,'[1] *EARLDOM OF* (Fraser), created 14th March 1740, with '*FRASER*,' *DUKEDOM OF*, which see.

WALSH, Earl [I].

1745 – 1763

I. ANTHONY VINCENT WALSH, third son of Philip Walsh of St. Malo,[2] by Anne, daughter of James Whyte of Waterford; born at St. Malo, and baptized in the Cathedral Church there, 22nd January 1703. Began life in the French Navy, but subsequently became a shipbuilder or 'marchand à 'la fosse' at Nantes. He provided the Prince Regent in 1745 with two vessels at his own expense, the one, the *Du Teillay* (Captain Durbé), on which he escorted the Prince to Lochnanuagh, on the west coast of Scotland, and the other, the *Elizabeth* (Captain Douaud), captured by him from the British, but which was so disabled in a fight with the *Lion*, a British man-of-war, on 20th July 1745, that she was forced to return to Brest. In recognition of these services[3] he was, by King James III and VIII, on 20th October following, created *LORD OF* [   ], *VISCOUNT OF* [   ], and *EARL OF* [*WALSH*] [I]. He was subsequently appointed by Louis XV to the command of an expedition that was to have landed eighteen battalions of infantry and two regiments of cavalry in support of the Prince Regent, 1746. This expedition never sailed, being probably stopped by the news of the defeat of Culloden. His pedigree and noble birth were recognised by Louis XV, November 1753, the decree being registered in the Parliament of Brittany, 9th January 1754. He held for some time the office of Secrétaire du Roi, and afterwards settled at Cap Français, in the island of

---

[1] Probably 'Abertarff,' the parish in the Lovat country in which Fort Augustus lies. *Ex inform.* the Rev. Sir David Hunter-Blair, Baronet.

[2] Where he had settled after the capitulation of Limerick, 1691.

[3] The patent recites that: 'Whereas we are thoroughly sensible of the great and 'good service rendered to us by our trusty and well-beloved Anthony Walsh, Esq., 'in his undertaking with uncommon zeal and disinterestedness the transporting our 'dearest son Charles, Prince of Wales, into Scotland, which was happily effected 'through manifold risks and dangers, for which signal service, and to perpetuate the 'memory of it to posterity, we, not only out of our inclination but also at the request 'of our dearest son, thought fit to bestow on him as a mark of our royal favour.' The titles are all blank.

WALSH

San Domingo, where he died, 2nd March 1763.[1] His will, dated 11th November 1758, was proved at the Châtelet in Paris, 13th September 1763. LORD WALSH married, in the Chapelle du Sanitat, at Nantes, 10th January 1741, Marie, daughter of Luke O'Sheill of Nantes, by Agnes Vanasse, his wife, and had issue :—

1. Luke Patrick Walsh, born and baptized at St. Nicholas' Church, Nantes, 24th May 1744, died young.
2. HON. Anthony John Baptist Walsh, his successor.
3. LADY Mary Anne Agnes Walsh, baptized at St. Nicholas' Church, Nantes, 12th October 1741 ; married, in the Chapel of la Maison de la Placelière there, her cousin-german, the Chevalier Anthony Anthisme Walsh de Chassenon, by whom she had issue.
4. LADY Helen Agnes Walsh, baptized at St. Nicholas' Church, Nantes, 9th November 1742.

II. ANTHONY JOHN BAPTIST (WALSH), second EARL WALSH, second but only surviving son and heir of the preceding; baptized at St. Nicholas' Church, Nantes, 22nd June 1745 ; succeeded his father, 2nd March 1763; appointed Chamberlain to the Empress Maria Theresa, 31st December 1772. He was compelled to emigrate at the time of the French Revolution, and according to the *Souvenirs de Cinquante Ans*, by his son, the HON. Joseph Walsh, settled first at Sclessin, near Liége, then in London, before leaving Europe to look after the remnants of his family property in San Domingo. He died at Kingston, Jamaica, 26th April 1798, and was buried in the Catholic cemetery there, aged fifty-three. He had married at St. Georges-sur-Loire, 28th October 1765, his cousin-german, Marie Josephine Dorothea, eldest daughter of Francis James (Walsh), first Count of Serrant [F], by Mary, daughter of Thomas Harper. She was born 6th October, and baptized in the Cathedral, Cadiz, 7th October 1748, and died in the parish

1763
–
1798

---

[1] *Lord Walsh* remained in constant correspondence with Prince Charles until his departure for San Domingo, his cipher name being Monsieur Legrand, to whom most of the letters are addressed. They are now in possession of the Duke of La Tremoïlle. He was also a regular correspondent of Colonel Warren, who brought Charles from Scotland in 1746, and of George Kelly, the Prince's secretary. The latter letters are in possession of Mr. V. Hussey Walsh.

WALSH

of St. Julien, Angers, June, and was buried at Serrant in Anjou, 18th June 1785. They had issue :—

1. *Hon.* John Baptist Paul Oliver Walsh, commonly called Count Theobald Walsh, born at St. Georges-sur-Loire, 29th January 1768; married at St. Vincent's Church, Nantes, 24th March 1791, his cousin-german, Agatha, second daughter of Anthony Anthisme, Chevalier Walsh de Chassenon, and the LADY Mary Anne Agnes Walsh. She was baptized at Sainte Croix, Nantes, 17th March 1769. He was killed in the massacre of the whites in San Domingo, 6th August 1792, leaving issue :—

   (1) Theobald Walsh, succeeded as third EARL WALSH.

2. *Hon.* Edward Walsh, born at St. Georges-sur-Loire, 28th October 1770; Canon of St. Peter's, Rome, 6th April 1794 to 6th October 1817; Private Secretary to Henry IX; died at Tivoli, 27th June 1822; buried in the Church of St. Michael there.

3. *Hon.* Charles Walsh, born at St. Georges-sur-Loire, 14th February 1773; died of yellow fever in San Domingo, July 1795.

4. *Hon.* Francis Thomas Joseph David Walsh, born 4th, baptized at St. Georges-sur-Loire, 5th February 1777; author of a *Journal of the Late Campaign in Egypt*; Lieutenant 88th regiment, 18th October 1798; Captain 93rd regiment, 24th June 1802; Major Queen's Rangers, 15th December 1804; Lieutenant-Colonel on service, 16th May 1805; Major 56th regiment, A.A.G. under Sir E. Coote. He was thrown from his gig in driving from Farnham to Guildford on 21st, and died 23rd August 1810. Will dated 24th July 1809, proved 2nd November 1810.

5. *Hon.* Philip Walsh of Sandpits, co. Kilkenny, baptized at St. Julien in Angers, 12th January 1780, died in Paris, 22nd February 1829.

6. *Hon.* Joseph Alexis Walsh, commonly called Viscount Walsh, born 25th April 1782 in the parish of St. Julien at Angers; author of *Les Lettres Vendéennes, Gilles de Bretagne, Lettres sur l'Angleterre, Explorations en Normandie, Histoires Contes et Nouvelles,*

WALSH

Voyage à Prague et Léoben, Voyage de Henri de France en Ecosse et en Angleterre, La Providence, Journées Mémorables de la Révolution Française, Souvenirs de Cinquante Ans, and a large collection of other works; Royal Commissioner at the Nantes Mint 1815, and afterwards Postmaster there, which office he resigned rather than take the oath of allegiance to Louis Philippe, 1830. Proprietor of *La Mode*, a weekly Legitimist paper started that year. He died in Paris 11th February 1860. He had married at Nantes, 5th December 1804, Pauline, daughter of Paul Martin Bouhier de la Bréjolière, by Madelaine Jeanne Sabry de Montholy. She died 27th April 1847. They had issue :—

(1) Edward Walsh, succeeded as fourth *EARL*.

(2) Arthur Walsh, Knight of the Legion of Honour, born at Nantes 29th May 1808, died at Nice 17th January 1880.

(3) Oliver Walsh, Chamberlain to Napoleon III, born at Nantes 27th July 1817; died 7th April 1883; married, 15th December 1857, Marie Louise, daughter of Francis Claude Fourmand-Desmazières. His widow remarried, 12th June 1884, the Viscount de Chemilier, and died at Angers 15th April 1889.

7. *Hon.* Francis Stephen Walsh, born at Angers 13th May 1784; entered the French army, Sergeant 112th regiment, left the Ecole Militaire, 21st November 1803; Sergeant-Major, 26th March 1804; Sub-Lieutenant 18th regiment, 1st April 1805; Lieutenant, 27th March 1809; Knight of the Legion of Honour, 17th July 1809; Captain, A.D.C. to General Bonnassi, 22nd June 1811; on leave on account of wounds, 28th December 1812; Colonel of royal volunteers of La Vendée; fought in the campaigns of 1805 and 1812; dangerously wounded at Wagram, 6th July 1809; Colonel in the Leroux regiment in La Vendée, 1815; afterwards Colonel 23rd regiment and Knight of St. Louis; died at Bayonne 17th November 1821. He married, at Nantes, 17th February 1813, Frances Adelaide, daughter of Francis Hippolyte d'Achon, by

WALSH

Jane Louise Catherine, daughter of Francis Delisle du Fief, by whom, who was born at Ecueilles, Seine-et-Marne, 28th January 1793, and died at Nantes 27th September 1814, he had issue :—

(1) Alfred Walsh, born 20th March 1814, married first, at St. Georges-sur-Loire, 20th September 1839, Sophia, Dowager-Countess of Serrant, daughter of John Francis Legrand and Marie Anne Balduc, by whom, who was born in Paris 26th December 1801, and died at the Château de Plessis-Macé, near Angers, 2nd April 1872, he had issue :—

(1) Robert Walsh, born in Paris 12th December 1840; died there, 7th February 1841.

(2) Alfred Walsh, born at Serrant 20th April 1846; died 20th October 1863.

He married secondly, at Vieux Rouen, 3rd June 1873, Matilda, Dowager-Baroness de Taintignies, second daughter of Count Alfred Isidore Walsh, and died as Conseiller-General of the Maine-et-Loire, at Angers, 21st October 1876. His widow, who was born 3rd September, and baptized at the Catholic Church at Ramsgate 6th October 1821, died May 1903.

8. *Lady* Mary Annie Walsh, born at St. Georges-sur-Loire 25th November 1766; married there, 19th May 1788, Pierre Constant, Marquis of Certaines.

9. *Lady* Dorothy Walsh, born 22nd April 1769; died 1st September 1787.

1798 — 1881

III. THEOBALD ANTHONY OLIVER (WALSH), third *Earl Walsh*, grandson and heir of the preceding, born at Sclessin, near Liége, 24th May 1792, and baptized at Notre Dame des Fonts, at Liége, the next day. He died *s.p.* in Paris, 23rd January 1881. He married at Anthien (Nièvre), 7th October 1818, Anne-Marie-Adèle, daughter of Pierre Constant, Marquis of Certaines [F]. She, who was born at Aix-la-Chapelle, 10th March 1794, died 2nd June 1858 in Paris, and was buried at Anthien, in the Certaines family vault.

WARREN

IV. EDWARD (WALSH), fourth *Earl Walsh*, first cousin and next heir-male of the preceding, born at Nantes 24th April 1806 ; sometime editor of *La Gazette de Normandie*, and from 1st October 1835 of *La Mode*, the organ of the elder branch of the Bourbon family. The violence of his attacks on Louis Philippe led to his being imprisoned five times during his reign, and to frequent fines. He married first, 17th September, 1835, Marie, daughter of Joseph Bernard Gouze of Bayonne and Josephe Desaa, widow of M. de la Juminière of Tours, who died 30th May 1843. He married secondly, 30th August 1848, Pauline Marie Georgina, Dowager-Countess of Aramon, daughter of [   ] du Bois de La Touche. She died 9th October 1872. *Lord Walsh* lived at the historic Château of Chaumont in Loir-et-Cher until his wife's death, when he settled in Paris, where he died 26th October 1884, when all his titles became extinct.[1]

1881
–
1884

WARREN, Baronet [I].

I. Colonel RICHARD WARREN was on 3rd November 1746 created by King James III and VIII a *Knight* and *Baronet* [I] for his services in bringing the Prince of Wales safely back to France. He was third son of John Warren of Corduff, co. Dublin, by his first wife, Mary, daughter of Richard Jones, retired to France, and after devoting himself for a short time to commercial pursuits at Marseilles, entered the regiment of Lally as a volunteer with the honorary rank of Captain, being afterwards transferred to the regiment of Rothe. He was a zealous Jacobite, and he was given command of one of the two vessels sent by the French King with men and arms to the assistance of Prince Charles. He landed at Stonehaven October 1745. After being employed on the erection of batteries on each side of the Forth, he joined the Prince's army in Edinburgh, and received his commission as Colonel, 12th November, being appointed Aide-de-camp to Lord George Murray. He distinguished himself at the siege of Carlisle, and after the retreat from Derby he was intrusted with the important mission of

1746
–
1775

---

[1] For the above account of the *Earls Walsh* the Editor is indebted to Mr. V. Hussey Walsh, the author of a most able and exhaustive account of the French and Austrian branches of the family of Walsh in *The Genealogist*, vols. xvii. and xviii.

WESTMINSTER

making an appeal to Louis xv for assistance. While in Paris he so ably exerted himself that he was able to despatch two frigates laden with arms and ammunition and £40,000 to Scotland. After the defeat of Culloden he was intrusted with the perilous enterprise of rescuing the Prince, and with the frigate *L'Heureux* (thirty-six guns) and the *Prince de Conti* (twenty-four guns) he, after many hair-breadth escapes, succeeded in rescuing the Prince and many of his adherents from Lochnanuagh in Moidart, and landed them at Roscoff near Morlaix, in Brittany, 10th October 1746. For this special service he was, as above, created a BARONET [I] by King James, 3rd November 1746, and received a pension of twelve hundred livres from Louis xv. He now rejoined the French army, and served as Aide-de-camp to Marshal Saxe up to the Treaty of Aix-la-Chapelle in 1748. Brigadier-General in the English army, 1750; Captain of a company in the regiment of Rothe, 1754; Knight of St. Louis, August 1755; Colonel, 15th February 1757; and Brigadier of Infantry, 10th February 1759, in the French army. He was one of the general officers appointed to take command of the expedition for the invasion of England that year, and had charge of the embarkation of the Irish regiments of Clare, Dillon, and Rothe at Lorient. Major-General in the English army, 10th February 1760; Maréchal-de-camp in France, 25th July 1762; Governor of Belle Isle and the adjoining islands, 1763-1775. He died there unmarried 21st June 1775, when the baronetcy became extinct.[1]

WESTMINSTER, Earl of [E].

1759 – 1777

I. HON. ALEXANDER MURRAY, M.P., fourth son of Alexander (Murray) fourth Lord Elibank [S], by Elizabeth, daughter of George Stirling, Surgeon, M.P. for Edinburgh; was an officer of some distinction, and having taken an active part against the Government in the Westminster election of 1750, was committed to Newgate, 6th February 1751; and as he declined

---

[1] See a *History and Genealogy of the Warren Family*, by the Rev. Thomas Warren, F.S.A. (Ireland), London, 1902, p. 261, etc. Two of his brothers, William and John, were also Captains in the French army, and served through the '45. James Warren, sub-Lieutenant in the regiment of Dillon, 1790, and [ ] Warren, sub-Lieutenant in the same regiment 1784, and Lieutenant 1790, were probably nephews of his.

WESTMINSTER

to receive sentence on his knees, was remanded there, and only obtained his release on the prorogation of Parliament, 25th June following. He afterwards retired to France and for some time managed King James's affairs at the French Court. On 12th August 1759 he was created[1] by King James EARL OF WESTMINSTER, co. Middlesex, VISCOUNT OF [   ], and LORD OF [   ] [E], with remainder to the heirs-male of his body, whom failing to Lord Elibank and the heirs-male of his body, whom failing to George, Gideon, and James Murray, and the heirs-male of their body, respectively, and thenceforth he was generally called Count Murray. He was allowed to return to England by letter under the King's Privy Seal, April 1701, and died unmarried 1777.

II. PATRICK (MURRAY), second EARL OF WESTMINSTER, etc. [E], fifth LORD ELIBANK [S], elder brother and heir, born 1703, and died *s.p.* 3rd August 1778.[2]

1777 – 1778

III. GEORGE (MURRAY), third EARL OF WESTMINSTER, etc. [E], 6th LORD ELIBANK [S], next brother and heir, born 1706, died *s.p.m.* 12th November 1785.

1778 – 1785

---

[1] Lumisden writes to him as follows, August 1759: 'Having had the honour to
' deliver to the King the letter you sent me for him, inclosed you will find H.M.'s
' returns. He has been graciously pleased to sign and deliver to me the warrant for
' your being an Earl, which, pursuant to your desire, I shall keep till I have the
' pleasure of seeing you, or receive your further directions how I shall dispose of it.
' The patent is to you and the heirs-male of your body, whom failing, to your brother,
' Lord Elibank, and the heirs-male of his body, and whom failing, to all your brothers
' respectively and the heirs-male of their bodies. Such an uncommon mark of H.M.'s
' approbation of your past services will, no doubt, engage you to give daily fresh proofs
' of your gratitude, zeal, and attachment to him and his royal family. The titles are
' left blank in the warrant, because as the title of Westminster has never been
' conferred on any one, H.M. was apprehensive that there might be some reason for
' it, especially as it is the seat of the court. But if, after enquiry, you find that there
' can be no objection to the title, you may insert it, otherwise you may assume any
' other title you judge proper, and against which no objection can ly. As it is of the
' utmost consequence to you to conceal your having obtained this patent till affairs are
' as we wish them in England, I send this letter under Mr. Gordon's cover, with
' directions to him that he may deliver it to you out of his own hand, or consign it to
' any person whom you shall desire, that it may safely reach you. And until it is a fit
' time for you to use your title I shall continue to write and address to you as formerly.
' You will do me, sir, but justice to believe that I have not been wanting on this
' occasion to represent your merit to H.M. in its true and proper light.'

[2] For a fuller account of this Peer and his successor see the extant peerages under Elibank.

WINCHENDON

1785 – 1820
IV. ALEXANDER (MURRAY), fourth EARL OF WESTMINSTER, etc. [E], seventh LORD ELIBANK [S], nephew and next heir-male, being the eldest son of Rev. the Hon. Gideon Murray, next elder brother to the first Earl, born 24th April 1747, and died 24th September 1820.

1820 – 1830
V. ALEXANDER (MURRAY), fifth EARL OF WESTMINSTER, etc. [E], eighth LORD ELIBANK [S], eldest son and heir, born 26th February 1780, and died 9th April 1830.

1830 – 1871
VI. ALEXANDER OLIPHANT (MURRAY), sixth EARL OF WESTMINSTER, etc. [E], ninth LORD ELIBANK [S], eldest son and heir, born 23rd May 1804, died 31st May 1871.

1871
VII. MONTOLIEU FOX OLIPHANT (MURRAY), seventh EARL OF WESTMINSTER, etc. [E], tenth LORD ELIBANK and tenth BARONET [S], eldest son and heir, born 27th April 1840, succeeded his father 31st May 1871.

WINCHENDON, Viscount of [E].

i.e. '*WINCHENDON*,' co. Bucks, VISCOUNTY OF (Wharton), created 22nd December 1716, with '*NORTHUMBERLAND*,' DUKEDOM OF, which see.

WOBURN, Marquis of [E].

i.e. '*WOBURN*,' co. Bucks, MARQUISATE OF (Wharton), created 22nd December 1716, with '*NORTHUMBERLAND*,' DUKEDOM OF, which see.

WOGAN, Baronet [I].

1719 – 1752?
I. SIR CHARLES WOGAN, second son of William Wogan of Rathcoffy, and Anne Gaydon his wife, was born about 1698. He took part in the rising of 1715, and was taken prisoner at Preston, 14th November. In the following April the Grand Jury of Westminster found a true bill against him, and his trial for high treason was appointed to take place 5th May 1716. At midnight on the eve of the trial Wogan took part in the successful escape from Newgate planned by Brigadier Macintosh, and

WOGAN

he was one of the seven (out of the fifteen) who made good their escape and for whose apprehension a reward of £500 was vainly offered. He went to France and entered the Dillon regiment, in which he served till 1718, in which year he followed James III and VIII to Rome. At the end of the same year he accompanied the Duke of Ormonde on a diplomatic mission to win the hand of a Russian princess for King James, and this failing, he was instrumental in selecting the Princess Mary Clementina Sobieska. This Princess, on her way to join the King, was arrested by order of the Emperor and imprisoned in the Castle of Innspruck, whence Wogan and his three kinsmen, Richard Gaydon, Captain John Missett, and Ensign Edward O'Toole, released her in a romantic manner, 27th April 1719. In reward for this King James created[1] him, 1719, a *KNIGHT* and *BARONET* [I], with remainder to his heirs-male, and the Pope conferred on him, 13th June 1719, the title of Roman Senator. Sir Charles afterwards entered the Spanish service, and in 1723 distinguished himself at the relief of Santa Cruz, besieged by the Moors. He was appointed Captain of the Irish regiment of infantry, 30th October 1725, and before 1730 was promoted to the rank of Brigadier-General, and made governor of La Mancha. In 1746 he was with the Duke of York at Dunkirk in the hope of being able to join the Prince Regent in Ireland, but this hope being disappointed, he returned to La Mancha. The 14th May 1750 he was appointed Governor of Barcelona, when he appears as General de Brigade. He died in Spain *s.p.* soon after 1752.

II. *SIR* EDWARD WOGAN, second *BARONET*, nephew and heir-male, being elder son of Patrick Wogan of Richardstown, by Thomasine Chamberlaine, his third wife, which Patrick was elder brother of the preceding. He died *s.p.* at Manilla between 1771 and 1782.

III. *SIR* FRANCIS WOGAN or DE WOGAN, third *BARONET*, brother and heir of the preceding, baptized 1st June 1720 in the parish church of Clane, in the diocese of Kildare, entered the French army and was Lieutenant in Dillon's regiment, 6th October 1733; Ensign, 20th September 1734; and

---

[1] The patent is printed in full in *Mémoire Historique et Généalogique sur la Famille de Wogan*, par Le Comte Alph. O'Kelly de Galway, Paris, 1896, p. 68, from which the above account of the family is taken.

WOGAN

afterwards, 6th October 1744, in that of Lally; Aide-Major, 27th March 1746; retired, 8th December 1747. Greatly distinguished himself with the Irish Brigade at the battle of Lauffeld, 2nd July 1747, where he was severely wounded; Knight of the Royal and Military Order of St. Louis; naturalised in France, February 1764. Married, first, Geneviére Charlotte de Boisadam; secondly, Marie Anne de Vaughan, widow [*s.p.*] of Pierre de Laborde; and thirdly, 28th February 1772, at Dinan, in Brittany, Reine Henrietta Claire Céleste, *dite* Mademoiselle de la Coninais, only daughter of Louis John Julien du Chastel, Seigneur de la Rouandais, de la Gaudière, and de Beaumont, in France, Knight of St. Louis, by his wife, Frances Geneviére de la Vallée, daughter and heiress of Francis de la Vallée, Seigneur de la Coninais, in France. She was born at the Château de la Coninais 27th April 1747, and baptized in the parish church of Taden 1st May following. He had issue:—

1. Francis John Patrick de Wogan, born 1st September 1774, died *s.p.v.p.*
2. S*IR* Edward John Peter de Wogan, his heir.
3. Cæsar Augustus Francis John de Wogan, born at Dinan 19th October 1781, died unmarried.
4. Jane Eleanor Reine de Wogan, born 28th January 1777, died at the Château de Bois de la Motte 1827.

1
-
1854

IV. S*IR* EDWARD JOHN PETER DE WOGAN, fourth B*ARONET*, second but elder surviving son and heir of the preceding, born at Dinan 29th March 1778, died 1854. He married first, at Dinan, Anne Scott, daughter of Andrew Scott and Anne du Pontavice. He married secondly, at Dinan, May 1815, Elizabeth Rose de Querhoëut or Kerhoëut, by whom he had issue:—

1. S*IR* Emile Edward de Wogan, his heir.
2. Edward de Wogan, died unmarried.
3. Zenaïde de Wogan.

1854
-
1891

V. S*IR* EMILE EDWARD DE WOGAN, fifth B*ARONET*, elder son and heir of the preceding, born at Dinan 13th March 1817, succeeded his father 1854, named Knight of the Legion of Honour 11th August 1850. Member of la Société des Gens de Lettres; died in Paris 23rd June 1891. He married, 3rd March 1848, Isabelle de Chamberlaine, and had issue:—

1. Emile Tannequy, his heir.

YORK

2. Emile Tannequy Edward de Wogan.
3. Jane de Wogan, married 26th June 1893 the Count Just de Plauzolles.
4. Alice de Wogan, married M. Nordin.
5. Eva de Wogan, died young.

VI. S*IR* EMILE TANNEQUY DE WOGAN, sixth *Baronet*, Baron de Wogan [F], elder son and heir of the preceding, born 23rd November 1850, succeeded his father 23rd June 1891. A well-known *littérateur* and member of the Yacht Club of France, etc. etc. He married, 17th October 1888, Griselle Anne Marie Hutchinson de Loyauté, only child of Alexander Hutchinson and Henrietta Emma Aimée de Loyauté, eldest daughter and co-heir of Henry Louis, last Count de Loyauté, [F]. She was born at the Château de Langlée, near Montargis (Loiret), 2nd March 1860. He has issue :— 1891

1. Yvonne Betsey Isabella de Wogan, born 22nd November 1893.

WORTH, Baronet [I].

I. PATRICK WORTH, E*sq*. 'of the Kingdom of 'Ireland, Lieutenant-Colonel in the service of his Imperial and 'Catholic Majesty, and Town-Major of Ghent,' was on 12th September 1733 created by James III and VIII a *Knight* and *Baronet* [I]. 1733 -

YORK, Duke of [E].

I. H.R.H. HENRY BENEDICT MARIA CLEMENT, Prince of England and Scotland, younger son of James III and VIII by Mary Clementina, daughter and co-heir of Prince James Lewis Sobieski, born 6th March 1725 in the Muti (afterwards Savorelli) Palace at Rome, and was created by his father, probably at or shortly after his birth, and certainly before 28th March 1733, *Duke of York* [E]. In 1745 he was at Dunkirk for the purpose of commanding the French expedition, which was on the point of sailing for England when news arrived of the fatal retreat from Derby. On the 3rd July 1747 he was created a Cardinal Deacon of the Holy Roman Church by Pope Benedict XIV, and 13th July 1761 was made Bishop of Frascati *c.* 1733 - 1788

YORK

and Cardinal Bishop. By the death *s.p.l.* of his elder brother Charles III, 31st January 1788, he became *de jure* King of England, Scotland, France, and Ireland, as Henry IX and I, when all honours merged in the Crown. He died unmarried at Rome, 13th July 1807, when the male line of the Royal House of Stuart and the whole of the issue of James II and VII became extinct.

NOTES

ADDITIONAL NOTES

There are also two warrants in which the names are blank, the one creating a Duke [E], dated 2nd October 1716, and the other an Earl [E], dated 10th March 1718.

P. 5. The Editor is indebted to Mr. Blackburne Daniell for the following extract regarding the Countess of Alberstrof from the MSS. of Sir John Coxe Hippesley, now in the possession of his descendant, Mr. Horner of Mells Park : 'I visited the 'Countess d'Alberstrof (she had been created a Countess of the Empire by the 'Emperor Francis) at Paris in a convent, accompanied by Mr. Andrew Stewart, a few 'days after the demolition of the Bastille, 1789. She then produced many letters of 'Prince Charles, evidently denoting their connection as man and wife. She died in 'Switzerland.' Note by Sir John Hippesley : 'Lady Hippesley's mother, Lady Stewart 'of Allanbank, was a cousin-german to the Countess d'Alberstrof.' In another place Sir J. Hippesley states that 'the late Emperor offered to create the daughter (the late 'Duchess of Albany) a Countess of the Empire, as he had previously conferred that 'rank on her mother, but her father declined accepting this boon, himself designating 'her Duchess of Albany.'

P. 15. By the courtesy of John Venn, Esq., F.R.S., F.S.A., Fellow and President of Gonville and Caius College, Cambridge, the Editor is able to add the following additional particulars concerning the Ashtons:—John Ashton was a member of the family of Ashton of Penketh, being apparently a son of Captain Andrew Preston of Liverpool. He was married (Lic., Vic. Gen. Office, 15 December 1685, to 'John 'Ashton, Esq., aged about 32, of St. Martin's-in-the-Fields, and Mary Rigby, aged 'about 19, daughter of Edward Rigby, Mercer, of St. Augustin [*i.e.* "St. Faith under '"St. Paul"]') at Great St. Helens, and had issue: (1) John, baptized at St. Faith under St. Paul, London, 29th June 1686, buried there next day; (2) James, created a *Baronet*, died before 1698 ; (3) Edward, buried at St. Faith, 20th May 1689; (4) [   ], buried at St. Faith, 11th August 1691 ; (5) Mary Ann Isabella Margaretha Beatrix, a godchild of Queen Mary Beatrix, married the Rev. Richard Venn, M.A., Rector of St. Antholin's, London, and died 25th June 1762, leaving issue. John Ashton was buried at St. Faith's 28th January 1691. Admon. P.C.C. to Edward Rigby, 20th September 1698.—See also *Notes on the Family of Ashton of Penketh*, by J. Venn, F.R.S., F.S.A., Liverpool, 1887, and *Annals of a Clerical Family, etc.*, by the same author, London, 1904.

P. 37. Sir Toby Bourke, writing to Lord Caryll, 28th October 1705 (Carte MSS. 180, f. 120b.), says of Sir Timon Connock : 'He deserves anything, for he is a man of 'excellent principle ; ye King and Queen of Spain have a true kindness for him, ye 'Princes and ye Ambassador do esteem him very much.'

P. 168. Colonel John Roy Stewart, created a *Baronet* by Charles III, 4th November 1784, had two nephews at Culloden, Donald and James. Donald was a Major in the French service, and was wounded and taken prisoner at Culloden, but escaped to France and resided for many years at St. Omers. It seems possible that he was created a Marquis

ADDITIONAL NOTES

by Charles III, for on the 31st January 1784 William Robertson of Lude, writing to his father from St. Omers, says: 'But here talking of acquaintances, I must not so slightly 'pass over two of my grandmother's friends—that is, gentlemen who were "out," as 'they say here. They are both Stewarts, but Marquis Stewart,[1] by his grave deport-'ment and formal address, besides his great alliances in Strathspey (which has the 'honour of his nativity), claims the precedency. The Marquis is a half-pay Captain in 'the French service, and has lived here about thirty years in exactly the same routine. 'His hair in the morning being dressed in a methodical curl with a huge bag behind. 'The hat, as it were by instinct, finds its place on top. Then, slipping both hands into 'an antiquated muff, forth issues the great Marquis—on one side hangs the Croise de 'St. Louis, from the opposite button dangles the necessary cane. It is well known the 'Marquis would rather be crucified than eat flesh on a Friday, and it is confidentially 'reported that he shaves with thirteen different razors upon the same occasion, regularly 'paraded for that purpose. Had the Prince been King of Great Britain, the Marquis 'was undoubtedly to have been the Lord Chamberlain.'—See *In the Shadow of Cairngorm*, by the Rev. W. Forsyth, M.A., D.D., Edinburgh, 1900, p. 182, where there is also a reproduction of a pen-and-ink sketch entitled 'The Marquis of Strathspey.'

---

[1] Dr. Forsyth tells me that John Roy Stewart's nephew was always known as 'Marquis of Strathspey.'

PART II

KNIGHTAGE, APPOINTMENTS GRANTS OF HONOUR ETC.

KNIGHTS

1705.[1] *a* Apr. 16. Toby Bourke, afterwards first *Baron Bourke* [I].
1707.[2] *a* Mar. 21. Timon Connock.
1709.   June 15. James Sarsfield of Nantes.[3]
1710.[4] *a* Nov. 12. Captain George Colgrave.
1713.[5] *a* Sept. 13. Thomas Higgons.
1714.[6] *a* Dec. 9. John Forrester, afterwards first *Baronet* [S].
1715.   Dec. 29. Patrick Bannerman, Provost of Aberdeen.[7]

---

[1] He is designated Sir Toby Bourke in his letters of appointment as James's Ambassador to the Court of Madrid. See p. 20.

[2] See p. 37.

[3] The patent recites that he is a native of Nantes, and the son of Paul Sarsfield, and grandson of James Sarsfield, natives of Limerick, who were descended from the branch of the Viscounts Kilmallock, and continues 'that in consideration of the services ' of the old and gentle family of Sarsfield, and particularly of those of Patrick, Earl of ' Lucan, Captain of the 2nd company of the King's Guards and *Maréchal des camps* ' of the Most Christian King, and of Dominick, Viscount Kilmallock, Colonel of a foot ' regiment in France, who, after distinguishing themselves by many deeds of bravery in ' Ireland, followed the late King into France, where they were killed, after distinguishing ' themselves in the service of the Most Christian King, and also in consideration of his ' personal merit,' he had conferred the honour of Knighthood, etc.

[4] On¦ the 22nd January 1705 he had letters of recommendation as George Colgrave, and on the 12th November 1710 he has a testimonial as Sir George. See pp. 203, 205. He was son of Lieutenant-Colonel Colgrave of Lee's regiment, who was killed at Hochstedt.

[5] He is designated Sir Thomas in a letter from Queen Mary of this date. He was the second son of Sir Thomas Higgons, M.P., diplomatist and author, by his second wife, Bridget, widow of Simon Leach of Cadeleigh, co. Devon, daughter of Sir Bevil Granville of Stowe, and was for some time (December 1713 to July 1715) James's Secretary of State. Biographies of his father and of his younger brother Bevil (born 1670, died 1st August 1735) are in the *Dictionary of National Biography*.

[6] On which date he is spoken of as Sir John in a letter from the Duke of Berwick to King James.

[7] He was knighted on the occasion of the presentation of an address to King James at Dunnottar, congratulating him 'on his arrival in his ancient Kingdom of Scotland,' and this title was retained by him, and he is so designated on his tombstone in St. Nicholas's Churchyard in Aberdeen. He was the fourth son of Sir Alexander Bannerman of Elsick, first Baronet [S], by Margaret, daughter of Patrick Scott of Thirlstone, was born 1678, admitted a burgess of Guild 10th August 1687, elected Provost of Aberdeen 28th September 1715, ejected 10th April 1716, and sent a prisoner to Carlisle, where he was tried for high treason, and narrowly escaped hanging. He died 4th June 1733. He married, 1714, Margaret, daughter of Sir Charles Maitland of Pitrichie, and by her, who died 31st October 1750, aged sixty-three, he had two sons and three daughters. His grandson succeeded as sixth Baronet [S] in 1796. See *Memorials of the Aldermen, Provosts, and Lord Provosts of Aberdeen*, 1272-1895, by Alexander M. Munro, F.S.A. (Scotland), printed for the subscribers, Aberdeen, 1897, p. 208.

KNIGHTS

1716. Jan. ? . Henry Crawford, Portioner of Crail, Fifeshire.[1]
1717. „ . John Walkinshaw of Burrowfield, Lannockshire.[2]
1717. „ . George Jerningham.[2]
1717.[3] *a* Dec. 20. Peter Redmond, afterwards first *Baron Redmond* [I].
1719. June . Richard Gaydon, Knight of St. Louis, Major in Dillon's regiment.[4]
„ „ . John Missett, Captain in Dillon's regiment.[4]
„ „ . Edward O'Toole, Ensign in Dillon's regiment.[4]
1722.[5] *a* July 6. Luke O'Toole.
1728.[6] *a* June 28. John Hely, afterwards first *Baronet* [I].
1734. *a* Jan. 22. Mark Forstal, afterwards first *Baronet* [S].
1747.[7] *a* Apr. 17. John William O'Sullivan, afterwards first *Baronet* [I].

---

[1] See *List of Persons concerned in the Rebellion*, Scottish History Society Publications, vol. viii., 1890, where he is said to have 'furnished the rebels with money and ' welcomed them to the Town [St. Andrews], advised them to secure the Excise officers and their Books, was in the Rebellion and knighted by the Pretender 1715, yet has ' a pension of 55 lib. p. annum from the Trustees for Improvment of Manufactors.'

[2] They are designated Knights in their letters of appointment as James's Ambassadors at Vienna and The Hague respectively. Sir George Jerningham afterwards (14th June 1737) succeeded his elder brother as fifth Baronet [E], and died 21st January 1774. He married, 1733, Mary, daughter and heiress of Francis Plowden, Comptroller of the Household to James II and VII and James III and VIII, by his wife, Mary, daughter and in her issue heiress of the Hon. John Stafford-Howard, younger son of William (Howard), Viscount Stafford [E], the last victim of Titus Oates. His grandson, Sir George William, seventh Baronet, was restored as eighth Viscount Stafford, 1824.

[3] He is designated a Knight in the warrant creating him a Baronet.

[4] For assisting their kinsman, Sir Charles Wogan, in effecting the escape of the Princess Clementina Sobieska from Innspruck, 27th April 1719. See p. 187.

[5] On which day he has a commission of Brigadier-General as Sir Luke O'Toole.

[6] They are designated Knights in the warrants creating them Baronets.

[7] See p. 143.

KNIGHTS OF THE GARTER

K.G.'s

1692. Apr. 19. James, Prince of Wales, Duke of Cornwall [E] and Rothesay [S].
„ „ „ William (Herbert), first *Duke of Powis* [E].
„ „ „ John (Drummond), first *Duke of Melfort* [S].
„ „ „ Francis Nompar (de Caumont), first Duke of Lauzan [F].[1]
1706. June 21. James (Drummond), first *Duke of Perth* [S].
[1714. ? Piers (Butler), first *Earl of Newcastle* [I].[2]]
1716. Apr. 8. John (Erskine), first *Duke of Mar* [S].
1723. July 30. James (Douglas-Hamilton), fifth Duke of Hamilton [S], and second Duke of Brandon [G B], K.T.
1726. Mar. 5. Philip (Wharton), first Duke of Wharton and *Northumberland* [E].
1727. Apr. 3. James (Fitzjames), Duke of Liria [Spain], Earl of Tynmouth.
1742. ? Charles, Prince of Wales, Duke of Cornwall [E] and Rothesay [S].
1747. Nov. . Daniel (O'Brien), first *Earl of Lismore* [I].

---

[1] So created a few weeks previously. He was fifth Count (1570) and fifteenth Baron (*c.* 1211) of Lauzan, and died in Paris 19th November 1723, aged ninety.

[2] The Duke of Berwick writes to King James, 26th January 1714:—'Lord Melford 'is dead, upon which subject my Lord Newcastle told me that, though he believed your 'Majesty would not give that Garter on this side of the water, yet he did designe on this 'occasion to begg your Majesty will be mindfull of him in proper time. So I thought 'it necessary to acquaint your Majesty with it, that you may have your answer ready, 'though indeed if he spakes in the termes he told me, you will easily know what to 'say.'

KNIGHTS OF THE THISTLE

K.T.'s

1705. Mar. . James (Drummond), *Marquis of Drummond*.
   „   „   „ Charles (Hay), thirteenth Earl of Errol [S].
   „   „   „ William (Keith), ninth Earl Marischal [S].[1]
1708. Feb. ? William (Keith), ninth Earl Marischal [S].
   „ May 10. John Baptiste (Gualterio), first *Earl of Dundee* [S].
1716. Apr. 8. James (Butler), second Duke of Ormonde [E and I], Baron Dingwall [S], K.G.
   „   „   „ James (Maule), fourth Earl of Panmure [S].
1722. May 26. Arthur (Dillon), first *Earl* [S] and *Viscount* [I] (? *Dillon*).
1723. July 30. James (Douglas-Hamilton), fifth Duke of Hamilton [S] and second Duke of Brandon [G B], K.G.[2]
1725. Dec. 29. George (Keith), tenth Earl Marischal [S].
   „   „ 31. James (Hay), first *Earl of Inverness* [S].
   „   „   „ William (Maxwell), fifth Earl of Nithsdale [S].
   „   „   „ James (Murray), first *Earl of Dunbar* [S].
1739. May 15. James (Drummond), third *Duke of Perth* [S].
1740. July 27. James (Douglas-Hamilton), fifth Duke of Hamilton [S] and second Duke of Brandon [G B].[3]
1742. ? Charles, Prince of Wales, Duke of Cornwall [E] and Rothesay [S].
1768. . John (Caryll), third *Baron Caryll of Dunford* [E].
1784. Nov. 30. Charlotte (Stuart), *Duchess of Albany* [S].

---

[1] The Warrant for investing the Marquis of Drummond has a note that two similar Warrants of the same date were granted to the Earl of Errol and the Earl Marischal, but the latter, at least, would seem not to have been acted upon, as there is a fresh Warrant three years afterwards as above.

[2] This would seem not to have been acted upon; see under 27th July 1740, when there is a fresh Warrant to the same man.

[3] Noted as antedated at Rome, 1st January 1725.

DECLARATIONS

DECLARATIONS OF NOBLESSE, ETC.

1692. Oct. 15. Certificate of the nobility of the family of Zouche [E] on the application of the Sieur Zouche de la Lande, who represents that he is descended from said family.

„ Dec. 31. Declaration that Francis Leslie, Seigneur du Clisson, is legitimately descended from the noble family of Leslie [S], 'which we recognise to be really noble and illus-' trious for many centuries back.'[1]

1693. Feb. 1. Certificate of character of Father Dominick White, a Capuchin, formerly the King's Chaplain.

1694. Apr. 15. Declaration that Sir Dominick Knowles [I], now residing at Nantes, is a gentleman descended from the noble and ancient family of Knowles of Orchardstone [I], which is descended from an old family [E].

„ June . Warrant to James Therry, Herald, to examine the pretensions of John Jacquenot Jackson, Sieur des Auches, a Captain in the French army, to bear the arms of the family of Jackson of Hickelton, co. York, Baronet [E], of which he pretends to be a cadet, and if he shall appear to be descended, to grant him the arms thereof with the proper distinctions.

---

[1] This sets forth that whereas Francis Leslie Lesloy du Clisson, Seigneur de Ricordières and de la Besselière, Gentleman in Ordinary to his Most Christian Majesty, born in Anjou, besought us about five years ago in our Privy Council [S] to testify the nobility and arms of the family of Leslie, lairds of Balquain, from which the Counts of Leslie in Germany are descended, and which is of the same stock as the family of Rothes; and whereas we thereupon directed several noble persons to examine the genealogy of the said family, who reported the descent of Philip Leslie, great-grandfather of the said Francis, and the first of his ancestors who emigrated from Scotland to France, and settled there, on which the said Council empowered the Earl of Perth, Lord Chancellor [S], to pass letters-patents under the Great Seal containing all the genealogy of the said Philip Leslie and verifying his nobility, but in consequence of the sudden outbreak of the rebellion all the documents and the order of the Council remained in the Chancery, from which the said Francis Leslie cannot get them without receiving them under the Seal of the Prince of Orange, which he has refused to do, and has besought us to grant him under our Great Seal, for these reasons, and especially because the said Francis Leslie especially needs these, our present letters, that one of his sons may be knighted, who had his arm broken at the head of his company at the battle of Steinkirk; we therefore, etc. etc. With note that a French translation of the foregoing declaration granted by His Majesty on the attestations produced from Scotland, proving the several contents thereof, was given to the said Sieur du Clisson, dated 9th January 1693.

DECLARATIONS OF NOBLESSE

1694. Dec. 1 and 30. Certificate that John Robertson [S], a Catholic, is a very faithful subject, who was forced on account of his religion and loyalty to seek refuge in France with his wife Magdalin Hepburn, where they arrived only five months ago.

1695. May 9. Certificate of the fidelity and services of the Marquis de Kerjan during the three years he has served as captain of a ship, with permission to him, since at present the King has no employment at sea to give him, to take service when he pleases, except with the King's enemies.[1]

„ Aug. 30. Certificate of the noblesse of the Hanmer family, and that they have long enjoyed the honours and privileges of Baronets [E].

„ Sept. 16. Certificate of the nobility of the family of Ogilvie [S], and that James Ogilvie, Sieur de la Perriere, has shown the King vouchers of noblesse granted in Scotland to his deceased father, John, certified by several lords [S], and particularly by the Earl of Airlie, head of the said family.

1696. Jan. 21. Certificate that the Countess of Grammont is descended from the families of Hamilton and Ormonde, which are among the most considerable in Scotland and Ireland.

„ Oct. 7. Certificate of the nobility of the family of Cary [E], and that Mademoiselle Cary is descended therefrom.

1697. Mar. 14. Certificate that Matthew Crone is a gentleman descended from a good family [I].

1698. Apr. 11. Certificate that the Sieur George Christopher Kast, a native of Strasburg, has always behaved in his dominions as a man honest and zealous for the King's service.

„ Apr. 12. Certificate that Colonels Johnston and Livingston have served the King faithfully on all occasions, that Colonel Johnson is a person of the first rank [S], and has served him faithfully for fourteen years, and was imprisoned by the Usurper; that Colonel Livingston belongs to an old family [S], and has served him and his late brother twenty-four years, was several times wounded in his service, was imprisoned by the Usurper and sentenced to be hung and quartered, and after being imprisoned for three years was banished to France; and understanding that the said Colonels were anxious to serve the Republic of Venice, granting them leave and recommending them to the Senate.

„ June 15. Certificate that Captain Arnold, after serving for a long time at sea, served in England as a foot Captain, where

---

[1] Noted as copy of that date of a certificate, dated 14th January 1691.

DECLARATIONS OF NOBLESSE

    he did his duty faithfully, and that having followed the King to France he has served for seven years on the ships of H.M.C.M., where he has always behaved to the satisfaction of his superior officers.

1698. June 17. Certificate that the Sieur Trohy [I], living at Antwerp, having lost his parents in the rebellion [I], was forced to learn the profession of surgeon, declaring the said Trohy to be such as he could have been, before the practice of the said profession, in order that he might enjoy all the privileges and advantages he might have claimed by his birth.

„ July 18. Certificate that James Bignon [E] has long served the late King and himself as a servant, and has always lived as an honest man and good Catholic.

„ Nov. 18. Certificate that Thomas Bragg served as a Captain of horse [I] with much zeal and capacity.

1699. Mar. 23. Certificate that Colonel Solomon Slater had been Commissary-General of the Musters [I] since 13th May 1690, and that he had since been expelled [E] for his loyalty.

„ Apr. 30. Certificate that Robert Sumerville [S] is a good Catholic and a faithful servant of the King, whom he has served with loyalty and distinction as Captain of the Scots Guards, and giving him leave to go to Rome.

„ Aug. 3. Certificate that Sir Terence Macdermot, being Lord Mayor of Dublin when the King was there, discharged his duties with much zeal and fidelity, and having come to France after the battle of Aughrim, has suffered much loss in Ireland, in the island of Montserrat, and elsewhere.

„ „ 7. Certificate that Morgan Price, having served the King as Captain and Major [I], and having gone to England with the King's leave on his private affairs, has been banished for having been in the King's service.

„ „ 15. Declaration that George Waters, eldest son of John Waters of Newcastle, co. Limerick, is descended from a good old family [I]. A copy was given by Lord Caryll, 29th March 1704.

„ „ 18. Warrant to James Therry, Athlone Herald, to examine the pedigrees of Julian Campain, Seigneur de St. Julian, who desires to be authorised to bear the arms of the family of Campain [E], and if he proves to be descended from them, to grant him the arms of that family with proper distinction; and of Louis Matthias Becquet, Seigneur de Beffe, and Peter Thomas Becquet, Seigneur de Moulin le Compte, who claim to be descended from the family of Becquet [E].

„ Nov. 26. Certificate that Mademoiselle Jeanne Macarty, now at

DECLARATIONS OF NOBLESSE

Lisbon, is descended from the ancient house of the Macartys, and that three of her brothers have been slain in the King's service.

1699. Nov. . Certificate that Francis Scott is descended from a noble family [S], being brother to the Earl of Tarras, that he has been Ensign-Colonel in the regiment of Buchan, when he did good service in the last revolution [E], and has since served the King in France, and that he has become a Catholic.

1700. Jan. 2. Declaration that Luke Comerford is a gentleman, the issue of parents of gentle blood [I].

„ „ 31. Certificate that John and Thomas Lyons [I], Catholics, have served with credit twelve years in Ireland and France, under Colonel Dominick Sheldon, and that, having been discharged at the recent muster of the armies of H.M.C.M., they cannot return home, being banished for their loyalty.

„ Feb. 3. Declaration that Mr. Thomas O'Clary of Fedan, co. Tipperary, is a gentleman and the issue of gentle parents [I].

„ „ 4. Declaration that Mr. James Fagan, a native of co. Dublin, now residing in Bordeaux, is a gentleman, and is descended in a direct line from the noble and ancient family of Fagan of Feltrum [I].

„ „ 24. Certificate that John Carroll and Daniel Macevay [I], Catholics, etc., identical with that to John and Thomas Lyons, 31st January.

„ Mar. 1. Certificate that John Osland [E], a Catholic, served faithfully as Major of dragoons in the King's army [I], and that he has suffered much and cannot return to England, having been banished for his faith and loyalty.

„ „ 15. Certificate that Louis Matthew Becquet, Seigneur de Beffe, and Peter Thomas Becquet, Seigneur de Moulin le Comte, his brother, now living in Flanders, are descended from the noble family of Becquets [E], and are therefore of gentle descent.[1]

„ „ 17. Certificate that Bartholomew Morrogh, now living in Spain, is descended from a family of gentle blood in co. Cork.

„ May 8. Declaration that Nicholas Geraldin, son of Nicholas, now living at St. Malo, is descended from the ancient and noble family of the Geraldines of Gurtins, co. Kilkenny, which is descended from the very ancient and noble family of the Earls of Desmond, as appears by a letter of the late Duke of Ormonde and by a genealogy of the Geraldines drawn up by Richard Carny, Ulster King of Arms.

---

[1] A copy certified by Lord Caryll and Mr. Nairne was given 28th March 1702.

DECLARATIONS OF NOBLESSE

1700. May 10. Declaration that William O'Brien of Tullo Garnony and Cross, co. Limerick, is the son of Terence O'Brien and Elizabeth Power, Catholics, descended from the noble family of O'Brien of Cuonagh, in that county.

„ June 2. Declaration that William Bourke [I] is a gentleman and the issue of parents of gentle birth.

„ „ 14. Certificate that the bearer, James Axton[1] [E], a Catholic and loyal subject of the King, left his country for his religion and took refuge in France, where he only asks permission to continue to work at his trade of weaver at Paris, where he has already worked for several years.

„ July 10. Certificate[2] that Catherine Fitzgerald, wife of Stephen Simon, Sieur du Bourg, is descended paternally from the very ancient and noble family of Fitzgerald, Earls of Desmond, and maternally from the noble family of Magraghs.

„ „ 15. Certificate that Thomas Browne has served in the regiment of Douglas, that the King has seen certificates that he was wounded in the left arm at Treves, and has lost the use of it, and that he has always been a loyal subject.

„ „ 28. Certificate that Patrick Hicky, now living in the Rue St. Marguerite, Fauxbourg St. Germains, left Ireland with the Irish troops, after the capitulation of Limerick.

„ Aug. 31. Certificate[3] that Paul Leonard, now living in Spain, is the son of parents of gentle birth of co. Waterford.

„ Sept. 1. Similar certificates in favour of Stephen Leonard,[4] of Cadiz, elder brother of the above-named Paul, and of Nicholas Aylward, of Port St. Marie in Spain.[5]

„ „ „ Certificate that Catherine Macarty, now in a convent at Nancy, is of gentle birth and is descended from the ancient and gentle family of Macarty Reaghs, co. Cork.

„ „ „ Certificate that Cornelius O'Sullivan, formerly a foot Captain in the King's troops [I], afterwards a reformed officer in the same troops in France, and now of the

---

Noted as solicited by Dr. Betham, in order to procure Mons. Argenson's protection for the said Axton, that he might continue his trade in Paris.

[2] Noted as granted on the attestations of the Archbishop of Tuam, Lords Clare, Brittas, and Enniskillen, three priests, Dr. Lehy, and Therry, and the original one being lost, it was renewed 22nd October.

[3] Noted as granted on the attestations of Sir Andrew Lee, Colonel Power, Captain Fr. Grant, Counsellor Robert Power, and Therry, and delivered to Mr. Waters.

[4] Whose birth is attested by Lords Slane, Clare, Brittas, and Enniskillin, and Therry.

[5] Whose birth is attested by Lords Brittas and Enniskillin, Colonel Power, Captain Frank Grant, and Therry.

DECLARATIONS OF NOBLESSE

Duke of Lorraine's Bodyguard, is a gentleman descended from the ancient and gentle family of O'Sullivan More, co. Roscommon.

1700. Sept. 25. Certificate[1] that Edmund Barry, formerly a foot Captain [I], and afterwards Lieutenant in H.M.'s Guards in France, is a gentleman descended from the ancient and noble family of the Earl of Barrymore, co. Cork.

„ „ 25. Certificate that Peter Hanley, formerly a Captain-Lieutenant [I], afterwards a reformed officer in the King's troops in France, and now of the Duke of Lorraine's Bodyguard, is a gentleman, the son of gentle parents in co. Roscommon.

„ Nov. 5. Certificate that John Coyle, now living in Paris, is the legitimate son of parents of gentle birth, Eugene Coyle and Catherine Barnewall, Catholics, and is descended from the gentle family of Coyle in Connaught, and that he and his father, in consequence of their religion and loyalty, forfeited all their property [I] and followed the King to France, where they served in the armies of the M.C.K. till the said Eugene fell in action.

1701. Jan. 4. Certificate that Stephen Gillet served in the King's troops [E] as one of the Bodyguard and afterwards as Ensign of infantry, and was made Cornet of dragoons [S], since serving in Ireland and France.

„ „ 19. Certificate that John O'Hanlon, now living in Paris, is the son of Edmund O'Hanlon and Honora Hodnett, both of gentle birth [I].

„ Feb. 26. Declaration[2] of the pedigree of Thomas Drummond, second son of the Earl of Melfort, tracing back the descent of the family of Drummond to Maurice, the commander of the fleet in which Edgar Atheling and his mother Agatha and his sisters Margaret and Christina took refuge in Scotland and who was of gentle parents in Hungary.

„ July 20. Certificate[3] that John Ryan, Captain in Lee's Irish regiment, is a gentleman descended from the Ryans of Glanogaha, Tipperary, a family that has been always Catholic and loyal.

„ Aug. 17. Certificate that Charles Russell, now living at Cadiz, is a gentleman descended from the ancient and noble family of Russell, Earls of Bedford.

1702. Mar. 26. Certificate that Daniel O'Rierdane, Captain in Dillon's regiment, and Aide-de-camp to the Duke of Vendome, is

---

[1] Noted as solicited by and given to Mr. Barry, the King's Page.
[2] Noted as antedated by the King's order, 19th August 1688.
[3] Noted as solicited and delivered to Mr. Ryan, the priest.

DECLARATIONS OF NOBLESSE

of gentle birth, being descended paternally from the old and gentle family of O'Rierdane of Banmore, co. Cork, and maternally from the Nolans of Balenoche, co. Galway.

1702. Mar. 26. Certificate in the same form to Theobald Roche.

„ Apr. 6. Certificate that Oliver Brindijone, *avocat* in the Parliament of Rennes, is of gentle birth, being the grandson of Ralph Bermingham, *alias* Brindijone, a cadet of the old and gentle family of Bermingham of Carrick, co. Kildare, who left Ireland about 1564 on account of the persecution, and settled in Brittany.

„ „ „ Certificate that George Morogh of Morlaix is descended from the gentle family of Moroghs of the city of Cork, who lost considerable property in the time of Cromwell for their loyalty.

„ „ 24. Certificate that Daniel O'Dun[n]e, Captain in Dorington's regiment, formerly Lieutenant-Colonel in the regiment of Charles O'Moore in Ireland, is descended from an old and gentle family in the Queen's county, being son of Francis Dun[n]e of Tinehinch, who was killed at Aughrim with two of his sons, after raising two foot-companies at his own expense for the service of the late King.

„ „ 28. Certificate that Thomas Grace, son of Edmond Grace of Ballynily, co. Limerick, is descended from the old and gentle Catholic family of Grace of Courtstown, co. Kilkenny.

„ June 9. Certificate that Christopher Hyrde, of Querellon, of the parish of Chateuneuf, diocese of Quimper, is of gentle birth, being the grandson of John Hyrde, naturalised in France 1606, who was son of John Hyrde of Drogheda, descended from the old and gentle family of Hyrde, otherwise O'Hyrde of Ladarath, co. Louth.

„ Aug. . Certificates that James Rice, now in Spain in the service of H.C.M., is descended from a gentle family of co. Limerick, and that Toby Bourke, now in Spain in the same service, is descended from the old and noble family of Bourke of Clanrickard.

„ „ . Warrant to James Therry to examine the claims of Francis Richmont, *alias* Richardson, Lieutenant of dragoons in H.M.C.M.'s service, to bear the arms of the family of Richardson of Glasgow, and if he proves his descent to grant him the said arms.

„ Oct. 31. Declaration of the noblesse of Nicholas Luker, now residing at Bordeaux, who is the son of gentle parents in co. Waterford.

„ „ „ Declaration of the noblesse of Daniel O'Brien, now

DECLARATIONS OF NOBLESSE

serving with the troops in France, who is the son of gentle parents in co. Cork.

1702. Oct. 31. Declaration of the noblesse of James Kelly, who formerly served in Dorington's regiment in France, and who is the son of gentle parents in co. Limerick.

„ Nov. 23. Declaration of the noblesse of Miss Mary Charlotte Fleming, daughter of Richard Fleming of Ardagh, co. Meath, who is descended from the old and noble family of the Barons of Slane.

1703. Jan. 13. Declarations of the noblesse respectively of Daniel Cunigane, son of gentle parents in co. Tipperary; of John Martin, son of gentle parents in co. Limerick; and of Francis de Richemont, *alias* Richardson, Lieutenant of dragoons in H.M.C.M.'s service, who is descended from the gentle family of the Richardsons of Glasgow.

„ Mar. 28. Declarations of the noblesse respectively of Peter Nagle, formerly Alderman of Cork, the son of gentle parents of co. Kerry; of Micheal Macegan, M.D., residing at Dormans in Champagne, the son of gentle parents of co. Clare; of Garrett Fitzgerald, the son of gentle parents of co. Kildare; of Richard Butler, the son of gentle parents of co. Kilkenny; and of Patrick Terry, now in the service of H.C.M. at Cadiz, the son of gentle parents of the city of Limerick.

„ Apr. 28. Declaration of the noblesse of Philip Francis Becquet, Seigneur of Saleppe and Counsellor in the county of Douay in similar terms to that granted to his cousins.

„ May or June. Declaration of the noblesse respectively of Arthur O'Brien and Denis Macarty.

With note that when signing the above, the King, with the advice of his Council, resolved to grant no more, without very strong reasons, but that notwithstanding he had the kindness to grant the one which follows at the request of a widow.

„ June 14. Grant to Elizabeth Tricot, widow of David Bourke, formerly Captain of dragoons in Ireland and afterwards an officer in the Dublin regiment in France, where he was killed in the service of H.M.C.M., who was the son of gentle parents in Clare and descended from the old and noble family of Bourkes, Lords Castle Connell, and Brittas, of a declaration of the noblesse of her said husband, that she and her son, Augustine Bourke, may avail themselves of it if necessary.

1704. Mar. 12. Declaration of the noblesse of Malachy O'Laughlin, Lieutenant in Dorington's regiment, the eldest son of Denis O'Laughlin, younger son of Anthony O'Laughlin, Lord of the Barony of Burren, and head of an old and

DECLARATIONS OF NOBLESSE

                 gentle family in co. Clare, and of Honora Clancy, daughter of the head of the Clancy family and descended in the fourth degree from the Earls of Thomond.

1704. Mar. 13. Declaration that the family of Cunningham, Earls of Glencairn, is one of the noble and old families among the peers [S].

„ Apr. 7. Declaration of the noblesse of John Macnamara, residing at Port Louis in Brittany, who is descended from the old and gentle family of Macnamara, who possessed considerable property [I].

1705. Jan. 14. Declaration of the noblesse of Roger O'Conlean, formerly a Captain [I], and now Lieutenant in Lee's regiment, descended paternally from a family who lost their considerable property in co. Cork for their religion and loyalty, and maternally from the old and gentle family of Mulronny O'Carroll in Queen's county, head of the O'Carrolls [I].

„ „ 22. Letters of recommendation to George Colgrave, son of Colonel Colgrave, who served with distinction for several years in the army of H.M.C.M., and was lately killed at Hochstadt, and who has himself served ten years in the same service, and who now wishes to travel.

„ „ . Declaration of the noblesse of Matthew Dowdall, Cornet in Sheldon's regiment, son of John Dowdall of Athlumney, co. Meath, formerly Captain of horse, and Elizabeth Macmahon, who belonged to the illustrious family of Macmahon of Carrickmacross, co. Monaghan.

„ Apr. 6. Declaration of the noblesse of John O'Cahane, an Irish officer now at Strasburg, eldest son of Colonel Roger O'Cahane, head of the old and gentle family of O'Cahane, and of Catherine O'Neil, daughter of the late Phelix O'Neil, who belonged to one of the principal branches of the noble family of O'Neil.

1705. May . Declaration of the noblesse of Toby Geraldin, who belongs to the old and gentle family of Geraldin of Gurteen, co. Kilkenny, a branch of the very noble and old family of the Geraldins of Desmond, and who is a relative of the Nicholas Geraldin of St. Malo, to whom the King granted a declaration of noblesse in 1700.

„ June 6. Certificate that Sir Richard Bulstrode served Charles I, Charles II, and James II and VII, in many honourable employments both civil and military, that he was for many years English Envoy at Brussels, and continued there after the usurpation till 1704, when, his correspondence with France being discovered, he was obliged to fly to France, leaving his family in Brussels, when his

DECLARATIONS OF NOBLESSE

property and his wife's, which consisted of houses there, was either confiscated, or burnt by the bombardment, and she and all her children were obliged to seek refuge at St. Germains with her husband, who after his long and faithful services, being now advanced in years and having a very numerous family, is a fit object for the charity of H.M.C.M.

1707. Sept. 13. Declaration of the noblesse of Edmund Butler, Major in Nugent's regiment of horse, he being descended from Lord Cahir's family.

„ „ „ Declaration of the noblesse of John O'Mara, an officer in Nugent's regiment of horse.

„ „ 20. Certificate to two young gentlewomen [I], Cecile and Mary Furlong, that their father James Furlong was of gentle birth.

„ Dec. 10. Declaration to Claude Francis Girardin, sieur of Mont Gerald, counsellor of the sovereign council of Martinique, who, following the genealogical tables certified by Therry, herald for Ireland, and by Chevillard, genealogist to the M.C.K., is descended from the old family of the Giraldins [I], and belongs to the same branch as that from which M. de Vauvray, Intendant at Toulon, and his brother, the late Marquis of Lery, who served in Ireland under James II and VII, descend, that the said family of Giraldin is very old and noble.

1708. May 4. Declaration of the noblesse of Thomas O'Leyne, now living in Paris, who is descended on both sides from Catholic and loyal families, who possessed considerable estates in Kerry and Limerick.

„ „ 17. Declaration of the noblesse of Valentine Fitzgerald, and of the loyalty and attachment of his family to the King's service, his father having been killed in Ireland in the service of the late King, and his uncle and two brothers having been killed in Italy in the service of H.M.C.M.

„ . Note of certificate to Colonel Fountaine.

1709. Jan. . Declaration of the noblesse of Mr. O'Roerk, an officer [I].

„ Mar. 7. Declaration of the noblesse of Charles Macarty, an Irish priest settled in the Diocese of Seéz in Normandy, who rendered good service to the late King and belongs to one of the noblest and oldest families [I].

„ Apr. . Declaration of the noblesse of Mr. Gough of Dunkirk.

„ Dec. 3. Declaration of the noblesse of Donough Macnamara, who followed James II and VII to France, and is now a reformed Captain in Lee's regiment, and who is head of the very old and gentle family of Macnamara, and is descended maternally from the very old and gentle family of Odueri (? O'Dwyer).

DECLARATIONS OF NOBLESSE

1709. Dec. 3. Declaration of the noblesse of Neal Mackean, who followed King James II and VII to France, where he served many years at sea, and is now settled at Rochefort.

„ „ 31. Declaration of the noblesse of Winifred Macmahon [I], wife of John de Chardon de St. Arques.

1710. Feb. 17. Declaration of the noblesse of Margaret Roche, descended from gentle parents in co. Cork.

„ Apr. 25. Testimonial from King James III and VIII that he has seen a certificate from several persons of understanding and credit that Colonel O'Donnell of Ramalton is nearest kinsman to the Earl of Tyrconnel of that name, forfeited in the reign of James I and VI, that his father and eldest brother had one after the other the command of the Tyrconnel regiment by commission of the Earl, afterwards Duke of Ormonde, then Lord-Lieutenant, for the service of Kings Charles I and II, wherein one of them lost his life fighting against Cromwell, and that he himself was very faithful and zealous in his own country against the late usurper, and had afterwards brought his regiment to France, and that he has on all occasions served with honour and distinction.

„ May 8. Declaration of the noblesse of David Trant, formerly a Major [I], and at present ex-Captain of foot in Bourke's regiment.

„ Nov. 12. Testimonial that the late Mr. Colgrave served fifteen years in France as Lieutenant-Colonel of Lee's regiment and was killed at the battle of Hochstadt, and that his son, Sir George, has been and now is serving in the same regiment as reformed Captain, and that he has always done his duty as a good officer and loyal subject.

„ „ 29. Certificate that Bryan Dermot, an Irish merchant at Rouen, served the late King during the Irish wars as a foot Captain, and that after the capitulation of Limerick he left his property and country to follow James II and VII to France, and served there as an officer till the troops were reformed at the Peace of Ryswick, after which he was obliged to take to trade to maintain himself, while his four brothers who came to France with him continued to serve as officers, and have all died during the present war.

1711. May 8. Declarations of the noblesse of Joseph Fitzgerald, Captain in O'Donnell's regiment, and of Richard Barry,[1] residing at Bayonne.

---

[1] With note that a duplicate of this last was signed by the King, June 1759, and sent to Mr. Marjoribanks at Montpellier.

DECLARATIONS OF NOBLESSE

1711. May 20. Declarations of the noblesse of Laurence Macmahon [I], born and settled at St. Malo, who is descended from the very old and gentle family of the Macmahons of Rosdingtoum, co. Galway, and of Catherine Duvoye, at present residing in the district of Montferrat in Italy, under the protection and charitable care of the Count and Countess of Pro.

1712. Feb. 27. Declaration of the noblesse of William, Francis, and Xavier Sarsfield, natives of the city of Limerick, sons of Ignatius Sarsfield, Major of foot, who after distinguishing himself by his services in Ireland, followed the late King to France and died in Savoy in the service of H.M.C.M., and who was the son of Patrick Sarsfield, gentleman, of the same city, who was descended in a direct line from the branch of the Viscounts Sarsfield of Kilmallock.

„ Mar. 17. Declaration of the noblesse of John O'Callaghan, late Captain in O'Brien's regiment, who died lately in H.M.C.M.'s service, granted to his widow.

„ May 11. Declaration of the noblesse of Robert Sempill, Captain in Lord Galmoye's regiment, who is grandson of the late Hugh, Lord Sempill, Peer of Scotland and sole heir-male of the property and the ancient title of the said lord, whose fourth son Archibald, father of the said Robert, is the only one who left any living male child.

1712. June 1. Declaration of the noblesse of Edmond Cotte, Captain of a free company of one hundred fusiliers in the service of H.M.C.M. in Languedoc.

„ „ „ Certificate that all the brothers of the late Sir Ignatius White [I], a Baronet [E] and Marquis of Albeville [H R E], formerly Envoy-Extraordinary to Holland from James II and VII, and his Secretary of State [I], have died, and that the sole heirs of all these brothers are the daughters of the said Marquis of Albeville, who are at present with their mother in the service of the Queen of Spain and the Prince of the Asturias at Madrid.

„ „ 15. Declaration of the noblesse of Miles MacSwiney, Captain of dragoons in Mahony's regiment in Spain, who is the eldest son and heir of [   ] MacSwiney of Ballymacrice, co. Limerick, and of Jane O'Brien, daughter of Demetrius O'Brien, of Derry, who is descended paternally from the old and illustrious family of MacSwiney, and maternally from the old and noble family of O'Brien, Earl of Thomond.

„ July 18. Declaration of the noblesse of Richard Butler, residing at St. Malo, descended from the old and gentle house of Paulstown, co. Kilkenny.

DECLARATIONS OF NOBLESSE

1714. Oct. 17. Declaration of the noblesse of Constantius Egan, Captain in Berwick's regiment.
1715. Mar. 18. Declaration of the noblesse of Clara Devereux, paternally descended from the house of Devereux of Ballymaguire [I], and maternally is allied to the Earls of Kildare and Westmeath [I], and Lord Montague Brown [E].
1717. Aug. 8. Declaration of the noblesse of Charles Macarty, gentleman [I], Captain of foot in Dorington's regiment, issue of the ancient and illustrious family of Macarty Reagh.
1726. Feb. 19. Declaration of the noblesse of the Abbé William Thomas Tyrril.
„ Mar. 18. Declaration of the noblesse of Edward Warren, Lieutenant of artillery in the service of the Duke of Lorraine.
„ Apr. 12. Attestation in favour of Charlotte Whyte, Countess of Alby, Marchioness of Albeville of the Empire, Lady of Honour to the Queen of Spain, and the legitimate daughter of the late Sir Ignatius Whyte of Ireland, Baronet [E], Count of Alby and Marquis of Albeville, late Ambassador to Holland from James II and VII, and his Secretary of State, wife of the Sieur Antoine de Sartine, Knight of the Order of St. Michael, and Count of Alby and Marquis of Albeville in right of his marriage.
„ July 2. Confirmation of the declaration of the noblesse (dated 7th March 1691) of Nicholas Geraldine FitzTheobald.
„ Sept. 28. Declaration of the noblesse of Colonel William Lacy of the Spanish service, descended from the Lacys of Kilminere, co. Limerick.
1727. Jan. 31. Declaration of the noblesse of William FitzGibbon, Lieutenant-Colonel in the Imperial service.[1]
1728. Jan. 17. Declaration of the noblesse of Redmond Roche, Captain of a regiment of fusiliers in the Sardinian service.
„ Feb. 16. Declaration of the noblesse of the children of the late Anthony de Mannery, Lieutenant-Colonel of the Dillon regiment, viz. :—John Anthony and Justin, foot Captains in the said regiment, and John Vincent and Arthur Mannery, Captains *réformé* in the said regiment, and Marie Elizabeth de Mannery.
„ Oct. 18. Declaration of the noblesse of Daniel Ohaguerty, gentleman, living at Nancy in Lorraine.
1729. May 18. Declaration of the noblesse of [   ] Higgons.
1730. Feb. 3. Declaration of the noblesse of Peter Barrel, Captain in the regiment of the Duke of Saxe Weimar in the service of the King of Poland.
„ Aug. 18. Declaration of the noblesse of Florence Macarty, Captain of a regiment in the Imperial service.

---
[1] Endorsed: 'Renewed Feb. 1732.'

DECLARATIONS OF NOBLESSE

1730. Nov. 15. Declaration of extraction to Charles Evans, son of the late William Evans [E].
1731. June 20. Declaration of the noblesse of Arthur Magenis, Captain in the regiment of Lee, descended from an ancient and noble family [I].
„ July 31. Declaration of the noblesse of George Francis de Ward Barry, and of Thomas Charles de Ward Barry, his brother, of a family living in Lorraine, since 1673, issue of the Earls of Barrymore.
1732. Feb. 15. Declaration of the noblesse of Lieutenant-Colonel William FitzGibbon.
„ Mar. 26. Declaration of the noblesse of Elizabeth Bridget, Frances Catherine Julia, Anne Marie Xaviere and Josepha Marie de Jesus, daughters of Sir Peter Redmond and Dame Anne Parker or Redmond.
„ Aug. 13. Declaration of the noblesse of Peter Dorington, Captain *réformé* in the regiment óf Rothe, and nephew of the late [William] Dorington, Lieutenant-General of our armies, descended from a noble family [E].
1733. Mar. 27. Declaration of the noblesse of William de FitzGibbon, Lieutenant-Colonel in the French service, Governor of Isola, son of Maurice de FitzGibbon and Emilia Power, and of his wife Anastazia, daughter of Florence Macarty and Anna FitzGerald of Coblentz.
„ May 15. Declaration of the noblesse of Dorothy Mildmay [E].
„ Jan. 13. Protection accorded to Marjoribanks, Main, Bowman, and Black, 'our subjects living at Cadiz.'[1]
1735. Oct. 20. Declaration of the noblesse of Thomas Gardiner, Lieutenant of a hundred Swiss in the service of the Queen-Dowager of Spain, and eldest son of William Gardiner of Mollonohne, co. Tipperary.
1736. Feb. 21. Declaration of the noblesse of James O'Hanlan, esquire *avocat* to the Parliament of Paris, descended from a noble family of Ulster.
„ Apr. 20. Declaration of the noblesse of John Machugo de Burgo or Burke de Ballinbrouder, Major in the regiment of Lorraine in the Imperial service, lineally descended from the family of Burke of the co. of Clanricarde, and that Theresa Roche, his spouse, is daughter of the late John Roche, uncle to the present Lord Roche, Viscount of Fermoy, and of Anne Sarsfield, 'nommé de la cour de ' Sarsfield,' from which family is descended the Earl of Lucan and the Viscount Sarsfield of Kilmallock.[2]

---

[1] Endorsed: 'Renewed of the same to the two first only at Mr. Marjoribanks' request.'
[2] Endorsed : 'The King signed a duplicate of this in December 1752, and it was sent ' to Mr. Machugo.'

DECLARATIONS OF NOBLESSE

1736. Oct. 15. Declaration of the noblesse of James Smith (in the Irish language MacGavan), Doctor of Philosophy and of Medicine, and an Associate of the University of Prague.

1737. Aug. 7. Declaration of the noblesse of Alexander Ogilvy, living at Autun in Burgundy, son of Patrick Ogilvy, an officer in the service of King James II and VII, descended from the family of Ogilvy of Boyne.

1738. Mar. 7. Declaration that the Irish regiment now commanded by Edward Bourk, Brigadier in the French service, was raised in 1688, by order of James II and VII, and named the Queen's regiment.

1739. Mar. 3. Declaration of the noblesse of Maurice FitzGerald, Captain in the Irish regiment of Buchy, son of Edmond, son of Richard, son of Edmond, son of the Chevalier John FitzGerald of Cloyne.

„ Apr. 3. Declaration of the noblesse of John Power, now of Liége, one of a family very ancient and noble in co. Waterford.

„ „ 15. Declaration of the noblesse of Frances Christian Butler, daughter of James Butler of Killcop [I], of a good and Catholic family, nearly related to Lord Cahir and to Butler of Killeagh, and who was distinguished at the time of the Revolution for his loyalty to King James, and passed into France, with the rank of Major of the Irish cavalry regiment of Sheldon, afterwards commanded by the Duke of FitzJames, in which he served as Major and Colonel with distinction.

1740. May 4. Declaration of the noblesse of Thomas Bourk, Lieutenant in the regiment of Foot Guards in the service of the King of Sardinia, son of Lord Castleconnel [I].

„ Nov. 9. Protection by the King to Charles Smith [S], established at Boulogne.

1741. Mar. 3. Declaration of the noblesse of John O'Sullivan, Captain of the infantry regiment of Dauphiny.

1743. Oct. 7. Declaration of the noblesse of Demoisille Evers [E], now in the 'la communanté de l'enfant Jésus à ' Paris.'

1745. Feb. 2. Declaration of the noblesse of James Grant, descended in a direct line from the old Barons of Iverque and Chevaliers of Glynnegrant.

„ Apr. 20. Declaration of the noblesse of Charles Macarthy, born at Brest, son of Timothy Macarthy, surnamed Latousche, and of Dame Eleanor Shèe of the house of Shèe of Kilkenny, and grandson of Denis Macarthy, Seigneur de Themolegue, descended from the illustrious family of Macarthy Reagh, Lords of Carbery.

DECLARATIONS OF NOBLESSE

1745. May 10. Declaration of the noblesse of Henry Fitzmaurice, native of Listonhill [I], Knight of the Military Order of St. Louis of France, and one of the gentlemen of our service, descended from one of the most illustrious families, and nephew maternally of Richard Pierse, late Bishop of Waterford, who was for some years an exile in France for his religion, 'and we farther certify and ' attest that he had a brother named Richard, who ' passed into the service of H.C.M., and was killed as ' Captain of dragoons in the regiment of Vallejo, leaving ' two daughters, one a nun at Madrid, now dead, and the ' other named Jane Frances, widow of Don Anthony ' Movante, who died Governor of Auza.'

„ July 5. Declaration of the noblesse of [ ] Rutlidge, *armateur* living at Dunkirk, son of James Rutlidge, Esquire, of the family of Rutlidge of the province of Leinster [I], and of Dame Juliana Blake, daughter of the Knight Baronet, Thomas Blake of the province of Connaught.

„ „ 19. Declaration of the noblesse of Marie O'Haugherne, daughter of Simon O'Haugherne, who was Lieutenant in the 2nd company of the Body Guards of James II, and afterwards Major of the regiment of the Guards of the same King, known as Dorington's and now Rothe's regiment, who was son of William O'Haugherne, Lord of Cairgirea and other places, and of Elizabeth Tobin, daughter of John Tobin of Garienuelly, son of John O'Haugherne and Eleanor Wanton, daughter of Maurice Wanton of Kiluatounig, son of Maurice O'Haugherne and Mary O'Brien, daughter of Denis O'Brien of Cummurugh.

1746. May 23. Declaration of the noblesse of Francis Balthazar Walle, Knight, Lord of Mesnutz in the diocese of Chartris in Beauce, late Lieutenant in the regiment of French Guards, Governor of the town and castle of Hain in Picardy for H.M.C.M., descended from the Walles of Johnstown, etc.

1747. Oct. 4. Declaration of the noblesse of William Power, captain in Ireland, and Aide-de-camp to H.S.H. the Duke of Modena, son of the late John Power, son of John Power Lord of Ballylinane and of Ballinebanoge, co. Waterford, and of Dame Mary O'Ryan of Limerick, which John Power was son of Marish Power, son of John Power, descended from Lord Power, Baron of Donoyle.[1]

1748. July 17. Declaration of the noblesse of James Macdonald [S], Captain of a company in the Royal Farnese regiment,

---

[1] Endorsed : 'Duplicate sent March 1749.'

DECLARATIONS OF NOBLESSE

1748. Oct. 4. descended from the family of Macdonald of Inverghysevan, cadet of that of Clanranald.[1]

Declaration of the noblesse of the late Anthony de Mannery, father, by his marriage with Marie Nicole, daughter of the Count of Rantzau, of John Anthony de Mannery, Justin de Mannery, John Vincent de Mannery, Arthur de Mannery, and Elizabeth de Mannery, who was Lieutenant-Colonel and Brevet-Colonel of the Irish infantry regiment of Dillon, and was killed at the battle of Chiary, having been born a gentleman, the issue of a family illustrious and ancient in Ireland.

„   „   „ Declaration that James Anthony Thaddeus Omehegan, Captain and Aide-Major in the regiment 'de la Couronne,' William Alexander Omehegan, priest, and Mary Catherine Omehegan, are the children of the late Chevalier Omehegan, late commandant by brevet at La Salle, in Cevennes, and Dame Elizabeth Russell Omehegan, daughter of William Russell of Ballymanseanlan [I].

1749. July 8. Declaration that Lawrence Ley, now residing at Cadiz, is the legitimate son of Nicholas Ley and of Anne Langton, natives of Kilkenny.

1750. Jan. 4. Declaration of the noblesse of Bartholomew Joseph Mahony, Esquire, one of the Doctors in Ordinary to the King, son of Eugene Mahony and Eleanor FitzMaurice.

„ Apr. 20. Declaration of the noblesse of James White [I], now living at La Rochelle.

1751. Feb. . Declaration of the noblesse of Andrew O'Carroll [I], now living at Cordova.

1752. Dec. 7. Declaration of the noblesse of Marianne Macmanus Maguire, daughter of Charles Macmanus of Lough Earne, and of Mary Maguire of Crohan, widow of James Egan of Kilbaran, son of Eustace, and grandson of O'Caroll, who was captain of an Irish infantry regiment in the service of the King of the two Sicilies.

1753. Nov. 3. Declaration of the noblesse of Charlotte Michel Russell, Countess of Tressan, wife of Louis Elizabeth de l'Avergne, Count of Tressan, Lieutenant-General of the armies of H.M.C.M., descended from the family of Russell, of whom the great-grandfather left England and established himself at Vitri in Champagne, as is attested by documents under the hand and seal of Sir Charles Russell of Waltham, Baronet.

1754. Mar. 18. Declaration of the noblesse of Thomas O'Kean, M.D., living at Chalons-sur-Soane, in Burgundy.

---

[1] Endorsed : 'In July 1752 there was a duplicate of this declaration, sought by and sent to Captain Macdonald.'

DECLARATIONS OF NOBLESSE

1754. July 5. Declaration of the noblesse of Anthony Arthur Boduel, living at Tarifee, in Spain, *avocat du Conseil Royale et subdélégué de la mer*, son of John Arthur Boduel, who was born at Tangiers in 1667, when it belonged to Charles II, and whose father, Thomas Boduel, was a native of England.

„ „ 27. Declaration of the noblesse of Henry Scrope [E], now living at Livourne.

„ Sept. 13. Declaration of the noblesse of Stephen Francis Remond, of a family established for several years in the province of Brittany in France, descended from the ancient and noble family of Remond or Redmond [I].

1755. Aug. 8. Declaration of the noblesse of Louis Kennedy, living at Perpignan, son of Louis Daniel Kennedy, who died at Perpignan, and grandson of Philip Kennedy [I], captain of grenadiers in the regiment of Lee in the French service.

1756. Dec. 18. Declaration of the noblesse of John Brigeat, Postmaster at Ligny in Barrois, descended through Jane Lambert, his mother, from the ancient and noble family of Lambert of Ballyhire [I].

1757. May 7. Declaration of the noblesse of Anne Coghan, native of St. Germains-en-Laye, and legitimate daughter of Terence Coghan, Knight of the Royal and Military Order of St. Louis, late Captain of the cavalry regiment of FitzJames, who was descended from the ancient and noble family of MacCoghan [I], and of Helen Evers, daughter of Richard Evers, Knight of the Royal and Military Order of St. Louis, colonel *réformé à la suite d'Arras* in Artois, descended from the ancient and noble family of Evers [E].

1763. May 19. Declaration of the noblesse of Richard Thomas FitzGerald, priest, now at Rome, son of Richard FitzGerald and Eleanor Tyrrell, descended on both sides from families of gentle birth.[1]

„ Nov. 15. Declaration of the noblesse of Richard Thomas FitzGerald, Canon of St. Martin's at Liége and Superior of St. Julian at Rome, legitimately descended from Richard FitzGerald and Eleanor Tyrrell, his father and mother, and from John FitzGerald and Mary Dempsey, his paternal grandfather and grandmother, and from Richard Tyrrell and Cecilia Duksinfield, his maternal grandfather and grandmother.

---

[1] Endorsed: 'The above declaration not being thought sufficiently full for Mr. FitzGerald's reception into the chapter of St. Martin's at Liége, the King was pleased to grant the [one] following.'

DECLARATIONS OF NOBLESSE

1760. Jan. 27. Declaration of the noblesse of Charles[1] and Clementina Erskine, children of Colin Erskine, arm., son of Dominus Alexander Erskine of Cambo, Knight Baronet, son of Charles Erskine of Cambo, Knight Baronet, second son of Dominus Alexander Erskine,[2] Earl of Kellie, son of Dominus Thomas Erskine, first Earl of Kellie, son of Dominus Alexander Erskine of Gogar, Knight, second son of John, Earl of Mar.

---

[1] He afterwards held the office of *Avvocato del diavolo* at Rome, and died *s.p.* 19th March 1811.

[2] This Alexander Erskine, styled Viscount Fentoun, was never Earl of Kellie, having died *v.p.* February 1633.

APPOINTMENTS

SECRETARIES OF STATE

1689. Jan.	-1689. Aug. 25.	John (Drummond), first Earl of Melfort, K.T., principal Secretary of State.[1]
1689.[2]	-	. Hon. Henry Browne,[3] Secretary of State for England.
		Father Lewis Innes, Principal of the Scots College at Paris, Secretary of State for Scotland.
		Sir Richard Nagle, Secretary of State for Ireland.
1690.	-	. Sir James Montgomery[4] of Schermarley, Secretary of State for Scotland.
1693.	-1694. June	. John (Drummond), first *Duke of Melfort* [S], K.T. ⎱ Joint Secs. of State.
		Charles (Middleton), second Earl of Middleton [S]. ⎰
1694. June	-1696.	. Charles (Middleton), second Earl of Middleton [S]. ⎱ Joint Secs. of State.
		John Caryll.[5] ⎰
1696.	-1702.	. Charles (Middleton), second Earl of Middleton [S].[6]
1702.	-1703.	. [? John Caryll.]
1703.[7]	-1713. Dec. 24.	? Charles (Middleton), second Earl of Middleton [S], first *Earl of Monmouth* [E].

---

[1] On 25th August 1689 he was sent on a mission to Louis XIV.

[2] Clarke, *Life of James II*, ii. p. 411, quoting Kennet, i. p. 601.

[3] Afterwards (1708) fifth Viscount Montagu [E].

[4] Clarke, ii. p. 427. He and the Earl of Annandale, who had at the same time been appointed Commissioner to the Scots Parliament, almost immediately submitted to the Government.

[5] Caryll appears to have been acting (or possibly Under-) Secretary of State from about 1690 to his death, 4th September 1711. On 5th October 1706 he had a promise from James to pay to him, his heirs or assigns, six months after his return to England, the sum of   livres for salary due to him as Secretary of State, and what further sum shall then be due. This is endorsed: 'Lord Caryll transferred this promise to ' the Benedictine nuns of Dunkirk, who are in possession of it, he having sent it to ' the abbess 17th October 1706' (*Calendar of Stuart Papers*, i. p. 208).

[6] Middleton resigned the secretaryship on becoming a Catholic, and was not reappointed till the following year. Caryll probably acted as sole Secretary during this period.

[7] On the death of Lord Caryll, 4th September 1711, David Nairne succeeded him as Under-Secretary of State.

SECRETARIES OF STATE

1713. Dec. 24	-1715. July	.	Sir Thomas Higgons.
1715. July	-1716. Mar.	.	Henry (St. John), first *Earl of Bolingbroke* [E].
1716. Mar.	-1724.	.	John (Erskine), first *Duke of Mar* [S], *K.G.*, *K.T.*
1724.	-1725. Mar. 25.		John (Hay), first *Earl of Inverness* [S], *K.T.*, temporary Secretary of State.
1725. Mar. 25	-1727. Apr. 3.		John (Hay), first *Earl of Inverness* [S], *K.T.*
1727. Apr. 3-		.	Sir John Græme, first *Baronet* [S].[1]
1727.[2]	-1747. Oct.	.	James (Murray), first *Earl of Dunbar* [S], *K.T.*
1747. Nov.	-1759. Oct.	.	Daniel (O'Brien), first *Earl of Lismore* [I], *K.G.*
1759. Oct.	-1763.	.	John (Græme), first *Earl of Alford* [S].
1763.	-1764. Sept. 24.		James Edgar, Secretary untitled.[3]
1764. Sept. 24	-1768. Dec. 8.		Andrew Lumsden, Secretary untitled.
1768. Dec. 8	-1777.	.	John Baptist (Caryll) third *Baron Caryll of Durford* [E], *K.T.*

---

[1] This was probably only a temporary appointment.
[2] John Murray of Broughton was Secretary of State to the Prince Regent while in Scotland, 1745-1746.
[3] He had been secretary to the King since 1716.

APPOINTMENTS

HOUSEHOLD APPOINTMENTS

JAMES II AND VII

1689. May 6. Sir John Sparrow, mentioned as Clerk Controller of the Household.
,, ,, ,, Nathaniel Gautherne, to be Clerk of the Kitchens and Spicery.
,, ,, ,, Richard Crump, to be Yeoman of the Pantry and Ewry.
,, ,, ,, Francis Miner, to be Yeoman of the Pastry.
,, ,, ,, Jeremiah Broomer, to be First Yeoman of the Kitchen.
,, ,, ,, Charles Macarty, to be Yeoman of the Butteries and Yeoman of the Chaundry.
,, ,, ,, Thomas Atkins, to be Master Cook in Ordinary to His Majesty's person.
,, ,, ,, James Menzies, to be Yeoman of the Silver Scullery.
,, ,, ,, John Read, to be Yeoman of the Confectionary.
,, ,, 13. William (Herbert), *Duke of Powis* [E], mentioned as Lord Chamberlain of the Household.
,, ,, ,, Walter, Lord Dungan (eldest son of William (Dungan), first Earl of Limerick [I]), to be a Gentleman of the Bedchamber.
,, June 1. John Prieur, to be Page of the Bedchamber.
,, ,, ,, Charles Forestier, to be Page of the Bedchamber.
,, ,, 29. Arthur Magennis, to be Equerry to the King.
1691. Dec. 13. Bevil Skelton, mentioned as Comptroller of the Household.
,, ,, ,, Francis Gaultier, to be Gentleman of the Butteries and Yeoman of the Chaundry.
,, ,, ,, Charles Macartie, to be Gentleman and Yeoman of the Cellars.
1692. Feb. 1. Father Dominick White and Father Manusat, Capuchins, mentioned as lately the King's Chaplain and Confessor respectively.
,, Mar. 13. Dr. Daniel Day, to be Physician to the family and household, with all the privileges thereunto belonging, and, after the Restoration, with all the fees, salaries, etc., usually enjoyed therewith.
,, ,, 20. [   ] Ginnari, to be His Majesty's first Painter.
1694. Dec. 24. William (Herbert), first *Duke of Powis* [E], Lord Chamberlain, Bevil Skelton, Comptroller of the Household,

HOUSEHOLD APPOINTMENTS

Robert Strickland, Vice-Chamberlain to the Queen, and Henry Conquest, to be Commissioners of the Household. Renewed 24th December 1695.

1694. Jan. Don James Ronchi, mentioned as having been First Almoner to the Queen since her arrival from England, and Don Pellegrino, his brother, as Almoner to the Queen, and with having been several years in her service.

1695. June 2. Francis Plowden and Edmund Perkins, to be Under Governors in Ordinary; Thomas Nevil, Thomas Belasis, and Walter Strickland, to be Grooms of the Bedchamber in Ordinary; and James Symes and Lawrence Dupuy, to be Gentlemen Waiters in Ordinary to the Prince of Wales.

„ „ 25. Sir William Waldegrave, to be first Physician to the King.

„ „ 27. John Constable, to be Clerk of the Kitchen in Ordinary.

„ Aug. 28. Denis Granville, Dean of Durham, mentioned as Chaplain to the King.

„ Oct. 22. Henry Parry, to be Clerk of the Kitchen in Ordinary in the room of Nathaniel Gauthern, deceased.

1696. Mar. 7. Richard Hamilton, to be Master of the Robes.

„ June 20. David Nairne, to be Clerk of Her Majesty's Council, of her Revenue, and of the Registrar of her Court, commonly called the Queen's Court, and Keeper of the Seal of her Council.

„ July 30. James Porter, mentioned as Vice-Chamberlain of the Household.

„ „ „ Hon. John Stafford Howard, to be Comptroller of the Household.

„ Aug. 12. John Stafford [? Howard], Comptroller of the Household, Robert Strickland, Vice-Chamberlain to the Queen, and Henry Conquest, to be Commissioners of the Household.

„ „ 19. James (Drummond), fourth Earl of Perth [S], to be Governor of the Prince of Wales.

1697. Feb. 1. William Berkenhead, to be Clerk of the Kitchen, in the room of John Constable.

„ May 8. Mr. Lewis Inese, Principal of the Scots College in Paris, mentioned as Almoner to the Queen.

1698. Jan. 23. John Stafford Howard, Comptroller of the Household, Robert Strickland, Vice-Chamberlain to the Queen, Sir Richard Nagle, Henry Conquest, and Sir William Ellis, to be Commissioners of the Household.

„ Feb. 14. Dudley Bagnall [? of Newry, Ireland], to be Groom of the Bedchamber.

„ Sept. 22. Pierce (Butler), third Viscount Galmoye [I], to be Gentleman of the Bedchamber.

HOUSEHOLD APPOINTMENTS

1699. Feb. 10. Father Naish, a Recolet, mentioned as Chaplain to Queen Mary.

„ „ 23. [ ] Riva, brother of Louis Riva, an Olivetan, cellarer of St. Michael in Bosco, mentioned by Queen Mary as having served her well for many years as an officer of her Wardrobe.

„ Oct. 17. John Stafford Howard, Comptroller of the Household, Robert Strickland, Vice-Chamberlain to the Queen, Henry Conquest, Sir William Ellis, and Thomas Sheridan, to be Commissioners of the Household.

„ „ 18. Innocentio Fede, to be Master of the Music of the Chapel Royal.

„ „ 22. Innocentio Fede, to be Master of Her Majesty's private Music.

1700. Apr. 19. Count Charles Molza, to be a Gentleman Usher of Her Majesty's Privy Chamber.

„ June 12. Roger North, mentioned as Attorney-General to Queen Mary.

„ „ „ Robert Strickland, late Vice-Chamberlain to the Queen, to be Treasurer and Receiver-General of all her rents and revenues.

„ Aug. 2. Francis Plowden, to be Comptroller of the Household.[1]

„ „ 4. Dominick Sheldon and William Dickeson (Dicconson), to be Under Grooms to the Prince of Wales; Charles Leyburne, Thomas Sakvill, and Sir John Gifford, Bart., to be Grooms of the Bedchamber.

„ „ 14. Francis Plowden, Comptroller of the Household, Henry Conquest, Sir William Ellis, Thomas Sheridan, and Sir Richard Bulstrode, to be Commissioners of the Household.

„ „ 23. Henry Conquest, to be Clerk of the Green Cloth.

1701. Jan. 5. Nestor Helme, to be Watchmaker to the King. Renewed 24th April 1702.

„ Mar. 24. Christopher Chilton, to be one of the Clerks of the Green Cloth. Antedated 24th March 1695.

„ June 28. Harcourt Berkenhead and John Simpson, to be Clerk of the Kitchen and Yeomen of the Ewry respectively.

„ July 20. Robert Power, mentioned as King's Counsel.

„ Aug. . Warrant to Henry Conquest to pay all bills relating to the Household, though only signed by Thomas Sheridan and Sir Richard Bulstrode, during the absence of Francis Plowden and Sir William Ellis, the other Commissioners of the Household.[2]

---

[1] He died before 21st April 1714, when Mary Plowden, widow of Francis Plowden, the Comptroller of the Household, had a discharge from all claims and demands for money put into his hands for the King's use.

[2] Noted as the last warrant signed by King James II and VII.

HOUSEHOLD APPOINTMENTS

JAMES III AND VIII
MARY OF MODENA, QUEEN-REGENT,
16TH SEPTEMBER 1701–21ST JUNE 1706

1701. Oct. 17. James Porter, to be Vice-Chamberlain of the Household.
,, ,, ,, James (Drummond), first *Duke of Perth* [S], to be Governor of the King.
,, ,, ,, Dominick Sheldon and William Dickeson, to be Under Governors of the King.
,, ,, ,, Richard Hamilton, to be Master of the Robes.
,, ,, ,, Thomas Neville, Charles Leybourne, Thomas Sackville, Sir John Gifford, David Lloyd, Richard Biddulph, Sir Randell Macdonnell, Richard Trevanion, Dudley Bagnell, Daniel MacDonnell, George Rattrey, and Charles Booth, to be Grooms of the Bedchamber.
,, ,, ,, Dennis Carney, John Ronchi, Thomas Wivell, and John Copley, to be Gentlemen Ushers of the Presence.
,, ,, ,, Francis Plowden, to be Comptroller of the Household.
,, ,, ,, John Stafford, to be Vice-Chamberlain to the Queen.
,, ,, 20. Timothy Doyle and John Nash, to be King's Messengers in Ordinary and Riding Messengers.
,, ,, 24. John Constable, to be First Physician in Ordinary to the King.
,, ,, ,, Calahan Garvan, to be Physician to the Household.
,, ,, ,, Henry Conquest, to be Clerk of the Green Cloth.
,, ,, 26. Henry Parry, to be Clerk of the Kitchen in Ordinary.
,, ,, 27. John Dutton, John Baggot, James Neagle, Thomas Higgins, James Symes, and Lawrence Dupuy, to be Gentlemen Ushers of the Privy Chamber.
,, ,, 29. Harcourt Berkenhead, to be also Clerk of the Kitchen in Ordinary,
,, ,, ,, Christopher Chilton, to be Clerk of the Green Cloth.
,, ,, ,, Christopher Williams, to be Yeoman of the Accompting House.
,, ,, ,, Patrick Owens, to be Messenger of the Accompting House.
,, ,, ,, Humphrey Prescot, to be Yeoman Baker.
,, ,, ,, Richard Pemberton, to be Yeoman of the Pantry.
,, ,, ,, Charles Macartie, to be Gentleman and Yeoman of the Wine Cellar.
,, ,, ,, John Read, to be Yeoman Confectioner.

HOUSEHOLD APPOINTMENTS

1701. Oct. 29. John Sympson, to be Yeoman of the Ewry.
,, ,, ,, Francis Gautier, to be Gentleman of the Buttery and Yeoman of the Chaundry.
,, ,, ,, Jeremiah Broomer, to be Master Cook.
,, ,, ,, John de la Roche, to be First Yeoman of the Mouth.
,, ,, ,, Thomas Fox, to be Groom of the Privy Kitchen.
,, ,, ,, Matthew Creagh, to be Child of the Privy Kitchen.
,, ,, ,, John Martinash, to be Yeoman of the Larder.
,, ,, ,, John Menzies, to be Yeoman of the Scullery.
,, ,, ,, Doctor John Betham, to be Preceptor to the King.
,, ,, ,, Doctor John Ingleton, to be Under Preceptor to the King.
,, ,, 30. The Duchess of Perth [S], and the Countess of Almond [S], to be Ladies of the Bedchamber in Ordinary to the Queen.
[1701. Oct. 30.] The Countess Molza, Lady Strickland, Mrs. Strickland, and Mrs. Biddulph, to be Bedchamber Women to the Queen.
,, ,, ,, Mr. Cane, Mr. Hatcher, Count Molza, and Mr. Caryll,[1] to be Gentlemen Ushers of the Privy Chamber.
,, ,, ,, Guy Foster, Joseph Persico, Edmund Barry, and Matthew Turene, to be Gentlemen Ushers of the Presence.
,, ,, ,, Roger Strickland, to be Page of Honour.
,, ,, ,, [   ] Person, [   ] Battiste, [   ] Haywood, and [   ] Prieur, to be Pages of the Backstairs.
,, Nov. 4. Ralph Sheldon and Richard Biddulph, to be Equerries.
,, ,, ,, Robert Buckenham, to be Equerry of the Great Stables.
,, ,, ,, John Lewin, to be Riding Purveyor.
, ,, ,, Gerald Devereux, to be Purveyor of the Stables.
,, ,, ,, Captain Henry Griffith, to be Yeoman Saddler.
,, ,, ,, Jolie Falvie, to be Harbourer of the Deer.
,, ,, ,, John Dixey, to be Body Coachman.
,, ,, ,, Henry Kerby, } to be Chairmen.
,, ,, ,, Thomas Umsworth,
,, ,, ,, Thomas Connor, to be Farrier.
,, ,, ,, Bryan O'Bryan, Denis O'Bryan, Alexander Stewart, Nicholes Milner, Lovell Webb, John Perry, and Andrew Symes, } to be Footmen.
,, ,, ,, Leonard Wait, Patrick Maguirk, Denis Ryan, Edward Douglas, Edward Hogan, Nicholas Clark, and Joseph Walden, } to be Grooms.
,, ,, . Henry Kerby, to be Body Coachman.
,, ,, 10. James Labadie, Closet Keeper to the King, to be Purveyor of the Wine.

---

[1] John Caryll, a nephew of the first Lord Caryll.

HOUSEHOLD APPOINTMENTS

1701. Nov. 10. James Bailly, to be Purveyor of His Majesty's Poultry.
,, ,, ,, Sir Charles Cartaret, to be Gentleman Usher of the Black Rod.
,, ,, 13. Peter Moyry, to be Gallery Keeper.
,, ,, 14. Louis du Monninx and Peter Monsett, to be Trumpeters in Ordinary.
,, ,, ,, Joseph Nosetto Dumont, to be First Kettledrummer of the Household.
,, ,, 17. Mary Callanan, to be Laundress and Starcher of the Body.
,, ,, ,, Elizabeth Leserteur, to be Seamstress.
,, ,, ,, John White, to be a Pursuivant of the Kingdom of Ireland.
,, ,, ,, Elizabeth Symes, Mary Plowden, Rose Lee, and Bridget Nugent, to be Bedchamber Women
,, ,, ,, Elizabeth Martinash, to be Nurse
,, ,, ,, Mary Neville, to be Laundress
,, ,, ,, Christian Plunkett, to be Seamstress
,, ,, ,, Daniel Fullan, John Wilkie, to be Pages of the Backstairs
,, ,, ,,
,, July 4. Mary Smallwood, to be Necessary Woman

to Her Royal Highness the Princess Louisa.

,, Nov. 25. The Countess of *Monmouth* [E] and Middleton [S], to be Governess to the Princess Louisa.
,, Dec. 6. Francis Plowden, Comptroller of the Household; Henry Conquest, Sir William Ellis, Thomas Sheridan, and Sir Richard Bulstrode to be Commissioners of the Household.
,, ,, 12. Francis Gaultier, to be Gentleman of the Buttery and Yeoman of the Chaundry.
,, ,, ,, Benedict Gennary, to be First Painter.
,, ,, ,, Dominick Rougé, to be Tailor.
1702. Jan. 9. James Therry, to be Athlone Pursuivant [I].
,, ,, William Weston, to be Printer and Stationer to the King's Household and Chapel.
,, Feb. 6. Count Anthony Davia, to be Groom of the Bedchamber.
,, ,, 12. Walter Strickland (saving his rank next to Thomas Neville), James Falvey, Oliver Nicholas, [   ] Finch, James Griffen, and Richard Bagott, to be Grooms of the Bedchamber.
,, ,, 24. John Shaw and Peter Halpeny, to be Saddlers to the Stables, with note that two new warrants were afterwards given, one to Shaw, of Esquire Saddler, and one to Halpeny, as Groom Saddler.
,, Mar. 1. Thomas Godert, Francis Neper, Richard Fermer, and Richard Waldegrave, to be Gentlemen of the Privy Chamber.

HOUSEHOLD APPOINTMENTS

1702. Apr. 29. Denis Granville, D.D., Dean of Durham, Chaplain to the last two Kings, received into the Royal Household.
,, ,, 30. Sir William Ellis, to be one of the Clerk Comptrollers or the Green Cloth.
,, May 6. Richard Richardson, to be Keeper of the Privy Garden at Whitehall.
,, June 19. Sir John Lidcot, to be Latin Secretary.
,, July 4. James Connock and Thomas Lee, to be Gentleman and Groom of the Privy Chamber respectively.
,, Oct. 14. Garret Fitzgerald, to be the King's Barber.
,, Nov. 13. Francis Grant, to be one of the Harbingers.
,, Dec. 4. Father Ruga, mentioned as the Queen's Confessor.
1703. Feb. . [Robert] Strickland, mentioned as Treasurer of the Queen's Household.
, ,, 14. James (Drummond), first *Duke of Perth* [S], and Piers (Butler), first *Earl of Newcastle* [I], to be Gentlemen of the Bedchamber.
,, Aug. 4. Donough (MacCarthy), fourth Earl of Clancarty [I], to be Gentleman of the Bedchamber.
1704. Jan. 7. Theobald Butler, Knight of the Spanish Order of St. James, to be a Gentleman of the Privy Chamber.
,, ,, ,, Joseph du Chaumont, to be a Gentleman of the Privy Chamber.
,, Feb. 14. Captain John Ryan, to be a Gentleman of the Privy Chamber.
,, ,, 26. Anne Nugent, to be a Bedchamber Woman to the Princess.
,, July 9. Patrick Fitzgerald, to be a Gentleman of the Privy Chamber.
,, Aug. 25. Pere La Chaise, mentioned as the King's Confessor.
,, Nov. 25. [   ] Delâtre, to be Equerry of the Great Stables.
1706. Apr. 19. Alexander Knightly, to be Gentleman of the Privy Chamber.
,, June 21. Robert Power, mentioned as King's Council.
,, ,, ,, David Nairne, to be Clerk of the Council.
,, ,, ,, James Murray and David Nagle, to be Gentlemen Ushers.
,, July 20. Calaghan Garvan, ⎫ to be Physicians in Ordinary to His
,, ,, 23. Lawrence Wood, ⎭ Majesty.
,, Aug. 15. Hon. Richard Bourke,[1] ⎫ to be Gentlemen of the Privy
,, Sept. 13. Thomas Napier, ⎭ Chamber.
,, Nov. 13. Lady Carteret, wife of Sir Charles Carteret, mentioned as a Maid of Honour to Queen Mary.
,, ,, 29. Roger Strickland, to be Groom of the Bedchamber.
1707. Mar. 21. Dame Conock, lately married to Sir Timon Conock, mentioned as formerly Maid of Honour to the Queen.

---

[1] Son of the late Lord Brittas.

HOUSEHOLD APPOINTMENTS

1707. Sept. 20. John Thomas Woodhouse, one of the Ushers of the Privy Chamber, to be Oculist to the King.
„ Nov. 15. John Sheridan, to be Riding Purveyor of the Stables.
„ Dec. 9. John Nugent, to be Equerry of the Stables.
1708. Feb. 18. Teresa Strickland, daughter of Robert Strickland, Treasurer of the Queen's Household, lately married to John Stafford, Vice-Chamberlain to the Queen, mentioned as having been a Maid of Honour.[1]
„ Mar. 5. Walter Strickland, to be Groom of the Bedchamber, 'con-' form to and of the same date with,' the former warrant granted him with five other Grooms, 15th February 1702.[2]
„ May . John Pyraube, to be Gunmaker in Ordinary.
„ „ 10. George Joyce, to be Clockmaker and Watchmaker in Ordinary.
„ „ 17. Francis Plowden, Comptroller of the Household, William Dickonson, Sir William Ellis, Thomas Sheridan, and Sir Richard Bulstrode, to be Commissioners of the Household.
1709. Jan. 10. Mr. Macghie, M.D., a Scotsman, who served the late King and suffered in Scotland for his zeal and loyalty, to be Physician to the King.
„ Mar. 11. William Dicconson, to be Treasurer of her Household and Receiver-General of all the Queen's rents and revenues.
„ Nov. 23. Lord Edward Drummond, to be Gentleman of the Bedchamber.
„ Dec. 2. Henry Conquest, deceased, mentioned as late Paymaster of the Household.
1710. Apr. 7. Edmund Fitzgerald, to be Gentleman of the Privy Chamber.
1711. Feb. 27. John Faure, dancing-master, who has taught the King dancing for seventeen years, to be the King's Dancing Master.
„ May 7. Lieutenant-General Dominick Sheldon, to be Vice-Chamberlain of the Household, admitted 2nd June.
„ June 15. Captain Janus Goolde, to be Gentleman of the Privy Chamber.
„ Nov. 7. Randal Macdonnel, to be Equerry of the Stables.
„ „ 13. Lady Mary Carteret, to be Bedchamber Woman to the Princess.
„ „ 14. Lady Murray, to be Bedchamber Woman to the Princess.
1712. May 20. Daniel Huoluhan, M.D., an Irishman, to be His Majesty's Physician.

---

[1] King James promises to pay her £2000, and Queen Mary £1000, within one year of the Restoration.
[2] Noted as signed 5th March 1708, and delivered to Lady Strickland two days before the King departed for Dunkirk.

HOUSEHOLD APPOINTMENTS

1713. Nov. 29. David Nairne, Clerk of the Council, to be Secretary of the Closet for the King's private letters and despatches.
„ „ 30. David Inese, to be H.M.'s Almoner.
„ Dec. 15. John Middleton, Lord Clermont, to be a Gentleman of the Bedchamber.
1714. Mar. 17. Lewis Inese, to be Lord Almoner.
1715. July 24. Jeremy Broomer, to be Clerk of the Kitchen.
1716. Feb. 21. John (Erskine), first *Duke of Mar* [S], to be Gentleman of the Bedchamber.
„ Apr. 7. Dr. John Blair, to be one of the Physicians in Ordinary.
„ May 12. Bernard Howard, Esq., to be a Groom of the Bedchamber.[1]
„ Aug. 1. Espri Joseph Parrelly, Doctor of Medicine of the Faculty of Avignon, to be one of His Majesty's Physicians Extraordinary.
„ Dec. 11. Patrick Abercromby, to be one of His Majesty's Physicians Extraordinary.
„ „ 21. Dr. Martin Guerin, to be one of His Majesty's Chirurgeons Extraordinary.
1718. Jan. 13. James Hay, to be one of His Majesty's Chirurgeons.
„ „ . John Hay, to be a Groom of the Bedchamber.
„ Mar. 21. Anthony David, painter in Rome, to be one of His Majesty's Painters.
„ „ „ John Peter Straglia, to be one of His Majesty's Musicians.
„ Apr. „ John Baptist Ronchi, to be Preacher to the King.
„ Aug. „ William Dugud, to be His Majesty's Jeweller.
1723. Sept. 5. James Hay to be Surgeon to the Household.
1724. Nov. 30. The Rev. Father Bernardin Mombruie, to be Theologian to the King.
1726. Feb. 18. Sir William Ellis, to be Cofferer [Treasurer] of the Household.
„ Sept. 28. Sir William Ellis, His Majesty's Resident in Rome, to be Keeper of the King's Palace in Rome.
1727. Jan. 20. Jerome Benozzi, Doctor of Medicine, to be one of His Majesty's Physicians Extraordinary.
„ June 4. James Murray, *Earl of Dunbar* [S], to be Governor of the Prince of Wales.
„ „ „ Sir Thomas Sheridan, to be Under Governor to the Prince of Wales.
„ „ „ Laurence Mayers, Priest, to be Preceptor to the Prince of Wales.
„ „ „ The Countess of Nithsdale, to be Governor to the Duke of York.
„ Nov. 18. Captain William Hay, to be a Groom of the Bedchamber.
„ „ 26. Dr. Thomé, to be one of His Majesty's Physicians Extraordinary.

---

[1] Noted as antedated 11th December 1713.

HOUSEHOLD APPOINTMENTS

1728. Feb. 18. Dr. Græme, to be one of His Majesty's Physicians Extraordinary.
 „   „ 26. Joseph Anthony Ragazzi, to be Theologian to the King.
1729. Sept. 17. Rev. [   ] Ormes, to be one of His Majesty's Chaplains.
 „ Nov. 23. Louis Du Val, to be one of His Majesty's Chirurgeons Extraordinary.
1732. Jan. 29. Dr. Farrelly,[1] to be one of His Majesty's Physicians Extraordinary.
1733. June 13. Dr. John Jennings, to be one of His Majesty's Physicians Extraordinary.
 „ Aug. 10. Patrick O'Shiel, M.D., to be one of His Majesty's Physicians Extraordinary.
1739. Oct. 18. Simon Lyons [I], to be one of His Majesty's Chirurgeons Extraordinary.
1740. Feb. 17. Bartholomew Joseph Mahony [I], Doctor of Physic of the Faculty of Rheims, to be one of His Majesty's Physicians Extraordinary.
 „ July 20. [   ] Guerin, Chirurgeon of Paris, and Master Chirurgeon of the Charity Hospital in Rome, to be one of His Majesty's Chirurgeons Extraordinary.
1742. July 7. Dr. John Howard, M.D., to be one of His Majesty's Physicians Extraordinary.
 „   „   „ James Power, D.D., Canon of the Collegiate Church of Mont Cassel in Flanders, to be one of His Majesty's Chaplains Extraordinary.
 „   „   „ [   ] Carteret, D.D., Canon of the Collegiate Church of Lisle in Flanders, to be one of His Majesty's Chaplains Extraordinary.
1743. Oct. 19. Teige O'Connel, to be one of His Majesty's Physicians Extraordinary.
1745. May 3. [   ] Bellew, to be one of His Majesty's Physicians Extraordinary.
1746. July 4. [   ] Michel of Ireland, M.D., to be Doctor Extraordinary.
 „ Dec. 20. Mr. John Maitland, to be one of His Majesty's Chaplains in Ordinary.[2]
1749. Aug. 16. Charles Guattani, to be one of His Majesty's Chirurgeons Extraordinary.

---

[1] At Sir Peter Redmond's request.
[2] 'We being desirous to give you a mark of our royal favour for the zealous and 'active part you acted in our cause in the late unfortunate affair in our ancient Kingdom 'of Scotland.'—Extract from warrant.

NOMINATIONS

ECCLESIASTICAL NOMINATIONS

1694. Mar. 28. Thomas Brown, B.D., Fellow of St. John's College, Cambridge, collated to the Archdeaconry of Norwich, vacant by death of the late Archdeacon, by William Lloyd, deprived Bishop of Norwich.

1702. Oct. 11. Dr. George Witham, to be Vicar-Apostolic [E], in place of John Leyburne, deceased.

1706. Aug. ? Joseph René, Cardinal Imperiali, to be Protector of the Kingdom of Ireland; appointed before 31st August.[1]

„ Sept. ? Cardinal Sacripanti, to be Protector of the Kingdom of Scotland; appointed before 4th October.

1707. ?[2] Dr. Ambrose Madin, to be Bishop of Kilmacduagh.

„ „ Dr. Denis Moriarty, to be Bishop of Ardfert and Aghadoe.

„ „ Father Thaddeus O'Rourke, a Franciscan, to be Bishop of Killala.

„ Apr. . Ambrose MacDermot, a Dominican, penitentiary of S. Maria Maggiore, to be Bishop of [Elphin.].

1709. June 16. John Verdun, D.D., Vicar-General of the Diocese of Armagh, to be Bishop of Ferns in Leinster.

„ „ „ Ambrose O'Conor, Master of Theology, Provincial of the Irish Dominicans,[3] to be Bishop of Ardagh and Clonmacnois.

1711. Mar. 2. Abbé Christopher Butler, Doctor of the Sorbonne, now in Rome, a near relation of the Duke of Ormonde, to be Archbishop of Cashel.

„ Aug. 24. Philip Anthony, Cardinal Gualterio,[4] to be Protector of England in succession to Alexander, Cardinal Caprara, deceased.

---

[1] Born at Genoa, 29th April 1651, died at Rome, 4th January 1737. See Migne, *Encyclopédie Théologique*, vol. xxxi.

[2] On 7th February 1707 King James writes to Cardinal Imperiali, Protector of Ireland, about the great need of increasing the number of Bishops [I], now reduced to two, of whom but one is at liberty to exercise his functions, the other being in prison, and mentioning that three years ago, at the desire and request of the Pope himself, he nominated the above three, after consulting the Irish Bishops, etc., but that up to the present he has no answer.

[3] Who is aged about fifty-five, and immediately going to Ireland.

[4] Died at Rome, 24th April 1748.

NOMINATIONS

1713. **Feb.17.** Abbé Melchior de Polignac, to be Cardinal.[2]
1715. **May 24.** Dr. Hugh MacMahon, Bishop of Clogher, to be Archbishop of Armagh, which Archbishopric has long been vacant; translated before August 16.[3]
„ **Aug. 16.** Edward Murphy, Vicar-General of the Diocese of Dublin, to be Bishop of Kildare.
„ **Oct. 18.** Edward Murphy, Bishop of Kildare, to be Administrator of the Bishopric of Leighlin.
1721. **Mar.18.** Benjamin Petre, Bishop of Prusa, to be coadjutor to Bishop Bonaventura Gifford, Vicar-Apostolic for the district of London.[4]
1722. **July 22.** William O'Daly, to be Bishop of Kilmacduagh.
1723. **Dec.15.** Bernard Ogara, D.D., to be Archbishop of Tuam, in succession to Fr. de Burgo.
1724. **Aug.24.** Edward Murphy to be Bishop of Kildare.
„ **Nov. 25.** Bernard Dunne to be Bishop of Kildare, with the administration of the Bishopric of Leighlin, the same as his predecessor had it.
„ „ „ Terence Macmahon, to be Bishop of Killaloe.
1725. **July .** James Gallihurium [? Gallagher], D.D., to be Bishop of Raphoe.
„ **Sept.12.** Father Stephan MacEgan, Dominican, to be Bishop of the Seven Churches (Clonanmaen).
„ „ „ Father Dominick Dalny, Dominican, to be Bishop of Achadoe.
„ **Dec.11.** Thomas Dominick Williams, an English Dominican Father, to be Bishop of Tiberiopolis, and Vicar-Apostolic of northern district of England.[5]
1726. **Aug.17.** Bernard Macmahon, to be Bishop of Clogher.
„ „ „ Thaddæus Macarty, to be Bishop of Cork.
„ „ „ Neil Conway, to be Bishop of Derry.
„ „ „ John Armstrong, to be Bishop of Down and Connor.
„ **Nov. 6.** Alexander John Grant, to be a Bishop and Vicar-Apostolic in the North of Scotland.
1727. **Jan. 8.** John Anthony, Cardinal Davia,[6] to be Protector of Scotland, in place of Joseph, Cardinal Sacripanti.[7] Noted as not made use of.

---

[1] James writes to Pope Clement XI on this day, thanking him for having raised the Abbé de Polignac to a Cardinalate on his nomination.
[2] Died at Paris, 20th November 1741.
[3] On which date James writes to Pope Clement XI, thanking him for preserving in his last letter his royal right of nominating to the churches of Ireland unimpaired.
[4] Henry Howard, Bishop-elect of Utica, previously nominated coadjutor, having died before consecration, 22nd November 1720. Bishop Petre was consecrated 11th November 1721, became Vicar-Apostolic of London on the death (aged ninety-two) of Bishop Gifford, 12th March 1734, and died 22nd December 1758, aged eighty-one.
[5] Consecrated 30th December 1725, died 3rd April 1740, aged eighty.
[6] Died 10th January 1740.   [7] Died 4th January 1727.

ECCLESIASTICAL

1728. . John Anthony, Cardinal Davia, to be Protector of Scotland.
„ May 22. Peter Guerin de Tencin, Archbishop of Embrun, to be a Cardinal in succession to Cardinal de Polignac.
„ Aug. 27. Sylvester Louis Lloyd, Franciscan, to be Bishop of Killaloe.
„ Nov. 24. Michael Macdonagh, Dominican, to be Bishop of Kilmore.
1729. Jan. 12. Stephen MacEgan, Bishop of the Seven Churches, to be Bishop of Ferns, in succession to John Verdun, dead.
„ Mar. 21. Alexander, Cardinal Falconieri, to be Protector of Scotland.[1] Noted as antedated, 8th January 1727.
„ Sept. 14. Lucas Fagan, Bishop of Meath, to be Archbishop of Dublin, in succession to Edward Murphy.
„ „ „ Stephen MacEgan, Bishop of the Seven Churches, to be Bishop of Meath, in succession to Lucas Fagan.
„ „ „ Ambrose O'Callaghan, Franciscan, to be Bishop of Ferns.
1730. Aug. . Peter Muligan, Augustine, D.D., to be Bishop of Ardagh, in succession to Thomas Flynn.
„ Sept. 17. Hugh Macdonnel, to be a Bishop in Scotland.
1731. July 19. Patrick Shee, Vicar-General, to be Bishop of Ossory.
„ Nov. 9. Patrick French, Franciscan, to be Bishop of Elphin.
1732. Nov. 11. Martin Bourke, to be Bishop of Kilmacduagh.
1733. Feb. 22. Monsignor Dominick Riviera, to be a Cardinal.[2]
„ Aug. 3. Peter Donnelan, to be Bishop of Clonfert.
„ Dec. 16. Stephen Dowdal, to be Bishop of Kildare, in succession to Bernard Dunne.
1734. Jan. 29. Cardinal Riveria, to be Protector of Scotland.
„ Mar. 9. John Linegar, to be Archbishop of Dublin, in succession to Lucas Fagan.
1735. Sept. 18. Alexander Smith, to be coadjutor to Bishop James Gordon, Vicar-Apostolic in Scotland.[3]
„ „ 24. John O'Hart, to be Bishop of Killala.
1736. „ 22. Colin O'Shagnussy [O'Saugnessy], to be Bishop of Ossory.
1737. Jan. 19. Nerée Marie, Cardinal Corsini, to be Protector of Ireland in succession to Cardinal Imperiali.
„ Apr. 21. Dr. James Gallihurium [? Gallagher], Bishop of Raphoe, to be Bishop of Kildare in succession to Stephen Dowdal.
„ Aug. 19. Dr. Robert Lacy, to be Bishop of Limerick.
„ Nov. 6. Dr. Bernard Macmahon, to be Archbishop of Armagh.
„ „ 30. Father Bonaventura Gallagher, to be Bishop of Raphoe, in succession to Dr. James Gallagher.

---

[1] Died 26th January 1734.   [2] Died at Rome, 3rd November 1752.
[3] He was consecrated 13th November 1735, succeeded on Bishop Gordon's death, 1st March 1746, as Vicar-Apostolic of the Lowland District, and died 21st August 1767, aged eighty-three.

NOMINATIONS

1738. May 13. Dr. Roche Macmahon, to be Bishop of Clogher.
1739. Feb. 21. Monsignor Peter Guerin de Tencin, Archbishop of Embrun, to be a Cardinal.
„ „ „ Eugenius O'Sullivan, to be Bishop of Kerry.
„ Apr. 10. Michael O'Reilly, to be Bishop of Derry.
„ „ „ Dr. Bernard O'Rourke, to be Bishop of Killala.
„ May 13. Sylvester Louis Lloyd, Bishop of Killaloe, to be Bishop of Waterford and Lismore.
„ July 10. Richard Challoner, Bishop of Doberus, to be coadjutor to Dr. Benjamin Petre, Bishop of Prusa, Vicar-Apostolic of London.[1]
„ „ 26. Patrick Macdonnagh, to be Bishop of Killaloe.
„ „ „ Dr. Walter Blake, to be Bishop of Achaden.
„ Sept. 9. Dr. Thomas O'Brien, to be Bishop of Ardagh in succession to Peter Muligan.
1740. Jan. 25. Cardinal Pico, to be Protector of England.
„ Aug. 29. Michael O'Gara, to be Archbishop of Tuam.
„ „ „ Father Francis Stewart, to be Bishop of Down and Connor.
„ Sept. 3. Edward Dicconson, Bishop of Mallus, to be Vicar-Apostolic of the Northern Province of England.[2]
1743. July 8. Father John Brett, to be Bishop of Killala.
„ Aug. 20. Dr. Thomas Stistch [? Stretch], to be coadjutor to Bishop Sylvester Lloyd.
„ Sept. 19. William O'Meara, D.D., Deacon of the Cathedral Church of Waterford, to be Bishop of Kerry in succession to Eugenius O'Sullivan.
1744. Jan. 1. Father Peter Killikelly, D.D., to be Bishop of Kilmacduagh.
„ Sept. 20. Dr. Nicholas Sweetman, Vicar-General of the Diocese, to be Bishop of Ferns.
1745. Mar. 23. Frederic Marcello, Cardinal Lante, to be Protector of England.
„ Apr. 3. Peter Creveo, to be coadjutor to Bishop Sylvester Lloyd.
1747. Feb. 23. Lawrence Richardson, to be Bishop of Kilmore.
„ Apr. 5. Monsignor Armand de Rohan, Abbé de Ventadour, to be a Cardinal.[3]
„ „ 20. Thomas Macdermot Roe, to be Bishop of Ardagh in succession to Dr. Thomas O'Brien.
„ July 19. Dr. Roche Macmahon, Bishop of Clogher, to be Archbishop of Armagh in succession to Archbishop Bernard Macmahon.
„ Aug. 9. Anthony Garvey, to be Bishop of Dromore.
„ Sept. 2. Daniel O'Reilly, to be Bishop of Clogher.

---

[1] He was consecrated 29th January 1741, and succeeded as Vicar-Apostolic on Bishop Petre's death, 22nd December 1758. He died 12th January 1781, aged ninety.
[2] Consecrated 19th March 1741, died 24th April 1752, aged eighty-two.
[3] Died 23rd July 1759.

ECCLESIASTICAL

1747. Dec. 13. Richard Walsh, to be Bishop of Cork.
,, ,, ,, John O'Brien, to be Bishop of Cloyne and Ross.
1748. Aug. . John Brett, Bishop of Killala, to be Bishop of Elphin.
,, Oct. 23. Michael O'Reilly, Bishop of Derry, to be Archbishop of Armagh.
,, Nov. 20. Dr. James Dunne, to be Bishop of Ossory.
,, ,, ,, Dr. Mark Skerret, to be Bishop of Killala.
1749. Apr. 21. Dr. Mark Skerret, Bishop of Killala, to be Archbishop of Tuam.
,, ,, ,, Dr. John Brullagham [? Bruligan], to be Bishop of Derry.
,, ,, ,, Father Bonaventura, *alias* Melchior, Macdonnel, to be Bishop of Killala.
,, Nov. 20. Dr. James Butler, to be coadjutor to Dr. Christopher Butler, Archbishop of Cashel.
1750. Jan. 3. Father Anthony O'Donnell, to be Bishop of Raphoe.
,, July 27. Francis Petre, Bishop of Amorium, to be coadjutor to Bishop Edward Dicconson, Vicar-Apostolic of the Northern Districts of England.[1]
1751. Jan. 6. Patrick Bradley, *alias* Brolcau, to be Bishop of Derry.
,, ,, 16. Dr. Edmond O'Doran, to be Bishop of Down and Connor.
,, July 2. Father Augustine Chevers, to be Bishop of Ardagh in succession to Dr. Thomas Macdermot Roe.
,, Nov. 10. Dr. James Keeffe, to be Bishop of Kildare and Leighlin.
,, ,, 22. John Hornyold, Bishop of Philomelia, to be coadjutor to John Talbot Stonor, Bishop of Thespiæ, Vicar-Apostolic of the Midland District.[2]
,, ,, ,, John Colgrave, to be Bishop of Derry, in succession to Patrick Bradley, resigned.
1752. May 5. Patrick O'Naughton, of the Irish College at Duact in Belgium, to be Bishop of Killaloe, in succession to Patrick Macdonnagh.
,, Nov. 10. Nicholas Madgett, D.D., late of the College of St. Barbara in Paris, to be Bishop of Killaloe.[3]
1753. Feb. 8. William O'Meara, Bishop of Ardfert, to be Bishop of Killaloe, and Nicholas Madgett, nominated Bishop of Killaloe, to be Bishop of Ardfert.[4]
,, Mar. 25. Andrew Campbell, to be Bishop of Kilmore.
1754. Feb. 14. Joseph Cardinal Spinelli, to be Protector of Scotland.
1755. Jan. 18. James Scott, to be coadjutor to Bishop Alexander Smith.
,, June 27. Nathaniel O'Donell, to be Bishop of Raphoe.

---

[1] He was consecrated 27th July 1751, and succeeded as Vicar-Apostolic on Bishop Dicconson's death, 24th April 1752. He died 24th December 1775, aged eighty-five.

[2] He was consecrated 10th February 1752, succeeded Bishop Stonor 29th March 1756, and died 26th December 1778.

[3] Patrick Naughton having asked to be excused accepting this Bishopric in order that he might complete his work in Belgium.

[4] They having prayed leave to exchange.

NOMINATIONS

1755. Sept. 19. Richard Lincoln, Archdeacon of Dublin, to be coadjutor to John Linegar, Archbishop of Dublin.
1756. Mar. 19. Paul Albert de Luynes, Archbishop of Sens, to be a Cardinal.
„ May 1. Charles Walmesley, Bishop of Rama, to be coadjutor to Lawrence William York, Bishop of Nisiba, Vicar-Apostolic of the West of England.[1]
„ July 21. Dr. Augustine Chevers, Bishop of Ardagh, to be Bishop of Meath.
„ „ „ Dr. Anthony Blake, to be Bishop of Ardagh.
„ Aug. 3. Dr. James O'Fallon, to be Bishop of Elphin.
1758. Apr. 19. Dr. Anthony Blake, Bishop of Ardagh, to be Archbishop of Armagh.
„ July 28. Patrick Robert Kirwan, to be Bishop of Achonry.
„ „ „ James Brady, to be Bishop of Ardagh.
„ Dec. 17. Father Thomas de Burgo, to be Bishop of Ossory.
„ „ „ Philip O'Reilly, to be Bishop of Raphoe.
1759. Feb. . James Talbot, Bishop of Birtha, to be coadjutor to Bishop Richard Challoner, Vicar-Apostolic of London.[2]
„ Sept. 12. Dr. Daniel Kerney, to be Bishop of Limerick.
1760. Aug. 27. Theophilus Macartan, to be Bishop of Down and Connor.
„ Sept. 18. Dr. Philip Philips, to be Bishop of Killala.
1763. Apr. 11. John Butler, Archdeacon of Cashel, to be Bishop of Cork.
„ May 5. Cardinal John Francis Albani,[3] to be Protector of Scotland in succession to Cardinal Spinelli.
„ Sept. 13. Patrick Fitz Simons, to be Archbishop of Dublin.
1765. May 16. Father Michael Peter MacMahon, to be Bishop of Killaloe.
„ Dec. 21. Philip MacDavett, to be Bishop of Derry.

---

[1] He was consecrated 21st December 1756, and succeeded as Vicar-Apostolic on Bishop York's death, 14th April 1770. He died 25th November 1797, aged seventy-six.
[2] He was consecrated 24th August 1759, and died 26th January 1790, aged sixty-five.
[3] Nephew of Pope Clement XI.

APPOINTMENTS

DIPLOMATIC APPOINTMENTS

1689. Aug. 25. John (Drummond), Earl of Melfort [S], sent on a mission to the Court of Paris.
1696. Mar. 18. Hon. John Stafford[-Howard], to be Ambassador to the Court of Paris.
1705. Apr. 16. Sir Toby Bourke, to be Ambassador to the Court of Madrid.
1711. Dec. 26. Cardinal Gualterio, to be Ambassador to the Court of Rome.
1716. Jan. 31. [   ] Cockburn, to be Ambassador to the Court of Sweden.
„ May ? [   ] Bagnols, to be Envoy to the King of Sicily.
„ „ 26. Thomas Southcot, to be Ambassador to the Court of Vienna.[1]
„ July 17. Sir John Erskine of Alva, Baronet, to be Plenipotentiary to the Court of Sweden.[2]
„ Sept. 21. [   ], to be Resident in England.
„ Nov. 6. John Walkinshaw of Burrowfield, to be Envoy to the Court of Vienna.
„ „ . James Carnegy of Boysack, to be Envoy to the States of Switzerland.
1717. Jan. . Sir John Walkinshaw of Burrowfield, to be Ambassador to the Court of Vienna.
„ „ . Sir George Jerningham, to be Ambassador to The Hague.
„ Feb. 1. Lieutenant-General Arthur Dillon, to be Plenipotentiary to the Court of Paris.
„ „ 14. The Duke of Ormonde, to be Plenipotentiary to the Court of Sweden.
„ Dec. 30. [   ] Obryan, to go to Vienna.
1718. June 4. Hon. James Murray, to be Plenipotentiary for negotiating the marriage with the Princess Clementina.
„ July 14. Mr. William Fraser, to be Plenipotentiary to The Hague.

---

[1] This is endorsed : 'Not made use of,' and at end : '*N.B.*—Upon Mr. Southcot's not 'going a copy of these Instructions, all but the two articles relating to Lorain, sent to 'Mr. O'Rourk, sealed and signed by the King, and countersigned by Lord Mar, for his 'going to Vienna. But that was afterwards found inconvenient, and so Mr. Walking-'shaw of Burrowfield sent thither.'

[2] Endorsed : 'Sir John got no further than Lubeck.'

DIPLOMATIC APPOINTMENTS

1721. Jan. 21. George Granville, Lord Lansdown, to be Plenipotentiary to the Regent of France.
1722. May 29. John Menzies, to be continued as Plenipotentiary for one year from date.[1]
„ June ?. [   ], to be Plenipotentiary to the Regent of France.
1723. Jan. 8. Thomas Sheridan, to be Envoy to Prince James Sobieski.
„ Aug. . Colin Campbell of Glenderule, to be Agent in Scotland.
„ „ 4. David Kennedy, to be Plenipotentiary to the States of Holland.[2]
„ „ 7. Full powers to Thomas Sheridan to treat with Prince James Sobieski regarding certain estates.
„ „ 31. [   ], to be Envoy to States of Holland.
1725. Feb. 24. Full powers in blank to the Emperor of Russia sent to Admiral Gordon by Captain William Hay.
„ June 15. Full powers to the Bishop of Rochester to represent the King, and to give instructions to all his subjects now residing in France, relative to the expedition to Scotland now impending.[3]
„ „ 16. Allan Cameron, to be Agent in the Highlands.
„ Aug. 22. Philip (Wharton), first Duke of Wharton [E], to be Plenipotentiary to the Court of Vienna.
„ Dec. 15. New full powers in blank to the Empress Catherine of Russia sent to Admiral Gordon.
1726. Sept. 6. John Græme, to be Plenipotentiary to the Court of Vienna.
„ „ 28. The Sieur Jerome Belloni, to be Agent at Rome.
„ „ „ Sir William Ellis, mentioned as the King's Resident at Rome.
1727. Apr. 18. Audeonus O'Rourke, to be Plenipotentiary to the Court of Vienna.[4]
„ May 2. Full powers to the Court of Muscovy sent in blank to Admiral Gordon to fill up with name of person to be left in charge during his absence.
1728. Feb. 6. New blank powers sent to the Duke of Liria to be left with Admiral Gordon on his leaving Muscovy, to be filled up by Admiral Gordon, or as they may agree.
„ Apr. 27. Cardinal Davia, to be Minister at Rome.
1731. Mar. 29. William Leigh, to be Plenipotentiary to the States of Holland.[5]

---

[1] Endorsed: 'Never used.'
[2] Endorsed: 'Never used, David Kennedy being dead before they came to Paris.'
[3] Endorsed: 'Writ with the King's own hand.'
[4] Endorsed: 'August 18, 1731. Renewed at his desire, of the same date, with the change of the name "Audeonus" to Eugenius.'
[5] Endorsed: 'Never made use of.'

DIPLOMATIC APPOINTMENTS

1732. Apr. 1. George Waters, Banker, to be Agent in Paris.
1733. Feb. 27. William (Keith), Earl Marischal [S], to be Minister to the Court of Madrid.
„ July 21. Colonel John Obryan, to be Minister to the Court of Paris.
1735. May 20. Dr. King, to be Agent to the States of Holland.
1736. „ 28. Colonel James Urquhart, to be Agent in Scotland.
„ Sept. 19. Full powers to Colonel John Obryan to treat with the Court of Madrid.
1745. Nov. 15. Colonel Daniel Obryan, to be Minister to the Court of Paris.
1746. Feb. 7. Full powers to Colonel Daniel Obryan to treat with the Court of Madrid.

APPOINTMENTS

CONSULAR APPOINTMENTS, ETC.

1689. July 17. Gregoire Fitzgerald, to be Consul at Nantes, Croisie, and all other ports and creeks belonging to the harbour of Nantes.
„ Aug. 9. John Porter, to be Consul at Rouen, Honfleur, and Havre de Grace.
„ „ 16. Nicholas Geraldin Theobald, to be Consul at St. Malo's and the ports and creeks belonging thereto.
1691. Nov. 6. Peter Nagle, to be Consul at Cadiz and all the ports and creeks belonging thereto.
1692. Feb. 13. Thomas Stratford, to be Consul at Brest, or any other port of Brittany.
„ Apr. 20. John, Count of Bonarelli [Italy], to be Consul at Ancona.
1694. Feb. 5. William Ploughman, to be Consul at Leghorn and all the ports depending thereon.
„ Mar. 6. William Chapman, to be Consul at Marseilles, Toulon, and Nice, and all the ports, etc.
„ June 9. Sir James Geraldin, to be Comptroller and Commissioner in the port of Dunkirk, and all other ports and places in Normandy and Picardy, of all accounts, etc., relating to the tenths, etc., due to the King from the capture of prizes, etc.
„ „ . John Constable, to be Agent and Receiver of the tenths of prizes at Dunkirk.
1695. Mar. 1. Thomas Stratford,[1] to be Agent, Consul, and Commissary, and also Receiver-General, in the Province of Brittany and in all ports and places in France southward of the said Province.
„ „ „ John Nimport, to be Vice-Consul in the port of St. Malo.
„ „ „ Francis Browne, to be Vice-Consul in the port of Brest.
„ June 1. Louis Raulin, Receiver of the Count of Toulouse, Admiral of France, to receive the tenth of prizes at Dunkirk.
1697. Mar. 19. Sir William Ellis, to be Agent, Consul, and Commissary, and also Receiver-General for France and its dependencies.
1702. Dec. 7. Dominick Lynch,[2] to be Consul in the ports of Ostend, Nieuport, and Bruges.

---

[1] Cancelled 6th March 1697, when the King pardoned him the debts due by him.
[2] Noted as solicited by, and given to, Lady Strickland.

CONSULAR APPOINTMENTS

1718. Jan. 1. Sir Peter Redmond, to be Consul-General for Portugal.
1731. Nov. 9. Richard Gawen [I], to be Consul at Civitia Vecchia.
1734. Nov. 23. Thomas Chamberlain, to be Consul at   .[1]
1762. Mar. 2. Ambrose, Count Tomasium, to be Consul at Ancona, vacant by the death of Joseph Storani.

---

[1] Endorsed: 'Recalled in 1740.'

PARDONS

PARDONS, ETC.

1689. Apr. 29. Reprieve, for one month from the date of their last reprieve, to Sir Lawrence Parsons of Birr, Bart., James Roscoe, and Jonathan Darby, lately indicted at Philipstown for rebellion and sentenced to death.

„ May 9. Pardon to Richard Close, Vernon Parker, etc., for high treason.

„ „ 16. Warrant, after reciting that William (Bourke), eighth Lord Castle Connell [I], was indicted and outlawed for high treason on account of the rebellion that broke out 23rd October 1641, and that, the outlawry being reversed, the said indictment is in being, for entering a *nolle prosequi* on the same, in consideration of his faithful services at home and abroad.

„ „ 25. Protection to John Otway of Ballyneclogh and Cloghanane, in cos. Limerick and Tipperary, with his houses, families, tenants, etc.

„ „ 29. Order that Henry (O'Brien), seventh Earl of Thomond, be not molested in his estates by the Commissioners for inquiring into rebels' or absentees' estates, his loyalty and affection, his old age and incapacity to attend His Majesty, being well known.

„ June 8. Pardon to John M'Mahon for high treason.

1692. Oct. 4. Pardon to Thomas Graham, Brigadier of the troop of Guards in Scotland, for the manslaughter of John Cleeland.

1694. June . Pardon under the Great Seal [E] to John (Drummond), Earl of Melfort, for all treasons, etc., committed against the King or against Charles II.

„ „ „ Similar pardon under the Great Seal [S].

1721. Sept. 28. Pardons under the Great Seals [E and S] to Simon (Fraser), Lord Lovat [S], and James Campbell of Auchinbreck, 'upon their returning to their duty.'

COMMISSIONS

MILITARY AND NAVAL COMMISSIONS

1689. June 7. George Anderson, to be Master and Commander of the yacht *Swiftsure*.
1690. May 13. Colonel Solomon, Commissary-General of the Musters [I].
1691. Dec. 8. Colonel Sir Andrew Lee, to go to Brittany and inspect troops lately arrived from Ireland.
„ „ 14. James (Fitzjames), first Duke of Berwick [E], to be Captain and Colonel of the First Troop of Guards [E].
1692. [Jan.]. The Modelment of the Irish Troops.
    Cavalry—First Company of Guards, commanded by James (Fitzjames), first Duke of Berwick [E].
    „ Second Company of Guards, commanded by Patrick (Sarsfield), first *Earl of Lucan* [I].
    2 Regts. First commanded by [　　] Sheldon.
    „ Second commanded by Piers (Butler), third Viscount Galmoye [I].
    The Royal Regiment of Dragoons, commanded by Maxwell.
    The Queen's Regiment, commanded by [　　] Carroll.
    Infantry—Regiment of Guards, commanded by Colonel Dorington.
    Queen's Regiment, commanded by Colonel Wachop.
    Marine Regiment, commanded by Henry Fitzjames, 'the Grand Prior.'
    Dublin Regiment, commanded by Colonel Simon Luttrell.
    Limerick Regiment.
    Charlemont Regiment.
„ Jan. 3. First Troop of Guards, commanded by the Duke of Berwick.
    Major-Gen. Sutherland, to be first Lieutenant.
    Col. Christopher Nugent, to be second Lieutenant.
    Matthias (Barnewall), tenth Baron Trimlestown [I], Lieutenant and Ensign; succeeded by Francis La Rue as second Ensign.
    Matthew Cook, to be second Ensign; succeeded Lord T. as first Ensign, and in 1696 as Lieutenant.

COMMISSIONS

Robert Preston,
Maurice Dillon, } Corporals (*Brigadiers*).
Brian Carroll,
George Rivers,
Thomas Bietagh, Staff-Sergeant.

1692. Jan. 4. Second Troop of Guards, commanded by the Earl of Lucan.
Charles O'Brien, to be first Lieutenant.
Nicholas Cusack, to be second Lieutenant.
John Gaydon, to be first Ensign.
Robert Arthur, to be second Ensign.
Edward Broghall,
[   ] Plunkett, } Corporals.
[   ] O'Brien,
George White,
Francis Bada, Staff-Sergeant, succeeded by E. Broghall.

„ Feb. 13. Jasper Strafford, to be Captain of the *Benediction*, asked by Tobie Gerardin.

„ „ 22. Patrick Lampert, to be Captain of *La Providence*, asked by Mr. Du Livier.

„[1] „ 23. Lawrence Hore, to be Captain of the *Prince of Wales*, asked by Mr. Doé.

„ „ „ James Wilson, to be Captain of the *Aran*, asked by Mr. Doé.

„ „ „ Terence Dermott, to be Captain of the *Sarsfield*, asked by Mr. Doé.

„ Mar. 6. Ignatius Cleere, to be Captain of the *Dolphin*, asked by Mr. Doé.

„ „ 10. William Herbert, Earl[2] (? Marquis) of Montgomery, to be Colonel of a regiment of horse to be raised in England.

„ „ 13. John Gooldin, to be Captain of the *Sun* of St. Malo.

„ „ „ Thomas Vaghan, to be Captain of the *Damiant*.

„ „ 20. Patrick Troy, to be Captain of the *Berwick*.

„ May 19. Alexander Nairne, of St. Foord (Samford), to be Captain of a troop of horse.

„ „ „ Colonel Canon, to be Major-General.

„ „ „ William Keith, Lord Keith, to be Colonel of horse.

„ „ „ Colonel Brown, to be Colonel of foot.

„ „ „ Colonel Scot, to be Lieutenant-Colonel of Colonel Brown's regiment.

„ June . List of officers, subsisted after the failure of La Hague expedition.

---

[1] After this, in 1693 and afterwards, commissions were given either by the King of France or the Admiralty.

[2] The next day William, *Marquis* of Montgomery, has a warrant empowering him to grant commissions for the subalterns of his regiment.

MILITARY AND

Note.—After His Majesty's return from La Hague, the officers not provided for in the Irish corps were joined together on several different lists, and paid so for some time.

Colonel Johnston's list[1] (Scottish)—
Capt. Achmouty.   Capt. Livingstone.
„ Deane.   „ Farmour, etc., in all 49.
Colonel Trapp's list[2] (English)—
Sir Alphonso Mottet.   Capt. Povay.
Major Feilding.   „ Arnald.
Mr. Price.   „ Adams.
Capt. Laysenby.   M. de Tangis, etc., in all 38.
Colonel La Rue's list[3] (80 guards or thereabouts).
Colonel Reinolds' list[4] (47 Irish officers).

1692. June . English at Havre under Colonel Skelton[5]—
Col. Chatham.   Capt. Wray.
„ Gifford.   „ Booth.
„ Napeir.   „ Byerley.
„ Throgmorton.   „ Delaval.
„ Latton.   „ Monson.
„ St. Ange.   „ Hall.
„ de Bussie.   „ Staveley
Capt. Stytch.   „ Oldfield.

„ „ „ Scots at Dunkirk under Major-Generals Buchan and Canon.[6]
[James (Seton), fourth] Earl of Dunfermline [S].
[David (Graham), third] Viscount Dundee [S].
Sir G   Barklay.
Sir W   Wallace.
[Alexander Robertson of] Struan.
Sir Alexander M'Lane.
[John (Fleming), sixth] Earl of Wigtoun [S].

---

[1] A part were to join the Scots companies in Roussillon and have fifty days' pay, the rest were to be subsisted by the King.

[2] Some to choose where they will serve or have passes, others to continue to be entertained by His Majesty, but none to come to St. Germains without leave.

[3] To join the Irish and have thirty days' pay.

[4] To march to Savoy to join Colonel Talbot's regiment and have forty days' pay.

[5] These were continued in subsistence at 30 *sols* a Colonel, 25 a Lieutenant-Colonel, and 20 Captains ; other thirteen officers at 10 *sols* a day were ordered to join regiments or take passes. All the Irish officers were to march with Colonel Bourke to join Irish regiments.

[6] The pay of 30 and 25 *sols* a day was continued to the Colonel and Lieutenant-Colonel, and the rest (with some exceptions) were to take service with the troops. A great many Captains and other subaltern Scots officers and cadets, at His Majesty's desire, voluntarily ranked themselves in a new Scots company of which Colonel Brown got the command, with Colonel Scot and Alexander Gordon for his lieutenants. They marched in September from St. Germains to Roussillon, and were at the siege of Roses with the other two brigades of Captains Rutherford and Haye.

NAVAL COMMISSIONS

[James (Galloway), third] Baron Dunkeld [S].
Patrick Graham.
Colonel Brown.
Lieutenant-Colonel Sir G Maxwell.
Colonel Scot.
„ Gordon.
„ Fitzsimons.
Major Farcherson [Farquharson].
„ James Buchan.
Captain Thomas Dunbar.
„ Fr. Scott.
„ Maitland.
„ King.
„ Bradel.
Priest, Nichols.
Minister, Edwards.

1692. Dec. . List of Field-Officers to whom subsistence was paid by the King's order :—

Col. Buchan.	Lt.-Col. Knightley.
„ St. Ange.	„ Fountain.
„ Bussy.	„ Scott.
„ Ingram.	„ Throgmorton.
„ Fitzsimons.	„ Bynns.
„ Gifford.	„ Robeson.
„ Oliphant.	„ Grace.
„ Robertson.	„ Graham, Bass.
„ Græmes.	„ Delaval.
„ Butler.	„ Malcome.
„ Rycaut.	„ Davidson.
„ Joseph.	„ Dicconson for A,
„ Farcharson.	B, C, D, E, F.

1693. May 20. Christopher FitzGerald, to be Brigadier of the Irish Troop of Guards, with brevet, dated 22nd September 1693, to command Brigadier George White, notwithstanding the date of the latter's commission.

„ „ „ Edward Broghall, to be Aide-Major of the Irish Troop of Guards, vice Bada, retired.

„ Aug. 14. Donogh (MacCarthy), fourth Earl of Clancarty [I], to command the Irish Troop of Guards, vice Patrick (Sarsfield), first Earl of Lucan [I], killed at Nerwinden (Landen), 29th July 1693.

„ „ 21. Captain Richard Middleton, mentioned as Governor of the Bass, when Lieutenant-Colonel Graham [commander of the garrison?] has leave to come to France.

„ Sept. 20. Colonel Garrett Dillon, to be second Ensign of the Irish Troop of Guards, vice Robert Arthur, died at Namur.

MILITARY AND

1693. Oct. 10. Captain Donnell M'Donnel, to be Brigadier of the Irish Troop of Guards, *vice* Christopher Fitzgerard, removed.

„ Dec. 22. [   ] Donnoghe,[1] mentioned as Sub-Lieutenant in Irish Troop of Guards.

„   . At the end of this year the list of Colonels and Lieutenant-Colonels subsisted at 30 and 25 *sols* a day was fixed at fourteen Colonels and sixteen Lieutenant-Colonels as under:—[2]

Col. Buchan.	Lt.-Col. Gifford.
„ Canon.	„ Latton.
„ Barclay.	„ St. Ange.
„ Murray.	„ Bussie.
„ Cunningham.	„ Trapps.
„ Wallace.	„ Ennis.
„ Skelton.	„ Benys or Bynus.
„ Graham.	„ Butler.
„ Lord Dunkeld.	„ Farrell.
„ M'Lane.	„ Fitzsimons.
„ Capt. Clanranald.	„ Lacy.
„ Owen Macartie.	„ Michael Bourke.
„ Tangis.	„ Reinolds.
„ Struan.	„ Napier.
Lt.-Col. Chetham.	„ Oliphant.

1694. Mar. 19. Major Robert Middleton, to repair to the Bass, and in case of the sickness, death, or absence of the Governor, to command in his place.

„   „   „ Father Nichols, sent as Priest to the garrison.

„ Apr. 28. [   ] M'Carty, mentioned[3] as Lieutenant in the regiment of Clancarty.

„ [Nov. ?]. Edmund French, to command the *Spy*.

„ Dec. 20. Father John Dillon, to be Chaplain to the Irish Troop of Guards, whereof Donough, Earl of Clancarty, is Captain.

1695. Feb. 22. Captain Peter Nagle, to command the *Marin* of Brest.

„   „   „ Captain Philip Welsh, to command the *Trompeuse* of Brest.

„ June 9. Captain Andrew White, to command the *Trompeuse*.

„ July 14. Captain Thomas Vaughan, to command the *Loyal Clancarty*.

„   „ 16. Edmund Kearney, to command the

---

[1] When Queen Mary writes to the Archbishop of Cambray recommending the bearer, his wife, who is going with her family to find her husband, who is in garrison at Cambray. In another letter, dated 21st September 1695, mention is made of her having four children.

[2] A great many officers were continued in subsistence by His Majesty, some at 20 *sols*, viz. Majors and others, and the rest at 10 *sols* a day.

[3] When Queen Mary writes to the Bishop of Valence recommending his wife, who intends to live in his diocese with her three children.

NAVAL COMMISSIONS

1695. Aug. 6. Edmund Ffrench, to command the *Marin*, cancelled in favour of Richard Geraldin, who had been chosen by the *armateurs* of the said frigate.
„ „ 10. Commission for a second Captain (not named) to command the *Marin*.
„ Sept. 16. Roger O'Cahane, to be commander of the *John* of Dunkirk.
„ Dec. 27. John Counter, to be Brigadier of the 1st Troop of Guards. Noted as delivered to George Berkeley.
1696. Mar. 8. [   ], Marquis of Harcourt [F], to be Captain-General of the Army [E].
„ „ 8. Richard Hamilton, to be Lieutenant-General of His Majesty's forces [E].
„ May 24. Edward Cooke, to be Brigadier of the 1st Troop of Guards. Noted as sent to Colonel Nugent.
„ Dec. 7. Peter Condroy, to be Chirurgeon of the 2nd Troop of Guards.
1697. Aug. 8. Bernard Berne, mentioned[1] as formerly Quartermaster of the 2nd Troop of Guards.
„ „ 17. Michael Dunn, mentioned[2] as formerly trooper in the 2nd Troop of Guards.
1703. May 19. Patrick Grahame, to be Colonel of a regiment of dragoons to be raised [S], and Captain of a troop thereof.
1708. Apr. 25. M . . . . A . . . . [? John (Murray), first Duke and second Marquis of Atholl], to be Lieutenant-General and Commander-in-Chief in Scotland till the King's arrival.
1711. May 19. Charles B . . . . , to be Colonel of a foot regiment to be raised [E], and Captain of a company thereof.
1715. Mar. 27. Captain David George, to be Captain of the *Speedwell* galley.
„ „ „ John Aberdeen, to be 1st Lieutenant of the *Speedwell* galley.
„ „ „ Alexander Gordon, to be 2nd Lieutenant of the *Speedwell* galley.
„ Sept. 7. John Erskine, Earl of Mar, to be General and Commander-in-Chief of the forces [S] both by sea and land, renewed 22nd October.
„ Sept. 1/12. John Gordon of Glenbucket, Bailie to the Marquis of Huntly, to raise the Marquis of Huntly's men.
„ Oct. 24. Thomas Forster, to be a Major-General.
„ „ 25. Thomas Forster, to be Commander-in-Chief [E] until the arrival of the Duke of Ormonde.
„ Oct. 15/26. Alexander Gordon, to be Lieutenant-General of His Majesty's forces (by Mar).

---

[1] When Major-General Sheldon, Colonel of a regiment of horse, is directed to inquire into the complaints of the Earl of Clancarty against him.
[2] When Major-General Sheldon is directed to examine a report upon his petition.

MILITARY AND

1715. Oct. 22/Nov. 2. John Gordon of Glenbucket, to be Colonel of a foot regiment, and Captain of a company thereof (by Mar).
1716. Feb. 4/15. Lieutenant-General Alexander Gordon, to be Commander-in-Chief [S].
„ Apr. 6. Peregrine (Osborne), second Duke of Leeds [E] and first Viscount Dunblane [S], to be Admiral and Commander-in-Chief of His Majesty's fleet.[1]
„ July 23. Lord Arran, to be Commander-in-Chief of all His Majesty's forces both by sea and land in the kingdom of England and Ireland, in the absence of the Duke of Ormonde.
„ Oct. 12. Harrie Lesly, Esq., to be a Major of foot.
„ „ „ Alexander Gordon, Esq., to be a Major of foot.
1717. Jan. 29. Colonel John Livingston, to be a Brigadier of foot.
„ Feb. 3. Colonel Colin Campbell of Glenderule, to be a Brigadier of foot.
„ Apr. . James, Marquis of Drummond, to be Lieutenant-General of the horse. Antedated 22nd October 1715.
„ May 10. The Honourable James Keith, brother to the Earl Marischal, to be a Colonel of horse.[2]
„ Aug. 7. Lancelot Ord, Esq., to be a Colonel [E].
„ Oct. 13. Sir John O'Brien, to be a Colonel of foot.
„ Dec. 20. Captain MacMahon to be a Colonel of horse.
1718. Feb. 2. Lieutenant-Colonel John Stuart, to be a Colonel of foot.
1721. June 26. Lord George Murray, to be Brigadier-General of the army.
„ „ „ William (Murray), *Duke of* [*Rannoch*], to be Lord High Admiral [S].
„ „ „ Arthur (Dillon), *Earl of* [*Dillon*], to be General and Commander-in-Chief of all our forces [I].
„ Dec. 15. George (Granville), *Duke of Albemarle* [E], to be Commander-in-Chief in Cornwall.
1722. Jan. 2. [Lord North], to be a Lieutenant-General.[3]
„ „ 4. Thomas Wentworth [*Earl of Strafford*], to be Commander-in-Chief of His Majesty's forces north of the Humber.
„ „ 5. William North [Lord North], to be Commander-in-Chief in and about the city of London and Westminster.
„ „ 31. Brigadier Græme, to be a Major-General.
„ „ „ Captain Alexander Urquhart, to be a Lieutenant-Colonel.
„ Mar. 1. Sir Charles Wogan, to be a Brigadier-General.
„ „ 10. Lord Lovat, to be a Major-General.
„ „ „ Sir Henry Goring, to be a Major-General.

---

[1] Endorsed, which commission the Duke of Leeds delivered back to the King at the Baths of Lucca, 28th August 1723.

[2] Endorsed: 'Renewed as a Col. of Dragoons, of the same date, and sent him from 'Bologne, Dec. 3, 1726.'

[3] Endorsed: 'Renewed, of the same date, and given to him June 17, 1727.'

NAVAL COMMISSIONS

1722. Apr. 1. Sir John Messit, to be a Brigadier-General.
,, ,, 2. Marcus Gealeagh, Esq., to be a Colonel.
,, July 6. Sir Luke O'Tool, to be Brigadier-General.
,, ,, 14. Lord Orrery, to be a Lieutenant-General.
,, ,, ,, ? to be a Brigadier-General.[1]
,, Aug. 24. Honourable John Dalziel (brother to Lord Carnwath), to be a Lieutenant-Colonel.[2]
1723. June . Mr. Colin Campbell of Glenderule, Major-General of our forces, to proceed to Scotland.
,, July 30. Sir James Campbell of Auchenbreck, to raise a regiment and be Colonel thereof.
,, Oct. 9. James Ogilvy, to be a Colonel.
,, Dec. 19. John Anselm Grossin, to raise a regiment and be Colonel thereof.
1726. Apr. 22. Andrew Ramsay, formerly ensign in the late Earl of Strathmore's regiment, to be a Captain of foot.
1732. May 22. The Duke of Ormonde to be General and Commander-in-Chief of all His Majesty's forces both by sea and land [E and I].
,, ,, ,, ? for Scotland.
,, ,, ,, Captain Charles Hardy, to be a Vice-Admiral.
1733. June 13. The Earl Marischal to be a Lieutenant-General.
1736. Oct. 29. The Duke of Berwick, to be a General of foot.
1740. Feb. 2. The Duke of Ormonde, Captain-General and Commander-in-Chief of all His Majesty's forces in Great Britain and Ireland.
,, ,, ,, The Earl Marischal, General and Commander-in-Chief of all His Majesty's forces in Scotland.
1741. May 17. Lord Fraser of Inveralochy, to be Colonel of a regiment of the name and clan of Fraser.
,, ,, ,, [ ] Chalmers of Galliard, to be a Colonel of foot.
1743. Dec. 23. Lord Lovat, to be a Lieutenant-General.
,, ,, ,, Sir James Campbell of Auchenbreck, to be a Major-General.
,, ,, ,, William Macgregor of Balhaldeis, to be a Colonel.
,, ,, ,, Blank Commission as Commander-in-Chief [E and I], designed for the Earl of Barrymore, in absence of Duke of Ormonde.
1745. Oct. 25. The Duke of York, to be Generalissimo of the King's forces in Great Britain and Ireland.
,, ,, ,, The Duke of Ormonde, to be Commander-in-Chief in Great Britain and Ireland under the Prince and the Duke of York.
1753. Apr. 13. Anthony Langley Swymmer, to be a Colonel of foot.
1759. June 11. Alexander Macleod, Esq., late Aide-de-camp to the Prince of Wales in Scotland, to be a Colonel of foot.

---

[1] Endorsed: 'Sent to Lord Orrory at his request for a friend.'
[2] Endorsed: 'Renewed Ap. 5, 1728, and sent to D. Ormonde.'

APPOINTMENTS

VARIOUS APPOINTMENTS

1689. Apr. 8. John Cusack, to be Deputy-Chancellor of the Exchequer [I], in the absence of the Chancellor, Bruno Talbott, who has leave to be absent from Ireland till Michaelmas term.

„ „ 25. Matthew Kennedy, LL.D., to be Master in Chancery [I].

„ „ 27. Sir Patrick Trant, Baronet, Francis Plowden, John Trinder, William Dickenson, and Richard Collyns, to be Commissioners of the Revenue, with a salary of £1000 per annum each; and James Nihill, to be agent or solicitor to the said Commissioners, *vice* Sir William Talbott and Charles Pleudell, Commissioners, and John Tapson, their agent, whose commission is recalled. Noted as renewed 6th May 1689, with the clause as to Nihill's being agent left out.

„ „ „ Richard Butler, LL.D., to be Master in Chancery [I].

„ „ 29. Randle M'Daniel, to be Clerk of the Crown and Peace and Prothonotary and Clerk of Common Pleas in the Court of King's Bench [I], and to keep all the records thereof.

„ May 1. Dr. Michael Plunkett, to be Master in Chancery [I].

„ „ 6. John Kearny, to be Clerk of the House of Commons [I].

„ „ 8. James Nagle, to be Sergeant-at-Arms [I].

„ „ 14. Lieutenant-General Justin M'Cartie, to be Master of the Ordnance [I].

„ „ „ John Shee, to be Commissary of the Musters [I].

„ „ „ Colonel William Mansel Barker, to be Lieutenant of the Ordnance [I].

„ „ 16. Richard Nagle, mentioned as Attorney-General [I].

„ „ „ Richard Talbot of Malahide, to be Auditor-General [I].

„ „ „ Order to Sir Richard Kearny, Ulster King of Arms, that the Barons of Ireland and their heirs for ever shall bear or use a circle of gold, with six pearls equally distant from each other on the said circle, for a coronet, to be marshalled with their arms.

„ „ 31. Thomas Arthur, to be Clerk of the Hanaper and Clerk of the Crown in the Court of Chancery [I].

„ „ „ Donnogh (Macarty), fourth Earl of Clancarty [I], to be Clerk of the Crown and Peace of Munster.

„ June 22. Thomas Peppard, to be continued as Mayor of Drogheda for the ensuing year.

„ „ 26. Francis Stafford, to be Clerk of the Pipe in the Court of Exchequer [I].

VARIOUS APPOINTMENTS

1689. June 30. James Nagle, to be Cursitor or Clerk and Engrosser of all original writs issuing out of the Court of Chancery [I].

„ July 1. Richard (Talbot), first Duke of Tyrconnell [I], Henry (Jermyn), first Baron Dover [E], Bruno Talbot, Chancellor of the Exchequer [I], and Sir Stephen Rice, Chief Baron of the Exchequer [I], to be Commissioners of the Treasury [I].

„ „ 4. Roger (Maguire), fifth Lord Inniskillin [I], to be Lord-Lieutenant of Fermanagh.

„ „ 5. Walter Dungan, Lord Dungan, to be Prothonotary of the Common Pleas of the Exchequer [I].

„ „ 23. William Dorington, to be Registrar of the Court of Chancery [I].

„ Aug. 16. Sir Michael Creagh, mentioned as Paymaster of the Army.

1691. Feb. 17. Commission to Henry Arundell, George Holeman, and Edward Perkins, authorising them or any two of them to promise a pardon to such subjects as shall return to their duty and such rewards as they shall think proportionate to the service they shall perform, etc.

1692. Feb. 13. Thomas Stratford, to be Receiver-General of the tenth due to H.M. of all the prizes taken by privateers.

1695. Aug. 24. Sir William Ellis, to be Commissioner and Comptroller-General of the revenue from prizes, etc.

„ Nov. 9. John Roettiers and his sons James and Norbert to be Engravers-General of the Mint [E]. *With note that the above was renewed to John and Norbert Roettiers, 6th June 1703.*

„ „ „ Joseph and Norbert Roettiers, to be makers of all instruments, tools, and engines fit and necessary for edging and milling all sorts of gold and silver to be coined in the Mint, etc. *With note that the above was renewed by James III and VIII, 6th June 1703, and again to Norbert Roettiers alone, 6th May 1710.*

„ Dec. 18. Warrant to John, James, and Norbert Roettiers to make puncheons and dies for coining five-pound pieces, etc.

1701. Oct. 31. Warrant to Norbert Roettiers for making and engraving the Great Seal of England.

1702. „ 15. Similar warrant for making the Great Seals of Scotland and Ireland.

1708. May 4. Similar warrant to Norbert Roettiers, Engraver-General of the Mint [E], to the one dated 18th December 1695.

1721. June 28. John (Erskine), first *Duke of Mar*, to be Lord-Lieutenant and High Commissioner [S].

1722. Mar. 24. Sir Henry Goring, to be Governor of Bristol.[1]

---

[1] Endorsed: 'September 1728. This commission and that of Major-General for Sir 'Henry Goring renewed, and both dated   day of   1722.'

VARIOUS APPOINTMENTS

1722. Mar. 26. James (Butler), first Duke of Ormonde [E and I], Charles (Butler), first Earl of Arran [I], Thomas (Wentworth), first Earl of Strafford [E], Robert (Harley), first Earl of Oxford and Mortimer [E], Charles (Boyle), fourth Earl of Orrery [I], Francis (Atterbury), Bishop of Rochester [E], ? Lord Gore, William (North), sixth Lord North and second Lord Grey [E], and George (Granville), first Lord Lansdown [E], to be Lords Regent [E] during the King's absence, with power (five making a quorum) to add four to their number.[1]

1723. July 30. Simon (Fraser), Lord Lovat [S], to be Lord-Lieutenant of Inverness, Nairn, and Sutherland.

„   „   „ Order for Lord Lovat to seize Inverness and be Governor thereof.

„   „   „ Order for Colonel John Stewart of Kinnachin to raise Atholl men, 'whereas we are resolved to make an 'attempt for the recovery of our Kingdoms,' etc.

„   „   „ Commission for Colonel John Stewart of Kinnachin to seize Castle of Blair in Atholl, to be Governor thereof.

„   „   „ Sir James Campbell of Auchenbreck, to be Lord-Lieutenant of Argyll.

„   „   „ Commission for Sir James Campbell of Auchenbreck to seize Inverary, to be Governor thereof.

„   „   „ James (Hamilton), fifth Duke of Hamilton [S], to be Lord-Lieutenant of the 'Shyres of Lannerech, Clidesdale 'and Renfrew.'

„   „   „ Alexander (Montgomerie), tenth Earl of Eglinton [S], to be Lord-Lieutenant of Ayr.

„   „   „ William (Cunningham), twelfth Earl of Glencairn [S], to be Lord-Lieutenant of Dumbarton.

„   „   „ William (Cunningham), twelfth Earl of Glencairn [S], to be Governor of Dumbarton Castle.

„   „   „ James (Fleming), sixth Earl of Wigton [S], to be Lord-Lieutenant of Stirlingshire.

„   „   „ John (Erskine), first *Duke of Mar* [S], to be Commissioner to the Parliament [S].[2]

1727. June 23. [   ] Roettiers, to succeed his father, Norbert Roettiers, as Engraver-General to the Mint [E].

„ July 4. Power to James (Murray), *Earl of Dunbar* [S], to open all letters addressed to the King or to Sir John Græme.

1732. May 22. James (Butler), Duke of Ormonde [E and I], to be Regent [E and I] during the King's absence.

1743. July 29. Le Sieur Jean Corroye Liegois, to be Expeditionaire du Roy (? copying-clerk) at the Court of Rome.

---

[1] Endorsed: '29 August 1722. This commission was returned and is destroyed.'
[2] Endorsed: 'Recalled.'

VARIOUS APPOINTMENTS

1743. Dec. 23. Commission of Regency to Charles, Prince of Wales.

,, ,, ,, Simon (Fraser), Lord Lovat [S], to be Lord-Lieutenant north of the Spey and to the head of the Spey to the north side of Loch Lochy.

,, ,, ,, Sir James Campbell of Auchenbreck, to be Lord-Lieutenant south of Appin in Lorne, including the isles of Lismore, Mull, Coll, etc.

1750. Aug. 5. Commission of Regency to Charles, Prince of Wales.

1757. Sept. 5. New Commission of Regency to the Prince of Wales.

1759. Aug. 12. James Edgar, Esq., to be Clerk of our Councils, Registers, and Rolls [S], with reversion to his nephew, John Edgar of Keithock, Esq.[1]

---

[1] The warrant sets forth that 'Whereas our Trusty and well-beloved James Edgar, 'Esq., has served us these great many years as our Clerk and Secretary with great 'fidelity, integrity, and diligence, of which we being very sensible, we therefore, as a 'mark of Our Royal favour and of Our Royal appreciation of the faithful services he 'has rendered to us, Do hereby constitute and appoint the said James Edgar to be 'the Clerk of our Councils, Registers, and Rolls in Scotland during all the days of his 'lifetime, and after that we also constitute and appoint our trusty and well-beloved 'John Edgar of Keithock, Esq., his nephew, to be our said Clerk of our Councils, 'Registers, and Rolls during all the days of his lifetime. To have and to hold to them, 'and the longest liver of them two,' etc. A note attached to a copy of the *Scottish House of Edgar*, formerly belonging to a granddaughter of John Edgar of Keithock, states that he was created a Baronet by King James III and VIII. James Edgar was a younger son of David Edgar of Keithock by his second wife, Elizabeth Guthrie, and was born at Keithock, 13th July 1688. He was out in the '15 with his brother John (who was taken prisoner and died in Stirling Castle), and afterwards fled to Rome, when he became Private Secretary to King James and so continued till his death, 24th September 1764. His nephew, John Edgar of Keithock, the son of his elder brother Alexander, by Margaret, daughter of the Rev. John Skinner, was out in the '45, and after the defeat of Culloden took ship for America, but being captured by a French privateer, was taken to France, where he obtained a commission in Ogilvy's regiment. He afterwards joined his uncle in Rome, but after the Act of Indemnity in 1756 he returned to Scotland, where he died 4th April 1788. He married, February 1762, Catherine Ogilvy, and had issue seven sons and three daughters. The sixth son and eventual heir, Thomas, born March 1775, died unmarried 7th September 1831, and was succeeded by his brother James, born 4th April 1777, died 1841, having married, 1813, Anne Barbara, daughter of J. Hamilton, merchant in Glasgow. He had issue two sons and three daughters : John, a monk, died unmarried ; James, of whom presently ; Anne Hamilton, married J. G. Plomer of Helstone, Cornwall, and had issue ; Catherine, died unmarried 1871 ; and Mary Caroline, who died unmarried 1896. James, the younger son, born 1819, emigrated to Canada, and died 6th April 1851, leaving by his wife, Grace, daughter of the Rev. David Fleming, with two daughters (Eliza Catherine, wife of W. P. Wilkie of Edinburgh, advocate, who died 5th September 1872, and Grace, wife of Richard Thome, merchant in Toronto), an only son, Sir James David Edgar, M.P., P.C., K.C.M.G., sometime (19th August 1896-31st July 1899) Speaker of the Canadian House of Commons, who was born at Hatley, Quebec, 10th August 1841, and died at Toronto 31st July 1899, leaving issue six sons and three daughters. Information taken from *The Family of Edgar*, published by the Grampian Club, 1873, supplemented by notes kindly supplied by Lady Edgar.

ALPHABETICAL LIST OF SURNAMES OF PEERS AND BARONETS

ASHTON, ... Baronet [E], 1692.
BUTLER, Charles, Earl of Arran [I], . Duke of Arran [E], 2nd Jan. 1722.
BORLASE, Humphrey, ... Lord Borlase, Baron of Mitchell [E], 16..?
BOURKE, Hon. John, afterwards Earl of Clanricarde [I]. Baron Bourke of Bophin [I], 2nd Apr. 1689.
—— Toby, ... Baron Bourke [I], 3rd Feb. 1727.
DE BOZAS, Joseph, Count of Castelblanco, Duke Castleblanco, and Duke of St. Andrews, Marquis of Borland, Earl of Fordan, Viscount of the Bass, Lord Divron [S], 4th Feb. 1717.
BROWNE, George, ... Baron, Viscount, and Earl of Browne [I], 12th Apr. 1726.
—— Sir Valentine, third Baronet [I], . Baron Castlerosse, Viscount Kenmare [I], 20th Apr. 1689.
BUTLER, Richard, ... Baron Butler [I], 1st Apr. 1727.
—— James, ... Baronet [E], 23rd Dec. 1743.
—— Piers, Viscount of Galmoye [I], . Earl of Newcastle [I], co. Limerick, 1692.
CAMERON of Lochiel, John, . . Lord Lochiel [S], 27th Jan. 1717.
CARY, Lucius Henry, sixth Viscount Falkland [S]. Earl of Falkland [E], 13th Dec. 1722.
CARYLL, John, ... Baron Caryll of Durford, co. Sussex [E], a. 29th Jan. 1699.
CHEEVERS, Edward, ... Baron Bannow, co. Wexford, Viscount of Mount Leinster, co. Carlow [I], 23rd Aug. 1689.
CHIFFINCH. See Villiers.
CONNOCK, William, ... Baronet [E], 22nd Feb. 1732.
CONSTABLE, John, ... Baronet [E], 17th Sept. 1753.
COTTINGTON, Francis, . . . Baron Cottington of Fonthill Gifford, co. Wilts [E], Apr. 1716.
CRONE, Matthew, ... Baron Crone [I], 16th Feb. 1728.
DAVIA, née MONTECUCULI, Anna Victoria. Countess of Almond [S], 3/13 Jan. 1689.
—— Virgilio, ... Lord Davia, Viscount of Moneydie and Earl of Almond [S], 9/12 Apr. 1698.
DILLON, Hon. Arthur, . . . Baron and Viscount Dillon [I], 1st Feb. 1717; Earl, Viscount, and Lord Dillon [S], 24th June 1721.

LIST OF SURNAMES

DORINGTON, Lieut.-Col. William, . Earl of Macclesfield [E], 17 . . ?
DRUMMOND. See Macgregor.
—— John, Earl of Melfort [S], . . Baron Cleworth [E], 7th Aug. 1689; Duke of Melfort, Marquis of Forth, Earl of Isla and Burntisland, Viscount of Rickerton, Lord Castlemains and Galston [S], 17th Apr. 1794.
—— James, Earl of Perth [S], . . Duke of Perth, Marquis of Drummond, Earl of Stobhall, Viscount Cargill, Baron Concraig [S], *a.* 17th Oct. 1701.
ERSKINE, John, Earl of Mar [S], . . Duke of Mar, Marquis Erskine, Earl of Kildrummie, Viscount Garioch, Lord Alloa, Ferriton, and Forrest [S], 22nd Oct. 1715; Baron [——] and Earl of Mar, co. York [E], 10th Nov. 1717; Duke of Mar [I], 13th Dec. 1722.
EVERARD, Sir Redmond, fourth Baronet [I]. Viscount Everard [I], 20th June 1723.
FITTON, Sir Alexander, . . . Baron Fitton of Gosworth [I], 1st Apr. 1689.
FITZJAMES, Henry, ... Baron of Romney, Earl of Rochford, and Duke of Albemarle [E], 13th Jan. 1696.
FORESTER, Sir John, ... Baronet [S], 31st Mar. 1729.
FORSTAL, Sir Mark, ... Baronet [I], 22nd Jan. 1734.
FRASER of Inveralochy, Charles, . . Lord Fraser of Muchalls [S], 20th July 1723.
—— Simon, Lord Lovat [S], . . Duke of Fraser, Marquis of Beaufort, Earl of Stratherrick and Upper Tarf (Abertarf), Viscount of the Aird and Strath-Glass, Lord Lovat and Beauly [S], 14th Mar. 1740.
GAYDON, Sir Richard, ... Baronet [I], 29th July 1743.
GORING, Sir Henry, fourth Baronet [E], Baron Bullinghel, Viscount Goring [E], 2nd Jan. 1722.
GRÆME, John, ... Baronet [S], 6th Sept. 1726; Lord Newton, Viscount of Falkirk, and Earl of Alford [S], 20th Jan. 1760.
GRAHAM, Richard, Viscount Preston [S], Baron of Esk [E], 21st Jan. 1689.
GRANT of Grant, James, . . . Lord Grant [S], 24th June 1721.
GRANVILLE, George, Lord Lansdown [E], Lord Lansdown, Viscount and Earl of Bath [E], 6th Oct. 1721; Lord Lansdown of Bideford, Viscount Bevel, Earl of Bath, Marquis Monk and Fitzhemon, Duke of Albemarle [E], 3rd Nov. 1721.
GUALTERIO, John Baptist, Count, . Earl of Dundee [S], *a.* 12th Nov. 1705.
HALES, Sir Edward, Baronet [E], . Baron Hales of Emley, co. Kent, Viscount Tunstall, and Earl of Tenterden [E], 3rd May 1692.

PEERS AND BARONETS

HAY, Col. William,	Baronet [S], 31st Jan. 1747.
—— John,	Baronet [S], 31st Dec. 1766.
—— Hon. John,	Earl of Inverness, Viscount of Innerpaphrie, and Lord Cromlix and Erne [S], 5th Oct. 1718; Baron Hay [E], 3rd Apr. 1727; and Duke of Inverness [S], 4th Apr. 1727.
HELY, Sir John,	Baronet [I], 28th June 1728.
HERBERT, William, Marquis of Powis [E].	Marquis of Montgomery and Duke of Powis [E], 12th Jan. 1689.
—— Sir Edward,	Earl of Portland [E], 1689 (?).
HIGGINS, Dr.,	Baronet [I], 6th May 1724.
HOOKE, Nathaniel,	Baron Hooke of Hooke Castle [I], 19th Feb. 1708.
JERMYN, Henry, Lord Dover [E],	Lord Jermyn of Royston, Baron of Ipswich, co. Suffolk, Viscount of Cheveley, co. Cambridge, and Earl of Dover [E], 9th July 1689.
LALLY, Gerard,	Baronet [I], 7th July 1707.
—— Sir Thomas Arthur, Baronet [I],	Baron Tollendally, Viscount Ballymole, and Earl of Moenmoyne, 1746.
LUMISDEN, John,	Baronet [S], 5th Jan. 1740.
MACCARTY, Hon. Justin,	Baron of Castleinch, Viscount Mountcashell, co. Tipperary [I], 1st May 1689.
MACDONALD. See Mackenzie.	
—— of Clanranald, Ranald,	Lord Clanranald [S], 28th Sept. 1716.
—— John,	Baronet [I] or [S], 1745.
—— of Sleat, Sir Donald, Baronet [S],	Lord Sleat [S], 23rd Dec. 1716.
MACDONELL of Glengarry, Alexander,	Lord Macdonell [S], 9th Dec. 1716.
—— of Keppoch, Alexander,	Baronet [S], 6th June 1743.
MACGREGOR, otherwise Drummond, Alexander.	Baronet [S], 14th Mar. 1740.
MACKENZIE, otherwise Macdonald, Penelope Louisa.	Baroness Clanranald [S], 28th Sept. 1716.
—— Kenneth, Earl of Seaforth [S],	Marquis of Seaforth, Earl of Fortrose [S], 1689.
MACKINTOSH of that ilk, Lauchlan,	Lord Mackintosh [S], 21st Jan. 1717.
MACLEAN of that ilk, Sir Hector, fifth Baronet [S].	Lord Maclean [S], 17th Dec. 1716.
MACLEOD of that ilk, Norman,	Lord Macleod [S], 8th Dec. 1716.
—— John,	Baronet [S], 5th Sept. 1723.
MIDDLETON, Earl of Middleton [S],	Earl of Monmouth, Viscount Clermont [E], 1701.
MURRAY, Hon. James,	Earl of Dunbar in East Lothian, Viscount Drumcairn, co. Fife, and Lord Hadykes, co. Dumfries [S], 2nd Feb. 1721.
—— William, Lord Nairne [S],	Lord [——], Viscount of Stanley, Earl of Nairne [S], 24th June 1721.

LIST OF SURNAMES

MURRAY, William, Marquis of Tullibardine. — Duke of Rannoch, Marquis of Blair, Earl of Glen Tilt, Viscount Glenshie and Lord Strathbran [S], 1st Feb. 1717.

—— Hon. Alexander, M.P., . . Earl of Westminster, co. Middlesex, Viscount and Lord [——] [E], 12th Aug. 1759.

NORTH, William, Lord North and Grey [E]. — Baron, Viscount, and Earl North [E], 6th Jan. 1722.

NUGENT, Hon. Thomas, . . . Baron Nugent of Riverston, co. Westmeath [I], 7th May 1689.

O'BRIEN, Col. Daniel, . . . Baron Castle Lyons [I], 17th Mar. 1726; Baron [——], Viscount Tallow, and Earl of Lismore [I], 11th Oct. 1746.

—— Col. John, ... Baronet [I], 19th Jan. 1723.
O'CALLAGHAN, ... Earl O'Callaghan [I], 17 . . (?).
O'GARA, Lieut.-Col. Oliver, . . Baronet [I], 2nd May 1727.
OGLETHORPE, Theophilus, . . Lord Oglethorpe of Oglethorpe [E], 20th Dec. 1717.

—— Anne, ... Countess of Oglethorpe [I], 6th Oct. 1722.

OLIPHANT of Gask, Lawrence, . . Lord Oliphant [S], 14th July 1760.
O'ROURKE, Owen, . . . Baron O'Rourke of Carha, co. Leitrim [I], 24th May 1727; Viscount of Breffney in Connaught [I], 31st July 1731; Baron Carha and Viscount of Breffney [I], July 1742.

O'SULLIVAN, Sir John, . . . Baronet [I], 9th May 1753.
PAYNTER, James, ... ? Marquis of Trelessick [E], 20th June 1715.

PURCELL, Col. Nicholas, . . . Baron Loughmore [I], 1689.
PYE, Walter, ... Baron Kilpee [E], 1690 (?).
RAMSAY, Andrew Michael, . . Baronet [S], 23rd Mar. 1735.
REDMOND, Sir Peter, . . . Baronet [E], 20th Dec. 1717; Baron Redmond [I], 15th Dec. 1721.

ROBERTSON of Struan, Alexander, . Baronet [S], 1725.
—— of Fascally, Alexander, . . Baronet [S], 10th May 1725.
ROCHE, Dominick, ... Baron Tarbert and Viscount of Cahiravahilla [I], c. 1689/90.

RONCHI, Joseph, ... Baronet [E], 24th July 1715.
—— Joseph, ... Baronet [E], 5th Oct. 1722.
RUTLEDGE, James, ... Baronet [I], 23rd Dec. 1748.
ST. JOHN, Henry, Viscount Bolingbroke. — Earl of Bolingbroke [E], c. 26th July 1715.

SARSFIELD, Col. Patrick, . . . Baron Rosberry, Viscount of Tully, Earl of Lucan, co. Dublin [I], Jan. 1691.

SEMPILL, Robert, ... Lord Sempill [S], 1725 (?).
SHERIDAN, Thomas, ... Baronet [I], 17th Mar. 1726.
SHERLOCK, Sir Peter, . . . Baronet [I], 9th Dec. 1716.
STEWART of Appin, Dugald, . . Lord Appin [S], 6th June 1743.

254

PEERS AND BARONETS

STEWART, Col. John Roy, . . . Baronet [S], 4th Nov. 1784.
STUART, Charlotte, ... Duchess of Albany [S], *c.* 23rd/24th Mar. 1783.
—— Prince Charles Edward, . . Prince of Wales and Earl of Chester [E], *c.* 1720.
—— Prince Henry, ... Duke of York [E], *a.* 28th Mar. 1733.
TALBOT, Richard, Earl of Tyrconnell, . Marquis and Duke of Tyrconnell, co. Tyrone [I], 30th Mar. 1689.
VILLIERS, Barbara, *née* Chiffinch, Countess of Jersey [E], Apr. 1761.
Countess of Jersey [E].
—— William, Earl of Jersey [E], . Baron of Hoo, co. Kent, Viscount of Dartford, co. Kent, and Earl of Jersey [E], Apr. 1716.
WALSH, Anthony Vincent, . . . Lord, Viscount, and Earl of Walsh [I], 20th Oct. 1745.
WARREN, Col. Richard, . . . Baronet [I], 3rd Nov. 1746.
WENTWORTH, Thomas, Earl of Strafford [E]. Duke of Strafford [E], 5th Jan. 1722.
WHARTON, Philip, Duke of Wharton [E]. Viscount Winchendon, co. Bucks, Earl of Malmesbury, co. Wilts, Marquis of Woburn, co. Bucks, Duke of Northumberland [E], Oct. 1716.
WOGAN, Charles, ... Baronet [I], 1719.
WORTH, Patrick, ... Baronet [I], 12th Sept. 1733.

INDEX

OF NAMES IN THE SECOND PART

(KNIGHTS, DECLARATIONS OF NOBLESSE, APPOINTMENTS, ETC.)

ABERCROMBY, Patrick, 224.
Aberdeen, John, 243.
Achaden, Bishop of, Dr. Walter Blake, 229.
Achadoe, Bishop of, Dominick Dalny, 227.
Achmouty, Capt., 240.
Achonry, Bishop of, Patrick Robert Kirwan, 231.
Adams, Capt., 231.
Airlie, Earl of, 196.
Albani, Cardinal John Francis, 231.
Albany, Charlotte, Duchess of, 194.
Albemarle, George, Duke of, 244.
Albeville, Marquis of, 206.
Alford, John, Earl of, 215.
Almond, Countess of, 220.
Amorium, Bishop of, Francis Petre, 230.
Anderson, George, 238.
Ardagh and Clonmacnois, Bishops of: Ambrose O'Conor, 226 ; Peter Muligan, 228 ; Dr. Thomas O'Brien, 229 ; Macdermot Roe, 229 ; Father Augustine Chevers, 230, 231 ; Dr. Anthony Blake, 231 ; James Brady, 231.
Ardfert, Bishops of : William O'Meara, 230; Nicholas Madgett, 230.
Ardfert and Aghadoe, Bishop of, Dr. Denis Moriarty, 226.
Argenson, Mons., 199.
Armagh, Archbishops of : Dr. Bernard Macmahon, 228 ; Dr. Roche Macmahon, 230 ; Michael O'Reilly, 230 ; Dr. Anthony Blake, 231.
Armstrong, John, 227.
Arnold, Capt., 196, 240.
Arran, Charles, Earl of, 248.
Arthur, Robert, 239, 242.
—— Thomas, 246.
Arundell, Henry, 247.
Atholl, Duke of, 243.
Atkins, Thomas, 216.
Axton, James, 199.
Aylward, Nicholas, 199.

BADA, Francis, 239.
Baggot, John, 219.
Bagnall, Dudley, 217, 219.
Bagnols, [——], 232.
Bagott, Richard, 221.
Bailly, James, 221.
Bannerman, Sir Patrick, 191.
Barclay, Col., 241.
Barker, Col. William Mansel, 246.
Barklay, Sir G., 240.
Barnewall, Catherine, 200.
Barrel, Peter, 207.
Barry, Edmund, 200, 218.
—— Richard, 205.
—— See de Ward Barry.
Barrymore, family of the Earl of, 200.
—— Earl of, 208, 237.
Battiste, 220.
Becquet, the family of, 197, 198.
—— Seigneur de Beffe, Louis Matthew, 197, 198.
—— Seigneur de Moulin le Comte, Peter Thomas, 197, 198.
—— Seigneur of Saleppe, Philip Francis, 202.
Belasis, Thomas, 217.
Bellew, 225.
Belloni, Sieur Jerome, 233.
Benozzi, Jerome, 224.
Benys, Lieut.-Col., 241, 242.
Berkeley, Sir George, 242.
Berkenhead, Harcourt, 218, 219.
—— William, 217.
Bermingham, family of, 201; Ralph, 201.
Berne, Bernard, 243.
Berwick, James, Duke of, 238 (3), 245.
Betham, Dr. John, 220.
Biddulph, Richard, 219, 220.
—— Mrs., 220.
Bietagh, Thomas, 239.
Bignon, James, 197.
Birtha, Bishop of, James Talbot, 231.
Black, [——], 208.
Blair, Dr. John, 224.

257

INDEX

Blake, Dr. Anthony, 231 (2).
—— Dame Juliana, 210.
—— Thomas, 210.
—— Dr. Walter, 229.
Boduel, Anthony Arthur, 212.
—— John Arthur, 212.
—— Thomas, 212.
Bolingbroke, Henry, Earl of, 215.
Bonarelli, John, Count of, 235.
Booth, Charles, 219 ; Capt., 240.
du Bourg, Stephen Simon 199.
Bourke, family of, 202.
—— Augustine, 202.
—— David, 202.
—— Edward, 209.
—— Martin, 228.
—— Lieut.-Col. Michael, 241.
—— Col., 240.
—— Hon. Richard, 222.
—— Thomas, 209.
—— Sir Toby, 191, 201, 232.
—— William, 199.
—— of Clanrickard, family of, 201.
Bowman, [——], 208.
Bradel, Capt., 241.
Bradley, Patrick, 230 (2).
Brady, James, 231.
Bragg, Thomas, 197.
Brett, John, 229, 230.
Brigeat, John, 212.
Brindijone, Oliver, 201.
Brittas, Lord, 199 (3), 202, 222.
Broghall, Edward, 239 (2), 242.
Broomer, Jeremiah, 216, 220, 224.
Browne, Francis, 235 ; Hon. Henry, 214.
Browne or Brown, Thomas, 199, 226.
Brown, Col., 239 (2), 241.
Brullagham, Dr. John, 230.
Buchan, Major James, 241.
—— Col., 241 (2).
—— Major-Gen., 240.
Buckenham, Robert, 220.
Bulstrode, Sir Richard, 203, 218 (2), 221, 223.
Burgo, Thomas de, 231.
Burke or de Burgo, John Machugo, 208.
—— family of, 208.
de Bussie, Col., 240.
Bussie, Lieut.-Col., 241.
Bussy, Col., 241.
Butler, Christopher, 226, 230.
—— Edmund, 204.
—— Frances Christian, 209.
—— of Killcop, James, 209.
—— Dr. James, 230.

Butler, John, 230.
—— Richard, 202, 206, 246.
—— Col., 241 (2).
—— of Killeagh, 209.
—— Theobald, 222.
Byerley, Capt., 240.
Bynns. See Benys.

CAHIR, Lord, 204, 209.
Callanan, Mary, 221.
Campain, family of, 197.
—— Seigneur de St. Julian, Julian, 197.
Campbell, Andrew, 230.
—— of Auchinbreck, Sir James, 237, 245 (2), 248 (2), 249.
—— of Glenderule, Col. Colin, 233, 244, 245.
Cambray, Archbishop of, 242.
Cameron, Allan, 233.
Cane, [——], 220.
Canon, Col., 239, 241.
Cardinals nominated by King James : Abbé Melchior de Polignac, 227 ; Peter Guerin de Tencin, 228 ; Monsignor Dominick Riviera, 228 ; Peter Guerin de Tencin, 229 ; Monsignor Armand de Rohan, Abbé de Ventadour, 229 ; Paul Albert de Luynes, 231.
Carnegy of Boysick, James, 232.
Carney, Dennis, 219.
Carnwath, Lord, 245.
Carny, Richard, 198.
Carroll, [——], 238 ; Brian, 239; John, 198.
Carteret, [——], 225.
—— Lady Mary, 222, 223.
—— Sir Charles, 221, 222.
Cary, family of, 196.
—— Mademoiselle, 196.
Caryll, John, first Lord, 194, 198, 220, 214 (5).
—— John Baptist, third Lord, 215.
—— John, 220.
Cashel, Archdeacon of, John Butler, 231.
—— Archbishops of : Abbé Christopher Butler, 226 ; Dr. James Butler, 230.
Castle Connell (Bourkes), Lords, 202, 209.
—— —— William, Lord, 237.
Chaise, Pere La, 222.
Challoner, Richard, 229, 231.
Chalmers of Galliard, [——], 245.
Chamberlain, Thomas, 236.
Chapman, William, 235.
Chardon de St. Arques, John de, 205.
Charles, Prince of Wales, 193, 194, 249 (3).
Chatham, Col., 240, 241.

INDEX

Chaumont, Joseph du, 222.
Chevers, Dr. Augustine, 230, 231.
Chilton, Christopher, 218, 219.
Clancarty, Earl of, 222, 243.
—— Donough, Earl of, 242, 246.
Clancy, family of, 203.
—— Honora, 203.
Clanranald, Capt. of, 241.
Clare, Lord, 199 (2).
Clark, Nicholas, 220.
Cleeland, John, 237.
Cleere, Ignatius, 239.
Clermont, Lord, 224.
Clogher, Bishops of : Dr. Hugh Macmahon, 227 ; Bernard Macmahon, 227 ; Dr. Roche Macmahon, 227 (2) ; Daniel O'Reilly, 229.
Clonfers, Bishop of, Peter Donnelan, 228.
Close, Richard, 237.
Cloyne and Ross, Bishop of, John O'Brien, 230.
Cockburn, [——], 232.
Coghan, Anne, 212.
—— Terence, 212.
Colgrave, [——], 205.
—— Col., 203.
—— Capt., Sir George, 191.
—— George, 203.
—— John, 230.
Collyns, Richard, 246.
Comerford, Luke, 198.
Condroy, Peter, 243.
Connor, Thomas, 220.
Connock, Conock, Dame, 222.
—— —— James, 222.
—— —— Sir Timon, 191, 222.
Conquest, Henry, 217 (3), 218, 219, 221, 223.
Constable, John, 217, 219, 235.
Conway, Neil, 227.
Cook, Matthew, 240.
Cooke, Edward, 243.
Copley, John, 219.
Cork, Bishops of : Thaddæus Macarty, 227 ; Richard Walsh, 230 ; John Butler, 231.
Corroye, John, 248.
Corsini, Nerée Marie, Cardinal, 228.
Cotte, Edmond, 206.
Counter, John, 242.
Coyle, family of, 200.
—— Eugene, 200.
—— John, 200.
Crawford, Sir Henry, 192.
Creagh, Matthew, 220.

Creagh, Sir Michael, 247.
Creveo, Peter, 229.
Crone, Matthew, 196.
Crump, Richard, 216.
Cunigane, Daniel, 202.
Cunningham, Earls of Glencairn, the family of, 203.
—— Col., 241.
Cusack, John, 246.
—— Nicholas, 239.

DALNY, Father Dominick, 227.
Dalziel, Hon. John, 245.
Darby, Jonathan, 237.
Davia, Count Anthony, 221.
—— Cardinal, 227, 228, 233.
David, Anthony, 224.
Davidson, Lieut.-Col., 242.
Day, Dr. Daniel, 216.
Deane, Capt., 240.
Delâtre, [——], 222.
Delaval, Capt., 240 ; Lieut.-Col., 242.
Dempsey, Mary, 212.
Dermot, Bryan, 205.
Dermott, Terence, 239.
Derry, Bishops of : Neil Conway, 227 ; Michael O'Reilly, 229 ; Patrick Bradley, 230 ; John Colgrave, 230 ; Philip MacDavett, 231.
Desmond, Earls of, 198.
Devereux, Gerald, 220.
Dicconson, Dickenson, Dickeson, Dickonson, etc., Edward, 229, 230 ; William, 219, 223 (2), 246.
Dillon, Arthur, Earl and Viscount, 194, 232, 244 ; Col. Garrett, 242 ; John, 242 ; Maurice, 239.
Dixey, John, 220.
Doberus, Bishop of, Richard Chaloner, 229.
Doé, [——], 239 (4).
Donnelan, Peter, 228.
Donnoughe, [——], 242.
Dorington, Dorrington, Col., 238 ; Peter, 208 ; William, 208, 247.
Douglas, Edward, 220.
Dover, Henry, Lord, 247.
Dowdall, John, 203 ; Matthew, 203 ; Stephen, 228 (2).
Down and Connor, Bishops of : John Armstrong, 227 ; Edmond O'Doran, 230 ; Theophilus Macartan, 231.
Doyle, Timothy, 219.
Dromore, Bishop of, Anthony Garvey, 229.

INDEX

Drummond, Lord Edward, 223 ; James, Marquis of, 194, 244 ; Thomas, 200.
Dublin, Archbishops of: Lucas Fagan, 228 ; John Linegar, 228 ; Patrick Fitz-Simons, 231.
—— Archdeacon of, Richard Lincoln, 231.
Dugud, William, 224.
Duksinfield, Cecilia, 212.
Dumont, Joseph Nosetti, 231.
Dunbar, James, Earl of, 194, 215, 248.
—— Capt. Thomas, 241.
Dundee, John Baptist, Earl of, 194.
—— David, Viscount of, 240.
Dunfermline, James, Earl of, 240.
Dungan, Walter, Lord, 216, 247.
Dunkeld, James, Lord, 241 (2).
Dunn, Dunne, Bernard, 227, 228 ; James, 230 ; Michael, 243.
Dupuy, Lawrence, 217, 219.
Durham, Dean of. See Granville.
Dutton, John, 219.
Duvoye, Catherine, 206.

EDGAR, family of, 249 ; Alexander, 249 ; Anne Barbara, née Hamilton, 249 ; Anne Hamilton, 249 ; Catherine, née Ogilvy, 249 ; Catherine, 249 ; David, 249 (2) ; Eliza Catherine, 249 ; Grace, 249; Grace, née Fleming, 249 ; James, 215, 249 (2) ; Sir James, 249 ; John, 249 (3); Lady, 249 ; Margaret, née Skinner, 249 ; Mary Caroline, 249 ; Thomas, 249.
Edwards, [——], 241.
Egan, Constantius, 207.
Egar of Kilbaran, James, 211.
Eglinton, Alexander, Earl of, 248.
Ellis, Sir William, 217, 218 (3), 221, 222, 223, 224, 225, 233, 235, 247.
Elphin, Bishops of: Ambrose MacDermot, 226 ; Patrick French, 228 ; John Brett, 230 ; Dr. James O'Fallon, 231.
Embrun, Archbishop of, Peter Guerin de Tencin, 228, 229.
England, Protectors of : Cardinal Gualterio, 226 ; Cardinal Pico, 229 ; Cardinal Lante, 229.
—— Vicars-Apostolic for the Northern District of: Thomas Dominick Williams, 227 ; Edward Dicconson, 229, 230.
—— Vicar-Apostolic of the West of, Lawrence William York, 231.
—— Vicar-Apostolic of Midland District of, John Talbot Stonor, 230.
Ennis, Lieut.-Col., 241.

Enniskillen, Lord, 199 (3).
Errol, Charles, Earl of, 194.
Erskine, Charles, 213 ; Clementine, 213 ; Colin, 213.
—— of Alva, Sir John, 232.
—— of Cambo, Charles, 213.
—— of Gogar, Alexander, 213.
Evans, Charles, 208 ; William, 208.
Evers, Demoiselle, 209 ; family of, 212 ; Helen, 212 ; Richard, 212.

FAGAN of Feltrum, family of, 198 ; James, 198 ; Lucas, 228 (3).
Falconieri, Alexander, Cardinal, 228.
Falvey, James, 221.
Falvie, Jolie, 220.
Farcharson, Farcherson, Col., 241 ; Major, 241.
Farmour, Capt., 240.
Farrell, Lieut.-Col., 241.
Farrelly, Dr., 225.
Faure, Jean, 223.
Fede, Innocentio, 218 (2).
Feilding, Major, 240.
Fermer, Richard, 221.
Ferns, Bishops of : John Verdun, 226 ; Stephen MacEgan, 228 ; Ambrose O'Callaghan, 228 ; Dr. Nicholas Sweetman, 229.
Finch, [——], 221.
FitzGerald, Anna, 208 ; Catherine, 199 ; Christopher, 242 (2) ; Edmund, 223 ; Garrett, 202, 222 ; Gregorie, 235 ; John, 209, 212 ; Joseph, 205 ; Maurice, 208, 209 ; Patrick, 202 ; Richard, 212 (2) ; Richard Thomas, 212 (3); Valentine, 204.
—— Earls of Desmond, 199.
FitzGibbon, Maurice, 208 ; William, 207, 208.
FitzJames, Duke of, 209.
—— Henry, 238.
FitzMaurice, Eleanor, 211 ; Henry, 210.
FitzSimons, Col., 241 (3) ; Patrick, 231.
FitzTheobald, Nicholas Geraldine, 207.
Fleming, Rev. David, 249 ; Mary Charlotte, 202 ; Richard, 202.
Flynn, Thomas, 228.
Forstal, Sir Mark, 192.
Forrester, Charles, 216 ; Sir John, 191.
Forster, Thomas, 243 (2).
Foster, Guy, 220.
Fountain, Fountaine, Col., 204 ; Lieut.-Col., 242.
Fox, Thomas, 220.

INDEX

Fraser of Inveralochy, Lord, 245.
—— William, 232.
French, Edmund, 242, 243 ; Patrick, 248.
Fullan, Daniel, 221.
Furlong, Cecile, 204 ; James, 204 ; Mary, 204.

GALLAGHER, Gallihurium, Bonaventura, 228 ; James, 227, 228.
Galmoye, Piers, Viscount, 217, 238.
Gardiner, Thomas, 208 ; William, 208.
Garvan, Calaghan, 219, 222.
Garvey, Anthony, 229.
Gaultier, Gautier, Francis, 216, 220, 221.
Gautherne, Nathaniel, 216.
Gawen, Richard, 236.
Gaydon, John, 239 ; Sir Richard, 192.
Gealeagh, Marcus, 245.
Gennary, Benedict, 221.
George, Capt. David, 243.
Geraldine, Geraldin, Giraldin, Girardin, of Gurteen, 198, 203 ; of Desmond, 203 ; Claud Francis, 204 ; Sir James, 235 ; Nicholas, 198 (2), 203 ; Toby, 203, 239.
Gifford, Col., 240, 241 (2), Sir John, 218, 219.
Gillett, Stephen, 200.
Ginnari, [——], 216.
Glencairn, William, Earl of, 248 (2).
Glynnegrant, Knights of, 209.
Godert, Thomas, 221.
Goolde, Capt. James, 223.
Gooldin, John, 239.
Gordon, Admiral, 233 ; Alexander, 240, 243, 244 (2) ; Bishop James, 228 ; Col., 241.
—— of Glenbucket, John, 243, 244.
Goring, Sir Henry, 244, 247.
Gough of Dunkirk, 204.
Grace of Courtstown, 201 ; Edmond, 201 ; Lieut.-Col., 242 ; Thomas, 201.
Græme, Brigadier, 244 ; Col., 241 ; Dr., 225 ; Sir John, afterwards Earl of Alford, 215, 233, 248.
Graham, Col., 241, 242 (2) ; Patrick, 241, 243 ; Thomas, 237.
Grammont, Countess of, 196.
Grant, Alexander John, 227 ; Francis, 222 ; James, 209.
Granville, Dean of Durham, Denis, 217, 222.
Griffen, James, 221.
Griffith, Capt. Henry, 220.
Grossin, John Anselm, 245.
Gualterio, Cardinal, 226, 232.

Guattani, Charles, 225.
Guerin, [——], 225 ; Dr. Martin, 224.
Guthrie, Elizabeth, 249.

HALL, Capt., 240.
Halpeny, Peter, 221.
Hamilton, family of, 196 ; James, Duke of, 193, 194 (2), 248 ; [——], 249 ; Richard, 217, 219, 243.
Hanley, Peter, 200.
Hanmer, family of, 196.
Harcourt, Marquis of, 242.
Hardy, Capt. Charles, 245.
Hatcher, [——], 220.
Hay, Capt., 240 : James, 224 (2) ; John, 224 ; Cap   m, 224, 233.
Haywood, [-   „ -20.
Helme, Nestor, 218.
Hely, Sir John, 192.
Hepburn, Magdalin, 196.
Hicky, Patrick, 199.
Higgins, Higgons, Sir Thomas, 191, 215 ; Thomas, 219 ; [——], 207.
Hodnett, Honora, 200.
Hogan, Edward, 220.
Holeman, George, 247.
Hore, Lawrence, 239.
Hornyold, John, 230.
Howard, Bernard, 224 ; Dr. John, 225 ; Henry, 227 ; John Stafford (see also Stafford), 217 (2), 218.
Huntly, Marquis of, 243.
Huoluhan, Daniel, 223.
Hyrde, O'Hyrde, of Ladarath, family of, 201 ; Christopher, 201 ; John, 201.
—— of Drogheda, John, 201.

IMPERIALI, Cardinal, Joseph Rene, 226.
Ingleton, Dr. John, 220.
Ingram, Col., 241.
Innes, Inese, David, 224 ; Lewis, 214, 217, 224.
Inniskillin, Roger, Lord, 247.
Inverness, John, Earl of, 194, 215 (2).
Ireland, Protectors of the Kingdom of : Joseph Rene, Cardinal Imperiali, 226 ; Nerée Marie, Cardinal Corsini, 228.
Iverque, Barons of, 209.

JACKSON of Hickelton, family of, 195 ; Sieur des Auches, John Jacquenot, 195.
James, Prince of Wales, 193.
Jennings, Dr. John, 225.
Jerningham, Sir George, 192, 232.
Johnston, Col., 196, 240.

INDEX

Joseph, Col., 241.
Joyce, George, 223.

KAST, Sieur George Christopher, 196.
Kearny, Edmund, 243; John, 246; Sir Richard, 246.
Keeffe, Dr. James, 230.
Keith, Hon. James, 244; William, Lord, 239.
Kellie, Alexander, Earl of, 213; Thomas, Earl of, 213.
Kelly, James, 201.
Kennedy, David, 233; Louis, 212; Louis Daniel, 212; Matthew, 246; Philip, 212.
Kerby, Henry, 220 (2).
Kerjan, Marquis de, 196.
Kerney, Dr. Daniel, 231.
Kerry, Bishops of: Eugenius O'Sullivan, 229; William O'Meara, 229.
Kildare, Bishops of: Edward Murphy, 227; Bernard Dunne, 227; Stephen Dowdal, 228; Dr. James Gallihurium, 228; Dr. James Keeffe, 230.
Killala, Bishops of: Father Thaddæus O'Rourke, 226; John O'Hart, 228; Dr. Bernard O'Rourke, 229; Father John Brett, 229; Dr. Mark Skerret, 230; Father Bonaventura Macdonnel, 230; Dr. Philip Philips, 231.
Killaloe, Bishops of: Terence Macmahon, 227; Sylvester Louis Lloyd, 228; Patrick Macdonnagh, 229; Patrick O'Naughton, 230; Nicholas Madgett, 230, 231; Father Michael Peter MacMahon, 231; William O'Meara, 231.
Killikelly, Father Peter, 229.
Kilmacduagh, Bishops of: Dr. Ambrose Madin, 226; William O'Daly, 227; Martin Bourke, 228; Father Peter Killikelly, 229.
Kilmore, Bishops of: Michael Macdonagh, 228; Lawrence Richardson, 229; Andrew Campbell, 230.
King, Capt., 241; Dr., 234.
Kirwan, Patrick Robert, 231.
Knightlley, Knightly, Alexander, 222; Lieut.-Col., 241.
Knowles of Orchardstone, family of, 195; Sir Dominick, 195.

LABADIE, James, 220.
Lacy of Kilminere, family of, 207; Dr. Robert, 228; Col. William, 207; Lieut.-Col., 241.

Lambert of Ballyhire, family of, 212; Jane, 212.
Lampert, Patrick, 239.
Langton, Anne, 211.
Lansdown, George Granville, Lord, 233, 248.
Lante, Frederic Marcello, Cardinal, 229.
La Rue, Col., 240; Francis, 238.
Latton, Col., 240, 241.
Lauzan, Francis Nompar, Duke of, 193.
Laysonby, Capt., 240.
Lee, Rose, 221; Sir Andrew, 199, 238; Thomas, 222.
Leeds, Peregrine, Duke of, 244.
Lehy, Dr., 199.
Leigh, William, 233.
Leonard, Paul, 199; Stephen, 199.
Lery, Marquis of, 204.
Leserteur, Elizabeth, 221.
Leslie, Lesly, family of, 195; Harrie, 244; Seigneur du Clisson, Francis, 195.
Lewin, John, 220.
Ley, Lawrence, 211; Nicholas, 211.
Leyburne, Charles, 218, 219; John, 226.
Lidcot, Sir John, 222.
Limerick, Earl of, 216.
—— Bishops of: Dr. Robert Lacy, 228; Dr. Daniel Kerney, 231.
Lincoln, Richard, 231.
Linegar, John, 228, 231.
Liria, James, Duke of, 193, 233.
Lismore, Daniel, Earl of, 193, 215.
du Livier, [——], 239.
Livingtone, Livingston, Capt., 240; Col., 196; Col. John, 244.
Lloyd, David, 219; Sylvester Louis, 228, 229 (3); William, 226.
London, Vicars-Apostolic for the district of: Bishop Bonaventura Gifford, 227; Dr. Benjamin Petre, Bishop of Prusa, 229; Bishop Richard Challoner, 231.
Lorraine, Duke of, 200 (2).
Lovat, Simon, Lord, 237, 244, 245, 248 (2), 249.
Lucan, Patrick, Earl of, 208, 238, 239, 242.
Luker, Nicholas, 201.
Lumsden, Andrew, 215.
Luttrell, Simon, 238.
de Luynes, Paul Albert, 231.
Lynch, Dominick, 235.
Lyons, John, 198 (2); Simon, 225; Thomas, 198 (2).

INDEX

MACARTON, Theophilus, 231.
Macarty, M'Carty, Macarthy etc., Catherine, 199 ; Charles, 204, 207, 209, 216 (2), 219 ; Denis, 204, 209 ; Florence, 207, 208 ; Jeanne, 197 ; Justin, 246 ; Owen, 241 ; Thaddæus, 227 ; Timothy, 209 ; [——], 242.
—— family of, 198.
—— Reagh, family of, 199, 207, 209.
MacCoghan, family of, 212.
M'Daniel, Randle, 246.
MacDavett, Philip, 231.
MacDermot, Ambrose, 226 ; Sir Terence, 197 ; Thomas, 229, 230.
Macdonagh, Macdonnagh, Michael, 228 ; Patrick, 229, 230.
MacDonald of Clanranald, family of, 211.
—— of Inverghysevan, family of, 211.
—— MacDonnel, MacDonell, M'Donnel, Capt., 211 ; Bonaventura, 230 ; Daniel, 219 ; Donnell, 242 ; Hugh, 228 ; James, 210 ; Sir Randal, 219, 223.
MacEgan, Michael, 202 ; Stephen, 227, 228 (2).
MacEvay, Daniel, 198.
Macghie, [——], 223.
Macgregor, William, 245.
Machugo, [——], 208.
Mackean, Neal, 205.
M'Lane, Col., 241 ; Sir Alexander, 240.
MacLeod, Alexander, 245.
MacMahon, M'Mahon, Capt., 244 ; Bernard, 227, 228, 230 ; Elizabeth, 203 ; Hugh, 227 ; John, 237 ; Laurence, 206 ; Michael Peter, 231 ; Roche, 229 ; Terence, 227 ; Winifred, 205.
—— family of, 203, 206.
Macmanus, Charles, 211 ; Marianne, 211.
Macnamara, family of, 203, 204 ; Donough, 204 ; John, 203.
MacSwiney, family of, 206 ; Miles, 206.
Madgett, Nicholas, 230 (2).
Madin, Ambrose, 226.
Magennis, Arthur, 216.
Magragh, family of, 199.
Maguire, Mary, 211.
Maguirk, Patrick, 220.
Mahony, Bartholomew Joseph, 211, 225 ; Eugene, 211.
Main, [——], 208.
Maitland, Capt., 241 ; John, 225.
Malcome, Lieut.-Col., 242.
Mallus, Bishop of, Edward Dicconson, 229.

de Mannery, Anthony, 207, 211 ; Arthur, 207, 211 ; Elizabeth, 211 ; John Anthony, 207, 211 ; John Vincent, 207, 211 ; Justin, 207, 211 ; Marie Elizabeth, 207, 211.
Manusat, [——], 216.
Mar, John, Duke and Earl, 193, 213, 215, 224, 243, 247, 248.
Marischal, George, Earl, 194 ; William, Earl, 194 (2), 234, 244, 245 (2).
Marjoribanks, [——], 205, 208.
Martin, John, 202.
Martinash, Elizabeth, 221 ; John, 220.
Maxwell, Sir G., 241 ; [——], 238.
Mayers, Lawrence, 234.
Meath, Bishops of: Lucas Fagan, 228 ; Stephen MacEgan, 228 ; Augustine Chevers, 231.
Melfort, John, Duke and Earl of, 193, 200, 214 (2), 232, 237.
Menzies, James, 216 ; John, 220, 233.
Messit, Missett, Sir John, 192, 245.
Michel of Ireland, [——], 225.
Middleton and Monmouth, Charles, Earl of, 214 (4).
—— John, 224 ; Capt. Richard, 242 ; Major Robert, 242.
Mildmay, Dorothy, 208.
Milner, Nicholas, 220.
Miner, Francis, 216.
Molza, Count Charles, 218, 220 ; Countess, 220.
Mombriue, Rev. Bernardin, 225.
Monmouth, Countess of, 221.
Monninx, Louis du, 221.
Monsett, Peter, 221.
Monson, Capt., 240.
Montgomery of Schermarley, Sir James, 214 ; Marquis of, 239 ; William, Earl of, 239.
Moriarty, Dr. Denis, 226.
Morrogh, Bartholomew, 198.
Mottet, Sir Alphonso, 240.
Movante, Anthony, 210.
Moyry, Peter, 221.
Muligan, Peter, 228, 229.
Mulronny O'Carroll, family of, 203.
Murphy, Edward, 227 (2), 228.
Murray, Col., 241 ; Hon. James, afterwards Earl of Dunbar, 222, 224, 232 ; Lady, 223 ; Lord George, 244.

NAGLE, David, 222 ; James, 246, 247 ; Capt. Peter, 202, 235, 242 ; Sir Richard, 214, 217, 246.

263

INDEX

Nairne, of St. Foord, Alexander, 239; David, 198, 214, 217, 222, 224.
Naish, Nash, Father, 218; John, 219.
Napier, Lieut.-Col., 240, 241; Thomas, 222.
Neagle, James, 219.
Neper, Francis, 221.
Neville, Nevil, etc., Mary, 221; Thomas, 217, 219, 221.
Newcastle, Piers, Earl of, 193, 222.
Nicholas, Oliver, 221.
Nichols, Father, 242; Priest, 241.
Nicole, Marie, 211.
Nihill, James, 246.
Nimport, John, 235.
Nisiba, Bishop of, Lawrence William York, 231.
Nithsdale, Countess of, 224; William, Earl of, 194.
Nolan of Balenoche, family of, 201.
North, Roger, 218; William, Lord, 244 (2), 248.
Norwich, Archdeacon of, Thomas Brown, 226.
Nugent, Anne, 222; Bridget, 221; Col. Christopher, 238.

O'BRIEN, Obryan, etc., Arthur, 202; Bryan, 220; Charles, 239; Col. Daniel, 234 (2); Daniel, 201; Denis, 210, 220; [——], 239; [——], 232; Jane, 206; Col. John, 234 (2); John, 230; Sir John, 244; Terence, 199; Dr. Thomas, 229 (2).
—— of Cuonagh, family of, 199.
—— of Derry, Demetrius, 206.
—— Earl of Thomond, family of, 206.
—— of Tullo Garnony, 199.
O'Cahane, family of, 203; John, 203; Col. Roger, 203, 243.
O'Callaghan, Ambrose, 228; John, 206.
O'Carroll, Andrew, 211.
O'Clary of Fedan, Thomas, 198.
O'Conlean, Roger, 203.
O'Connel, Teige, 225.
O'Conor, Ambrose, 226.
O'Daly, William, 227.
O'Donnell of Ramalton, Col., 205; Father Anthony, 230; Nathaniel, 230.
O'Doran, Dr. Edmond, 230.
Odueri, family of, 204.
O'Dunne, Daniel, 201; Francis, 201.
O'Fallon, Dr. James, 231.
Ogara, O'Gara, Bernard, 227; Michael, 229.

Ogilvie, family of, 196; Sieur de la Perriere, James, 196.
Ogilvy of Boyne, family of, 209; Alexander, 209; Catherine, 249; James, 245; Patrick, 209.
Ohaguerty, Daniel, 207.
O'Hanlon, Edmund, 200; James, 208; John, 200.
O'Hart, John, 228.
O'Haugherne, John, 210; Marie, 210; Maurice, 210; Simon, 210; William, 210.
O'Kean, Thomas, 211.
O'Laughlin, Anthony, 202; Denis, 202; Malachy, 202.
Oldfield, Capt., 240.
O'Leyne, Thomas, 204.
Oliphant, Col., 241 (2).
O'Mara, John, 204.
O'Meara, William, 229, 230.
Omehegan, Chevalier, 211; Elizabeth, née Russell, 211; James Anthony Thaddeus, 211; Mary Catherine, 211; William Alexander, 211.
O'Moore, Charles, 201.
O'Naughton, Patrick, 230 (2).
O'Neil, family of, 203; Catherine, 203; Phelix, 203.
Ord, Lancelot, 244.
O'Reilly, Daniel, 229; Michael, 229, 230; Philip, 231.
O'Rierdane of Banmore, family of, 201; Daniel, 200.
Ormes, Rev. [——], 225.
Ormonde, family of, 196; James, Duke of, 194, 198, 205, 232, 243, 244, 245 (5), 248 (2).
O'Rourke, O'Roerk, Audeonus, 233; Dr. Bernard, 229; Thaddeus, 226; [——], 204.
Orrery, Charles, Earl of, 245 (2), 248.
O'Shagnussy, Colin, 228.
O'Shiel, Patrick, 225.
Osland, John, 198.
Ossory, Bishops of: Patrick Shee, 228; Dr. James Dunne, 230; Father Thomas de Burgo, 231; Colin O'Shagnussy, 227.
O'Sullivan, Cornelius, 199; Eugenius, 229 (2); John, 209; Sir John William, 192.
—— More, family of, 200.
O'Toole, Sir Edward, 192; Sir Luke, 192, 245.
Otway of Ballyneclogh, John, 237.

INDEX

Owens, Patrick, 219.
Oxford and Mortimer, Robert, Earl of, 248.

PANMURE, James, Earl of, 194.
Parker, Anne, 208 ; Vernon, 237.
Parrelly, Espri Joseph, 224.
Parry, Henry, 217, 219.
Parsons of Birr, Sir Lawrence, 237.
Pemberton, Richard, 219.
Peppard, Thomas, 246.
Perkins, Edmund, 217 ; Edward, 247.
Perry, John, 220.
Persico, Joseph, 220.
Person, [——], 220.
Perth, Duchess of, 220 ; James, Duke and Earl of, 193, 194, 217, 219, 223.
Petre, Benjamin, 227, 229 ; Francis, 230.
Philips, Dr. Philip, 231.
Philomelia, Bishop of, John Hornyold, 230.
Pico, Cardinal, 229.
Pierse, Richard, 210.
Plomer of Helstone, [——], 249.
Ploughman, William, 235.
Plowden, Francis, 218 (4), 219, 221, 223, 246 ; Mary, 218, 221.
Plunkett, Christian, 221 ; Dr. Michael, 246 ; [——], 239.
Polignac, Abbé Melchior de, 227 (2).
Porter, James, 217, 219, 221 ; John, 235.
Povay, Capt., 240.
Power, Col., 199 (2) ; Elizabeth, 199 ; Emilia, 208 ; James, 225 ; John, 210(4); Marish, 210 ; Robert, 199, 218, 222 ; William, 210.
Powis, William, Duke and Marquis of, 193, 216 (2).
Prescot, Humphrey, 219.
Preston, Robert, 239.
Price, Morgan, 197 ; [——], 240.
Prieur, John, 216 ; [——], 220.
Prusa, Bishops of : Benjamin Petre, 227 ; Dr. Benjamin Petre, 229.
Pyraube, John, 223.

RAGAZZI, Joseph Anthony, 225.
Rama, Bishop of, Charles Walmesley, 231.
Ramsay, Andrew, 245.
Rannoch, William, Duke of, 244.
Rantzau, Count of, 211.
Raphoe, Bishops of : James Gallihurium, 227 ; Father Bonaventura Gallagher, 228 ; Father Anthony O'Donnell, 230 ; Nathaniel O'Donell, 230 ; Philip O'Reilly, 231.
Rattrey, George, 219.
Raulin, Louis, 235.
Read, John, 216, 219.
Redmond, Remond, family of, 212 ; Anne Marie Xaviere, 208 ; Elizabeth Bridget, 208 ; Frances Catherine Julia, 208 ; Josephe Marie de Jesus, 208 ; Sir Peter, 192, 208, 225, 236 ; Stephen Francis, 212.
Reinolds, Lieut., 240, 241.
Reudell, Charles, 246.
Rice, James, 201 ; Sir Stephen, 247.
Richardson of Glasgow, family of, 201, 202 ; Lawrence, 229 ; Richard, 222.
de Richmont, *alias* Richardson, Francis, 201, 202.
Riva, Louis, 218 ; [——], 218.
Riveria, Riviera, Cardinal, 228 ; Monsignor Dominick, 228.
Rivers, George, 239.
Robertson of Struan, Alexander, 240 ; Col., 241 ; John, 196.
Robeson, Lieut.-Col., 242.
de la Roche, John, 208, 220 ; Redmond, 207 ; Theobald, 201 ; Theresa, 208 ; Viscount of Fermoy, Lord, 208.
Rochester, Francis, Bishop of, 232, 248.
Roettiers, James, 247 (2) ; John, 247 (3) ; Joseph, 247 ; Norbert, 247 (7), 248 ; [——], 248.
de Rohan, Armand, 229.
Ronchi, James, 217 ; John, 219 ; John Baptist, 224 ; Pellegrino, 217.
Roscoe, James, 237.
Rougé, Dominick, 221.
Ruga, Father, 222.
Russell, Earls of Bedford, family of, 200 ; Charles, 200 ; Countess of Tressan, Charlotte Michel, 211.
—— family of, 211 ; Sir Charles, 211 ; William, 211.
Rutherford, Capt., 240.
Rutlidge, family of, 210 ; James, 210 ; [——], 210.
Ryan of Glanogaha, family of, 200 ; Denis, 220 ; Capt. John, 222 ; John, 200.
Rycaut, Col., 241.

SACKVILLE, Sakvill, Thomas, 218, 219.
Sacripanti, Cardinal, 226.
St. Ange, Col., 240, 241 (2).

INDEX

Sarsfield, Anne, 208; Francis, 206; Ignatius, 206; Sir James, 191; Patrick, 206; William, 206; Xavier, 206.
—— of Kilmallock, Viscount, 206, 208.
de Sartine, Antoine, 207.
Scotland, Protectors of: Cardinal Sacripanti, 226; John Anthony, Cardinal Davia, 228 (2); Alexander, Cardinal Falconieri, 228; Cardinal Riveria, 228; Joseph, Cardinal Spinelli, 236; Cardinal John Francis Albani, 231.
—— Vicars-Apostolic in: Alexander John Grant, 227; Bishop James Gordon, 228.
Scott, Scot, Col., 239, 240, 241, 242; Capt. Francis, 198, 241 (2); James, 230.
Scrope, Henry, 212.
Sempill, Hugh, Lord, 206; Robert, 206.
Sens, Archbishop of, Paul Albert de Luynes, 231.
Seven Churches, Bishop of, Father Stephen MacEgan, 227, 228 (2).
Shaw, John, 221.
Shee, Eleanor, 209; John, 246; Patrick, 228.
Sheldon, Lieut.-Gen. Dominick, 198, 218, 219, 223; Major-Gen., 243 (2); [——], 238; Ralph, 220.
Sheridan, John, 223; Sir Thomas, 218 (3), 221, 223, 224, 232 (2).
Skelton, Bevill, 216 (2); Col., 240, 241.
Skerret, Dr. Mark, 230 (2).
Skinner, Rev. John, 249.
Slane, Barons of, family of, 202; Lord, 199.
Slater, Col. Solomon, 197.
Smallwood, Mary, 221.
Smith, Alexander, 228, 230; Charles, 209; James, 209.
Solomon, Col., 238.
Southcot, [——], 232.
Sparrow, Sir John, 216.
Spinelli, Joseph, Cardinal, 230 (2).
Stafford, Francis, 246; John, 217, 219, 223; [——], 232.
Staveley, Capt., 240.
Stewart of Kinnachin, Alexander, 220; Francis, 229; Col. John, 248 (2).
Stistch, Dr. Thomas, 229.
Stonor, John Talbot, 230.
Strafford, Jasper, 239; Thomas, Earl of, 244, 248.
Straglia, John Peter, 224.
Stratford, Thomas, 235 (2), 247.
Strathmore, Earl of, 245.
Strickland, [——], 222; Lady, 220, 223; Mrs. 220; Robert, 217 (3), 218 (2),
223; Roger, 220, 222; Teresa, 223; Walter, 217, 221, 223.
Struan, Col., 241.
Stuart, Lieut.-Col. John, 244.
Stytch, Capt., 240.
Sumerville, Robert, 197.
Sutherland, Major-Gen., 238.
Symes, Andrew, 220; Elizabeth, 221; James, 217, 219.
Sympson, John, 220.
Sweetman, Dr. Nicholas, 229.
Swymmer, Anthony Langley, 245.

Talbot, Talbott, Bruno, 246, 247; Col., 240; James, 231; Richard, 246; Sir William, 246.
Tangis, Col., 241; Monsieur de, 240.
Tapson, John, 246.
Tarras, Earl of, 198.
Tencin, Peter Guerin de, 228, 229.
Theobald, Nicholas Geraldin, 235.
Therry, Terry, James, Athlone Herald, 195, 197, 199 (2), 201, 221; Patrick, 202.
Thespiæ, Bishop of, John Talbot Stonor, 230.
Thome, Dr., 224; Richard, 249.
Thomond, Henry, Earl of, 237; Earls of, 203.
Throgmorton, Col., 240, 242.
Tiberiopolis, Bishop of: Thomas Dominick Williams, 227.
Tobin, Elizabeth, 210; John, 210.
Tomasium, Ambrose, Count, 236.
Trant, David, 205; Sir Patrick, 246.
Trapps, Col., 240, 241.
Tresson, Louis, Count of, 211; Charlotte, née Russell, Countess of, 211.
Trevanion, Richard, 219.
Tricot, Elizabeth, 202.
Trimlestown, Matthias, Baron, 238 (2).
Trinder, John, 246.
Troy, Patrick, 239.
Trohy, Sieur, 197.
Tuam, Archbishops of: Bernard Ogara, 227; Michael O'Gara, 229; Dr. Mark Skerret, 230.
Turene, Matthew, 220.
Tyrconnell, Richard, Duke and Earl of, 205, 247.
Tyrrell, Tyrril, Abbé William Thomas, 207; Eleanor, 212 (2); Richard, 212.

Umsworth, Thomas, 220.
Urquhart, Capt. Alexander, 244; Col. James, 234.

INDEX

Utica, Bishop-elect of, Henry Howard, 227.

VAGHAN, Thomas, 239.
du Val, Louis, 225.
Valence, Bishop of, 242.
Vaughan, Capt. Thomas, 243.
de Vauvray, [——], 204.
Verdun, John, 226, 228.

WACHOP, Col., 238.
Wait, Leonard, 220.
Waldegrave, Richard, 221 ; Sir William, 217.
Walden, Joseph, 220.
Walkinshaw of Burrowfield, Sir John, 192, 232 (2).
Wallace, Col., 241 ; Sir [——], 240.
Walle of Johnstown, family of, 210; Francis Balthazar, 210.
Walmesley, Charles, 231.
Walsh, Richard, 230.
Wanton, Eleanor, 210 ; Maurice, 210.
de Ward Barry. See Barry.
Waterford and Lismore, Bishop of: Sylvester Louis Lloyd, 229.
Waters, George, 197, 234 ; John, 197.
Webb, Lovell, 220.

Welsh, Capt. Philip, 220.
Weston, William, 221.
Wharton, Philip, Duke of, 193, 233.
White, Whyte, Capt. Andrew, 243 ; Countess of Alby, etc., Charlotte, 207 ; Father Dominick, 195, 216 ; George, 239, 242; James, 211 ; John, 221 ; Sir Ignatius, 206, 207.
Wigtoun, James, Earl of, 248 ; John, Earl of, 240.
Wilkie of Edinburgh, [——], 249 ; John, 221.
Williams, Christopher, 219 ; Thomas Dominick, 227.
Wilson, James, 239.
Witham, Dr. George, 226.
Wivell, Thomas, 219.
Wogan, Sir Charles, 244.
Wood, Lawrence, 222.
Woodhouse, John Thomas, 223.
Wray, Capt., 240.

YORK, Duke of, 245 (2).
—— Lawrence William, 231.

ZOUCHE, family of, 195.
—— de la Lande, Sieur, 195.

www.ingramcontent.com/pod-product-compliance
Lightning Source LLC
Chambersburg PA
CBHW071809300426
44116CB00009B/1251